PERSONAL BRANDOLOGY

THE FIRST HUMAN REVOLUTION

JAYDEN KAFANELIS

B.Sc M. Biotech

Disclaimer

The material in this publication is of the nature of general comment only and does not represent professional advice. It is not intended to provide specific guidance for any particular circumstances, and it should not be relied upon for any decision to take action or not to take action on any matter that it covers. Readers should obtain professional advice where appropriate, before making any such decision. To the maximum extent permitted by law, the author and publisher disclaim all responsibility and liability to any person, arising directly or indirectly from any person taking or not taking action based on the information in this book.

ISBN: pbk: 978-0-6452141-0-9

First published July 2021 by Jayden Kafanelis.

The moral rights of the author have been asserted.

Editing and inside pages design by Claire McGregor, Kookaburra Hill Publishing Services.

From Mum: unconditional and unwavering love and support, universal compassion, selflessness, resilience, true happiness, virtue, the embodiment of human nature's finest qualities, an ideal.

From Dad: leadership, ambition, passion, family, morality, inspiration, "achieve your potential".

From Reice: strength of will, independence, discipline, kindness, generosity, wit.

From Kaitlyn M: companionship, compassion, kindness, unconditional positive regard, empathy.

From Aunty Vick and Uncle Luke: spirituality, philosophy, intellect, belief, support, family.

From Eddie C: entrepreneurship, philanthropy, inspiration, selflessness.

From Gemma S: creativity, strength, passion, novelty.

From Nick A: genuineness, a love of science, selflessness.

From Samy S: lifelong learning, a love of science, curiosity.

From Nick, Dylan, Jesse, Marco, PK, & James: friendship, loyalty, hustle, support.

Contents

Preface

Over the last decade, I have achieved a few things, which, in combination, have provided me the capabilities, insights, and knowledge required to craft this book. If I was to draw on some of them to paint myself as a credible author and help you justify the time and effort investment required to read this book, I'd probably start with my first business, Jaystar Fitness, where I've worked for the last nine years as an independent professional.

Soon after starting Jaystar, I went on to co-found two more companies: one in internship recruitment and one in personal branding, and in doing this I sold the résumé technology we'd developed to career professionals, recruiters, résumé writers, and employment agencies. During these ventures, I coproduced an interview course to improve employability, which is now being micro-credentialed by an Australian university and translated into different languages for delivery in different countries.

Within this time, I also completed a Bachelor of Science at Victoria University and a Master of Biotechnology at Melbourne University. During my science degree, I was awarded an innovation scholarship by the College of Business to represent Victoria University in Italy at the world-renowned European Innovation Academy; was asked to guest lecture for an innovation subject at La Trobe university; participated as a start-up mentor at Deakin's entrepreneurial SPARK program; and, most recently – and perhaps one of my biggest achievements – is that I completed this book. However, for every success outlined above there were 100 failures that I felt wholeheartedly, and I learned more, if not the most, from each of them.

It is the above highlight reel of my life, combined with years of hardship, stress, failure, introspection, learning, reading, and challenging experiences, that has led me to the realisations put forward in this book. Working as an independent professional while simultaneously being involved in start-ups focused on recruitment and personal branding, and concurrently studying science where I familiarised myself with academic literature, refined my critical-thinking ability, and gained a deep understanding of the biology and psychology underlying *Homo sapiens*, provided me the resources and realisations I needed to link up this framework of personal branding.

There are surprising links between biology, psychology, business, entrepreneurship, and the future of work, and, as evidenced in the proceeding pages, it's a link you can't ignore. The purpose of this book is to demonstrate a few key points:

1. In the 21st century you are part-business and part-biological organism.
2. Due to being part-business, you have a personal brand forever attached to you.
3. By observing how organisations behave, it's clear to see the most successful are those that *humanise* themselves.
4. The world of work is changing, from the primitive paradigms of the early industrial revolutions, which viewed employees as expendable, robotic workhorses, to a new age where the individual is placed at the centre of the universe and is given power.
5. The business of the 21st century world of work is the individual – it's you! Your personal brand that will drive your success is influenced by a framework of elements specific to you, which is entirely what this book is about.
6. A component of a flourishing life is a successful career.

This book will well-equip you for the emerging world of work through gaining a better understanding of your personal brand while simultaneously being exposed to a holistic approach to life, which will enable you to rethink what personal flourishing looks like in modernity. I hope you enjoy reading it as much as I enjoyed writing it.

To your success,

Jayden Kafanelis

Introduction

Biological business

You are a biological business. I'm not talking about a pharmaceutical or bioengineering company that manufactures biologics. Neither am I referring to those involved in livestock, agriculture, zoology, or farming. I'm talking about *YOU*, the individual. As the blood pumps around your body in celebration of evolution's meticulous engineering, it does a few things. One of these is to connect many vital organs, leveraging their highly specialised skillsets for the optimal running of your body. Another is to provide a transport service for your army of white blood cells in order to protect you against microscopic invaders. Finally, and arguably most importantly, your blood delivers necessary oxygen to tissues in the body and, in doing so, enables organs such as your brain – the seat of consciousness – to operate.

Because of the highly complicated symphony of chemical reactions and biological processes occurring inside the body, your psyche emerges fully formed with the ability to govern a highly functional organism – an organism that exists in a 21st century world driven largely by a capitalist ideology. Meaning, everything you need to succeed in today's world was given to you the moment you were born. Your biological self-healing, metamorphosing, adaptive, and extremely intelligent physical body is much more sophisticated and flexible than humanity's finest technological inventions, and it's yours to command and control at your will.

Your mind, with its capacity to reason, feel, think, and create is divinely powerful and still evades the global efforts of artificial intelligence researchers, neuroscientists, and psychologists in their quests to replicate, understand, and rewire it. Furthermore, the civilisational environment you currently exist in, and were likely born into, celebrates individuality, freedom, and human rights, and recognises the importance of personal flourishing, creating an atmosphere of support for you to freely progress toward your life's purpose, achieve your potential, and produce value to the world. A perfect storm! Beautiful, isn't it?

You operate daily as a biological business with a unique and powerful personal brand.

Being a higher-order conscious being with an able vehicle grants you the ability to pursue unique interests, function independently, participate in personal development, decide who to associate and spend time with, determine behaviours, habits, and day-to-day operations, and subscribe to any number of personal philosophies. The possibilities are endless. Throughout this book, I'll draw attention to the many activities you engage in throughout life that can be clearly viewed through a business lens and align with a successful life. Instead of "successful life" I could just have easily said "professional success"; however, one of the tenets of this book is that your professional and personal lives are inextricably linked, and success in one overlaps and manifests as success in the other. In fact, the aim of this book is to convince you that, fundamentally, you operate daily as a biological business with a unique and powerful *personal brand*. A brand that is becoming more salient, important, and valued in the 21st century's individualistic society we live in.

Of course, opposition will undoubtedly arise if this view is seen to "reduce" people to glorified commercial entities, and it's best to extinguish them early on. Certain critics may rebut the notion that individuals should be viewing themselves as biological businesses, and instead would claim we should ultimately strive for achieving happiness and developing meaningful relationships as there is more to life than money, work, and career ambitions. To this, I partially agree. Yes, meaningful relationships and the pursuit of happiness are extremely important, evidenced through psychological, medical, and philosophical studies, which I present in this book. But in the society we live in, being financially stable, living in accordance with your purpose, and engaging in productive work is equally important, necessary, and inseparably ties into psychological wellbeing and happiness, while providing important areas of personal relationships.

Dr James Suzman, a well-known anthropologist with a research focus on human relationships with work throughout history, in an interview with Harvard Business Review, confirms that working has been an integral part of human life since our earliest civilisations, including hunter-gatherer societies. His in-depth anthropological exploration of *Homo sapiens* leads him to emphatically claim in his interview: "We are a species born to work. We are the purposeful species".[1] My view is, areas of life usually exiled strictly to business settings, such as work, career, and income-related endeavours, when combined with other areas of life traditionally associated with intimate and personal matters, including family, relationships, and psychological wellbeing, come together and constitute a flourishing life in modernity. They are both equally important and inextricably linked.

You produce value

The concept of value in itself comprises a key link between these two seemingly diametric cross-sections of life. Producing value to others, the wider society, or globally, which is a by-product of pursuing interests, passions, and purpose – despite whether done selfishly or selflessly – contributes to better overall wellbeing for the producer and leads to improved living conditions and enhanced quality of life for people around the world. Our species benefits when individuals selfishly or selflessly offer up value they've created to society. Clearly, individuals' personal contributions of value to the world are what we can thank for innovations such as the internet, GPS technology, the concept of gravity, and electricity. Further efforts led to the discovery of penicillin, X-ray technology, and the structure of DNA, saving millions of lives annually and propelling human knowledge forward at lightning speed. Car manufacturers to doctors, online courses to lightbulbs, and from charities to supermarkets, each delivers value to people in some way and are born from the efforts of individuals or groups. The shift of value through society is described by economic flux because value – a personal judgement – is traded for dollars – a financial reward.

Dollars and recognition are what we use as a proxy for value in the 21st century, and these speak the language of businesses and organisations. If you produce something of value to someone, they will happily purchase it from you with dollars. Even charities, the most altruistic of organisations, require and attract money from others to sustain valuable activities. In this instance, dollars are being provided by those who can afford it to produce value on behalf of those who can't. Money makes the world go around, and without it the world stops spinning. However, value in life doesn't always translate into dollars. Meaningful relationships, exploring nature, and intimate encounters are examples of things valued in life that don't necessarily cost money (although lonely, wealthy people can pay others to provide them with company, in effect purchasing pseudo-meaningful relationships; adventurers can purchase tickets to travel the world; and intimate encounters can be bought from escorts).

On the commercialisation of value, I am not suggesting slapping a dollar figure on everything you do. You are not going to charge friends for things you would normally charge others for. You will not invoice your mum for labour if she asks for help around the house. And there will be times when you can afford to be altruistic, helping others for nothing in return except the self-manufactured pleasant feelings that bubble up from within. Yet, if you did not charge someone for the value you offer, at some point life as you know it inevitably comes crashing down. Not only this, but without being financially reimbursed for the creation of value, many inventors, researchers, capitalists, and workers would throw in the towel. Civilisation regresses.

In a capitalist economy, dollars and value largely overlap, and taking dollars away from value creation crumbles our world and inhibits innovation and advancement. Being commercially remunerated for value produced equates to formal recognition and signals a balanced and fair environment for economic participants. If you work harder and produce more value to more people, you will get more in return. The converse is true too. The point is, the capitalist system surrounding us is essential, effective, and morally fair. A fortunate state of affairs considering we can't escape it.

Citizenship in a country means agreeing to its terms and conditions, and it just so happens that signing up to a capitalist system works in our favour because we each possess unlimited potential to create any form of value, in whatever quantity we like, and to be reimbursed accordingly. Because of this foundational economic pillar of modern life, your ability to produce value, which is realised financially, is a necessary component of a flourishing life. Some of the world's most famed Ancient Greek philosophers also defined a flourishing life as one where seeking one's rational purpose is complimented by virtuous acts; those acts that benefit others. Even to them, being a valuable member of society was extolled and necessary.

As such, another main proposition of this book is that you should align your purpose in life with the production of value to others, which allows you to commercialise your unique capabilities while achieving heightened fulfilment in life.

Achieving this means:

- you live your values
- pursue your passion
- enhance your creativity
- improve your psychological wellbeing
- perform work to a higher standard
- produce value to others
- benefit the wider society
- attract likeminded people and develop higher-quality relationships
- have better career and life satisfaction.

Yet for you to fully realise your potential financially, I first have to convince you that you are a business. No, seriously.

You, the business

As mentioned, you, a human, produce value to others, and in the 21st century value is interchangeable with dollars. Therefore, it's plain to see: you are a business! Just kidding – there's more to this story. In this section I'm confident I will convince you of your inherent business nature. To do so, I want to start with a few questions:

- Have you ever charged anyone for goods or services you provide?
- Do you live your life in accordance with your own moral standards?
- Is there a goal or end state you are striving to achieve in your life?
- Do you have daily routines and habits?
- Is the way you interact, behave, and respond in life predictable and consistent?
- At this moment, do you own a phone, car, or house?
- Have you paid for goods and services before?

If you answered yes to any of these questions, it hints at your business capacity, but you will soon come to know you could have answered yes to many more. If you are already one of the people answering yes to all, I have a pretty solid case. First, no matter who you are, if you are over the age of 18 and living in a capitalist society it would be rare to answer no to "have you ever charged anyone for goods or services you provide?" Independent professionals provide the most obvious example of this. Tattooists charge for drawing on people, artists charge for artworks, graphic designers charge for designs, athletes charge for sport performance, singers charge for singing, and consultants charge for consulting. These are instances of goods and services being transacted between people.

Consultants, athletes, singers, and tattooists sell a service. Artists and designers predominantly sell goods. In the above examples, each independent professional, each individual, functions as the business, and whoever is purchasing off of them, the customer. What you may have missed though is that if you have ever been paid for anything, have previously been employed, or are still employed currently, you should also have answered yes to this question as well. Your employer is a customer paying *you* for the services you provide. You could easily quit your job and get a new one, effectively taking your services elsewhere. For example, if you're a cleaner working for a company, you could resign tomorrow, tell your boss thanks but no thanks and put yourself back on the market. You could offer cleaning services to an array of new clients whether they are individuals or small businesses. You may even opt for another large organisation that will once again function as your sole employer. In doing so, you are essentially selling your services to new customers.

If you said yes to living life in accordance with your own moral standards, you have just admitted you follow a code of ethics. Remember those? Companies and businesses enthusiastically virtue signal theirs and revert to them in times of unethical workplace behaviour. And that goal we asked about – the end state you're working toward in life – in corporate land they call it a 'vision statement' and usually it sits right next to the organisation's 'mission statement'. Those habits and routines of yours you answered yes to having, through another lens you could refer to them as your day-to-day operations.

The predictable and consistent way you behave, interact, and respond in life is described by psychologists as your personality. Every single person has one, although some are more noticeable than others. Having a personality is part of being human and is one of the many areas that contribute to a person's uniqueness. Again, this shines through in business settings. Modern-day corporate lingo simply calls it "culture", and in social psychology culture is widely viewed as a set of cognitions and practices that characterise a specific social group and distinguishes it from others. In fact, organisational culture heavily factors into corporate identity, much like personality contributes to your identity.

Obviously, the difference here is that culture refers to a group of people, whereby personality is an individual property, meaning social effects and emergent group properties seen in cultures aren't encompassed in the domain of personality. But I want to draw your attention to the uncanny similarities between the two: they both describe characteristic behaviours; both lead to characteristic styles of thinking; and both heavily influence identity. It seems that businesses and companies, in light of their enthusiastic advertisement of their organisation's unique "culture", are trying to humanise their business by drawing attention to the equivalent of their personality. All things considered, culture is a *human* property despite its application to corporate entities. If large multinational companies and aspiring businesses are trying to humanise their business in order to be more successful, isn't this already showing you that us humans are the epitome of a successful business entity?

Owning a phone, car, or house proves that, like businesses and companies, you have the capacity to own assets. You've paid for goods and services before? Of course you have. It could have been that time you paid a mechanic to fix your car, maybe even the person who did your gardening, or the professional who recently fixed your broken phone screen. Ahh, that is a business expense! After all, as the saying goes, your life is your "business". This explains why, if I intruded too far into another person's life, they would scold me and tell me to mind my own "business". Not to mention the moment someone finishes doing a job for you they usually pleasantly inform you that it was a pleasure doing business. In life, we're all just hustling and bustling going about our business. The book you're reading right now represents one of my own products and one of your business expenses. Utilising some insights I've stumbled across in my life, paired with academic literacy, has enabled me to deliver value to you in the form of a book, which you willingly exchanged dollars for. I really want to express my appreciation that you chose to do business with *me*. Thank *you*.

Still not convinced? Okay, here's some more food for thought. Business is defined as "commercial activity", and a company is defined as "a commercial business". Since we live in a capitalist society where we need money to live, our whole life is commercial activity. When we are born, we are a consumer, we just use Mum and Dad's money to purchase the products we need. They are the proverbial money tree, even though they try to claim otherwise and convince us they can't grow it. This offspring sponsorship period thankfully, for them, isn't forever.

As we transition through our developmental stages and mature, we reach a point where our ability to produce value to others manifests. It is here that we enter the workforce or engage in another form of work, effectively counteracting our consumption with production. Keep in mind: both consumption and production are inextricably tied to dollar amounts. If I produce value for someone else, they'll happily *pay* me to consume it if the value I can provide them is more than the value they place on the dollars they are trading for it. To not be involved in commercial activity we'd have to ask permission to join the hunter-gatherers of the world, although their bartering of food and resources may actually constitute a primitive form of trade.

Companies and businesses, as part of their obvious commercial activity, are subjected to taxes, albeit at different rates. Company tax rates hover around 30 percent of their taxable income, and business tax is bracketed at different earning levels. Doesn't this sound awfully familiar? As an individual you pay tax at tax brackets too. In fact, on the Australian Taxation Office website, if you set yourself up as a sole-trader business, you can use your *personal* tax file number and are prompted to pay tax at the same rate as individual taxpayers.[2,3] In effect, formally appointing yourself as a business requires minimal change, because you already are one! Notice how if you make any money as an individual, even in the event you are on state benefits and receiving government payments, you are required to pay tax on it?

Businesses and companies are legal entities though, which brings our person–business analogy to a jarring holt. Or does it? On Cornell Law School's website, an entity is defined as "a person or organisation possessing separate and distinct legal rights such as an individual, partnership, or corporation". It's the same the other way around when moving from a person to a corporate entity. A "legal person" in the Oxford dictionary is defined as "an individual, company, or other entity which has legal rights and is subject to obligations". In court cases this is why companies and organisations can be prosecuted like people can. We both have similar rights and legal standing. What is telling is the fact that two people can enter a legal contract with each other and both are treated as entities bound by legal jargon and business terminology.

To take it further, when you were born you were issued a birth certificate after your birth was recorded on a register, in much the same way companies are issued a certificate of registration upon their birth. To enforce the issuance of birth certificates, Australia passed a Births, Deaths and Marriages Act,[4] but other countries manage citizen registration processes in their own unique ways. On their website, Births, Deaths and Marriages Victoria confirms birth certificates are used for legal purposes, including your identity,[5] and on the Victorian Law Reform Commission's website, a birth certificate is described as an official document that outlines the particulars of a person's legal identity.[6] Upon birth, in addition to entering the world as a human being, a "natural person", you were dually made into a business-like entity, a "legal person", bound by the laws of the land. Surprise! And this is why I refer to you as a biological business. You're part biological organism, part commercial entity. In the 21st century, you are a chimera, a hybridised organism. It's time to reconcile the two and start acting like one.

All businesses have a brand

Considering you are part business, paying attention to your brand is of rising importance. Branding is an area taken seriously by organisations as it represents the perceptions people hold of them, some of whom are highly profitable current or future customers. The reality is, a brand can make or break a business. The biggest organisations in the world are those whose brands have captured the hearts of the masses. On the contrary, organisations nosedive if their brands are tarnished, evident in plummeting stock prices when distasteful news reaches media. A company's brand holds their story and purpose. It's what they are known for, who they are, who they want to be, and how they are perceived. It distinguishes one business from another and is reflected in everything from customer service to creativity; advertising and marketing to product offerings; and strategic partnerships to corporate culture. Even the research areas an organisation is interested in and their governing principles form unique elements of their brand.

The brand of a business creates impressions in the minds of its audience and in doing so crafts a powerful and hopefully meaningful experience. If brand experiences are processed positively by audience members, it leads to a host of benefits. Good brand experiences result in:

- loyal and satisfied customers
- tribes of advocates
- referrals through word-of-mouth advertising
- motivated, proud, and passionate employees
- a competitive business advantage

- a unique value offering to customers, especially in an experience economy.

The end result is a profitable, reputable, and respected enterprise.

You are a business, and the information provided above is directly applicable and intricately ties into your personal brand. People will create mental impressions of you based off your brand, then archive these experiences and subsequently form an attitude toward you that influences your relationship with them moving forward. In much the same way they would have companies. For example, if a company acted empathetically, listening intently to customers who contacted them with concerns, and then went above and beyond to make every effort to rectify and address the concerns, of course their customers would feel positively toward them, relay the experience to friends, and show hints of brand loyalty. The converse is true for cold, transactional companies who overtly treat people as commodities.

A good brand is an elevator to success; a bad brand is an anchor dragging you downward.

People will interact with and respond to you in a similar manner as they experience your personal brand and everything it encompasses. If you do right by people, people will do right back to you, and it is true that your world is a reflection of you. Branding, the advertisement of your personal qualities, is karma. A good brand is an elevator to success; a bad brand is an anchor dragging you downward. You can choose.

Take note that even when you are working for a company, their brand is not your personal brand. The company merely represents a transient customer of yours that is currently paying you for a service. At this moment you may be an employee for one company but in three years it's possible you might be employed somewhere else. Your current company, along with other companies you've worked for, are in fact a personal customer of yours that bought into your personal brand. Having this list of paying customers provides you with a form of social proof for your personal brand by providing evidence of your brand value.

The key to understanding the power of a brand is to realise that it forms the basis of an emotional connection between people and business. Fittingly, concepts such as "brand love" have garnered rising interest in recent times. As this book will explore, humans are emotional creatures driven primarily by feelings. Logic very much takes a back seat in most areas of our life, including business settings. To illustrate, think of things you've bought. Now think of things you bought that you didn't actually need. Every purchase in the second list you can thank emotions for.

Materialistic, consumerist societies such as ours capitalise on this fact and have conditioned us to indulge and spend impulsively on anything and everything. Over time, we've been trained in a lab-rat fashion to want more and more through advertising, propaganda, and psychological hijacking, with the end goal being the widespread adoption of mindless, emotionally driven spending. Now, people buy from brands simply because they like them. Employers only hire people they like. Emotional activation leads to other by-products as well. Colleagues work better together when they like each other; being emotionally invested in work and liking a job means professional performance improves. Furthermore, without relentless passion, the biggest companies in the world would not exist. Emotions and human traits drive consumer spending, factor into business profit and success, and facilitate productive relationships between people. Your personal brand is infused with potent emotions, and its ability to properly resonate with and activate emotions in others sends you skywards.

The false dichotomy of personal qualities and professionalism

If we break up the words "personal brand" you realise there are two implications here: the first word is "personal", which hints at natural human qualities; the second word "brand" is derived from the area of business. Considering you are a "natural person" – a biological organism – and a "legal person" – a business-like entity – it makes sense that your personal brand encompasses all your qualities and is omnipresent throughout life. You can't escape it because wherever you are, elements of your brand follow you. When you are in what could classically be defined as personal situations, such as family gatherings, parties with friends, or intimate interactions with another person, your personal qualities are more salient. Note: in the book I may refer to these personal qualities as "natural qualities" or your "natural essence". In these personal situations, qualities such as empathy, respect, and morals become more obvious. Then your unique communication style, social intelligence, philosophies, personal standards, and personality traits further influence and govern your interpersonal behaviour. Additionally, the content you discuss with friends, family, and lovers is influenced by personal interests, your inherent creativity, values, emotional intelligence, and cognitive abilities.

The opposite of these environments are traditional business environments; for example, an employee in the workplace. Professional qualities become more noticeable here such as your ability to develop a rapport with peers and the overall workplace behaviour you display. Professional qualities are further viewed in the commitment you demonstrate to the company vision and mission statements, and the code of ethics you adhere to. The technical skills utilised in your role, the professional networks you maintain, and the calibre of your job performance are other examples of your professional business-related qualities. However, notice how each of these stems from your personal qualities. The modern business environment and the professionalism it entails are an emergent layer of societal functioning; therefore, every professional quality touched on above arises from personal qualities that merely transform upon crossing into the 21st century world of business.

Before civilisation made us an advanced, interdependent, connected society reliant on currency exchange, we were *Homo sapiens* living a simple life. Each member possessed their own natural endowments and operated in a less-sophisticated environment, no more complex than the lives of our primate cousins. This is why every professional quality mentioned above can be directly traced back to natural human qualities, our personal qualities.

> Your professional brand appears when
> you look at your personal qualities
> through a business lens.

Developing rapport with peers and maintaining professional networks stems from respect, empathy, and social intelligence. Overall workplace behaviour is largely governed by personality and communication styles. The level of commitment to company vision and mission statements is dependent on personal alignment with the organisation's goals and purpose, because if it resonates on a personal level, individuals demonstrate much higher commitment. Adherence to the workplace code of ethics suggests personal morals are similar to the organisation's. The technical skills required for the role were acquired through idiosyncratic cognitive abilities. Attention was distributed toward learning a skill, which was then committed to memory, enhanced with creativity, then delivered in a professional capacity.

Job performance is directly linked to personal capabilities, standards, and values. Valuing high standards and diligently completing tasks manifests higher performance. Even the quality of professional work is directly determined by personal quality standards. The "professional brand" you wear in "business environments", including in traditional nine-to-five employment modes, independent contractor roles, or nonstandard work, is nothing more than a slightly filtered projection of your personal brand. Your professional brand appears when you look at your personal qualities through a business lens. What I want you to realise though is that your whole life is a business. It's your business, every single part of it. You can't afford to only give attention to your brand when you're in the classical conceptualisation of a "business environment". Successful professional brands shouldn't be isolated temporary facades; they should be a by-product of your consistently flourishing personal brand.

In addition to this, at any point in time, personal networks of family, friends, and acquaintances can cross over from the "personal domain" of your life to the "business domain". Your best mate may end up paying you to do work for him in the future, as may his mum, your cousins, or even the two people recently introduced to you at a friend's party. In a similar fashion, business associates may traverse boundaries too, becoming highly valued friends, personal connections, or a romantic partner. In fact, personal qualities are what initially drive people to do business with you in the first place, and can often deter it too. For example, let's say I had a friend who was talented at software engineering, dependable, creative, and set high personal standards. Out of the 100 available people in Melbourne I could choose to build a mobile application, I would choose them because their personal qualities, combined with the generic technical skills the 99 other people possess, lead to a better service. Personal qualities are unique value-adds and make a massive difference.

A real-world example demonstrating the opposite occurred when I was involved in my own start-up company. In essence, we had identified a certain investor as potentially being a big value-add to our business if we were to bring them onboard. They demonstrated access to large amounts of wealth, hinted at robust professional networks, possessed existing resources, and advertised themselves as having the skills needed to transform a start-up company into an established enterprise. However, after working closely for a few months, we came to the jarring realisation that this person lacked honesty, was condescending, had highly narcissistic traits, and if we squeezed them as hard as we could I don't think a single drop of integrity would have made its way out of their body. Because of their personal qualities, their professional abilities and value were reduced to zero. To us at the time – a supportive, open, and collaborative company – culture was of paramount importance, and dutifully we severed the relationship immediately and went our separate ways.

Cancerous individuals will destroy morale and stifle progress, and there's nothing more dangerous than a trojan horse who removes their professional mask and unleashes their pathological true colours. After all, technical skills can be taught or bought safely at arms-length from a contractor. For us, we place the value on the person and have to be sold on their personal brand if they are to come into our business ecosystem.

A new world of work

Currently, there is a pervasive belief in Western society that strictly isolates business and personal areas of life from each other. Often, work and professional endeavours are seen as an evil necessity of the human condition and a means to an end. Business is viewed as cold, impersonal, demoralising, and transactional. When someone screws someone over personally, they smile and say, "it's just business". This is wrong. Producing value to the world is an end in itself, and operating as a business is an inherent, inseparable part of you while living in an affluent, capitalist 21st century society. Business is fundamentally a human venture, and today this fact is becoming recognised and given due attention.

Recently, a massive push in the corporate world has seen businesses becoming more personal and customer-centric. Millions if not billions of dollars have been invested in crafting positive customer experiences, building authentic and meaningful connections with audiences, and in creating cultures where people feel safe, supported, and valued. Primitive business paradigms, like that of the industrial revolution – which saw employees as expendable robotic workhorses and viewed customers through a purely transactional lens – are dead. The world of work has evolved since then and is evolving rapidly again as we speak. Even the cornerstone of modern economies, traditional nine-to-five employment, has been caught in the crossfire and is under attack. Currently, unprecedented changes in the workforce are unfolding, an event sped up rapidly by the COVID-19 pandemic and contributed to by myriad factors including the onset of the Fourth Industrial Revolution, Generation Y's influx into the workforce, and the rise of independence and entrepreneurship.

Klaus Schwab, founder and executive chairman of the World Economic Forum, when talking on the Fourth Industrial Revolution, states that it builds upon digital technology seen in the Third Industrial Revolution and is heralded by innovations in artificial intelligence, genome editing, augmented reality, robotics, and 3D printing, profoundly transforming institutions, industries, and individuals. Effectively altering how humans create, exchange, and distribute *value*. For example, imagine going to work in virtual reality and not having to leave the house. The rise of automation, biotechnology, and emerging digital technologies, such as blockchain, redefines and blurs boundaries between the digital and physical world, further eroding traditional conceptualisations of employment. Modes of communication, interaction, learning, and entertainment will be innovated, each having a ripple-effect through the economy. The result is societal transformation at a global scale, influencing human identity, communities, and political structures.[7] In his book, Klaus highlights that in this new world where boundaries are disappearing and aspirations are changing, the younger generation are not only seeking work–life balance but are also opting for harmonious work–life integration. Purposeful engagement is becoming a major issue companies will face. People don't want to jeopardise their meaning and purpose in life, and the constraining nature of corporate life reminiscent of another era has lost its appeal.[8]

Klaus contrasts this generational perspective with the ramifications for the corporate world through the concept of "talentism"; a new form of capitalism. Convincingly, Klaus proposes that capital is being superseded by human talents, such as creativity and the ability to innovate; just as capitalism replaced manual trades, capital is now giving way to human talent. In the future world of work a company's talent base is an emerging and ultimately important competitive advantage. In light of this, organisational structures will need to be rethought and new strategies to attract and retain talent, formulated. Successful organisations will move from hierarchical structures to more collaborative and networked models. Motivation will be increasingly intrinsic, and management focus will shift toward fostering mastery, meaning, and independence.

Entangled in the Fourth Industrial Revolution, from my perspective, is the first human revolution. For the first time in history the power balance is shifting to the individual, whose creativity, ingenuity, critical thinking, expertise, and problem-solving capabilities are becoming the most highly valued and sought-after means of production. Combining Klaus's "talentism" with the me-centred mindset of the 21st century, which is further scaffolded by a socio-political landscape that enables and enforces this ideology, is a catalyst for this change. Since *you* are an organisation's greatest achievement, their winning product and competitive advantage, yielding to demands of flexibility, autonomy, and allowing you to pursue passions and interests, is a price that needs to be paid. This shift is in stark contrast to the worker who gave their life to the factories of the industrial revolution.

Millennials

Amidst the sea of technological and societal change, Generation Y – referred to as "millennials" – take centre stage. This generation, born between 1981–1996, and often referred to as "entitled", currently makes up over one-third of the global workforce and puts dramatic pressures on employers to adapt their ways. Not only are they the largest cohort in the workforce, but they are also the most educated, surpassing the former Gen-X leader. Nearly four in 10 millennials (39 percent), hold bachelor's degrees or higher, compared with Gen-X's rate of 29 percent.[9] A 2020 global report on millennials, conducted by Manpower Group, evidences the attitudes characteristic of this new wave of workers, and in doing so potentially uncovers where the "entitled" perception stems from. The report further highlights the subsequent effect on employer–employee relations.[10]

When looking for a job, among the top five priorities for millennials are money, time off, and flexibility. Upon losing their job, 62 percent are confident they could find equally good or better work within three months. Moreover, half would be open to non-traditional modes of work, and half would quit their job if they didn't feel appreciated. When probed about how long they expected to stay in a role before being promoted or moving to another, two-thirds said under two years and one-quarter said less than 12 months. This confirms a millennial bent toward challenging, engaging, and portfolio-style work. To top it off, 93 percent wanted lifelong learning, and, all things considered, millennials' second-highest priority in their search for work is job security.[10]

Being born into a humanitarian world concerned with promoting equality, morality, and psychological wellbeing has reprogrammed mindsets and lessened tolerance for bad bosses, toxic workplaces, and suboptimal experiences. In addition, having been exposed early to the internet, technology, and globalisation has offered increased accessibility to opportunities and has provided an echo-chamber for "entitled" millennial mindsets. Not only this but online companies such as Glassdoor exist purely to shift the power balance between companies and workers by providing an anonymous service that allows current or former employees to rate or review employers, publicly. Employee mistreatment can no longer be hidden or accepted. Finally, living in an era where autonomy and flexibility is valued and viable has opened up new avenues of professional life, further eroding the concept and necessity of traditional employment.

Entrepreneurs

Along with the generational impact on the workforce, society is further influenced by the glorification of entrepreneurship and self-governance. Entrepreneurs are pedestalled on social media platforms, hailed as idols, granted awards, amass tribes of followers, and boast lavish lifestyles. Universities noticed this trend early on and rushed to supply courses in entrepreneurship and innovation, arming people with formal qualifications and enriching environments. It's no surprise the masses are converging at destination innovation. In an article posted by entrepreneur.com, 550,000 new entrepreneurs enter the US workforce every month.[11] In 2020, a report published by the Global Entrepreneurship Research Association highlighted that 10.5 percent of Australian adults and 17.4 percent of American adults demonstrated early-stage entrepreneurial activity.[12] Respondents were those actively engaged in starting or running a business and were motivated by making a difference in the world, building wealth, continuing a family tradition, or earning a living in a scarce job market. The report further demonstrated a global upward trend in this space.

Pulses of entrepreneurial activity can additionally be measured through independent contractor metrics. Contractors, at minimum, are functioning as solo professionals requiring apt business skills, initiative, and self-governance; therefore, closely resemble entrepreneurs. In Australia, 1 million people identified as independent contractors in 2020, representing 8.2 percent of the workforce,[13] and America recorded 10 million in 2017, representing 6.9 percent of theirs.[14] Statistics like these, in conjunction with entrepreneur and gig worker metrics, provide proof of tectonic psychological shifts, being the internalisation of self-governing capitalistic mindsets, and hints at a changing economic landscape in the near future.

Gig workers

In an Australian discussion paper on the future of work and workers, the emergence of the gig economy was touted as being the biggest change in the American workforce in over a century. In 2020, 40 percent of the US workforce was estimated to participate in nonstandard jobs; falling under the looser definition of "gig work".[15] The gig economy describes economic activities related to short-term, project-based, outcome-defined work. It is comprised of gigs offered by those who need the work done, which are completed by workers, who are referred to as gig workers. Companies like Uber, Airbnb, Lyft, Freelancer, and Upwork epitomise the gig worker economy and have accelerated the adoption of this line of work. In addition to prototypical gig work, the gig economy may include parts of the sharing economy, such as renting out rooms; can be in the form of crowdsourced work offered on platforms; or in the broadest sense has been described as any work not included in a standard, permanent, full-time employment model, such as contractor work, temporary work, and casual work.

In 2014, 32 percent of the Australian workforce undertook freelance work, closely followed by 44 million Americans (29 percent of the US workforce), who also participated in some form of gig work during 2015.[15] Alongside millennial mindsets, dreams of entrepreneurship and self-governance, and the impact of the Fourth Industrial Revolution, other factors expediting the emergence of the gig economy are globalisation forces, digital talent marketplaces, and enabling information and communication technologies.[16] One last notable factor is the deeper, fundamental societal changes exposing the flaws of a primitive paradigm, which traded time for money. The old mode of employment was based on the concept of selling time and required employees to physically attend workplaces. However, there has been widespread disenchantment with this view paired with the realisation that it's not all that effective. These days, productive capital is viewed as knowledge, networks, resources, and talent, which may or may not include a time component.

The AI Workforce Development report, titled *The Emergence of the Gig Economy*, shows that not only does the gig economy benefit workers through increased autonomy, flexibility, and engaging work, but is of tremendous benefit to employers. Contingent workforces provide fluid human capital to companies, allowing them to dynamically scale up and down workers depending on project needs and timeline requirements. Another benefit is wider access to talent. Being part of a global village means organisations can reach every corner of the globe in their quest to find the best talent, unearthing specialised professionals who were once inaccessible. Third is a boost in productivity. Due to the individual nature of freelancing, access to better talent, and the associated increase in accountability, gig workers perform better than feet-dragging employees weighed down by corporate politics and veiled by a diffusion of responsibility. Lastly, the on-demand, competitively priced, less-obligated engagement of this pool of professionals allows smaller businesses who are unable to bring time-based employees onboard, the ability to capitalise on the skillsets they require. In effect, levelling the playing field.

The skills most sought after in future workers include critical thinking, problem-solving, and self-management.

Employers understand the changing world of work demonstrated in the World Economic Forum report *The Future of Jobs*.[17] Forty-one percent of employers planned to expand their use of contractors by the year 2025, while 34 percent planned to expand their workforce through technology integration. Furthermore, 84 percent of employers are set to rapidly digitalise working processes with the potential to move 44 percent of their workforce to remote operation. Not to worry – given that the human is now the centre of the universe, one-third of these employers expect to take measures to improve employee wellbeing and create a sense of community, connection, and belonging. Imagine telling a tycoon of the industrial revolution that they had to respect and value people! They would be completely bamboozled.

The skills most sought after in future workers include critical thinking, problem-solving, and self-management such as active learning, resilience, and flexibility. Note that these are all personal qualities. It appears the gig economy has been selected in the natural evolution of society, and in doing so humanises business, raising the importance of your personal brand to record heights. It's not just the five local professionals you're competing with; in some cases you're now up against everyone the internet touches, and your brand better bring you business.

The old order

Sadly, a remnant of the old world of work still has a stranglehold on the current employment landscape. One of the obvious downfalls of status-quo recruitment processes is that they are tied to archaic documents, technologies, and processes. Leonardo da Vinci started the résumé trend in the 15th century by writing his suitability for a position on ancient paper, and not much has changed since. Résumés are still written on a piece of paper. Granted, the structure of them has changed over time, and now we make them with MS Word and other technologies instead of writing them, but the concept, for the most part, is the same.

In the ancient world of work pre-technology, before individuality and personal identity became celebrated, and in the lead up to a radically evolved 21st century society, boring paper-based documents outlining historical employment, education, and technical capabilities that completely *dehumanised* job applicants, worked! But, embarrassingly, this is still how people are hired today. Statistics suggest that in 494 of the Fortune 500 companies, résumés are filtered through an Applicant Tracking System (ATS); a trying and anchored technology that copies résumé data from job applicants into a database, cross-references it with keywords employers have programmed it to look for, and delivers a shortlist of jobseekers to the hiring manager.

From the moment you apply for a job you are stripped of your individuality because traditional recruitment works on treating people as transactional commodities, utilises software anchored to the 15th century concept of employment, bases decisions off impersonal data on résumés, and then cries when new employees aren't a good cultural fit. Puzzlingly, personal qualities are of the highest importance yet usually come as an afterthought in employment. I'm not saying résumés are entirely bad; they're not. They are just primitive, boring, and could be improved, dramatically. Résumés do enable employers to select a candidate from a list of people that have the necessary technical capabilities required for the role, which would otherwise be hard if they didn't exist. If you need someone to create software, for example, it helps if you can gauge their proficiency in software development before you hire them. But in the 21st century this is not enough. Nowhere near it.

Proof evidencing the shortfalls of résumés shines through when employers dutifully journey over to personal social media profiles of applicants to understand who they are as a person. It's further demonstrated by the mandated process of reference checking, where employers call up an applicant's references to get a feel for the person. From these inquisitions, ideally interviews are only offered to those who possess the *necessary baseline personal qualities* required for the role, but with today's depersonalised CVs, a robotic selection process, social media profiles set to private, and references that are personally biased, how are employers to know who to interview? No wonder hiring is such a painful process. The panacea to this archaic and ineffective state of affairs is to radically evolve the concept of the résumé, rethink employment, and innovate recruitment-filtering technologies to better capture the personal qualities of a person, adapt to the new world of work, and improve the selection process of prospective employees, respectively.

To get around these obvious recruitment-related issues, many companies adopt employee referral programs, which prove much more successful than 15th century résumé-related processes because they put personal qualities first. I discuss these in-depth later in the book. Another glimpse of innovation in recruitment is offered through forward-thinking companies who prompt job applicants to upload video biographies, allowing them to get a feel for the person behind the résumé. Not to mention influencers on professional platforms like LinkedIn, who amass hundreds of thousands of likes and are enthusiastically applauded when they post seemingly platitudinal quotes such as, "You don't hire for skills, you hire for attitude. You can always teach skills." It seems that every member on LinkedIn agrees with the premise supporting the importance of personal qualities over technical capabilities, yet begrudgingly are forced to work with 500-year-old concepts. Unfortunately, the truth of today is that the best people aren't selected for jobs, just those who can navigate outdated technologies, list technical capabilities on résumés a pre-programmed machine can pick up, and are lucky enough to make their case in front of a pair of human eyes.

Depersonalisation

The argument against the advertisement of personal qualities in résumés is prejudice, discrimination, and unconscious bias. Recruitment professionals are quick to point out that, as humans, we can all be influenced by unconscious processes and cognitive heuristics, leading us to favour certain people over others based on their personal and social characteristics. Prejudice refers to the tendency for people to make unfavourable and sometimes hostile prejudgements about others based on their social group.[18] For the record, a social group can be defined as any two people who regularly interact, have mutual expectations, and share a common identity.[19] Therefore, an individual's family, religious communities, recreational clubs, universities, high schools, friendship groups, age, sexual orientation, race, social media network, ethnicity, and any other number of groups they belong to could be grounds for prejudice. Discrimination is prejudicial treatment, or, simply put, occurs when prejudice is acted upon. For example, if I was prejudiced toward green aliens because I perceived many of them to be disorganised, then excluded them from being hired at my company as a result, I'd be discriminating against green aliens. This can happen consciously or unconsciously.

As such, the recruitment and résumé-writing industry celebrates depersonalisation. It says no to putting photos on résumés due to the potential for personal characteristics of an applicant leading to unconscious bias in hiring managers; it may prompt people to change their name on their résumé if it hints at a minority cultural background; it warns against advertising oneself in a way that doesn't fit the mould; it takes out employment and education dates on résumés if they hint at outlying age ranges; it obfuscates any information pointing to minority ethnic origins; and, given the climate, I wouldn't be surprised if enforcing gender-neutral names soon became a thing too. We may as well give people ID numbers instead at this rate.

The only information that should be included in a résumé is that which is not social and cannot be used to categorise people.

This is done to eliminate grounds of discrimination; however, given any personal or social information can be used to discriminate, we may as well hide education levels, previous job roles, universities studied at, companies applicants have worked for in the past, hobbies, interests, areas applicants live in, bilingual or multilingual status, and any licences or certificates too, because each of these could be the basis of subjective discrimination. Perhaps employers would much prefer a prestigious education institution like Melbourne University and in effect demonstrate prejudice toward others? Sadly, this was confirmed when hiring managers confided university preferences to me when I had my first company, InternMe Australia. The poor, oppressed university goers who attended less-reputable universities were discriminated against. What an atrocity. Why are jobseekers not told to take out this data? In short, in line with current recommendations and discrimination-dodging advice, the only information that should be included in a résumé is that which is not social and cannot be used to categorise people, otherwise it has the potential to lead to discrimination.

Furthermore, if applicants are telephoned, should it only happen if voice-disguising technology is used by the recruiter or employer? We wouldn't want an accent or the use of mannerisms to lead to discrimination. Also, if personal qualities are such an issue, recruiters and employers should certainly not be allowed to look at social media, ask for personal data from an applicant's references, let alone probe for any personal information before or during an interview. Imagine if they actually saw the person for who they are, unfiltered, socially painted, wholly personalised, and not as anonymised, dehumanised data on a résumé!

The 87 percent of recruiters that use LinkedIn – a professional social media networking site that advertises its users as "talent" – should definitely be shamed because LinkedIn urges users to put up photos of themselves and warns that without photos profiles receive less engagement.[20] LinkedIn highlights that profiles with photos receive 21 times more views and nine times more connection requests than those without.[21] Independent professionals, when using social media platforms like Instagram and Facebook for business purposes, often feature photos of themselves, their customers, or their teams; reason being it personalises their businesses and helps people engage with them. Think about the fitness influencers and make-up artists clogging up Instagram feeds. Even gig economy platforms such as Upwork, Airtasker, and Freelancer ensure their talented workers feel pressure to upload profile photos.

Airtasker highlights profiles with photos are 10 percent more likely to get tasks and that photos help contribute to trust.[22] Upwork goes a step further, suggesting introductory videos are good for business. And what about the companies championing video résumés and asking for one-minute video biographies to be sent in alongside a candidate's job application. The grounds for discrimination here are endless. It's clear people want to see a person, not depersonalised data. The contradictions present in the résumé space and current recruitment processes amongst the backdrop of the 21st century world of work are puzzling.

If we are going to dehumanise people in recruitment and employment, at least let's be consistent? Dehumanisation can prevent discrimination, but until artificial intelligence and advanced robotics replaces humans, organisations are hiring *Homo sapiens* that walk through the door as holistic, flourishing individuals who should be celebrated for all they are; throughout the whole job application and recruitment process, not just when companies have figured out they can make money off them and have decided to onboard them.

I get it – part of being human means we have a higher affinity for people like us, and if a certain demographic of people is prevalent in hiring roles then of course, logically, a bias in hiring processes can arise. An Asian female may prefer another Asian female when hiring. As humans we like people we share a common group with, have similarities to, and are familiar with. This is evolutionary and looking out for "our own" is nested deep in our psychology. Historically, it most likely conferred a survival advantage because we knew how people in groups that we were familiar with interacted, so they were predictable. As such, we perceive people who share similarities or group identities with us as safe; they reflect aspects of us and we all like ourselves; the preferential treatment amongst group members creates and perpetuates a cycle of reciprocity; and, to further evidence the point, as humans we still currently show a natural affinity to cater to a group we identify with, even if the group is formed on meaningless grounds.[18] Evolution wired us this way for good reasons.

So, I understand the noble nature of applicant depersonalisation in traditional employment, but this is a band-aid solution and is still ineffective. Despite the evolutionarily shaped psychological processes that universally influence *Homo sapiens*, discrimination occurs subjectively at the individual level. If hiring managers really are going to discriminate against someone, they'll do it anyway, even if a person makes it all the way to interview and slips under their discrimination radar using an anonymised résumé. Systemic widespread depersonalisation of individuals is not the solution to 21st century business.

The problem is a lack of awareness and understanding by employment professionals about their own cognitive biases and psychology,[23,24] or if this is not the case and professionals do understand the inner-workings of their mind yet still discriminate for no good reason, the problem stems from misguided personal qualities. Therefore, the solution is education, and in the case of individuals who overtly discriminate based on personal or social qualities that shouldn't affect the job, then it's to put someone with better personal qualities in charge of employment. The résumé concept and traditional recruitment processes as they stand extinguish individuality and stifle personal brands.

Achieving your potential

You are brimming with potential, full of value, deserving of a flourishing life living in the enriching environment of the 21st century. This book aims to take you on a journey of brand discovery, starting with helping you to understand the importance of personal principles and to identify your own. Following this, we leverage the psychology of interest to improve creative success and facilitate innovation. From there, we dive deep into your personality to understand how your personal attributes manifest in what is viewed as professional success and details your day-to-day operations. After some introspection, we explore personal networks, strategic partnerships, and both of their ensuing benefits. Moving on to commercialising your potential, we tease apart your ability to identify, develop, and deliver your own personalised suite of products. Hijacking the human experience comes next as modern-day marketing is an experiential process grounded in biology and psychology. By understanding what makes humans tick, aligning these realisations with marketing insights, and then providing you with actionable, foundational knowledge, you are then taught the hidden art of experience engineering, which equips you with skills to alter the personal experience of people you interact with.

One of the best and most famous salespeople in history, Zig Ziglar, wrote a 400-page book titled *Secrets*, where he enthusiastically suggested that to be a good salesperson you had to be a good person. The tone of this book is similar, however, broader in scope, suggesting all forms of professional and personal success are inextricably linked, and both are heavily influenced by each other. My hope for this book is that it results in the achievement of your personal brand's potential, a hallmark of your biological business' success, and consequently provides you with a resource and perspective shift for a flourishing life in the modern world.

PART I

Chapter 1:
Principles

The DNA of your personal brand

Yuval Harari, a history professor from Oxford University who studied the roots of humanity, talks about the cognitive revolution and how the ability for humans to imagine things was the predecessor to modern civilisation. In his book *Sapiens*, Yuval proposes that our developed cognitive and metacognitive abilities allow us to flourish as a species by directing our efforts and improving our understanding in all areas of life. He demonstrates that just as imagination in the form of religion, myths, and social systems facilitated how *Homo sapiens* and their communities lived their life, imagination also affected and guided the development of fictional entities, such as the legal structures of businesses, partnerships, and companies.

The suggestion that humankind and the corporate world function within a shared imagined reality may seem outlandish, but if you were to discuss with an Amazonian hunter-gatherer tribe the legal structure of your disruptive tech company, you would be met with puzzled expressions (and perhaps an aggressive grumble coupled with a searching spear). Reality to them is much different to yours. They are in the business of survival, living day to day, and running a hunter-gatherer tribe. Why in the world would they exert mental effort or allocate precious time to coming up with something as complicated and abstract as a legal entity with human-like rights? Our reality, and the reality of an Amazonian tribe is based on the enaction and widespread adoption of our corresponding imaginations.

In the same way that fictitious thoughts can build countries, societies, legal entities, ancient ritualistic practices, and all-encompassing religious narratives, these inventive thoughts also dramatically influence our own individual realities and weave themselves into our personal philosophies. As a result of our evolutionarily fine-tuned minds, we can interrogate our own existence, analyse feelings bubbling up from deep within us, and create an imagined set of beliefs or rules that guide our behaviours, motives, interactions, and decisions. Higher-order thinking processes, born from humanity's cognitive and metacognitive abilities, allow each of us to develop, articulate, and adhere to our own personal philosophy.

Exactly as it sounds, personal philosophies are unique to individuals, directly stem from personal qualities, and form a fundamental component of our personal brand. For instance, Martin Luther King Jr's philosophy of nonviolence, born from his introspection and fundamental perspectives of the world, was key in differentiating him from other African Americans living during the times of the civil rights movement. The power of and support for his philosophy is also one of the main reasons for his fame.

As humans ventured further into the land of imagination, we even began to project these human-centric qualities onto our made-up entities; our companies and businesses. It's common to see organisations highlighting their company philosophy through tabs on their website, in the depths of their business plans, and through advertising and marketing campaigns. In a propaganda-like fashion, these same companies try to instil their philosophy into their employees, ensuring that workers feel pressure to voluntarily enrol themselves into the imaginary framework being presented to them. After all, you can't work for Justin Bieber if you're not a Belieber, and you'd find yourself misplaced if you joined forces with the leading animal rights organisation, PETA, while spending money on animal products manufactured through the cruel and unethical treatment of animals.

> Your guiding beliefs heavily influence your success in life and are inextricably linked with your professional potential in business.

As an aside, the projection of philosophies onto organisations, and the resulting propagation of them, means philosophical congruence is vital for employee–employer relations. Especially in an opportunity-dense and empathically fuelled 21st century world that places the individual at the centre of the universe. The corporate world will fast come to know that people in the modern world are "entitled", and having philosophical needs realised is no longer a "nice to have" but is increasingly becoming a precondition of engagement.

As such, in this chapter I focus on areas of philosophy, ethics, and values, and how they tie into personal principles, then finish off by exploring vision and mission statements. By the close of this chapter, I hope it will be clearer to you that your guiding beliefs – your philosophy, combined with its constituent components in your values, ethics, vision statements, and mission statements – heavily influence your success in life and are inextricably linked with your professional potential in business. This applies when you work for a company and are forced to align your personal philosophies with the company's philosophy, when you operate as an independent professional, or if you become the founder of your own company.

As mentioned, the further apart your personal philosophies are from your company's philosophies, the more dissatisfaction and pressure you will feel, which is why opting for philosophical congruence is conducive to your best professional self. In the case of working as an independent professional, you essentially function as a holistic business, integrating personal attributes of *you* directly into the services you offer your customers. If you are the business, your personal philosophy doubles as your business philosophy, and if not exactly similar, your business philosophy will be inextricably tied to your personal philosophy. After all, it would be unlikely for a well-natured individual with a life philosophy encompassing benevolence, financial freedom, and fairness, to run a company that blatantly cons vulnerable elderly people out of their life savings.

When, and if, you begin your own company and are a founder, your personal philosophies become the company's philosophies, which new employees will be governed by and pressured to enlist in. In any professional capacity, from employee to employer, or volunteer to independent professional, your philosophy remains fundamental and impactful. Without a match, flourishing is unachievable.

Prioritise to philosophise

The power of philosophy is evident through the current standing of the world we live in today. The Greek philosopher Aristotle, who lived between 384 and 322 BC, was known for defending reason, inventing logic, examining reality, and for placing an emphasis on human flourishing. It's true, surprisingly, that the ecosystem of modern society, from democracy to the scientific method, and from psychological wellbeing to the rise of reason, has largely been shaped by ancient philosophies such as Aristotle's. Not all philosophies traverse 2,000 years of human civilisation, but some do, and it is a testament to the power and penetrative nature of a sound philosophy.

You have the power to impact the zeitgeist of society and can even influence fundamental human realities.

Philosophy, if translated from its Greek roots, literally means the "love of wisdom". Nowadays in society, philosophy represents a much larger field of study and places emphasis on an individual's fundamental perspectives of the world. Philosophy is an activity that people engage in to learn the deep truths about themselves and understand the world in which they live. Additionally, it can be used to explore the relationships that exist between themselves and others, and themselves and the world. In recent times, the pedagogy of philosophy has matured, introducing subdomains including ethics, logic, value, and metaphysics, some of which we'll explore soon. An interesting thought here is that when a personal philosophy becomes adopted mainstream, it manifests as a social norm and subsequently becomes embedded in a shared reality.

Stemming from your mind, you have the power to impact the zeitgeist of society and can even influence fundamental human realities. Martin Luther King Jr, Aristotle, Plato, Newton, Darwin, Jobs and Wozniak, Larry Page and Sergey Brin are but a few individuals *who changed the world* because of their philosophies. Although you may not personally send global shockwaves that ripple over two millennia and come up with a human and societal framework like Aristotle, you still have the ability and right to generate, live, and propagate your own set of unique, fundamental beliefs. Many a time, the world will enthusiastically thank you for your contribution.

To illustrate a philosophy in action we can look at the example of "minimalism". This is a philosophy that rejects the consumerist nature that blankets most affluent countries, suggesting that instead of splurging on materialistic things that we don't need, the key to a happy, fulfilling life is to rid yourself of excess. It promotes a life free of stress, worry, and anguish, instead promising time for the more important things, such as family and freedom. Some individuals who choose to adopt this philosophy opt in to anoint themselves as a loyal minimalist, and completely alter their habits, routines, and behaviours to fit in with this ideological framework. This example shows the interactional nature of philosophies in that they can move from a person to a community, or from a community to a person, in much the same way as corporate philosophies behave. If you joined The Fred Hollows Foundation, for example, which is driven by the mantra to "restore sight", it wouldn't be long before your yardstick measurement for success transitioned from profits and losses to the number of people's eyes positively impacted. And if it didn't, you should probably quit.

Aristotle is famous for his views – his philosophy – on human flourishing and happiness. He proposed that each person's life has a purpose, and that the nature of one's life is to achieve that purpose.[1,2] The purpose of life, identified by Aristotle, was termed "eudemonia", otherwise known as "happiness" or "flourishing", and was thought to be achieved through the use of reason and the acquisition of virtues. Flourishing was identified by Aristotle as the "highest good" of human existence and described as a situation in which "a person is concurrently doing what he ought to do and doing what he wants to do". This view is both individualistic and universal to human existence. It is individual in that the wants and needs of one person are not necessarily present in another ("what he wants to do"). However, by extolling the moral development of individuals, societal functioning improves as people derive pleasure from enacting virtues such as generosity, honesty, integrity, and benevolence. "What he ought to do" relates to actions that universally benefit humanity.

Importantly, Aristotle noted, a precondition for individual happiness and flourishing is self-direction, otherwise known as autonomy, as this allows an individual freedom in their decision-making and behaviours. He endorsed the right of personal direction in your life, including the rational use of endowments, virtues, and energies for the pursuit of freely and rationally chosen values and goals. He suggested combining freedom with reason, and through the development of proper virtues taught by your experiences, you can identify your ultimate end in life and work toward it while using your abilities to their fullest. As you realise your talents in pursuit of your unique purpose, you undergo a process of self-actualisation, achieving your innate potential to become all that you can be. In addition, for you to flourish, your actions must be deemed "proper", as this signifies personal moral accomplishments.

Aristotle proposed that the combination of self-actualisation and moral achievements constitute a flourishing life and result in happiness and enjoyment for the individual. The idea of human flourishing encompasses a wide range of constitutive ends, such as pursuits of knowledge, productive work, the development of character traits, religion, love, self-efficacy, pleasurable sensations, and community building. It follows then, that to have a flourishing life as Aristotle suggested, you need to exercise your capacity to reason to develop your own set of uniquely fulfilling goals, values, and ultimate ends while behaving virtuously. All of which come under the umbrella of your own personal philosophy. Taking the time to introspect, explore, and truly understand yourself, while accounting for your relationship to the rest of the physical world – which includes other people – is a precursor to your existential success.

In doing this, not only would you be setting yourself on a path to success, achieving the highest state of human existence and validating the 2,350-year-old beliefs of an Ancient Greek, but you would also be appeasing the recommendations of modern-day psychology. Psychological wellbeing evidences many similarities with Aristotle's concept of "eudemonia" and refers to the inter- and intraindividual levels of positive functioning that constitute a meaningful, purposeful, and authentic life of self-realisation. As is mostly the case, anything immeasurable and ambiguous is vilified by the scientific community, and it wasn't long before an American psychologist crafted a comprehensive framework to accurately measure the psychological wellbeing of an individual.[3] The framework consists of six dimensions:

1. Self-acceptance
2. Positive relations with others
3. Autonomy
4. Environmental mastery
5. Purpose in life
6. Personal growth

High scores in each of these dimensions, in combination, symbolises an individual has arrived at a psychological utopia and attained fulfilment in life. The resemblance of this psychological wellbeing framework to Aristotle's philosophy is uncanny, which is why sometimes "psychological wellbeing" can be used interchangeably with "eudemonic wellbeing". As well as identifying the need to "become all that they can be" (comprised of autonomy, personal growth, and purpose in life in the modern framework), Aristotle also arrived at the conclusion that meaningful relationships are necessitated by the human condition (now measured via the scores in the dimension called positive relations with others), and that people can achieve their values if they recognise and adhere to the reality of their unique personal endowments and contingent circumstances (the environmental mastery dimension).

Understanding that the Aristotelian philosophy of flourishing is largely synonymous with 21st century conceptualisations of psychological wellbeing means taking advice from Aristotle will evidently improve your mental state, quality of life, and put you in the good books of any professional psychologist. Not only does this bring about psychological improvements, but notably influences your physical health and, weirdly enough, might even extend your lifespan.

"Health", as defined by the World Health Organization, is "a state of complete physical, mental, and social wellbeing and not merely the absence of disease or infirmity". Psychological wellbeing therefore receives plenty of attention in the world of health research. A recently published paper demonstrated links between psychological wellbeing and physical health outcomes, showing a significant relationship between the two evidenced through mortality rates.[4] Throughout the paper, the authors combined numerous studies demonstrating that increased scores on scales for "purpose in life", "personal growth", "mastery", "optimism", and "overall psychological wellbeing", led people to have lower mortality rates and, therefore, on average, live longer than their non-flourishing counterparts.

Potential mechanisms underlying these findings included the stress-buffering effects of positive mental states and the healthier behaviours, habits, and lifestyles of those who are psychologically well. For example, a depressed person may eat away their feelings only to end up with a skyrocketing BMI that becomes a risk factor for many life-threatening physical diseases. On the flipside, a positive, motivated, purposeful, or optimistic person may be more inclined to socialise, exercise, or engage in healthy activities conducive to better physical health. Both psychological states result in molecular cascades that underlie their associated emotions. Negative mental states increase cortisol, usually in a chronic manner, which has detrimental effects on the immune system[5] – the vigilant protection and surveillance system of our body. Whereas positive mental states do the opposite and boost immune system functioning through many different mechanisms,[6] while sidestepping the detrimental effects of mental negativity. Thoughtfully crafting your framework of governing thoughts using your imagination can demonstrably extend your life here on Earth. Beliefs and perspectives really are a lifesaver for you or the organisms they serve.

Organisations under the microscope

If we specifically apply an organisational lens to our current area of interest, it highlights the importance of philosophy in business. Ideally, organisational philosophies guide the internal and external processes of the business and provide an overarching framework for the whole ecosystem of the business to operate within. If a company philosophy is not formally established, it becomes an unsolvable puzzle, contributed to by many aspects of the organisation. Solving the puzzle and piecing together a company's philosophy that hasn't been explicitly articulated will involve observing and analysing the attitudes of employees, the company culture, the belief systems and values of organisational influencers, process guidelines, and the unwritten code of ethics that govern moral behaviours between employees and customers.

Corporate philosophies prove to be a huge differentiator when comparing businesses with each other. Let's explore an example contrasting two fictional companies: "Food Products" and "Bananas About Bananas". Food Products and Bananas About Bananas both operate in the same area of business – both sell bananas. The key difference between the two lies in their philosophies.

Food Products hasn't established its philosophy formally. As a result, the business and employees lack direction and have no insight into the company direction or its vision. Additionally, the moral guidelines – the unwritten laws governing internal company communications and external customer-facing interactions – are missing. An absence of identified values and an unclear mission means employees can't operate autonomously as they are unsure of what constitutes right and wrong. It does not help that new employees are not properly filtered based on personal qualities but are hastily accepted on baseline technical criteria. The result is a lacklustre business in an insidious nosedive.

Begrudgingly, employees drag themselves through their shift and resemble zombies on autopilot. Such an environment stifles the potential for meaningful relationships to develop between colleagues and peers, leading to less psychological security and suboptimal career experiences, both of which factor into organisational productivity and performance. Moreover, it is evident that initiative, independence, and individualism aren't fostered in this workplace culture, which could validly be summarised at times as chaotic and anarchic.

The apathetic employee experience is further projected onto other workers and customers, propagating an undesirable experience in all directions. In fact, customers are treated as purely transactional, and, consequently, their experience with the company is usually negative. Customer mistreatment, stemming from a lack of care, morals, and purpose in employees, is a frequent occurrence, but unfortunately mistreatment here doesn't discriminate. Employees too frequently raise concerns about bullying and toxic workplace behaviour to senior management. The corrective action and outcome of which is as nebulous as the company philosophy. The company makes money through the sale of bananas. This is what they do, and there is nothing exceptional to be found here. Food Products is ordinary.

In stark contrast, Bananas About Bananas is, quite literally, bananas about bananas. It started off as a passion project of an individual who enjoyed growing bananas on his farm, and who found further fulfilment when he could gift them to loved ones and friends. But the demand for the product grew exponentially, accelerating the transformation from passion project to incorporated company. The owner is a person who values food, values nutrition, and is imbued with integrity while possessing an admirable moral code. He sees bananas as fundamental to physical health and as an earthly gift. Especially since many people of the world are poverty stricken.

His work ethic and quality standards are second to none because of his commitment to deliver only the best produce. The company reflects and amplifies the characteristics and beliefs of its founder. Everyone who comes to work at the company meets him, and if they do not share his passion and appreciate the greater impact of their work, he won't hire them. Employees have no hope of being integrated into the organisation without a functioning moral compass. Additionally, if they can't navigate the sensitive blueprint that codes for humane interactions with others, then their future at the organisation vanishes. He is vigilant when it comes to workers. Extending from the greater vision, the company places customers on a pedestal and boasts manifestos that highlight the customer-centric nature of the business.

The people working at Bananas About Bananas, after being vetted, are empowered to make independent decisions, act on initiative, and be themselves. In a bushfire crisis, like the one seen in Australia in 2020, an astute employee would readily donate bananas to the affected areas and be commended for doing so. Employees have high degrees of psychological security and go above and beyond for the organisation, knowing they will be supported by management and peers when they base their decisions on company principles. Customers have a good experience when they purchase produce, and the awareness of the company is amplified by these people in society. Communities have started to form around the product, local businesses have rushed to integrate this healthy product into existing food delivery businesses, and locals enjoy gathering for a day on the banana farm while they sit in the sun drinking their coffee and bask in the positivity of the organisation's culture. The company has never initiated advertising or marketing campaigns, awareness has grown organically, much like their product through the word-of-mouth advertising that has resulted from inspired, satisfied, and happy customers.

The day and night difference between both banana-selling companies can be attributed to their philosophies. A philosophy is a moral, value-oriented, ethically imbued, and focused framework of beliefs, which, when properly crafted, ensures a company resonates with people and achieves peak productivity.

Power to the people

An example personal philosophy could be:

> *I believe engaging in life with an open mind, and a never-ending pursuit of knowledge can lead to the betterment of humanity through collaboration and discovery.*

Here's the thing though, when you're operating in a professional capacity, such as a business founder or an independent professional, more often than not your personal philosophy and the professional philosophy governing your business largely overlap. Often, they can be one and the same. If you're the founder of a company and you are driven to better the quality of people's lives, have an intense curiosity in science and technology, and adhere to a strong set of morals, guess what your business – the extension of yourself – will be known for? Probably an innovative biotechnology company that measures its success in the number of people that it's helped while pursuing the latest and greatest medical and scientific advancements in search of positive human impact.

If you are a compassionate and respectful individual operating on a philosophy of fairness and empowerment, when you step into your professional role as a freelance marketing consultant and offer services to a multitude of customers, guess how your services will be received in the market? Even as an employee, the professional projection of yourself is blueprinted by your personal principles including your philosophy. Your personality, beliefs, morals, experiences, and values underlie the delivery of your professional services. Commonly, employee–employer relationships break down due to mismatches in principles, exemplified by "value clashes", "attitudinal disagreements", or "philosophical incongruence", yet none of these relate to the technical delivery of professional services that an employer contracts an employee to do in a professional capacity.

To illustrate, a talented artist may not believe in equality, may be completely narcissistic, and may act contradictory to the beliefs of their company, but they can still deliver the work they are paid to do. However, because of their belief systems and other *personal* qualities, they will be fired. In business, personal qualities are always attached to professional services if a human is directly involved in their delivery. It's why understanding the intrinsic relationship between yourself-as-a-person and yourself-operating-as-a-business, is essential. Especially for the future landscape of work, which will be largely populated by independent professionals, entrepreneurs, and self-managing employees, foreshadowing an even greater overlapping of personal brands into professional spheres. Personal philosophies enormously affect your professional potential.

Valuable values

Values, an important area of your personal principles, are the things you hold to have worth. Values differ from person to person, organisation to organisation, and community to community, making this metaphysical concept somewhat challenging to investigate. However, us modern-day *Homo sapiens* are not scared of a challenge. To tackle this, a new area of study was birthed from the wider umbrella of philosophy, known as axiology. Axiology explores the concept of "value" and seeks to understand the nature and types of values that exist. For example, value can be explored in a variety of areas such as ethics, politics, and religion, and can be characterised as a subjective psychological state or purely objectively.[7] When explored as subjective phenomena it becomes apparent that everyone has different values; this is neither good nor bad but alters our interactions with objects, ideas, and people. For example, our love and dislike for objects, people, or other things is determined by how much we find that to be valuable to ourselves.

If others don't value similar things to us, our common ground with them diminishes, meaning the scope of collaborative and enjoyable activities that could be done together is reduced, along with the potential for a meaningful, fruitful, and long-lasting relationship to develop. The people we are most fond of usually share similar values to us, which is why we are most fond of them in the first place, and why we invest time and effort into building and fortifying our relationships with them. This is how meaningful friendships develop. If two people value mathematical science, a brighter future for humanity, friendship, and health, we could reasonably assume the two individuals will flourish in coexistence. They both have the underlying value architecture conducive for this to happen. Conversely, the people we despise or feel indifferent toward are usually the ones operating on a completely alien hierarchy of values. After all, a medical doctor probably wouldn't spend his Friday night with a serial killer; their life purposes governed by their values, are polar opposites. The Hippocratic oath is insoluble in a bath of maliciously spilled blood.

Objectively, bits of information are neither valuable nor valueless; however, certain pieces of information to certain individuals can be interpreted as such. Information made available to researchers foreshadowing answers to perplexing scientific questions and facilitating medical innovation in society could surely be deemed valuable, but only to those researchers or the people who benefit directly from it. To the people on the outskirts, like those living in poverty who are unreachable by these health-bolstering discoveries, this information has no value. The way we analyse information and how it makes us feel determines how we behave toward the source of it. For example, in employment settings, interviewers usually hire people they "like". In other words, they "like" the values – a subset of personal qualities being displayed by a person – that are being transmitted. As such, interviewers process this information about candidates favourably, it stirs up positive feelings from within them, and they act on these feelings accordingly. In this case, they hire the candidate.

In business, we engage with companies that we "like" and do deals with people we "like". Usually, we like them because there is a value match. Seeing them demonstrate our values is attractive because it reflects us and is a form of validation. Maybe this is why passionately experiencing your values can dramatically improve the extent to which you like your life. When you live your values, your life reflects you.

Evidently, this happens in your professional life. The extent to which you value your work, or your "work values", can significantly and solely affect your job satisfaction. This is related to job characteristics across dimensions such as:

- the intrinsic interest in your work
- the amount of independence you have in your role
- the relationships you have at work
- the opportunities to grow in your job
- how convenient your work is.

If your personal values are supported by your job characteristics, this results in increased job satisfaction because your values are being realised in your work environment. Are you working in an area you are interested in? Do you value professional growth? If you do and if your job has you on a progression plan you would score higher on job satisfaction. If you value autonomy and your job allows you to manage yourself independently, value congruence arises and, as such, job satisfaction improves. Similarly, if your moral values encompass fairness and equality, and promotions are handled in this manner throughout your organisation, then personal values, again, are being reflected at work and boost satisfaction.[8]

Logically, any aspects of your work that match your personal values should achieve a similar result. Job satisfaction has flow-over effects to your overall quality of life, which isn't hard to believe given that the traditional employment model nested in a capitalist society sees it making up a large portion of waking life.[9] Additionally, value patterns have been shown to distinguish successful managers from unsuccessful managers, with successful managers valuing aggressiveness, change, creativity, competition, and liberalism more than their counterparts. Value patterns have been proven to influence career choices, guide corporate decisions regarding strategy, and are shown to alter employee commitment to organisations.[10]

In the interest of avoiding a 20,000-word deep dive into mind-boggling value-related theories in philosophy, we can summarise values as subjective, internal, and malleable beliefs and opinions we hold regarding ideas, people, or objects that enable us to accomplish certain objectives. Unlike overarching philosophical belief systems, which may comprise many values, single values are more targeted, guide us in certain aspects of life, and essentially allow us to organise our behaviour across many situations. They include our moral, personal, cultural, and professional values.

Like humans, companies operate and behave according to their values. Our previous case study provides an example of how values manifest in professional settings at an organisational level. If we slide "Food Products" and "Bananas About Bananas" under the microscope, we can zoom in on their values and determine their correlations with the company's success. Food Products' values are entirely absent or peppered so thin that they are virtually non-existent. Nothing has been formalised, and autonomous professionals driven by their own fundamental beliefs about the world are not empowered in this environment. Professional autonomy, along with those workers who value it, is drowned out by prehistoric institutional norms that view employees as robotic, submissive work horses, and is just one example of where this organisation's misguided value system leads to turmoil.

In contrast, Bananas About Bananas demonstrates and operates on clear values, positively affecting the running of the business. The values instilled in this company from day one encompass integrity, quality control, respect, benevolence, autonomy, and equality. Employees who demonstrate these values are recognised, selected out, and supported. Those who need a refresher course receive the gentle propaganda necessary to invoke tectonic shifts in their value hierarchies to better align them with the value system of the organisation.

In our case study, the missing link between Food Products and Bananas About Bananas is a result of two reasons. First, Food Products may have values, but they aren't clearly defined, leading to ambiguity, decreased productivity, decreased employee job satisfaction, bad customer experiences, and a scatter-gunned company direction. A lack of awareness and introspection about values at the governance level can lead to this. This reinforces the idea that a company blueprint that fails to pinpoint clearly articulated values cannot have them be effectively distributed to, and actioned by, individuals throughout the organisation. Value incongruence is failure. Food Products evidences the consequence of this.

Second, the values they do have may be enacted the whole time but are just not honourable or conducive to modern interpretations of success, such as those that improve employee experience, an organisation's brand image, or customer satisfaction. Valuing money, valuing oneself disproportionately above others (think pathological narcissism), and valuing the status and power derived from different organisational roles could have been manifested by the owner of Food Products and then passed down its genealogy. People at the executive level and those in management may be driven by ulterior motives that are less than admirable because of their misguided value systems. The cancerous beliefs and values of these people affect all levels of the company and create a perpetuating cycle of mismanagement, which becomes the organisational norm to the detriment of everyone but the pigs of George Orwell's animal farm.

At an organisational level, clearly defining values and selectively filtering only those that are virtuous to enact are two ways to ensure that the value system is poised for success and immune to corporate cancer.

In the corporate world, values are organisation specific, much like they are personally subjective, and emanate throughout businesses that acknowledge and appreciate their existence. Importantly, they are subjectively shaped by an individual or group who are inextricably tied to the birth or governance of the organisation. After all, values are ingredients of the human condition, which are merely leveraged by these fictitious entities in an effort to humanise them. The mechanisms of value creation and value congruence are extremely important for achieving peak productivity in your own life, in partnerships, or in organisations. Values are a major differentiator in business, and in people.

Now that we know and understand the significance of properly defined values, it's important to apply these learnings to yourself. The accurate identification and realisation of your value system comprises a key element of your personal brand and represents a major differentiator for you. If you were to locate yourself a doppelganger who shared all your educational credentials, capabilities, career experiences, and major life events but did not share your value system, you could end up worlds apart as time goes on. Cloning a genius and swapping out value systems could result in anything from a broke professor to a revolutionary computer scientist, or a bestselling author to a billion-dollar megalomaniac company founder. This would depend on the unique value system that the clone operated on. The broke professor may have valued education, learning, and knowledge. The computer scientist may have valued societal evolution, a utopian future, and technological advancement. Becoming a bestselling author probably stemmed from values of deeply connecting with people, positively influencing others, and creativity. All of which are realised through the creation and distribution of a book. Lastly, a genius who values money, fame, and status may selectively pursue avenues that help her achieve her ends. Maybe she started a company to exploit a highly profitable product and then used her profits to buy power, expand her corporate portfolio, and subsequently enhance her status. The underlying genius capability existed in all these people but was focused through a specific value lens resulting in completely unique outcomes.

What are the fundamental beliefs that underlie your behaviours, decisions, and earthly interactions? What are your ideals? If you had to list all your values, how would you prioritise them? Are there values that are subsets of other larger universal values? If you had to choose only three, what would they be? Exploring these questions will help you align yourself with opportunities, people, educational endeavours, and business ventures throughout your life. At the top of your value hierarchy lies the key to your best life. For example, if you value helping others, learning about biological sciences, and appreciate humanity, a life as a research scientist on a quest for a cancer cure likely represents your best life. As you'll see, these values tie into your ethics, your vision, and your mission, and without them you are flying blind.

Ethical ethics

Ethics, also known as moral philosophy, involves the exploration of right and wrong behaviour and differs from values in key ways. Values are a set of ideals that guide our behaviours and influence our motivations in all areas of life. Ethics are a consistent moral standard of right and wrong. In some cases, ethics are said to be the "social values" of groups, with ethical recommendations for certain courses of social action mirroring the "guidance" that our subjective values impress on us, attesting to their similarity with values. In this context, ethics can be thought of as overarching moral values relating to human conduct. Unlike the subjective nature of values, ethics are more universal and absolutist, reinforced through institutions, countries, communities, and other people.

In the larger field of ethics there are three conceptually different subfields:

1. Metaethics
2. Normative ethics
3. Applied ethics

Metaethics investigates where ethical principles come from. In contrast, normative ethics is more practical, less philosophical, and aims to develop moral standards that can be used to regulate right and wrong conduct. Applied ethics is the application of ethics to a controversial topic such as abortion or animal welfare.[11]

Normative ethics is the field relevant to us. Moral standards, including our sensitivity to others and the acknowledgment of right and wrong consequences of behaviour, when operationalised in an organisation or professional setting, lead to a code of ethics. This code provides a general framework for what constitutes right and wrong behaviour. You should abide by a code of ethics that aligns with your values. When personal values and codes of ethics are aligned in organisations, research suggests that individuals are less likely to act unethically.[10]

Living your values, provided they are socially acceptable, may not only lead to a better quality of life, more work enjoyment, and higher job satisfaction, but also ensures you are consistently operating ethically and adhering to Aristotle's virtuous recommendations. To better understand normative ethics, it helps to draw an imaginary line between this concept and empathy. In philosophy, encyclopaedias, and professional ethics-related-PhD dissertations, strong links have been found between empathy and ethics.[12,13] Due to its nature, which is the ability to understand another's feelings and see situations from their point of view, empathy has been proposed by some researchers as a primal existential condition that makes ethical life possible.

Looking back at the previous example, Food Products, alongside clearly defined values and proper governance, lacks a code of ethics. This is evident through the mistreatment of customers and the internal bullying concerns that were raised to senior management. There are no guidelines on how humans should behave toward each other in this environment, nor are employees vetted on morality grounds when they are hired. Bananas About Bananas, however, has a strong ethical undercurrent that shapes the behaviours of people working there. It is observable in the customer-centric philosophy of the business and the treatment and respect seen between employees. The initial selection process helps filter out the wrong type of people, leading to an environment of well-meaning and interpersonally sensitive, ethical individuals. These employees reify the code through their practical adherence to it and reinforce it through social norms. Even if someone is rough around their moral edges when they enter the organisation, the environment soon conditions their behaviour accordingly.

Your ethics are ultimately important. If you can't decipher between right and wrong behaviour and then act accordingly, relationships will suffer. Opportunities and networks will be lost. People won't like or advocate for you. Society will frown on you, and your personal brand will become irreversibly tarnished. Such reasons are inferior to simply being an honourable citizen of humanity. In your personal quest for moral excellence, if you are interested in such an endeavour, psychological counselling, exploring philosophy, and online courses and books that focus on developing emotional intelligence and empathy would be extremely beneficial.

You're a visionary

Two further overarching concepts ensuring you have a clearly defined trajectory, and that you're continually moving forward, are your vision and mission statements. These are currently popularised in public and private organisational settings, and if you're an employee at a large company you've probably seen the company vision and mission statements plastered on the walls or advertised somewhere on the website. The mission statement simply outlines a pragmatic way to progress toward the vision.

Visions are personal and powerful. Realise yours.

To break these concepts down, visions, at their most foundational explanation, are vivid mental images of a future point in time. And a vision statement in the context of flourishing can be summarised as a statement that illustrates where something could and would like to be in the future.

It's aspirational and is as simple as answering any of the following:

- Where are we going?
- Where do we want to be?
- Who and what are we inspiring to change?
- What are our hopes and dreams?
- Who do I want to be?

The following are examples of company vision statements:

Google: *To provide access to the world's information in one click.*

Amazon: *Our vision is to be earth's most customer-centric company; to build a place where people can come to find and discover anything they might want to buy online.*

Nike: *To remain the most authentic, connected, and distinctive brand.*

Oxfam: *A world without poverty.*

The vision statements guide the companies through many situations and remain relatively stable over time. It keeps them on track and highlights the most important, all-encompassing, company objective. It is like a light at the end of the tunnel or a utopian end state with a magnetic attraction. Companies use this as a guide. On a personal level, without a vision you will ricochet through life being pulled in contradictory directions, wasting time and effort on meaningless, rather than meaningful, ventures. Your vision is what gives you a sense of purpose and meaning, and it helps to clearly articulate it and reference it over time.

The following are examples of personal vision statements:

Martin Luther King Jr (1963): *I have a dream that one day, on the red hills of Georgia, the sons of former slaves and the sons of former slave owners will be able to sit down together at the table of brotherhood. I have a dream that one day even the state of Mississippi, a state sweltering with the heat of injustice, sweltering with the heat of oppression, will be transformed into an oasis of freedom and justice. I have a dream that my four little children will one day live in a nation where they will not be judged by the color of their skin but by the content of their character…*

John F Kennedy (1961): *I believe that this Nation should commit itself to achieving the goal, before this decade is out, of landing a man on the Moon and returning him safely to Earth.*

The personal vision statements of two men dating back over 50 years completely changed the landscape of civil rights across the globe and slingshotted humanity into the abyss of space, landing us on satellite rocks orbiting the Earth. This is the power of a clearly articulated vision statement scaffolded by wholehearted conviction.

Generic examples based on professions could be:

A PhD student studying medicine: *To make a valuable addition to the medical research community in the global war on disease.*

A psychologist: *To help free people from the chains of their mind to better the quality of as many human lives as possible.*

Importantly, realise that even though a vision can be attached to a company and even a country, it was initially attached to and formulated by a person or group of people. They simply magnified their vision by attaching it to a non-human entity that other people could easily rally around. Visions are personal and powerful. Realise yours.

On a mission

The dictionary definition of a mission statement is: "a formal summary of the aims and values of a company, organisation, or individual." As you can see, the values discussed earlier are inextricably linked to your mission statement. Simply put, a mission relays "why something exists", or in other words, its "reason for being". This is determined by an underlying value structure because if it wasn't valuable to its creator, a mission wouldn't exist. Therefore, a mission statement is a short statement about you, or your company's purpose or reason for existence that highlights important values. If the vision is the endgame, your mission is how you live each day on your quest to get there.

The following are examples of company mission statements:

Tesla: *To accelerate the world's transition to sustainable energy.*

Kickstarter: *To help bring creative projects to life.*

Uber: *We ignite opportunity by setting the world in motion.*

Spotify: *To unlock the potential of human creativity—by giving a million creative artists the opportunity to live off their art and billions of fans the opportunity to enjoy and be inspired by it.*

Extending from the personal vision examples, their mission statements may have looked something like this (the following quotes from Martin Luther King Jr and John F Kennedy have been made up for the purpose of this exercise):

Martin Luther King Jr (1963): *To bring awareness to the current injustices plaguing African Americans, and to spend each and every day fighting for civil rights.*

John F Kennedy (1961): *To inspire confidence and belief in people and to engage the smartest and most passionate scientists who will collectively contribute to landing a man on the moon.*

A PhD student studying medicine: *To study diligently, work hard, and think creatively for the benefit of science and human health.*

A psychologist: *To empower people every day with valuable, freeing, and perspective-shifting knowledge that they can use to better their life.*

To sum up

As demonstrated above, the cognitive and metacognitive abilities that we have developed as humans are not only conducive to our success as a species and success in the corporate world of business but are necessary for us to flourish as individuals. In the same way that the powerful philosophies of the glorified deceased eternally radiate into the wider world and are continually adopted by communities, countries, and humanity, so too do we possess the ability to craft our own contagious philosophies.

For us to achieve the highest state of human existence, and simultaneously check off the criteria of modern-day psychological wellbeing, we need to identify, enact, and pursue our values while striving to fulfil our self-determined purpose in life. We need to align ourselves with that which we determine significant to ourselves while extinguishing everything that is contrary to our personal philosophies. In doing this, we focus our efforts on meaningful pursuits while improving our career satisfaction, relationships with others, physical health, and psychological wellbeing.

What we believe in, what we oblige ourselves to do, what we value, and the moral standards we hold ourselves accountable to stem from our personal qualities, our natural essence, and form the unique DNA of our personal brand.

Puzzlingly, it is our values, code of conduct, and beliefs that can lead us to be perceived as valuable by others. It is why employers hire people with similar values and why friendships are usually nested in similitude. Dollars, minutes, effort, and emotions are unhesitatingly invested into other people that we find valuable. In this vein, identifying our core values is one way to streamline our life because it shows us what is important, who is important, what is "worth" doing, and what should be prioritised. Operating as a social magnet, our values draw people toward us, expediting opportunistic connections, and can effectively filter our social world for us.

Our value hierarchies contribute to the discovery of our metaphorical destination and provide the architecture necessary to craft and live our mission. Many measures of success are a result of your ability to successfully introspect. A journey into your inner world sets the scene for your life on Earth. Your success heavily depends on this element of your personal brand. Prioritise to philosophise.

What's next?

In the following chapter we will shift our attention to "interests", the universal basic drive we share that motivates us to action. Drawing a line from interests to character traits shines light on the nature of curiosity, and from here we are able to see how both a drive state and a character trait are predecessors to creativity. Creativity is then explored in terms of its utility throughout history and even through to its place in our future. From creation, innovation flows, and knowing this companies seek out only those possessing this highly valued ability. Creativity is something we all possess, and apart from it being an innate feature present in each and every one of us, its potential can be maximised when interests take centre stage.

Chapter 2:
Interests, Creativity, and Innovation

21st century superpowers

Paul Sylvia, a leading researcher on the emotion of interest, views interest as a basic human drive. His rationale: babies are born knowing nothing and therefore must explore the world. If they do not, they will not learn much and this negatively impacts their chances of survival. Interest is the desire to learn new things, to seek out novelty, and to be on the lookout for change, all of which are necessary for adaptation and survival. Interest, therefore, is a basic drive.

Interests, although a universal trait, are key differentiators when comparing people with other people and organisations with other organisations. In fact, the word interest comes from the Latin word *interesse,* which means to differ. Interests are partly heritable and partly interactional, meaning there is a genetic component to interests; however, experiences with the outside world and other people further shape them. The latter part is important to emphasise because it is through these interactions with the outside world that interests are triggered. According to Angela Duckworth, a pioneering professor of psychology, even though you may be genetically predisposed to certain interests, engaging in a behaviour is what brings that interest to life.

Given their universality, interests are now examined in educational, developmental, and vocational psychology as well as personality and emotion research. In earlier times, before interest research gained popularity, psychologists had arrived at the conclusion that human behaviours were simply driven by innate biological urges such as sex, hunger, and thirst, and were further influenced by external factors like rewards and punishments. With this view, human behaviour was explainable through basic causal relationships and it made for a convincing argument in the underdeveloped and still-budding scientific climate. However, as the world tumbled forward it was only a matter of time before people became more interested in the state of "being interested". In the wiser years of psychology, following numerous scientific breakthroughs and paradigm-shifting discoveries, it was realised that not all behaviours are engaged in as a means to an end, and sometimes the behaviour is the end in itself and is associated with positive feelings of interest, satisfaction, and enjoyment.

Intrinsic motivation or "authentic motivation" leads to enhanced performance, persistence, and creativity.

Psychologists started to wine and dine the idea that interests were conceptually related to personality and suggested interests were merely "expressions of personality". They supported this proposition through evidencing weak similarities between the two, in that personality and interests could both influence behaviour through their effects on motivation.[1] The scientific community eventually exiled this theory and it fell by the wayside, making room for further impactful discoveries, which led to our current understanding. We're now at a point in our expedition into the psychology of interest where scientists strongly assert that interests form a central component of motivation and motivated behaviours.[2]

This motivation is the energising force that enables and guides behaviours and, contrary to traditional beliefs, it is not as simple as once thought. Humans aren't automatons that behave purely as a result of survival-based physiological urges and conditioned responses. A metaphysical attraction to certain ideas, objects, or people is enough to cause us to behave in certain ways, stirring us into action, and initiating a purposeful pursuit. In the same way that our survival-based instincts influence our behaviour, so do the widely misunderstood sparks of our interests.

As time has passed, our understanding of the role that interests have on motivation and performance has become robust and clearer. Researchers highlight that spontaneous interests are a driver of intrinsic motivation in life and suggest that humans are naturally inclined to pursue their interests. They propose that a life governed by intrinsic motivation leads to a life full of vitality and enjoyment. On this, it has been demonstrated that intrinsic motivation or "authentic motivation" – which is characterised by people being more interested, confident, and excited about what they are doing – in turn leads to enhanced performance, persistence, and creativity.[3] As an aside, it's strange to think that the objects and concepts in our mind can exert an influence on us so powerful that our whole life trajectory is jolted in its direction.

The above findings suggest that when you are truly interested in something, you will be more confident and perform better in tasks that encapsulate your area of interest. An easy way to remember intrinsic motivation is to think of it as motivation that stems from deep within you, driven by a universal set of internal rewards such as satisfaction, exploration, spontaneous interests, autonomy, and learning. Extrinsic motivation, on the other hand, is driven by external rewards like fame, social acceptance, money, and the avoidance of punishment.

A key differentiator between internal and external rewards is that the former is derived from present experiences that are pleasurable in themselves, whereas the latter are usually given after the fact. As human beings, satisfying our internal reward criteria is essential for our continued social and psychological development – interests, specifically, further lead us to explore and learn. Arising from this, sparks of our interest should be regarded with esteem and be given considerable attention. They represent a powerful metaphysical attraction we have formed to something that lurks in the dark corners of our mind, and we are hardwired to engage and pursue them.

Apart from being inherently enjoyable, representing an end in themselves, and contributing to psychological development, the ability for interests to ignite our intrinsic motivation transforms the workings of our mind. Intrinsic motivation, which is similar to "flow state", represents a psychological transformation that allows you to capitalise on your cognitive abilities through alterations to the normal functioning of your mental machinery. The pursuit of your interests is all that's required to bring about this tectonic psychological shift.

Even impressive external forces are unable to foster intrinsic motivation like personal interests can. Money, fame, social and material rewards, and incentives cannot transform your mental state into a psychological utopia in the same way that an intangible, highly subjective, metaphysical, and still poorly understood self-identified interest can. A scenario that explores internal and external interests is provided in the following paragraphs. A direct takeaway from understanding different types of motivations highlights that in order to promote motivation and commitment in yourself, or in employees, you need to have a supportive environment at work, university, or home that allows authentic interests to be fostered and pursued. A supportive personal network provides part of this foundation.[4]

Stepping back for a moment, before an interest synthesises, there is usually an experience preceding it. When you engage in an activity or behaviour, many a time you are exposing yourself to novelty. The unique feelings, atmosphere, people involved, and subjective overall experience resulting from engagement in novel behaviours or activities culminate and cause you to feel a certain way. If you process the combination of these factors favourably, it may represent one of the earliest stages of interest formation. Although it is true that the intrinsic pleasure you derive from these moments may be enough on their own to create meaningful interest pursuits, there are scenarios in which only the buds of interest are realised. If this is the case, such budding interests can be nurtured through supportive environments and repeated exposure to certain stimuli. This malleable aspect of interest formation presents a thought-provoking discussion because, as discussed toward the end of this chapter, an interest by itself creates a driving force that can lead to stratospheric successes and achievements. But, capitalising on the outcomes of interest first involves implementing mechanisms to foster new interests, and requires the nourishment of green interests, which are both discussed below.

The identification and realisation of your own interests is powerful, and engaging your interests can lead you to achieve the impossible. The seemingly complex hypothesis I've presented touting interest formation as a building block of success can be accurately captured in the following simple question: would Newton have discovered gravity if he was not first interested in its mechanisms and consequences? Another perplexing proposition on the power of interest is this: what would Newton have discovered if his interests were manipulated toward the world of psychology instead of mathematics and physics?

To summarise, an interest can be likened to a subjective attitude that motivates a person to perform a certain task. You may watch certain documentaries because they have piqued your "interest". Alternatively, you may talk to a person because they are "interesting". It is the initial interest that drives you to engage in a specific behaviour. This behaviour is intrinsically motivated, satisfying, and pleasurable to you, and has not been contrived by the needs or wants of others. Apart from the interest-driven behaviour you've engaged in being enjoyable and fruitful in itself – for example, watching documentaries may increase your knowledge and talking to interesting people may provide you with valuable insights – the mere fact that you are in an interested state leads you to unleash the cognitive potential that is usually hiding beneath the surface of your normally functioning brain. More specifically, it initiates a cascade of psychological benefits associated with the state of flow.

Flow state

To understand the benefits arising from being interested in something we need to understand "flow state". Flow state, also known as optimal experience within the domain of positive psychology, depicts the mental state of a person who is entirely immersed in an activity. When in flow state a person experiences energised concentration, optimal enjoyment, full involvement, and their intrinsic interests.[5] It seems that both spontaneous and intrinsic interests initiate intrinsic motivation and flow state respectively. However, the punchline here is that they are both one and the same.

Being intrinsically motivated is akin to entering a state of flow. Think back to a time when you were focused, motivated, energised, happy, and completely aligned with the task you were doing. It is likely that flow state had taken charge. Your normal cognition took a back seat and flow took the wheel, and in all honesty it's a much better driver of productivity and the quality of your work. Flow state can be achieved by everyone and may occur across many different types of activities. A basketballer may achieve flow as they practise free-throw shots; an academic while they familiarise themselves with the latest research in their field; and a musician while they practise a melody. The underlying factor linking the individuals is the metaphysical force that pulls them toward these activities. They engage in the activities not for external incentives like fame or money, but for the pure pleasure they derive from their participation in them.

Their sense of time becomes warped and hours of participation in their chosen activity may feel like 20 minutes. This is characteristic of flow state as it defies the objective nature of time by altering subjective perceptions of it. The people are wholeheartedly invested in their activity, so much so their sense of consciousness begins to fade. There is no room for anything but complete alignment with the task at hand because this activity challenges them. Their skillsets are balanced with the activity they are doing, warranting complete focus and leading to a sense of satisfaction and achievement. When these criteria are met, flow state is active, and flow state is nothing short of a mental hack.

The important ingredient necessary for us to achieve flow is our intrinsic interests. This is the metaphysical force pulling us toward certain behaviours, activities, and experiences. Intrinsic interests are those things we find interesting because of their basic nature or character, it is not because of their relationship with external factors like social rewards. Rather, they satisfy our internal reward criteria required for intrinsic motivation, which simply cannot be brought about by contrived incentives. For example, if someone was intrinsically interested in biology, the inherent pathogenic nature of microbial organisms may be fascinating to them in and of itself. Conversely, if they found biology interesting just because other people did, such as their highly influential lab manager, or because the world was converging on this area of science and there was a monopoly market on the horizon, then this is not an intrinsic but an extrinsic interest. Identifying and pursuing intrinsic interests are key to the transmogrification and elevation of your psychological state.

The path to success starts with a steppingstone called interest.

A controlled experiment comparing intrinsic to extrinsic interests and the subsequent effects of both on motivation and performance was conducted in organisational settings. It found that intrinsically motivated individuals performed better at work, were more committed to the organisation, had less burnout, demonstrated reduced turnover intentions, and had less family–work conflict.[6]

Extrinsic, otherwise known as "external", interests and motivations manifest in workplaces in the form of incentives, financial bonuses, and other lucrative social or material rewards that are used as a carrot to drive employee productivity and performance higher. However, these do not work. Aligning the work environment with the intrinsic interests of employees, along with appealing to the set of universal internal rewards, is the only way to capitalise on flow states, which generate a network of effects in the brains and minds of employees and stirs them into overdrive. It is this mechanism that leads to greater performance when compared with their puppeteered counterparts.

Autonomous, passionate, and supported employees are the cure to historical management philosophies that reduce the complicated behavioural and cognitive systems of humans to a function of material incentivisation, and it is through engaging their interests this is realised. If an employee's interest does not come from deep within and align with the basic essence of the object or experience that is being engaged in, then it is not a "true" interest but in most cases a poorly executed external attempt at manipulation. Flow state will not be activated and the panacea of benefits succeeding its activation are foregone. As an individual, a life devoid of intrinsic interests will be dry, tedious, and anticlimactic. As an organisation, ignoring the intrinsic interests of employees will cost enormous amounts of money, massively restrict productivity, and negatively impact culture.

The practical implications of achieving flow state are numerous. For example:

- Individuals in flow state lose self-consciousness, meaning they do not hesitate or second-guess themselves, allowing them to achieve peak performance.
- In flow, people are found to suppress and ignore negative thoughts while having higher self-esteem and confidence levels.
- Creativity soars, as evidenced in work-related flow studies,[7] and in studies of musicians and their compositions.
- Productivity improves, as seen through studies looking at the associations between flow and psychological capital in employees.[7]
- On a personal level, people in flow are filled with joy, are more satisfied, lose sense of time, are completely immersed, concentrated, and aligned with the task at hand, and operate with laser-like focus for their goals. This makes for fulfilling, high-quality, enduring, achievable, and rewarding work.

There is more to this than meets the eye. Persistence alone has been identified as a key ingredient in the DNA of mega-successful people, and here we can see that flow state feeds persistence through continually deploying motivation, undivided attention, and positivity to goal pursuits. Imagine working on something you weren't interested in! While undervalued and probably not widely understood, the path to success starts with a steppingstone called interest.

Interested in your career?

If we step out of the microenvironment of an organisation and look at career landscapes, we find that interests are prevalent in professional pursuits. This is supported by John Holland's Theory of Career Choice, which proposes that people's careers are heavily influenced by where their internal interests lie. In this theory, people's areas of interest are grouped into six categories:

1. Realistic
2. Investigative
3. Artistic
4. Social
5. Enterprising
6. Conventional

Individuals who fall into the realistic category are interested in hands-on types of work activities. Investigative-inclined people like intellectual, scholarly, and scientific types of work. Artistic types gravitate to creative, unconventional, and expressive work. Social types prefer work that involves teaching, helping, and caring for others. Enterprising individuals are drawn to work that includes leadership, assertiveness, and persuasion. Conventional types prefer work with well-ordered routines and activities.[8]

It's safe to assume that the majority of these career outcomes are due to intrinsic interests and are guided not by external rewards, but by the internal reward system of the individual. However, in some instances, it is possible that a combination of the two may factor in. For example, people with enterprising interests, driven by leading and inspiring people, experience internal rewards such as the realisation of their personal interests, yet external rewards such as social esteem and money could also prove influential.

In one study, individuals from different industries were categorised into these six domains. Measures of job performance, job knowledge, and continuance intentions were examined. It was demonstrated that when an individual's broader interests lined up with their job, they were more knowledgeable in their job area, performed better, and intended to continue it for longer.[1] The interest-related traits of people were found to be of more predictive value than their cognitive attitude and personality traits (measured via The Big Five – explored in *Chapter 3*) in determining job performance and tenure.

This is a huge finding considering the industry standard for recruitment is psychometric testing, which focuses on individuals' cognitive abilities and personality measurements. Despite the evidence cited above, the current recruitment paradigm is highly problematic in many ways already. Especially since the majority of personality testing for organisational recruitment processes is done via the free Myers-Briggs Type Indicator (MBTI) inventory, which is widely available to anyone online. Currently, 2 million people complete this assessment annually and it represents the "gold standard".

I recently participated in an insightful discussion with a personality professor at Deakin University about exactly this topic. First, it has been heavily debated in organisational psychology circles for quite a while now that the MBTI may not measure personality traits validly, and its effectiveness is continually being questioned.[9] This isn't surprising considering this assessment purports to test personality traits of people yet doesn't align itself with The Big Five personality framework that mainstream psychology has adopted as the gold standard approach to personality measurement.

In a way, MBTI is similar to the companies selling "fat-loss teas" online while nutritional and dietetic scientists, backed by vast amounts of published literature, point to the calorie in versus calorie out model of fat loss. If you listen to science, these fat-loss teas are a highly profitable scam that exploit the psychology of vulnerable people. Indeed, the reason they are sold is through the spread of misinformation and because people (secretly) want to believe they work. How reassuring the thought, *If I drink tea, I'll lose the 50kgs I put on from inactivity and woeful food choices over the last 10 years* must be. Similarly, a free online quiz that sums up the metaphysical concept of a human, pigeonholes them into a category, and matches them with numerous complicated attributes and environments present in the organisation, sounds like it could be handy too. The MBTI also claims to assess the motives, creativity, and thoughts of people. Wouldn't that be great? A telepathic test. Google and Facebook should just give up and stop spending billions of dollars on behavioural profiling and behaviour-prediction pursuits because, clearly, this free online quiz is superior.

Second, the MBTI does not provide an accurate and complete picture of an individual because it only focuses on positive traits. It uses warm and fuzzy adjectives for every category it pigeonholes a person into and omits any negative or troublesome traits. Considering this test claims to facilitate teamwork and collaboration, you would think the disagreeable, prickly traits of people would need to be given some attention and factored into team environments. Everyone can work with an intellectual, ambitious, energetic person. But can everyone co-work with an intellectual, ambitious, energetic person who's also narcissistic, disrespectful, racist, and disagreeable? Probably not, and this test won't help you here.

Third, since the inventory is widely available and accessible online, it means people can access it and prepare for it. In clinical psychology, proper personality inventories like the Minnesota Multiphasic Personality Inventory are hidden from the public so people cannot cheat them. As a result, the integrity of the assessment is maintained, which is important considering *real* personality tests are used to inform clinicians about potential mental health problems and personality disorders an individual may have.

Fourth, and probably the most perplexing of all, is that personality assessment scores can change based on how the questions are worded, the previous information the candidates have been exposed to about the organisation, and the motivation of the candidates as they complete the assessment. During my psychology degree, in my personality unit at Deakin University we tested this. The class participated in a personality assessment at the start of the semester and then participated in the same test again later. For the second sitting we were given job descriptions and company information to read beforehand and were then told to complete the test imagining that we were applying for the company we'd read about. What do you think happened? Our personality profiles changed! Everyone knew to answer in a more-conscientious, more-agreeable, and less-neurotic fashion when we knew our personality scores would judge our employability. Don't just take my word for it though, research shows that faking in high-stakes personality testing happens a lot.[10] Even medical students applying for internships manufacture their scores.[11]

There are definitely some benefits to understanding aspects of a future employee's personality. For instance, understanding that someone is neurotic, disagreeable, and lacks conscientiousness, means that when they apply for a job as a prison rehabilitation officer who specialises in behavioural interventions for offenders, it's probably in everyone's best interest this doesn't lead to employment. The aspiring employee would soon have a nervous breakdown, offenders would not be properly rehabilitated, and the employer would fast be looking for a replacement. This represents a highly nuanced example; however, in the wider world of employment, the problems with personality testing may outweigh the benefits. Real personality tests will become unreliable if used widely in the public domain as their integrity will be challenged.

Not only this, personality profiling tells you about the habits of people, but it does not necessarily "capture" the essence of an individual. Two people can be introverted, one can be a revolutionary computer scientist, the other, a young Mozart; the fact they both share in a similar personality characteristic doesn't tell you much more than a fleeting observation would if you were trying to guess at their career from some of their universal behavioural tendencies.

And, of course, people are not silly. If they know the organisation and they know the job description, they can manufacture answers. My whole class did. Medical interns do. And in high-stake situations this is common. These problems are not a big deal for "interest profiling" though. People would be inclined to answer honestly if there was potential for them to immerse themselves in a world of their choosing.

> The pursuit of properly motivated employees starts with the accurate identification and alignment of their intrinsic interests.

If we further explore this interest-matching concept in workplace settings, we can see there are arguable benefits to aligning the interests of organisations with individuals who work there. If you are currently job seeking, you, too, should take this into account. Psychologists claim that people are more satisfied with their job, and perform better, when they are doing something that aligns with their personal interests.[4] By interest-matching, employee tenure is positively affected, which reduces costs and productivity losses resulting from a higher staff turnover rate. Additionally, improvements in job tenure manifest for the organisation via the increased capitalisation of employee psychological assets and heightened creativity and innovation.[7] Not to mention the intangible benefits that a knowledgeable, satisfied employee passes on to the company.

Without being able to match interests with work and foster true motivation, we arrive at where we are now in society. A place where most people are merely surviving and counting the clock during their nine-to-five job that, truth be told, they could not care less about. They are there for an extrinsic reward, a monetary benefit they require to negate the punishing effects of being broke. A cold transaction of time for money. The true motivational force of an employee is always exuded by their behaviours and consistent actions. A contrived motivation leads to a poisonous attitude that infiltrates host organisations and manifests as a bad customer experience, toxic workplace dramas, sporadic bouts of negativity, and lapses in productivity. Not to mention it is a culture-killer!

The primitive recruitment paradigms governing organisational hiring decisions is evidenced by the fact that we have not even standardised the inclusion of interests in a traditional résumé, yet costly and time-consuming psychometric tests are dutifully administered by the "all-knowing" deities of recruitment. The pursuit of properly motivated employees starts with the accurate identification and alignment of their intrinsic interests. And, on a side note, if you're thinking of starting your own business or partnering up with someone in a new venture, it pays to factor interest congruence into your equation.

Sowing the seeds of success

Although interests arise from rather serendipitous interactions with the outside world and from infinitely complicated genetic mechanisms, they can be nurtured. By creating a supportive network of individuals and engaging with peers, early interests can receive the necessary fuel to transform into a consolidated and well-defined interest.[4] Discussing, collaborating, and receiving support for your newfound interests provides a form of social acceptance, psychological security, and intellectual stimulation, in turn further nurturing them.

It has been suggested that another way to develop an interest is to find meaning and value in the activities you engage in.[2] Coincidentally, finding meaning and value in activities is usually why you are interested in them in the first place. When interests are taken seriously, they evolve and snowball into a powerful passion. In fact, passion could even be described as an "eager interest". Passion and perseverance, according to leading psychologists, are the two attributes displayed by the world's highest achievers across many domains.[4] Academic leaders, entrepreneurial visionaries, special forces soldiers, Olympic athletes, and even professors who specialise in puzzles, known as enigmatologists, consistently display both.

Isn't it interesting that interests also facilitate perseverance – the second key ingredient for high achievement – through their relationship with flow state? Perseverance, remember, is the continued pursuit of purpose despite discouragement and difficulties. What type of person opts in to persevere through a lifetime of the necessary challenging, soul-sucking, and mentally taxing activities that precede any great discovery, notable lifetime achievement, or the rise of a revered company? Only those who are interested, of course. Perseverance is fed the resources and mental energy it requires through intrinsic motivation initiated and sustained by engaging our interests.

The challenging nature of something becomes pleasurable when engaged through the lens of flow. The energetic balance of mental states is not depleted by intrinsically motivated activities; rather, it is improved and vitalised by them. The dizzying time investment required for lifelong endeavours becomes achievable when it is no longer counted using objective painful hours, but is distorted, shortened, and ignored by a flow state possessing the capacity to warp it. Discouragement, an external factor and form of punishment, doesn't affect the internal fire that burns for your interests. Without interest guiding your activities, perseverance is futile.

Interests can be used to explain the achievement of excellence. In 1989, Daniel Chambliss formulated a theory known as the "mundanity of excellence", positing that excellence is accomplished through the repeated performance of ordinary actions, which are consistently and carefully executed, habitualised, and compounded over time. From this view there are no special talents or scale-tipping factors in the pursuit of excellence, only a dull combination of meticulously practised skills and behaviours that, when combined, give rise to exceptional levels of performance.

Only when someone is interested in something can the mundanity of excellence ever manifest. Without an internal interest, no one can, or would, persist for the time required to achieve excellence in any capacity. Overcoming an endless wave of obstacles and pushing through repeated bouts of hardship is unimaginably difficult and arguably unachievable without intrinsic motivation, born from interest, fuelling every step of the way.

Now, that is curious...

Curiosity is another trait intertwined with the overall field of interests. For starters, interests and curiosity, although mainly synonymous, differ slightly. Curiosity can be thought of as a specific subset of "interests" and is usually associated with more excitement and energy than interests, which are more stable and enduring over time. Leading authorities in curiosity research, Kashdan and Silvia, have defined it concisely:

> *Curiosity can be defined as the recognition, pursuit, and intense desire to explore novel, challenging, and uncertain events. When curious, we are fully aware and receptive to whatever exists and might happen in the present moment. Curiosity motivates people to act and think in new ways and investigate, be immersed, and learn about whatever is the immediate interesting target of their attention. This definition captures the exploratory striving component and the mindful immersion component. By focusing on the novelty and challenge each moment has to offer, there is an inevitable (however slight) stretching of information, knowledge, and skills. When we are curious, we are doing things for their own sake, and we are not being controlled by internal or external pressures concerning what we should or should not do. (p. 368)* [12]

The above definition highlights many similarities between curiosity and interest. By teasing out some of the key passages, we can clearly see that curiosity is related to interests and results in a flow-like state. People are "immersed" with the "immediate interesting object of their attention", and "fully aware and receptive to whatever exists and might happen in the present moment". We also do things for "their own sake", which is similar to the nature of experiencing intrinsic interests described in flow states. The "slight stretching of information, knowledge, and skills" is akin to the challenging nature of activities, enabling flow.

Prolonged activation of flow states is like a low dose of daily mental steroids.

When you understand this it becomes obvious why curiosity is a favourable trait in employees and why curiosity may be a superpower. Being a curious person means you are continually interested in things, which, of course, leads you to regularly engage in flow. Prolonged activation of flow states is like a low dose of daily mental steroids. You operate at a higher cognitive level as you journey through life, turning your already impressive mental machinery into a next-generation super processor with laser-like focus. Not to mention, curiosity leads to happiness,[13] academic achievement,[14] facilitates relationship bonding, and enhances empathetic abilities because people are genuinely interested in others.

Epistemic curiosity

For the purpose of this book, we're going to look at epistemic curiosity specifically. Epistemology relates to the theory of knowledge, so this form of curiosity is literally "a drive to know". Epistemic curiosity forks into two subtypes known as *diversive curiosity* – more easily conceptualised as broad curiosity – and *specific curiosity* – a narrower form of curiosity that can be context dependent.

Diversive curiosity results from an internal desire for knowledge that motivates us to eliminate information gaps, learn new ideas, and solve intellectual problems. As a result of nudging us to add new ideas or concepts to our repertoire of knowledge, it propels general exploration and involves feelings of enjoyment that are associated with our want to improve intellectual mastery.[15] This drive leads us to enthusiastically chase down knowledge, question things, and continually feed our minds with bits of information. Simply put, a "broad interest in learning and exploring" has been repackaged into the character trait "curious" and used to label people.

Specific curiosity motivates exploration in response to an unsolved puzzle due to the need to reduce uncertainty and create a sense of mastery.[16] The small pestering problem that has recently taken over your life, the one that you can't seem to figure out yet forever dances at the forefront of your mind and occupies precious attention, initiates this narrowly scoped form of curiosity. It sparks focused exploration, the aim being to uncover the solution that is proving elusive in the specific experience, interaction, or domain the problem stems from.

Specific curiosity commonly arises in engineers and designers. For example, if a designer is handed a brief that outlines three key outcomes that are required for a successful design, they may face a targeted set of problems that need to be overcome. How can they design a frame for a small drone that is lightweight but still performs its function in different weather conditions? How can they ensure the drone can support, and manoeuvre with, small packages? What is the trade-off between endurance and speed? In the process of designing something, a designer searches for a creative solution that will solve the challenge they are working on. As they formulate solutions, they encounter new problems and concurrently analyse and solve these problems, each of which can lead to new problems requiring new solutions. The new frame design of the drone makes it durable and functional across a wide range of weather conditions; however, now the ability to manoeuvre the drone with packages has been affected, creating a new problem longing for a new solution. Highlighted here are examples of specific curiosity, otherwise known as cycles of intentionality and exploration, which is purported to be central to human creativity.[17] This whole process takes place in a narrow or specific goal-oriented scope and is an intentional exploration of possible solutions to the vexing problems at the forefront of our attention.

This is what differentiates specific curiosity from diverse curiosity. Whereas diverse curiosity refers to a broad interest in learning and exploring, specific curiosity tunnel-visions our inquisitions. The distinctions are important for properly comprehending the research studies that will soon be presented. However, it is evident from the above information that each of these different forms of curiosity are just labels used to categorise interests that subtly differ from each other. Understanding the link between curiosity and the universal human drive of interest largely explains the benefits arising from curiosity research, and in organisational settings there are many.

The curiosity trait

Curiosity is a highly sought-after trait in employees for several reasons. Studies looking at curious people found that curiosity can help them adapt to an organisation if they are new and predicts job performance better than general mental ability and personality tests.[18] Other anecdotal research suggests that career-related curiosity is required for emerging leaders in the digital world as it motivates them to try new things and enables them to become more self-sufficient and autonomous. Acting in this manner allows them to adapt to disruptive technologies, changing landscapes, and global innovation, meaning they can always stay ahead of the curve.

A comprehensive study carried out across workplaces in different countries found curiosity to be positively correlated with job satisfaction, worker engagement, innovation, and proactive behaviours related to job tasks.[19] Additionally, organisations regularly knight curiosity as a core value, driver of innovation, and suggest it provides them with a competitive advantage.[20] Next time you sift through job ads online you may notice that some posts, despite sharing completely separate industry backgrounds and role requirements, band together in their quest to source the "naturally curious" and "inquisitive" individuals. Most likely, the aforementioned are reasons why.

Even though curiosity manifests in many organisational benefits, one of the most valuable has only been alluded to. Previously, it was mentioned that through our unique interests we activate intrinsic motivation, which in a roundabout way can lead us to perform better and be more creative. Further down the line we arrived at curiosity representing a fundamental process of intentionality and exploration, proposed to be central to human creativity. There seems to be a high degree of similarity between curiosity and interest, and a link from both traits to "flow states". Not surprisingly, a study that explored the connections between curiosity, flow, and creativity uncovered the direct link between curiosity and flow. The experiment also uncovered a direct link between flow and creativity. Through a sequence of psychological state changes, curiosity was proven to be a steppingstone to creativity.

Psychologists trained in creativity participated in the experiment and reviewed creative ideas put forward by participants in response to a novel problem they were presented with. It was found that when participants were engaged in the activity, they reported higher levels of curiosity and this was associated with greater levels of flow. More flow was in turn associated with higher levels of creativity. Flow, as a result of this experiment, was identified as the intermediate process between curiosity and creativity. Remember, in addition to flow's direct effect on creativity, flow is a psychological state that unlocks motivation, facilitates perseverance, pairs positive feelings with the activity, and achieves fulfilment. Even in organisations, work-related flow and work-related curiosity are significantly associated with employee creativity and innovation respectively.[7,21]

Curiosity and creativity

Curiosity and creativity are themselves inextricably linked, irrespective of the presence of flow state. In the world of academia curiosity is widely believed to be a key antecedent to creativity. The reason for this conceptual shift is drawn from the logic that the first part of the creative process relies on information seeking, and the second on the associations of novel and previously unrelated stimuli. This is exactly what curiosity enables. Curiosity is the driver of exploratory behaviour that leads us to interact and engage with novel ideas and objects. Such actions cause us to acquire and mentally store puzzle pieces of information; data that we can cross-reference with our existing knowledge banks. Additionally, it adds to the existing pool of our knowledge bank, which will be cross-referenced by the future information and data we acquire.

Curiosity preceding creativity is evidenced in studies of creative children where curiosity was found ubiquitously throughout the childhoods of exceptionally creative individuals.[22] In line with this, well-known entrepreneurs like Steve Jobs, Walt Disney, and Larry Page were historically known for their insatiable appetite for curiosity, and they gave rise to some of the most revered, creative, and innovative companies on the planet.

In one study, researchers set out to determine the most valid method of predicting creativity in employees.[23] In the study they recruited 122 undergraduate students from The University of Oklahoma. The experiment saw the students land a creative role in a fictional company. After being presented with a package of marketing materials, consumer research, and a demographic of their target market, the undergraduates, now acting as the "head of advertising", were tasked with the development and implementation of a marketing plan. Psychologists familiar with the fields of industrial psychology and creativity oversaw the study and scored participants on their creative abilities as the experiment unfolded. At the conclusion of the study, upon completion of numerous questionnaires, and after the students were subjected to a battery of psychological tests, researchers were able to pinpoint the source of creative performance.

The culprit, they found, was epistemic curiosity. More specifically, it was diversive epistemic curiosity. Those students who were naturally inquisitive, spent more time seeking information, and continually acquired knowledge, demonstrated more creativity. Instead of diving deep into areas of research with a narrow focus, they had begun broadly exploring all the information that was presented to them. This kept their minds open and allowed for new ideas and novel associations to form, and, as such, the trait curiosity is one of the biggest predictors of workplace creative performance.

As a result of broadening the focus of your attention, you are allowing yourself to be exposed to more information, which results in diverse global information processing in your mind. This is exactly what is needed for the generation of ideas. You need to think of all the different bits of information you consume as potential puzzle pieces that may or may not be required for your endgame. Only after the fact will you ever be able to know what information proved to be indispensably valuable. So, until then, stay curious. Stay open.

Specific curiosity was the focus of another study.[20] Here, it was thought that specific curiosity, despite being more narrowly focused than diversive curiosity, could still contribute to creative outcomes but through a different mechanism. Diversive curiosity influenced creativity through the broad information-seeking aspect of the creative process, resulting in novel concepts and experiences being creatively combined. Specific curiosity, remember, elicits an intense desire for individuals to seek out and explore information relevant to a puzzling problem or phenomenon that has surfaced in their field of focus and dances at the forefront of their mind.

The narrowed field of focus contrasts with the all-encompassing globalist view of diversive curiosity. When a specific problem arises for someone it draws attention to the "information gap" that exists, which refers to the gap between the information the individual knows and the information required for the puzzling problem or phenomenon to be explained, or "solved". This gap is the driver and motivates exploration. For example, a biological researcher may wonder how a certain species of jellyfish achieves immortality. There is a gap between the researcher's expertise and the phenomenon of immortality that the jellyfish demonstrates, which, by the way, is plenty enough to warrant a decade of heavily invested research.

Motivated by the information gap, an individual will engage in continued, directed exploration as they search for the solution, or the idea, that diffuses the apparent problem, which in this case is immortality. Individuals in this state will use the information they source to generate ideas relating to the puzzling problem they are facing. They move from one idea to another, and then to another. When shifting ideas in and out of focus, they still remember artefacts and aspects of previous ideas as these may serve to explain certain elements of the problem.

An initial idea the jellyfish researcher developed may have revolved around examining the genetic components of a jellyfish that changed throughout the lifespan to explain its immortality. In this instance, although proving unsuccessful in explaining this phenomenon, an aspect of this early genetic-related idea may be combined with another idea through a link. The genetics of the jellyfish throughout its life may then be mapped to changing protein levels in the jellyfish. The protein-mapping idea evolved from the first idea. Sequentially exploring key ideas through a loosely tethered mental web may hold the key for alleviating a mental gridlock and is a characteristic of specific curiosity.

It is through this process of idea linking that specific curiosity has also been linked to enhanced creativity. By being able to narrowly focus in an area while keeping creativity flowing through loosely associated ideas and concepts, a person can generate a targeted form of creativity. In this process the early ideas are necessary and provisional, serving as steppingstones for following ideas. Elements of early ideas are used to develop more sophisticated ideas, in turn potentially forming the basis for the evolution of the next most sophisticated idea. The end product of ideation, the "Aha" moment and the solution to a puzzling problem, is the summation and iteration of the pool of ideas generated in a narrow search radius, motivated by specific curiosity. This is how creativity is influenced by specific curiosity and is why we should attribute our most prized discoveries to the frustrating and attention-gripping problems we encounter and endlessly ruminate over.

Curiosity, a subset of interests, is the prerequisite for exploring the self and the outer world. This exploration results in the attainment and integration of novel perspectives and experiences, which go on to form the basic building blocks of creativity. As a matter of fact, if you did not have an urge to learn and explore, you would never encounter anything new, and without new information your creative potential can never be fully achieved. The world we live in today has largely been shaped by individual and societal interest pursuits that have led to innovation through thoughtful creation. Humanity, without curiosity and other interests, would be nothing short of unremarkable. Technological, social, and cultural advancements would cease to exist and the evolution of civilisation, if it did happen, would be an unforgivably long slow-burner. If you needed a reason to light and admire your own curiosity flame, hopefully somewhere in the paragraphs above you found it.

Creation and innovation

Creation and innovation, despite existing separately, are closely linked and in some cases inseparable. Psychiatrist John Young tackled the difficult and ambiguous question: "What is creativity?" Creativity, as he described it, occurs when people use their imaginations to come up with something new and valuable in a process of transforming something from its current state into something better.

It is said that in the process of creativity the individual adds their unique contributions to whatever it is they do and surpasses the old, outmoded, and traditional with innovation and improvement. While this view is largely adopted, other experts in creativity suggest that novel ideas or originality alone is enough to define creativity, suggesting that the outcome or value of an idea should not factor into its definition. They argue that creativity is still evident, even if it does not lead to innovation or improvement.[24] An obvious example of this train of thought comes in the form of an amateur painter who creatively expresses themselves through art. The end result of their painting is not really valuable, and it did not necessarily improve on any existing traditional processes or products, yet it was creative nonetheless. The outcomes of creativity don't define its nature but venturing into the area of innovation sees them as a fundamental criterion.

The creative employee is the driver of organisation-level innovation.

Innovation is like a socially validated and commercialisable form of applied creativity in the sense that it implements, exploits, and capitalises on original ideas. Creativity is one of its driving forces; however, it is not directly dependent on creativity because it can occur when innovative processes, products, technologies, business models, and services are adopted from elsewhere. Innovation, unlike creativity, can be copied. In the business world, a company may replicate a technology or business model but not create it, still earning them the label of innovative.

In this sense, innovative companies are synonymous with early adopters of disruptive technologies. They are both leveraging ground-breaking discoveries, are open to change, and are evidently neophiliacs. Companies can have an attitude that leads to innovation; however, in my view, they are not authentically innovative until they have created, implemented, and radiated their own solutions that are in turn taken up by others. Unlike this pseudo-form, true innovation is a result of the transmogrification of novel ideas from their metaphysical nature into a reality that can be integrated into the processes, technologies, and products of societies, organisations, and humanity in a way that has never existed before. True innovation happens once by authentic innovators, but pseudo-innovation occurs many times after.

It is the interpersonal adoption and reification of forward ideas by virtue of an agreed-upon value that delineates creativity and innovation. An idea, or originality, without direct utility stays in the realm of creativity in the mind of one individual, whereas those that are valuable and improve upon current standards, are implemented, adopted, and propagated through social systems, and lead to some new or improved form of value creation. The utility of a novel idea causes it to be innovative.[24]

Creativity can happen without innovation in the form of a painter and his valueless painting. Innovation can happen without creativity when companies adopt others' ideas and implement their discoveries. However, true innovation is dependent on creativity. Without a new idea that leads to a new process, new market, new technology, new product, or new service, true innovation is unachievable. This newness was born from creativity after people imagined, invented, and ideated. Without creativity, the state of society would be an infinite loop of pseudo-innovation, which after a point in time is no longer innovative but normal. The once-novel innovation would eventually stagnate society, and in the absence of creativity, there would be no hope for progress. True innovation is dependent on creativity applied, actioned, and accepted by people and companies, who agree on the value of the outcome.

This can often be viewed in workplaces; the following example illustrates one. If an employee at a university science lab was keenly interested in genetic engineering, or, say, specifically curious about the mechanisms that can be utilised to change genomic sequences, there is a high chance that this curious employee will end up generating a creative solution to vexing genomics problems. When the employee taps into their creative potential to solve the problem and discovers a solution, that solution will likely manifest as an innovative gene therapy. Creative thoughts reified in these settings become innovative behaviours. As a result of the employee's discovery, the lab now uses the gene therapy solution as a standard, in the process turning themselves into an innovative scientific laboratory. The creative employee is the driver of organisation-level innovation.

The value of creativity can be traced back to ancient civilisations. History shows that inventors and scientists like Archimedes and Leonardo da Vinci were treated like royalty and held in high esteem by aristocrats and their peers. Obviously, inventors are creative, but what may not be so obvious is the creative nature of a revolutionary scientist. For scientists to make, propagate, implement, and integrate ground-breaking discoveries, they must come up with something new. They create new technologies, new ways of thinking, new fields of study, new ways to test assumptions, new laws, and new applications of existing phenomena that challenge current assumptions, propel societies, and open minds to possibilities previously impossible.

Discoveries

Science is built on discoveries, each often representing the outcome of the creative problem-solving processes that go on in the minds of scientists. For example, the discovery of gravity occurred because Isaac Newton developed a new way of thinking. Similarly, natural selection was discovered by Charles Darwin, but it was his initial idea about it that led him there. The idea that nature was selective and only the fittest survived was something he formulated and refined over time. At the time it was a creative idea, now it is taught as a law of nature.

The discovery of penicillin – an antibiotic compound – by Alexander Fleming is as serendipitous and seemingly uncreative as a scientific discovery could be. On returning from vacation, Fleming noticed something strange happening in one of the agar plates in his lab experiment. An invading fungus had inhibited the growth of bacteria, creating a no-grow zone around the fungus. Experiencing a lightbulb moment, he isolated the mould, extracted its active compounds, and found penicillin, the active antibiotic agent. The dawn of antibiotics began, greatly impacting human health.

Despite Fleming stumbling upon an already-existing interaction between microorganisms, *he formulated the idea* that the invading mould possessed a unique compound responsible for an inhibitory effect on bacterial growth. Other scientists may have glazed over this agar plate, unaware of the lifesaving capabilities, underlying significance, or mechanism of action being demonstrated. Fleming, though, whose interests led him down a specific career path culminating in him becoming an expert bacteriologist, fortuitously ideated the process of extracting this compound and delivering it to the world as a novel therapy for bacterial infection. His expertise allowed him to form unique insights about a natural phenomenon that he observed, leading him to a new idea necessary for this discovery to be realised.

Perplexingly, a discovery is something that has always been, it is not created, yet, as illustrated above, discoveries are entirely dependent on creativity. Much of reality is built or confirmed with our imagination.

Testing ideas

In this sense, a discovery is a realised idea, and usually a creative one at that. This adds further fuel to the fire that warms the idea of science being of a creative nature; and, subsequently, scientists being creators, is provided through the mandated use of the scientific method. In this method, researchers are required to come up with a hypothesis, or an idea, that they can test through rigorous methodical procedures. The testing of the idea seeks to provide answers to perplexing problems and to generate new information for the wider scientific community. For this aim to be achieved, the hypotheses being tested must be original and testable.

Funnily enough, the creation of a hypothesis involves researchers building on existing theories, which, at the end of the day, are nothing more than ideas that were once created themselves. The difference between ideas and theories is simply the fact that theories are ideas that have passed the rigorous testing and interrogations carried out by the scientific community. After this they cement themselves in our world and form a tentative pillar of reality. There is, of course, one way scientists are not creative; and it mirrors pseudo-innovation. Scientists can take others' ideas and claim them as their own. There are many examples of this in the scientific world. Everyone knows Rosalind Franklin heavily factored into the discovery of the helical structure of DNA only to have Watson and Crick steal the Nobel Prize upon claiming her discovery as solely theirs. Even so, I would argue that the way fraudulent scientific discovery has and can be covered up, in fine scientific fashion, could still be called creative.

Shifting back to Archimedes and Leonardo da Vinci, kings and councils, as previously noted, demonstrated extreme generosity and respect for these individuals in light of their creative abilities. Ancient accounts suggest the king of France allowed Leonardo da Vinci to live with him, and that King Heiro II of Syracuse regularly called on Archimedes to help find solutions to problems. Even now, centuries later, it is hard to avoid these names, and they command the same amount of respect and awe now as they did back then.

Openness

In modern times, creative individuals, or in other words, individuals who choose to realise their natural creative abilities, are still celebrated and revered. Some of them include scientists who are awarded Nobel prizes after discovering major scientific breakthroughs; musicians who craft songs and tunes that top musical billboard charts; and artists who auction off paintings and artworks for millions of dollars. Other individuals try their luck at entrepreneurship, and, with the right mix of intrapersonal skills layered on top of creative abilities, they can also achieve tremendous success and stardom. A world-renowned psychologist, Jordan Peterson, draws attention to the fact that the second biggest predictor of entrepreneurial success is the trait of openness. This trait is explored in-depth in *Chapter 3*, but for now, this trait is notable as the single strongest and most consistent personality trait predicting creative achievement and is found to be high in visionary tech entrepreneurs, travellers, and original thinkers.

Creative benefits

Despite creativity not always leading to riches, fame, or a cult-like worshipping, it still boasts the ability to dramatically improve your quality of life. In fact, creativity is so important that around the globe it is becoming an inherent requirement of youth education. In 2008, Australia's federal and state ministers agreed to a landmark statement concerning the future of young Australians' learning. This statement, known as the Melbourne Declaration on Educational Goals for Young Australians, recognised the need for young Australians to "become successful learners, confident and creative individuals, and active and informed citizens".[25]

Creativity allows you to better solve problems, express yourself without limitations, and engage in flow states. It is protective against cognitive decline,[26] reduces anxiety, stress, and depression, and above all it's fun. In addition, creativity can lead you to better other people's lives by providing them with entertainment, aesthetic value, and potential remedies to their subjective problems. Creativity also enables innovation in your own life and can result in the development of unique commercialisable products that are realised by you financially. Creativity and imagination can even challenge the status quo – what we consider knowledge today, at one point in time was merely an idea that was tested, accepted, and then embedded in our universal rule book.

Finally, the pursuit of creative endeavours are inherently pleasant experiences, evidenced through their associations with flow state, and alone can contribute to purpose in life. To provide one practical example, creativity allows you to positively contribute to, and advance, niche fields of study, such as science, art, mathematics, or economics to name a few. Whatever your area of specialisation, it will benefit from your creative contributions. Computers, other forms of technology, medical advancements, psychological interventions, innovative companies, science in general, and the consciousness infused and transmitted through books, are creative inventions that have collaboratively saved and improved billions of people's lives.

As already established, creativity is valuable and necessary for us to flourish individually and as a civilisation. Understanding the nature of creativity, how we can hack it, and subsequently how we can achieve our creative potential, proves ultimately valuable. What's more, despite our pre-existing creative capabilities, a vast amount of experimental evidence suggests we can in fact improve it. Some studies hint at it being as easy as improving your mood, since positive moods can enhance creative ideation; a measurable and testable aspect of creativity.[27,28]

Creative ideation refers to an array of skills that include fluency (the production of ideas), originality (the uniqueness of ideas), and flexibility (the variety of ideas). Creative ideation literally refers to the continued *formation* of *multiple, unique* ideas. In the simplest of terms, a good mood sparks your creativity. Remember, when you are interested or curious about something your mood is positively affected through the activation of flow state. You tend to feel good, even satisfied, as you embark on your creative journey of exploration, knowledge seeking, and learning in pursuit of your intrinsic interests. This link is one reason why pursuing your interests sets the stage for creative success.

Creativity in business

It is not just individuals and civilisations; companies know the value of creativity too. In business settings, facilitating and benefiting from the creative potential of employees ensures companies remain nimble, innovative, and ahead of their competition. This is already being realised and actioned in some companies. Google employees regularly participate in ideation as part of their job roles to achieve this end. Furthermore, think tanks, creative workshops, and whiteboard sessions are run throughout all fields of business and scholarship with the aim of teasing out million-dollar creative thoughts and paradigm-shifting discoveries. Companies like Snapchat, Microsoft, Google, and Amazon ooze with creativity and, in a reciprocal fashion, creativity is the reason for their existence in the first place; a necessary constituent of their physiology and deeply ingrained in their DNA.

To add to this, the future of work, as highlighted by studies referenced in Klaus Schwab's book, *The Fourth Industrial Revolution*, sees 47 percent of the US workforce at risk of losing their jobs in the next decade or two while employment grows for high-income cognitive and creative jobs.[29] McKenzie Wark, another author commentating on the shifting economic landscape, goes as far as saying that capitalism is on its way out and two new class relations are already forming – the "vectoralist class" and the "hacker class". To McKenzie, the "hacker class" represents a new form of production and is replacing the worker class in the 21st century. Whereas workers clocked on, traded time for money, and stamped out repetitive units of commodities for industrial tycoons, the value of the hacker class stems from their ability to produce differentness out of sameness. Members of the hacker class produce value when they turn information into intellectual property through cognitive and creative abilities, which is then capitalised on by information aggregators.[30] The new class McKenzie describes solely relies on creativity. This conception makes even more sense when overlapped with Klaus Schwab's talentism. Creativity is the currency of the future and talented individuals embody it.

To not end up like the primitive and fossilised remnants of the past requires companies to keep inventing, and they know that if they don't, they will die. It really is that simple. However, despite artificial intelligence beginning to occupy board seats at some companies,[31] most companies are run by people, which means that for companies to be creative they need creative people at the helm and working in the trenches, explaining their search for "curious individuals", "critical thinkers", and "problem solvers". Innovation depends on creativity, which is the common factor attached to all these traits. A driving force behind the looming war for talent.

Creativity research

Apart from being in a good mood, there are three significant areas of research in the realm of creativity that are important to our understanding of it.[32] Gaining insight into these mechanisms positions us uniquely ahead of our peers in the same way that an economist navigating the stock market surpasses theirs. These areas are:

1. insightful problem-solving
2. creative cognition
3. expertise acquisition.

Insightful problem-solving, "Like a lightbulb"
During the process of insightful problem-solving, an individual overcomes a mental block and moves from a position of not knowing how to complete a problem to having a deep understanding of the problem and its solution.

This arises in the form of a spontaneous lightbulb or Eureka-like moment. Instances of this form of creativity have occurred many times in history, such as when Newton reportedly discovered gravity due to a falling apple, or when Archimedes leapt out of his bathtub shouting "Eureka" after having realised the displacement of water could be used to measure volume. This highlights how the solution to a perplexing problem can spontaneously arise. Insightful problem-solving is said to comprise four main characteristics:[33]

1. Solvers come to a mental block or impasse where they are no longer making progress toward a solution. In literature this is known as a "creative block". One of the most visible of these takes the form of "writer's block", where writers experience an inability to access their internal creativity.

2. The problem-solver cannot readily report the mental processing that enabled them to reinterpret the problem and overcome their brain's gridlock. In other words, people do not know how they came up with the idea, it is as if the solution appeared fully formulated.

3. People who solve a problem with insight report that they experience the solutions to their problems arising suddenly. The steppingstones to the idea do not present themselves in a sequential manner, appearing in a moment of clarity or a flash of inspiration.

4. Performances on insight problems are associated with the creative thinking ability of an individual. People identified as more creative usually present higher-quality creative solutions. In this way, insightful problem-solving can be idiosyncratic.

Interestingly, this form of creativity has been proposed to stem from unconscious deliberation about a problem, which, once solved, is sent to our consciousness as a fully formed solution that appears as a creative thought. Research suggests the incubation period – the period characterised by the absence of conscious thought on the problem – occurs via the unconscious processing of information and has been identified as the antecedent to creative thinking.[34]

Unconscious thought, when compared to conscious thought, is suggested to be more associative and divergent as opposed to focused and convergent.[35] This essentially describes a paradigm whereby unconscious thought leads to more wildish, abstract, and novel solutions to problems, which could be rephrased as a "more creative solution". Contrary to this, conscious thought will lead you to more convergent outcomes and depends on the objects or information you are consciously focusing on.

For example, if you are trying to solve a medical problem and are operating within a hospital, you may be inclined to look for solutions through a medical lens; therefore, only giving attention to those areas or potential solutions that fall into your predefined scope of interest. However, leaving the problem to simmer in your mind and directing your conscious thought toward something else will allow you time for the incubation phase of idea generation to work its magic. As you leave the hospital and stroll down the footpath after work, you may suddenly come to the realisation that the medical problem you are trying to combat requires experimental approaches derived from the field of physics or Buddhism. And that the solution you are trying to find in the deeply rooted genealogies of medicine does not actually exist.

The incubation period allows for your unconscious processing network, known as "the default mode network", to associate distantly connected categories of information into a meaningful, coherent, and well-formulated solution to your vexing problem. Fittingly, the "default mode network" demonstrates proven links between unconscious processing and creative abilities in individuals.[34] There is merit to the argument that after a period of rumination on a certain problem, the best thing to do may be to metaphorically push the problem to the back of your mind and continue with your day. Handing this task over to the unconscious is an underused yet superior method of creative problem-solving in some instances.

> Pursuing alternative mental states that enhance your creative abilities may be viable ways to improve creativity.

Another problem with consciousness is that it may literally be blocking your creativity. Terms such as "functional fixedness", "mental blocks" and "fixation" describe the tendency of the mind to adhere to the coherent behaviour of objects and functions, or to continuously revert to previous solution procedures. Consequently, your field of focus can become a limiting factor in creativity. In one experiment, participants failed to realise that a box could also be used as a mount for a candle if they had first observed the box functioning as a container. This represents functional fixedness and refers to when the predefined functionality of something causes you to perceive it in that light. If the box did not function as a container when subjects were first exposed to it, subjects were able to readily deduce that the box could double as a mount for a candle.[36]

Your mind gets stuck in context-dependent thought processes, essentially blocking the visibility of other, more creative, thought processes and solutions. This lends support to why pursuing alternative mental states that enhance your creative abilities may be viable ways to improve creativity. As this suggests, the mere fact that you are consciously trying to be creative may be hindering your creative progress and constraining your ability to formulate unique, original ideas, some of which evidently manifest in the unconscious. Of course, you could simply try to be more creative, but sometimes the most obvious solution to a problem is the solution to another. In this case, it's best to let your mind wander and connect the seemingly unrelated concepts for you.

Instead of chasing creativity, think about generating internal environments that facilitate the processes that creativity flourishes in. Being interested in something and remaining curious is one approach. Another is to let the problem simmer on the backburner of your mind.

Creative cognition – of course you're creative

In addition to the unconscious insightful problem-solving abilities of humans, there is the notion that all humans innately possess creative abilities despite their age, race, gender, personal characteristics, and physical attributes.[37] From this viewpoint, if your brain is working in a normal capacity, you will find creativity lurking in its corners.

Creative cognition relates to a different perspective of creativity. It is a theory developed as an extension of the field of cognitive psychology. The theory differs from others due to its overarching belief that creativity results from normal cognitive processes in the human brain. It argues that all brains are creative because creativity is part of normal functioning. Within this view there is no difference in the minds of people who make extraordinary, ground-breaking discoveries – sometimes termed creative geniuses – and the minds of everyone else, because both possess the same generative abilities. Quite simply, the generative ability refers to your capacity to construct organised mental concepts and infer information despite only being exposed to situations or information rarely. Your mind can use your existing knowledge as a scaffold, off which it builds more complicated ideas, enabling you to take the logical next step without first having to experience it.

As you move through life constructing concepts and inferring information, you can combine this with your existing knowledge bank, achieving even higher levels of creativity. In fact, this is already a frequent occurrence and core component in our everyday functioning. For example, after watching a documentary about data ethics and data ownership and combining it with my existing knowledge about marketing, technology, business, and the future trajectory of humanity, I had an idea around people being able to sell their data to companies for advertisement. Instead of companies like Facebook and Instagram forcing ads down our throats because advertisers pay them for the privilege, what if we could be paid to look at annoying, intrusive ads on our terms? Instead of going through a broker, why don't you pay me directly and I'll watch 11 seconds of your attempt to sell me something? Let's see if you're savvy enough to take my emotions hostage and manipulate me to purchase your product. It is a new way of data management, data monetisation, and data ownership. This idea may have been floated before, but the point is, it was a creative thought for me at that point in time that resulted from being exposed to new information and, subsequently, combining it with my existing knowledge. The generative ability resulted in what could appropriately be defined as the logical next step in marketing and data ownership from some angles.

Humans are evolutionarily fuelled organisms with an uncanny ability to categorise, repackage, and build complex ideas from small snippets of information. This feature allows us to generate some form of mental order from the chaotic and overwhelming amount of information presented by the external world. The fact that bits and pieces of information can allow someone to form a concept of the overall subject matter to which it belongs is what leads creative cognition scientists to emphatically exclaim that we are all naturally brimming with creativity.

A more generic example of the everyday generative capacity of individuals is demonstrated in our ability to form infinite and complex novel sentences using a small subset of rules relating to language. A sentence to illustrate this point is: "Amidst a backdrop of meteoric downpouring, a unicorn rode through Saturn's stratosphere, glowing from cosmic rays." The sentence utilises basic grammatical, syntactical, and semantic rules to achieve a creative outcome – a sentence that has likely never been written before now. This ability to generate new concepts, ideas, and outcomes, built from sets of rules, assumptions, and existing data, is a characteristic creative feature of the human brain.

Although everybody possesses this innate creative ability, it is influenced by individual differences, such as an individual's motivation, existing knowledge reservoirs, the timeliness of the idea, situational factors, and the value that a culture places on the idea. Each of these contribute to how "creative" something is deemed to be.[37] Another consideration regarding this take on creativity is the many ways we can be creative. Processes that can lead to the generative abilities of humans include:[37]

- the retrieval of existing thought structures in memory
- the associations between thought structures
- combining thought structures
- the mental synthesis of new thought structures
- the mental transformation of thought structures into new forms
- the transfer of information from one domain to another
- the reduction of existing thought structures into more primitive constituent parts.

Retrieving an old idea may prove creative at a different time, unique associations between two areas can lead to creativity, combining ideas leads to new ideas, using a different perspective when you categorise information changes its application, and reverse-engineering old constructs can manifest creative outcomes. This is what everyone does, all the time, because it is part of our daily life.

Creative cognition, as previously alluded to, indoctrinates the idea that everybody is a creative individual and possesses the same mental machinery as creative geniuses. To add credibility to this proposition, I'm going to examine individuals who could be aptly labelled a creative genius and deconstruct their world-renowned creative achievements. The Wright brothers – a famous duo from history who pioneered aircraft design in 1903 – did so because they wanted humans to achieve flight. Behind their ingenious inventions, and the creativity that made it possible, was their generative abilities in action. Specifically, they linked one thought structure to another that resided in a different domain of information, effectively synthesising a new idea from two previously unrelated thought structures. The information in these "thought structures" was simply derived from their observations.

Initially, the Wright brothers owned a bicycle shop, which meant they were familiar with the concept of momentum. During this time, their interest in flight had led them to ponder on the potential mechanisms that made it possible. As a result of this thought exercise, they concluded it had to be a combination of balance and momentum. They tilted their head upwards toward the sky, looking at birds for the answer to the balance component. After their observations and subsequent analysis of bird flight, they built a pulley system in an attempt to artificially engineer the balance that nature had so generously endowed the birds with. They combined existing mental concepts (momentum and balance) to a new field of interest (human flight) and will forever be prevalent in history as some of the world's most pioneering and creative aviation engineers. Some would even call them geniuses. Really, they were just two people – not so different from you – with an interest in flying that inevitably stumbled upon a solution they were looking for. The real creativity behind their achievement was when they decided to look for their answers to human flight in the realm of nature. This generative ability that sent them skyward forms a fundamental component of your mind that you, too, can easily wield at your will.

Even though you may not have discovered the molecular blueprint required to convert normal body cells into stem-like cells, you aren't going to potentially save millions of lives through organogenesis, and you haven't been awarded a Nobel Prize like Dr Yamanaka, you are still creative. There is no question you have the potential to come up with world-changing concepts, products, and business models, which, by virtue of their ability to change the world, generate ridiculous amounts of revenue, and create monopoly markets, are clearly creative.

Uber's simple and obvious business model represents a "creative" idea worth upward of $80 billion. The fact that Uber was the first mover in the personal transport industry knights the founders' idea as original and creative, but upon deconstructing it you would realise that someone need not have years of university education to arrive at a similar conclusion: people who drive cars can function as taxi drivers if there is a way they can connect with customers. Additionally, a company called Dollar Shave Club, leveraging a once-creative business model in the form of monthly razor blade deliveries for a dollar, and despite their net worth being over $1 billion, also does not boast any supernatural creative abilities. The creativity behind this extremely successful business was… delivering razor blades monthly.

Boost juice is another example of an average idea born from the mental machinery we all possess that turned into a rainmaker. After travelling to the US, a Melbourne woman with no formal business education noticed that the juice and smoothie industry was a big thing in America but had not yet blossomed in Australia. When she returned, she started a juice and smoothie business. That person is now worth over $50 million. People initially looked at Boost and thought, "Oh, what a great idea!" but putting fruit in a juicer and serving it in a green cup is not rocket science. "Fruit smoothies are big in America." "Fruit smoothies aren't done in Australia." "Fruit smoothies could be brought to Australia." That was the creative process underlying Boost Juice's success. Manipulating and transforming information we come across, otherwise known as creativity, is something we are all capable of. The founders behind some of the world's biggest organisations made their money and achieved ridiculous levels of success through this mechanism and you, too, own the world-changing machinery needed for such feats.

To reiterate, we all have the capacity to come up with concepts that others would label as creative genius. Once upon a time, sharing a picture with a friend (Instagram), generating an online profile of yourself (Facebook), sharing videos for strangers to see (YouTube), and sending text messages instantly to your friend via the internet (iMessage) were unheard of, possibly considered ludicrous, ideas. However, they were imagined and dreamed up in the minds of people no different to us. In hindsight, many new ideas and business models are obvious, and it doesn't take a creative genius to discover them. It is just an ordinary person with different life experiences and knowledge reservoirs that puts some mental energy toward a problem and eventually comes up with an individualised generative solution.

Entrepreneurs with hugely successful companies have usually leveraged this inherent form of creativity early on, and it's one of the reasons they are where they are. Now you know they are no different to you in terms of their creative potential*. In fact, you may be more creative than the founders of all the aforementioned start-ups. Open your eyes when you walk through life and you may end up knocking yourself out on a million-dollar business idea.

---

* To note, successful entrepreneurs, the creative people in business, also have high levels of motivation, ambition, discipline, and resilience... all of which you could acquire, if you so wished.

Here is a piece of Chinese wisdom for the road:

Genius can be recognised by its childish simplicity. —Chinese proverb

---

Expertise acquisition – becoming an expert in creativity

Expertise acquisition is another theory that has been mentioned as a potential precursor to innovative and creative ideas. Expertise acquisition is defined as being the direct result of extensive amounts of deliberate practice toward a focused goal – the outcome being that someone usually becomes an expert in their field. Examples of intense deliberate practice include a music student completing homework tasks with a focus of progressing in musical ability; a university student studying mathematics and undergoing tutoring to help them become proficient in understanding the structures of mathematical models. It can even include an up-and-coming footballer taking themselves to the oval for a certain amount of time each week to practise their goal-kicking ability with the aim of improving accuracy. All these individuals are participating in a deliberate form of practice and exerting effort toward a focused goal, which sees them on the path of expertise acquisition.

The concept of creative expertise was born after studies that looked at elite musicians and composers found there to be an expertise component that preceded most of their creative works. This finding proved similar for scientists and inventors; however, creativity in this case happened in a different domain.[38] This raises the question: how could expertise acquisition explain creative genius? In the case of creative expertise, it is suggested that the underlying construct binding expertise acquisition to creative genius is the notion that creative individuals do not simply come up with new ideas in isolation, but they arise from an arsenal of well-developed skills and a robust body of domain-relevant knowledge. The isolated and unrelated arcane thoughts lurking in the shadows of an expert's mind are weaved together and result in fully formed ideas that give rise to Eureka-like moments. It is through this mechanism that undiscovered ideas manifest as creative flashes of inspiration.

There is documented evidence linking expertise acquisition and creativity; however, this link can be observed and deduced from the achievements of those we deem to be experts. The vast amount of scientific, psychological, and philosophical breakthroughs that ripple through humanity are born from researchers' lifelong efforts in those fields. As researchers acquire expert knowledge, they are better able to see the novel links between unrelated concepts and information, leading to their creative ideas. These creative ideas become discoveries and, as a result, the researchers are awarded prestigious prizes, showered with admiration, and pedestalled by institutions. Perhaps borderline mental obsessions with topics that nobody seems to understand may sculpt you into a domain-specific expert full of knowledge, which, given the right ingredients and life experiences, manifests as the pinnacle of creativity. On that note, JK Rowling, thank you for being an expert in magic.

Another argument for expertise acquisition is evident in the form of unique associations between areas of study. If a music expert becomes an expert in biology, they may soon realise that the frequency of soundwaves can affect the functioning of physiological systems. This brings together two domains of expertise, and a new creative link emerges between the two. In science, interdisciplinary research is responsible for most of the ground-breaking discoveries that propel the field of medicine forward. In the 1980s, a well-known neuroscientist, Candace Pert, cofounded the field of psychoimmunoendocrinology after collaborating with her partner, who was an immunologist. The two fields, neuroscience and immunology, came together in the form of two experts collaborating, to facilitate the birth of a whole new field of science, which provided unprecedented insights into how the human body functions as an integrated system.[39]

As you can see, there are various processes and models that are used to describe creativity. Certain models place an emphasis on the innate abilities of all humans to be creative, while others suggest creativity comes from the domains of knowledge-rich experts. There is also evidence that showcases the differing roles that conscious and unconscious mental activity plays in creativity. The key takeaway from this information is that anyone, and everyone, can be creative. Creativity is a basic function of being human. We all have similar mental machinery, all have an unconscious domain lurking somewhere in the abyss, and we all have the capability to become an expert in a field, if we so wished.

The attainment of creative expertise is a logical sequence of events:

1. Following our interests can lead us to a pursuit of passion and being interested in "learning and exploring", or in solving a "puzzling problem", means we are labelled as curious.

2. Engaging in any activities that spark our curiosity, ignite our interest, or sees us pursuing our passions, transforms the normal workings of the mind through the activation of flow state.
3. Intrinsic motivation, synonymous with entering flow, subsequently leads to improvements in mood, general creativity, workplace creativity, musical creativity, productivity, self-esteem, concentration, and peak performance. By themselves, improvements in mood are already positively associated with creativity.
4. When engaging in the activities we find interesting, the pleasure, satisfaction, psychological transformation, and internal rewards we experience allow us to persevere through difficult times.
5. This perseverance can eventually lead to expertise acquisition, which further contributes to our creative abilities and brings us ever closer to achieving our creative potential. At the same time, in conjunction with passion, creating a recipe for elite performance.

Throughout our interest-pursuit, the amount of knowledge we acquire accumulates progressively as we reach differing levels of subject matter expertise, and this archived knowledge forms further fundamental pillars of creativity. First, the existing knowledge we possess guides our perspective in a targeted manner, allowing us to unveil the relevant bits of information we come across in life. Second, in conjunction with existing information, new information enters our super-intelligent unconscious and is processed in a divergent, associative fashion, cross-referenced with all of our other stored data, and it is offered up to our conscious mind after being painted with the brush of creativity. It is through these steps that interests facilitate our creative potential as humans, which, when capitalised on, leads to organisational innovation, improvements in global health, and the advancement of civilisation.

The flipside of this suggests that when companies hire new talent, they should seriously take into consideration an individual's existing interests and pay close attention to developing strategies and work environments conducive to the optimisation of individual interest pursuits. If a company is able to "interest match" prospective employees, the benefits include:

- increased job performance
- reduced staff turnover
- better employee satisfaction
- improved productivity
- increased capitalisation of psychological assets

- enhanced employee self-esteem and confidence
- notable improvements in creativity and innovation.

An innovative company, after all, is the result of human creativity.

Combined consciousness

To finish, I would like to share one more creativity-related concept that I have encountered through my involvement in a start-up company through an in-depth collaboration with another person. I call this combined consciousness. Without getting too philosophical, it is simply the realisation that when you put your head together with someone else's, or when you "combine consciousnesses", you arrive at unique destinations. By doing this, you are opening up the concepts and data residing deep in one another's brains to each other's consciousness and, in effect, allowing packages of processed and already analysed data to be seamlessly transmitted and downloaded by one another.

This is similar to the concept of collaboration but involves a purely mental expedition into the abyss of multiple minds. It differs from brainstorming as this usually takes place in a narrow scope, is goal directed, and can be limited by functional fixedness. Combining consciousnesses is an exercise most likely to happen when fields of interests between multiple parties are closely aligned, uniquely associated, progress in an unstructured discussion, and are tackled from vastly different backgrounds and areas of expertise.

Surrounding yourself with thinkers, intellectuals, disruptors, creators, and experts, can lead to discussions that naturally evolve through combining consciousnesses as a result of the input both parties enter. The consciousness of both manifest in unique concepts, creative solutions, and disruptive products when shared interests inspire action.

To sum up

Our interests are the ingredients unique to us that propel us forward on a certain trajectory. In the same way that personal interests help to differentiate people, the interest areas of companies set each apart from another. Interests are a driver of intrinsic motivation, a formidable force, and have the ability to spark a psychological transformation that sets our mind into overdrive. Flow state leads to energised concentration, optimal enjoyment, and complete alignment with the task at hand. In organisations this type of motivation leads to better performance, more commitment, less burnout, and reduced turnover intentions in employees. When employees' broader interests align with their jobs they are more knowledgeable and perform better, they stay longer, and companies reduce productivity losses and costs associated with staff turnover and languishing.

A "broad interest in learning and exploring" has been repackaged as the character trait "curious" and used to label people. Curiosity predicts job performance better than personality and general mental abilities, while helping new employees adapt to organisations. It's been correlated with worker engagement, job satisfaction, innovation, and proactive behaviours in the workplace. Organisations widely knight curiosity as a driver of innovation, referring to it as a competitive advantage. Apart from the benefits listed, curiosity has also been dubbed an antecedent of creativity due to its role in information gathering.

Creativity and innovation are intricately entangled, and only through creativity can true innovation manifest. Creativity is one of the most valuable abilities we as humans possess, and throughout history creative individuals have been held in high esteem by the ruling class. Even today, the organisations that in a way rule the modern world, are still chasing them down. They understand the competitive advantage, change to the bottom line, and innovation each creative individual represents. Apart from purely profitable endeavours, it is because of creative individuals that the world surges forward toward destination innovation, where utopian improvements to the quality of life, living conditions, and fulfilment of individuals can be realised.

There are three main theories on creativity, including insightful problem-solving, creative cognition, and expertise acquisition. And together these theories put the power of creativity squarely in your hands. Through the power of our unconscious mind, lightbulb solutions present themselves. In the everyday use of our mental machinery, we're lucky creativity comes inbuilt. An unrestrained pursuit of our interests fuels our path toward expertise acquisition, where in combination with our conscious and unconscious mind, a repertoire of robust information adds another layer to our creative capabilities. Your interests and creativity are a unique value proposition for your personal brand.

What's next?

Next we'll explore what your personality is and how it ties into success in life – whatever that is to you. Effectively, personality traits describe your day-to-day operations and by virtue of this we can glimpse the future they foretell. Personality describes human behaviour, and for us to master ourselves and control our future destination, we jump into the world of psychology, philosophy, and habit formation, leveraging them for our own behaviour change interventions. The amplification of personality traits manifests as company culture, and after our personality science expedition we apply our findings to corporate culture to understand exactly where personality sits in the world of business.

Chapter 3:
Personality and Culture

Your personality

Day-to-day operations

The individual and habitual practices that make you unique are aspects of your *personality*. More specifically, in psychological terms, personality describes a person's *usual* pattern of feelings, thoughts, and behaviours that distinguish them from others. The important word here is "usual" because if these characteristics are to be considered part of personality, they must persist across situations and over time. For example, if you are a well-known socialite with a magnetic attraction to people and festive events, it's likely these tendencies would earn you the label of extrovert. Yet, despite a bent toward outgoing behaviour, there will be times where you don't feel like going out. It may be the Friday after a long and stressful work week, rain pounding your windows, and your energy levels flatlining that causes you to opt for an evening in. Saying no to going out with your friends on this occasion is not your persistent, usual pattern of behaviour. Consequently, when exploring personality traits, this once-off introverted behaviour doesn't make the cut. It's not one of your characteristic tendencies, rather it represents more of an anomaly.

Similarly, if you are a thrill-seeker who loves chasing the feeling of rising adrenaline levels and enjoys death-defying activities, it's unlikely you'll wake up next week and refuse to go skydiving with your best friend. Over time and across situations, a unique combination of behaviours, thoughts, and feelings will consistently surface throughout your everyday life. This unique, core, consistent part of you is what personality refers to.

Your personality is like an electron cloud that surrounds the nucleus of an atom, except that instead of electromagnetic principles guiding probable electron positions, behaviour potentials guide the likelihood of certain actions, thoughts, and feelings occurring. Behaviour potentials are influenced by the situation you are in, other people, your internal bodily state, neurological activity, previous experiences, and genetics. These variables factor in to how we behave in specific situations and give rise to a range of potential behaviours, each with their own probability of manifesting. For instance, if you are in a psychologically stressed state, burdened by frustrating physical injuries, genetically prone to aggression, and currently being antagonised by your partner, there is a high probability that in response to one more slight provocation you might just punch a hole in the wall and spit venom. In the same situation, in the absence of psychological stress and annoying physical injuries, the likelihood of a hole in the wall may drop significantly and be substituted by another behaviour, such as a minor angry outburst that now has a higher probability of occurring.

There are some traits unique to you that provide the scaffold off which your potential behaviours are generated, meaning that if you have aggressive tendencies, it is likely your range of behaviours will include an aggressive undertone. In the same way that a core disposition for orderliness and scheduling would see you consistently micromanaging many areas of your life, including occupational responsibilities, exercise, eating habits, and study. These core dispositions are also conceptualised as personality "traits".

Although personality can't be used to precisely predict your behaviour and responses, it informs us about the cloud of likely outcomes in specific situations. The favoured behaviours, over time and when compounded, manifest as significant life events and successes. Through small daily habits you can glimpse future outcomes and personality traits – the habitual ways you operate – are no different. Certain personality traits can be correlated with a range of life outcomes, including personal characteristics, academic achievements, interpersonal communication styles, physical and mental health status, peer perceptions, and career success.

The whole world is beautiful when you put on a pair of rose-tinted glasses, yet despite the benefits of an optimistic outlook, substituting the lens of reality with a superficial quick-fix sometimes provides an unachievable illusion of beauty. What you see when you wear them is a state of bliss and satisfaction, an idealistic world resembling your personal utopia. However, these glasses merely show you an end state without informing you about how it is built day by day, action by action. Engineering your perfect life, a utopia where you're happy, satisfied, respected, supported, healthy, driven to achieve, emotionally stable, and accomplished requires you to understand how your day-to-day operations – a reflection of your personality – impact the coordinates of your future destination.

Mastering traits

When you master personality traits this is possible. The "mundanity of excellence" theory places habitualised, compounded actions as the core ingredient for success; personality traits then are a correlate of success. Consistent behaviours and thoughts over time are described by your personality. These habitualised patterns of behaviour predictably lead to a subset of outcomes. In some cases, excellence, achievement, and success result.

> You can formulate your own end state while identifying the goals you need to meet to get there.

Understanding links between personality traits and their subsequent outcomes in different areas of life grants you a high-level view of the playing field. It enables you to pick apart your life goals, map them to certain outcomes, and trace these back to underlying personality traits. When you've zoomed in on key personality traits conducive to your goals, your volition enables you to develop these so that day by day you act in accordance with your true purpose, slowly but surely progressing to your end state. For example, the goal of living a happy life could be mapped to certain outcomes, such as measures of "life satisfaction", "psychological wellbeing", and "physical health", which in turn could be tied to personality traits like *conscientiousness* and *emotional stability*.

By having the capacity for thought, being guided by your own personal philosophy, and regularly introspecting, you can formulate your own end state while identifying the goals you need to meet to get there. And given personality traits such as conscientious and emotional stability can be engineered through daily behaviours or acquired knowledge, you can arm yourself with behaviours and thoughts that form the building blocks of success.

This chapter will introduce some key outcomes associated with different personality traits so that you can trace a path to your goals through daily behaviours. All while ensuring that you live in accordance with the wider framework of your philosophy.

Personal operations

If your personal philosophy describes your ideals, fundamental beliefs, and aspirations, and your interests determine the sandbox you're playing in, your personality will outline your journey. Your personality is comprised of an array of traits, some beneficial, some not so much, and throughout your journey these traits can be viewed as a selection of tools. Certain tools are handy to have as you move through the academic jungle of universities, while others ensure you're well positioned to be an employer's top pick in the workplace.

Some tools are fashioned for creative success while others prove useful in altering others' perceptions. Contrarily, other tools are faulty and can be ticking timebombs posing a risk to you, the people around you, and threaten the overall achievement of your goals. Life is an obstacle course and your toolbelt dramatically influences your journey through it. For those with a pessimistic outlook, carrying the emotional baggage that accompanies high levels of neuroticism, this obstacle course will loom much larger. To an extrovert, the same obstacle course that sent someone spiralling into depression will be viewed as a fun challenge and something to be overcome.

Personality, on average, will predict how you respond to many of the events you face along the way. It will detail the "autopilot" psychological state that will fly you from this point in time to a point in the future where you can realise your ultimate vision. And, above all else, your personality will have the final say when determining if, how, and when you arrive at your personal utopian destination.

Your vision is the end point, and your mission statement idealistically outlines the necessary practices to get there. How you carry out your mission statement in reality, the lifeforce behind it, is governed by your personality and is further influenced by your personal values.

In the land of business, for an organisation, personality is akin to culture. It's all well and good if a cancer therapy company identifies their mission as "continuing to explore scientific breakthroughs in an effort to eradicate cancer once and for all", but how they *live* their mission matters. Will they explore these scientific breakthroughs thoroughly or superficially? Diligently or half-heartedly? Will they look for out-of-the-box ideas or remain tethered to conventional, widely accepted scientific dogma? Will they explore breakthroughs in a cooperative manner or with trailblazing scientists who divide and conquer? What are the underlying ethics and values that govern the scientific breakthroughs they deem worthy of exploration – is the ability for the science to be monetised and profitable second to the ability for it to cure a patient once and for all? The way a mission statement comes alive is heavily influenced by aspects of your personality, or in this case the combined sphere of employee behaviour – the organisation's culture.

Components of personality can be used to describe how people differ from each other, but it also considers many human tendencies we all share. There are many people who experience anxiety, daydream about travelling the world, walk on eggshells trying to please others, and many who dutifully complete their work to a high standard. However, of the many people who experience anxiety, they experience different levels of it. Whereas one person is housebound, paralysed by the crippling weight of a clinically diagnosed anxiety disorder, another has a fleeting moment of it, their feelings of worry find no foothold and slide like water off a duck's back. It is the degree to which these people experience the same thing that enables them to be separated out on the spectrum of a universal trait. Negative feelings like anxiety and depression help to characterise people on one spectrum. In the realm of personality research there are many other traits, each with their own spectrums used concurrently by psychologists to diagram your personality. The overall combination of these traits and their corresponding levels is how a snapshot of your personality is captured.

A history of personality

Arriving at this modern method to describe personality was no easy feat. From the birth of the field of personality to now, scientists from many disciplines have proposed unique theories attempting to explain personality development and describe the ways it can be measured. The oldest theories, one of which is based on the work of Sigmund Freud, suggests that personality arises from psychodynamic forces; the interactions between unconscious urges and impulses in your mind. Being old, this theory is loosely tethered to modern scientific findings in neuroscience and psychology; however, since its inception it has profoundly influenced popular thought in the area.

Freud's personality theory proposed the existence of three intangible components in the mind: the *id, ego,* and *superego,* which, in combination, are responsible for resolving psychological conflicts and determining our behaviour. The *id* is an unconscious structure operating on the pleasure principle, the *ego* operates on the reality principle, and the *superego* operates on morality principles. Unconscious evolutionary urges may arise from the *id*, such as sexual desire. This then interacts with the *ego* component of the mind, responsible for dealing with the real world and solving problems about how the urge can be satisfied. In this case, we may begin searching for potential mating partners and engage in behaviours that bring us closer to sexual satisfaction. The way in which we navigate reality to achieve this end is influenced by the *ego*. When we adhere to the universal codes that govern male and female interactions, and strive to achieve this outcome in a moral manner, you could attribute this to the work of Freud's *superego*. The combination of these three mental structures summarises the psychodynamic perspective on personality development, which says our personality arises from psychical conflicts in our mind.

Others propose that personality is a result of social learning and operant conditioning. These views fall under behaviourism, otherwise known as behavioural psychology, and suggests our behaviours are learnt through interactions with the environment. As someone progresses through life from birth to death, they are continually influenced to develop, behave, and adapt in certain ways through environmental cues such as social feedback, sensory stimuli, and the varying outcomes that result from their actions. One form of social feedback occurs when we observe other people's behaviours and the consequences that arise from them. There is some powerful research about this, showing how these observations consequentially influence how we behave. One of the most famous experiments highlighted how young children, when observing a violent role-model, went on to copy and enact their behaviours.[1]

Reward or punishment

Observing others' behaviour is one direct way that ours is influenced. Another way is through rewards or punishments. If we are rewarded for a behaviour, research in operant conditioning shows that our future behaviour will be positively influenced and is likely to increase in frequency. The easiest way to see this form of behaviour modification in action is to think about your beloved pet dog (or maybe you're a cat person?). If they are anything like my eternally hungry pug toddler Baxter, whenever you are sitting down at the dining table to eat your food, in some mysterious way, they end up magically appearing next to you. It is like they have a sixth sense for detecting activities relating to food. Have you noticed though that they are always on their best behaviour? My dog sits down, pumps his chest out, perks his head up, and then looks at me expectantly. When he was a puppy, like many other dog owners, we taught him to sit, rewarding him with food, praise, and cuddles. In his mind, even if he's long forgotten the initial reason for his sitting behaviour, he knows that by sitting (and making sure that I can see him) he's being a "good boy". Good behaviour is the best chance for getting whatever's on my plate. He knows it and never leaves emptyhanded.

The reverse of this mechanism holds true for punishment. Behaviours will be extinguished if paired with something undesirable, like time out. In Baxter's case he used to get a little crazy and devious when we watched movies in our theatre room. He jumped up on the couch and, silently, like a ninja, made his way onto the back supports, where he bade his time, calculating his next attack. A few minutes into stealth mode, when the unwitting audience were absorbed in the movie and completely unaware of the external world, he ran along the top of the couch and pug-bombed an unsuspecting victim. It was a shock to the system when a pug flew from the heavens and landed on your face, and it was definitely a behaviour that needed fixing. When my ex-girlfriend (a psychologist) was there, she'd promptly get up and take him outside, effectively putting him in time out so that he could reflect on his evil ways. Little pug and his bad behaviour were no match for her. Now, instead of pug-bombing during movies, he runs out and comes back, bringing with him toys and is much more content chewing his monkey in the corner.

Social environment

Evidence for the above personality view is provided through socialisation, a process whereby, over time, an individual's behaviour is shaped by societal expectations, parenting methods, and operant conditioning. The result, from years of governing feedback, is the creation of a mature individual who functions smoothly as a member of a group to which they belong, whether it be a family, organisation, or society. A societal expectation in Japan is that everyone operates in a respectful manner, adheres to similar moral principles, and abides by cultural norms such as bowing upon greeting. A Japanese individual's family, in addition to the wider society they are brought up in, shape them through social feedback in such a way that they end up functioning as a coherent unit in Japanese culture. Socialisation describes this process.

This process is continually happening in every domain of life, differing in magnitude, and being distributed by anyone and everyone. Relationships, family environments, professional settings, academic journeys, and recreational activities all provide behaviour-shaping social data. It is in this way that behaviours, beliefs, and consequently personalities are conditioned by your environment and are largely influenced through social information.

We are not just passive agents in our environment though. Our environment influences us, but we also influence our environment, which can further influence our future behaviours. The model for this is called reciprocal determinism and credits our personal choices and "free will" as integral parts of our personality development through our ability to choose and subsequently shape the environments we are in. Someone who chooses to spend all their time in libraries is going to develop different habits and traits than someone who spends the majority of their time partying at nightclubs. The people, scenery, experiences, and all other factors that vary across these environments will impact a person differently, in effect conditioning behaviours over time. However, this isn't the whole story.

Blame it on biology

Some personality theorists adopt a biological viewpoint, knighting human biology as the causal agent in the development of behaviours, thoughts, and feelings that are unique to us. Biology, to them, is the reason for our personality. Research supports this premise too, even at the most foundational level. In fact, evidence for genetic involvement in personality traits in some instances is obvious. Angelman Syndrome is one example. This disorder is characterised by a defect on chromosome 15 that results in excessively happy children who are reportedly filled with glee.

Other examples of the impact of biology on personality can be found in identical twin studies. Studies show that even when identical twins are separated at birth and have completely different upbringing environments (social information), they still exhibit striking similarities in their personalities. Through the above research it's apparent that changes in chromosomes can cause unique variations in personality traits, and that duplicating DNA, which is essentially what identical twin studies are examining, produces similar results in terms of personality.[2] Upstream of genetics, our hormone levels and internal bodily environment boasts further areas supporting biology's impact on personality variation. Males have more testosterone than females, and it's widely known that elevated testosterone levels can predispose a person to aggressive behaviour. Just ask someone on steroids if they have anger issues – politely of course, you don't want them to "roid rage" and burst a blood vessel.

Further biological underpinnings of personality have been identified through the *behavioural activation system* and *behavioural inhibition system* – a set of brain circuits common to all of us and discovered by neuroscientist Jeffrey Alan Gray. The characteristics of these brain circuits alter how we behave by influencing how sensitive we are to rewards or perceived punishments. For example, if you had an overactive *behavioural activation system*, you'd be more impulsive and constantly pursuing rewards. The overactivity in this circuit is the reason people respond differently to rewards than their properly regulated counterparts. Indeed, evidence supports that higher activity in this system is a risk factor for overeating and drug addiction, both of which stem from impulse regulation issues.[3]

How impulsive you are factors into your personality; it's one of your unique characteristics. Overly impulsive people act without thinking and make rash decisions they regret, and, not surprisingly, impulsivity is linked to obesity.[3] The opposite of this is someone who is highly conscientious and carefully plans and thinks about their actions. As such, the sensitivity of these brain circuits significantly affects our behavioural tendencies, which, when consistent over time, forms foundational components of our personality.

The real story

The truth about how our personality develops and evolves includes a combination of all three of the above theories. There is evidence that unconscious thoughts can influence how we behave and respond in situations, providing some support for Freud's psychodynamic theory. In addition, many experiments and longitudinal studies support the role of behavioural conditioning in shaping personality, which results from social learning, environmental feedback, and behavioural reinforcement achieved through rewards and punishments (remember Baxter the dive-bombing pug?). Furthermore, it is obvious that genetics, brain structures, and hormone levels – elements of our biology – demonstrably influence our behaviours too. Personality is complex but knowing about its super complexities isn't useful unless we can take advantage of our knowledge. That is where *trait theory* comes in.

Trait theory

In terms of measuring and tracking personality, trait theory is the gold standard and has been widely adopted throughout the world of psychology. Gordon Allport pioneered this area of enquiry and suggested that although people will behave differently at different times, in different situations, with different people, and at different ages, their core pattern of constant, predictable behaviours can be summarised by their personality traits.[4] Think of traits as predispositions to acting in a certain way across situations, which forms a baseline for responses, reactions, and thoughts toward events in daily life. For example, a person who tends to agree with people and focuses their energy toward helping others is widely perceived as a nice, soft-spoken, and kind person. People like this tend to avoid conflict, act in a way to please people, cooperate with others, and readily engage in prosocial behaviour. It doesn't matter all too much who they are with, where they are, what situation they are in, or if they have aged since you last saw them, this tendency will shine through; it is one of their core personal traits.

Trait theory stemmed from the work of early researchers who set out to identify each and every word in the English language that could be used to describe character. Gordon Allport databased a staggering 17,000 words that could be used for this end.[4] Doing this allowed researchers to understand and categorise different descriptive words, in turn creating an informed landscape for the study of personality traits. Having this foundational knowledge meant researchers could group people with each other but could also compare them against others, turning what was once an ambiguous activity into one with much more scientific rigour.

However, 17,000 words, as they soon realised, despite being thorough and enormously informative, was not a pragmatic way to measure and compare people's traits. There were simply too many words to manage, and how would you compare someone described as zealous and inquisitive with another described as magical and exuberant? What if one person has been described with 300 words, another 23? Even the attempted measurement of personality utilising this method presented problems. When a personality test is administered to 100 people, who each interpret questions differently and possess varying levels of IQ, and who are then asked to choose from thousands of words to describe themselves or other people, the results become meaningless and infinitely challenging to analyse. To generate meaningful insights in personality research, the way traits were measured and assessed needed to be standardised and relevant for all of us. A simpler structured framework was required, but researchers were faced with a problem: how could 17,000 words and the entirety of human functioning be concisely summarised into a few traits that could apply universally to everyone?

The Big Five

The answer was *factor analysis*, a statistical method whereby variables are grouped together based on their correlations and called a factor. For instance, joyful, cheerful, happy, gregarious, sociable, and pleasant are adjectives that are similar and, unsurprisingly, are correlated. Meaning that if someone is described as happy it is likely they could also be described as sociable, pleasant, or any of the other words above. In essence, each of these words, due to their relationship, describe and allude to a broader underlying trait called a factor, which in this case would be *extroversion*. Using this method, thousands of adjectives pulled from the world of personality research were simplified into five common traits (these are the factors) applicable to everyone. These universal traits are known as "The Big Five" and are assessed on a continuum.

Over the years, this framework has proven to be a useful, reliable, and valid way to investigate personality; however, it is still not perfect. A point of contention around it is that, to date, a biological basis has not been found for all five underlying traits, and in the current ecosystem of science, without physical evidence, hypothetical constructs remain theoretical and limited and are accepted with caution. Yet despite this, it has still proven extremely valuable. Resulting from this model, to plot your personality to the best of today's knowledge only requires you to answer some multiple-choice-style questions on a personality questionnaire and, almost magically, the mind-boggling complexity of your personality is distilled into meaningful and accurate results.

Throughout the test, your scores are used to position you at different levels of these universal traits, and in doing so hint at the pattern of core tendencies that make you, *you*! It is important to note that if you are interested in better understanding yourself, psychologists and psychiatrists are the only professionals who can access and administer valid clinical personality assessments. Don't waste your time on online quizzes or free personality tests, they're meaningless.

The Big Five framework, as mentioned, refers to a set of broad universal traits that people can be measured and assessed on. They are:

1. Openness to experience
2. Conscientiousness
3. Extroversion
4. Agreeableness
5. Neuroticism

As an ex-psychology student, an easy way to remember them is through the acronym OCEAN. Each of these large factors are then further broken down into sub-traits belonging to that cluster called facets.[5] As we unpack each of these five dimensions of your personality, see if you can recognise elements of your own. Being aware of your behavioural tendencies, patterns, and habits offers you an opportunity to objectively look into the state of your overall functioning while providing you a crystal ball through which you can glimpse the future your personality-driven practices foretell.

Personality traits and their facets can be used to predict behaviours, life outcomes, and other unique individual activities. For example, the university course you enrol in, the number of parties you attend, your dieting behaviours, smoking status, popularity, willingness to share money, general knowledge, job performance, physical health status, and academic success are but a few of the outcomes predicted partially or powerfully by personality attributes.[2,6]

Seeing how you measure up to everyone else from a bird's eye view allows you to think, respond, and behave differently.

When you understand your unique personality traits and their subsequent patterns of behaviour, you can make educated guesses about potential outcomes in your life. Consequently, using the following knowledge and applying relevant behaviour change strategies to tweak aspects of your personality profile so that you operate better can position you for a life of success, one of flourishing. Destination unknown becomes, "Ahh, I should have known."

It is important to realise that you are who you are, that your personality is a result of your biology, your acquired knowledge, and your social environment. How you measure up on traits is based on your personal nature, and there is nothing inherently wrong with you being *you*. Your individuality is cause for celebration. Diving into personality science in this way merely aims to help you recognise and describe your traits, identifying those that confer benefits. Knowledge is power, and understanding universal human operations gives you an ability to form an objective view on the operator of *your* life. Although we're not doing a comprehensive proper personality inventory here my aim is to offer you some insight that you hopefully find useful.

When you understand your mental and physical day-to-day operations at a higher level, seeing how you measure up to everyone else from a bird's eye view allows you to think, respond, and behave differently. You can draw links to the beneficial behaviours and outcomes associated with different personality traits so that if you want you can attempt to consciously tweak your personality profile to one that is more in line with what you value for yourself, your future, your goals, and your relationships. If being more open leads to enhanced creativity, and you value creativity, then consciously implementing techniques or behaviours to increase your openness will facilitate your creative ambitions. If managing emotions allows you to be a better partner, then identifying and implementing techniques that can help you improve aspects of trait neuroticism can lead to better emotional regulation and therefore healthier and fulfilling relationships. Through applied philosophy and psychological science, you can equip yourself with the right tools for your life journey because the most valuable tool is your mind, and you are its master!

Openness to experience

Openness to experience, also referred to as "trait openness", is the first of the five universal traits we are going to cross-examine. People scoring highly in this trait generally appear witty, original, imaginative, and artistic, commonly tending to daydream, fantasise, and lose themselves in thought. They have an appreciation for art and beauty and are moved by poetry and music. They participate in introspection, explore their inner feelings, are willing to try different activities, and prefer variety to routine. They are intellectually efficient, allowing them to process complex information,[7] and are curious, displaying a readiness to re-examine values, and bend toward anti-traditional and anti-authoritative views through their willingness to reconsider ideas and beliefs.

As previously mentioned, traits are measured across a spectrum. The above description describes someone at the upper limits of this openness dimension. Someone at the other end, scoring low in "openness to experience", would prefer routine, dislike change, abstain from daydreaming, may not be particularly curious, and might not have an appreciation for art. Of course, there is a middle ground too, where some descriptions may apply to you, others not so much. In this case, you would score relatively average in this dimension. Now that you know what this personality dimension is and can attempt a broad guess about where you sit on it, why is it important?

> When high openness is paired with good emotional regulation, creative potential becomes creative achievement.

High scores in openness leads people to have more life experiences, resulting in exposure to more positive and more negative events. Additionally, effective and transformational leaders who inspire, motivate, and lead and who foster innovation, change, and creativity, generally score highly in openness. In organisations, increased openness is connected to organisational citizenship behaviour, demonstrated by people who see areas for change and improvement and take the time to remedy them for the organisation's benefit.[2] Openness is linked to entrepreneurial intentions, representing one of the best predictors of entrepreneurship.[8] It is the trait most consistently studied in relation to innovation and creativity. In fact, leading personality scholars define openness as a personality disposition for creativity because of its associated tendencies for people to seek out new experiences, think imaginatively, tolerate ambiguity, and practise nonconformity.[9]

This shouldn't be surprising. In the previous sections we learned about the creative process and how an increase in the exposure to information, people, opinions, thoughts, and experiences provides the scaffolding off which new ideas are born and creativity can manifest. Openness simply describes the behavioural tendencies preceding it because people are living life in a curious, information-gathering mode. When high openness is paired with good emotional regulation, creative potential becomes creative achievement, with emotions being an integral part of the equation.[10] The likelihood of success diminishes when someone is unable to adequately manage, overcome, and endure emotional rollercoasters that spring up during creative pursuits. Having an idea is great but will you be able to put up with being broke, living in a bubble of uncertainty, stressed, time poor, and mentally burnt out as you try to bring that idea to life or turn it into a profitable business?

Research shows that, on average, scientists and artists are more open than non-artists and non-scientists.[11] High-school graduates higher in openness have more creative potential at age 27 and display greater occupational creativity at age 52.[12] Openness also predicts success in education and in the workplace more accurately than general intelligence.[13] Finally, it is notably correlated with optimism, self-efficacy (the belief that you can achieve what you set out to do), proactive personality (a disposition to control your environment and incite change), and general intelligence, meaning that people higher in openness usually score better in these variables.[7] However, high openness is not necessarily causal of the increase.

Conscientiousness

Scoring high in the trait of conscientiousness generally occurs when someone perceives themselves as competent, effective, prudent, and sensible. Additionally, people who score high in this trait are usually well-organised, methodical, and neat. Governed by their conscience, they have a sense of duty, demonstrate ethical behaviour, adhere to social norms and rules, and evidence high moral standards. Motivated and driven by the need to achieve and succeed, they work hard to realise their goals through self-discipline and persistence, from the initiation of a task through to its end. Part of this self-control sees them able to delay gratification, putting off short-term lucrative rewards for longer-term returns.

Thinking carefully before acting and cautious deliberation is another hallmark of someone high in conscientiousness. Whereas someone low in this trait would be the opposite, demonstrating impulsive, disorganised, irrational, immoral, and unmotivated behaviours. When discussing the associations below, keep in mind the opposite perspective. For example, if a highly conscientious person has more job success, a low-scoring counterpart tends to move in the opposite direction.

Conscientiousness boasts many beneficial links and outcomes for people displaying this trait, which is no surprise given the qualities of their character. Not only can you pick a conscientious person from their external behaviours, but you'd also be able to spot them through high-tech medical imaging technology because a conscientious brain looks different.

Researchers found an increased volume of grey matter in certain brain areas involved in redirecting attention from external stimuli back toward goal-driven behaviour. This makes sense given conscientious individuals regularly exert self-control to overcome distractions in their environment and need to focus their attention on goals in order to achieve them.[14,15] Grey matter is made up of neuronal cell bodies and is heavily involved in information processing. Having less of it is associated with a reduction in cognitive abilities.[16] The fact that conscientious people demonstrate higher amounts shows how thoughts and behavioural tendencies are linked to improvements in physical brain structure.

Later in this chapter I present information showing how thoughts themselves can rewire our brains, which suggests that by adopting conscientious tendencies you too can improve neural architecture. On this, conscientiousness is the only Big Five personality trait that is consistently related to better academic performance through increased academic effort and self-efficacy.[17] A fascinating finding building upon this shows the volume of conscientious-associated grey matter in certain areas of the brain, by itself, can even be linked to academic performance. Using these regions, from a brain scan, researchers could predict academic performance despite not knowing how conscientious the participants were.[18] Conscientiousness, academic performance, and cognitive abilities are biologically linked through the amount of this neural tissue you have!

Conscientiousness also predicts good life events, such as winning academic awards, getting promoted, or successfully quitting smoking.[19] Conscientious individuals are prone to having higher self-efficacy, equating to more confidence in their abilities.[20] Confidence – an output of this trait – attracts life partners, generates respect, fosters impressions of reliability, and lands you jobs. Not only will conscientiousness and its derivatives make you appealing to employers, but once in the job it becomes the best predictor of general work performance, success in sales roles, and is related to overall career success.[2,21] This is a logical finding considering pragmatism, discipline, responsibility, organisational skills, and ambition represent some of the core ingredients of an ideal employee.

Higher up in the organisational chain, effective leaders, emergent leaders (those who naturally move into leadership roles in organisations), and transformational leaders (those who inspire positive change in others) also score highly in this trait.[22] Self-oriented perfectionism – another correlate of conscientious high scorers – describes an individual's belief system that values striving for perfection and is linked to better goal progress and positive moods.[23] High standards and aspirations point you in the direction of perfection, discipline carries you through, and the purpose you derive from this process likely provides the reason for your positive moods.

Some authors propose that conscientiousness leads to flow states, which arise from the progression toward challenging goals, and attribute this to increases in life satisfaction.[24] Notably, purpose in life and positive moods are important dimensions of psychological wellbeing and life satisfaction. Through links to better self-control, the highly conscientious tend to live longer because they are more likely to eat better, get enough sleep, have better interpersonal skills, have smaller waistlines and are less likely to smoke, drink, use drugs, binge, or suffer obesity.[2,25] Evidently, detrimental impulsive behaviours are properly controlled through the deliberate and disciplined mind.

Extroversion

Extroversion comes in third. People scoring highly in this trait are generally warm, affectionate, friendly, and unreserved around others. They are filled with positive emotions, brimming with joy, laugh easily, and are cheerful, enthusiastic, and optimistic. These individuals are sociable, prefer company, and embody philosophies like "the more the merrier". Capabilities in leadership are born from their ability to take charge, be forceful, to function well socially, and to dominate their surroundings. Highly active, the extrovert prefers a fast-paced lifestyle, seeks excitement and stimulation, and is characterised by high energy levels.

The opposite side of the extroversion spectrum is introversion. The introvert is more reserved around others, preferring their own company. They may not experience positive feelings to the same extent and may appear timid, quiet, and socially inhibited. Instead of a bloodlust for adrenaline, the introvert is complete with relaxation and could be perceived as calm and dispassionate.

Note, this dimension of personality is a spectrum like the other four factors. The descriptions above paint the picture of the extremes that live on the opposite ends of this human trait, whereas reality is much less black and white. The majority of individuals lie somewhere in between and will exhibit both introverted and extroverted tendencies. What is important is that you can recognise the different types of tendencies, as they tie into the next section.

Not surprisingly, extroverts tend to smile more, speak louder, text more frequently, are more likely to smoke and drink, and have more sexual partners. On Facebook they have more friends, leave more comments, and post more pictures of themselves with other people.[2] Along with high openness and conscientiousness, high extroversion is also seen in effective and emergent leaders. In careers, extroverts are less likely to experience burnout in their job; a psychological syndrome characterised by emotional exhaustion, reduced personal accomplishment, and negative moods.[26]

Extroversion and its constituent tendencies are associated with positive emotional states, happiness, and life satisfaction.[27] Some theorists even suggest that positive emotional states are the core of extroversion and are a precondition. Being extroverted means you're more persuasive and less persuadable.[28] When presented with stressful academic events extroverts are more likely than introverts to perceive them as challenges due to being more sensitive to the potential rewards budding from the event, and rate themselves as more eager, confident, and hopeful.[29]

Interestingly, one group of researchers attempted to identify the purpose of extroversion by exploring existing personality theories, which suggested the five personality traits had underlying motivational, social, and cognitive explanations behind them. From this they found extroverted behaviours to be highly correlated with goals people were actively pursuing, and in doing so drew a bridge from personality traits to motivational states. When people's goals revolve around having fun, connecting with people, being entertaining, attempting leadership, drawing attention to oneself, giving a positive impression, or trying to make friends, they are more likely to demonstrate an extroverted personality state.[30] Understanding the functional aspects of this trait means we can view these associated behaviours as tools in our belt for an array of social goals.

Agreeableness

Agreeableness is the fourth dimension of personality. High agreeableness is characterised by a tendency to trust other people, believing them to be well-intentioned and honest. Agreeable types are sincere and unwilling to manipulate others through flattery or deception. Demonstrating altruistic tendencies, they express concern for others' welfare, are considerate, helpful, and generous. Operating in a cooperative, forgiving, and mild-mannered way, they showcase compliance and inhibited aggression. They are modest and tender-minded, sympathetic to the human side of social policies.

At the opposite end of this spectrum, disagreeable people may be manipulative, inconsiderate, callous, uncooperative, frugal with effort, uncompromising, and apathetic to the struggles of others. Whereas extroversion deals with social impact, agreeableness revolves around maintaining positive relationships with others. Very low scores on agreeableness, when paired with high neuroticism, usually manifest as personality disorders. Narcissists and power-corrupted leaders typify the extremes of low scores for the trait of agreeableness and high scores for extroversion.

As a result of the humanistic elements embedded in agreeableness, many researchers have examined it in numerous social contexts. Agreeable people, when faced with interpersonal conflict, move toward trying to maintain a positive relationship with the antagonistic agent. One way they attempt this is by generating positive perceptions and attributions toward their provocative behaviour. In times of conflict, they disagree with undermining the other's self-esteem and deem compromising and dropping the topic as appropriate methods of resolution. Due to this they are more likely to use constructive tactics like negotiation to diffuse disputes and are rated as better interpersonally adjusted than low scorers.[31]

Agreeable types show an affinity for prosocial behaviour through their tendencies to offer people help.[32] Furthermore, resulting from these lubricating social tendencies, it's likely that high scorers will spend more time in longer, committed relationships with partners.[2] Equally likely is them having a larger social support network distinguished by fulfilling relationships with friends and family members.[2] Both of these are linked to health and longevity through happiness studies.[33] Like extroverts, agreeable types share in positive moods, which may be why they tend to report lower depression.[24,34] The compliant and compassionate tendencies agreeable people display are sought after in face-to-face jobs; are heavily valued in occupations with frequent interpersonal interactions and environments where helpful behaviours are necessitated, such as nursing; and result in team members being viewed as more cooperative, likeable, and even-tempered.[2,35]

As you may have realised, the agreeable person is the archetype of an ideal employee, right next to highly conscientious people. Research showing career stability and reduced risks of unemployment over time supports this viewpoint.[34,36] Whereas prestigious leaders are high in agreeableness, dominant, micromanaging, power-hungry leaders score low.[2] The flipside of being too agreeable is that, on average, disagreeable people tend to have higher incomes. Three large surveys showed that less agreeable men make $9,772 a year more than their counterparts, and woman scoring low in agreeableness make $1,828 over theirs.[37] It seems that degrees of callousness, self-interest, and assertiveness do have a function, evidenced through salary differences. Someone too agreeable will avoid conflict across the board, even if it means settling for lower salaries, unhealthy relationships, or an unfulfilling lifestyle. Although, moving too far to the disagreeable end of the spectrum isn't good either. Low scorers have higher crime rates, can be extremely narcissistic, are more likely to engage in counterproductive workplace behaviour through unethical, illegal, or unwise workplace behaviours, and negatively impact social relationships.[2,36]

Neuroticism

The last dimension of personality is neuroticism and scoring highly here is notoriously negative. At the extreme end, a neurotic person is plagued with anxiety, tension, and fear. They are hostile, easily becoming frustrated and irritated by others. Being excessively self-conscious increases their sensitivity to shame and embarrassment. Unlike a cheerful, warm extrovert, neurotics are depressed and regularly feel negative emotions, such as guilt, sadness, and hopelessness. They demonstrate a susceptibility to temptation, being unable to control their cravings and urges, which results in impulsive and irrational behaviour. To top it off they are vulnerable, easily stressed, and prone to panic states.

Unlike the other dimensions of personality, where you get the sense that being pulled to the higher end of the spectrum seems constructive, higher scores on this dimension are certainly destructive. The opposite of neuroticism is emotional stability, meaning the lower your neurotic tendencies are the more emotionally stable you are. If a withdrawing drug addict plagued with aggression, depression, impulsivity, and volatility epitomises the highest levels of neuroticism, Buddha is the counter opposite, embodying emotional stability.

Aside from the glaringly obvious negative outcomes of being neurotic, such as experiencing emotional states of anxiousness, depression, and aggression, there is research to show where a neurotic trajectory can often take you. Neuroticism is widely regarded as a risk factor for developing anxiety and depression. It predicts first-time depressive episodes and is directly associated with increased risks of developing clinical depression, anxiety disorders, and mood disorders.[38] Depression is associated and exacerbated by rumination – a common practice of letting stressful thoughts overrun the mind for extended periods of time.[39] Ruminative thought patterns form the baseline mental environment for neurotics, continually delivering unwelcome messages that ripple and echo throughout the mind.

Negative emotional states and bad emotional regulation can detrimentally alter your DNA!

High neuroticism paired with low agreeableness is associated with many clinically diagnosed personality disorders; think egotistical narcissist, for example. Traversing the mind–body void provides more evidence of the destructive effect of neuroticism. Higher neuroticism has been linked to increases in all-cause mortality risk, and in one study neuroticism was significantly related to the risk of death from cardiovascular disease.[40] Neuroticism is significantly related to suicidal ideation, suicidal attempts, and suicide.[41]

Perhaps most damning is the fact that in studies that tracked men over an 18-year timespan, those with increasing neuroticism were much more likely to die during the study than those whose neuroticism levels decreased.[42] Stress is a killer. Neuroticism is linked to an increased probability of smoking, drinking, and drug use and predicts physical conditions such as heart disease, high blood pressure, personality disorders, and obesity.[2] It even affects you at the most basic level of life – your genetics. Increased hostility – a subdomain of neuroticism – has been linked to shorter telomere length.[43] Telomeres are repetitive nucleotide sequences that cap chromosomes, thereby maintaining genetic integrity and ensuring proper functioning. Simply put, they are protective sequences of DNA that ensure your body remains healthy. Longer telomeres are markers of healthy chromosomes; shorter telomeres resemble biological cellular ageing and point toward adverse health outcomes. Psychological stress, another facet of neuroticism, has also been linked to reduced telomere lengths.[44] Negative emotional states and bad emotional regulation can detrimentally alter your DNA!

In the workplace, low neuroticism and high conscientiousness predicts higher salaries. Leaders usually demonstrate lower levels of neuroticism. And employers preferentially select individuals lower in neurotic traits because no one wants a depressed, hostile, drama-fuelled employee who will negatively impact customers, colleagues, corporate culture, and business productivity.

Awareness of you

Where we sit on these five widely accepted dimensions of human behaviour summarises how we operate throughout our lives and predicts our career, health, wellbeing, psychological, social, recreational, and academic outcomes. Remember, these traits are not in isolation; the five combine to form your overall personality profile. For example, you may identify as someone high in *conscientiousness* and *openness*, average in *neuroticism* and *extroversion*, and low in *agreeableness*. As you can see from the research above, in isolation, certain traits you possess can hint at future destinations. From your personal snapshot of behavioural tendencies, you can forecast certain outcomes while having a deeper understanding of your dispositions and ensuing day-to-day operations. Awareness is the necessary first stage in behaviour change. Importantly, nothing is wrong with how you operate right now, but the above research does point toward a beneficial trend, suggesting that dialling up certain tendencies and turning down others is better for your health, wealth, and wellbeing. In the same way success is built from successful habits, a healthy, meaningful, fulfilling, and achievement-dense life arises from certain traits.

Openness seems to be a precursor to creativity, creative achievement, innovation, proactive organisational behaviour, self-belief, and predicts general intelligence. Striving to embody thoughts and behaviours associated with openness is no doubt a beneficial pursuit, which, for me, has no upper limit.

Conscientiousness, at its upper limits, describes someone who is neurologically enhanced with robotic levels of self-discipline and foreshadows a longer life decorated with positive events, academic success, healthier behaviours, better work performance, and overall career success. Dialling up this trait through its associated behavioural tendencies confers a great deal of benefits and, again, the sky is the limit.

Extroversion showcases the socialite whose life seemingly revolves around embedding their social impact throughout society. They are more likely to be popular, with bigger social media networks, immune to psychological burnout, happier, optimistic, and satisfied with life. All while radiating confidence, enthusiasm, and improved persuasive capabilities. As noted by personality researchers, extroverted behaviours serve a function in the form of helping people progress toward self-identified goals. To generate connections, build friendships, and gain popularity, acting like a model extrovert makes sense. On the flipside, if your goals take another form – perhaps studying, starting a company, or writing a book – becoming more introverted and giving up fun times, thrill rides, and waterslides is necessary. In this respect your behaviours on this "social" dimension of personality should reflect the goals you've currently set yourself. Choose behavioural tendencies wisely; they are tools for goals.

Agreeableness describes the archetype of an ideal employee. Agreeable people are characterised by having big social support networks; longer-lasting, committed relationships; report lower depression rates; are rated as cooperative, likeable, and even-tempered in the workplace; demonstrate career stability and lower unemployment rates over time; and constructively approach interpersonal relationship conflicts. However, being too agreeable and cooperative has drawbacks. If you don't stand up for yourself and aren't dogmatic (and sometimes uncooperative) in pursuit of your beliefs and standards, you'll transform into a "yes" person, could lose authority, could be seen as a pushover, and could lose out financially. The cost of extreme social facilitation in the form of altruism, philanthropy, and viewing others through rose-tinted glasses, is your self-interest.

Although an agreeable operating scheme is highly admirable due to its positive social ramifications, don't forget to factor yourself into the equation. Placing yourself and your beliefs firmly second to others can potentially bear a big cost to you that you need to live with in the form of time, effort, achievement, money, career direction, settling for less than you deserve, and status. When you are living solely to benefit and please others, putting their success, happiness, and wellbeing before your own, you will lose out. There is a happy middle ground where your self-interest and the interests of others lies – a place where your success can flourish and others are still respected, valued, and cared for – and it is up to you to determine where that is. In life, sometimes the crowd isn't always right; herd mentality has its flaws. Interestingly, only through the efforts of an uncompromising, uncooperative, disagreeable person will herd mentality ever be properly kept in check.

Neuroticism at high levels is unequivocally and evidently bad in every way. Demonstrating neurotic tendencies leads to many forms of clinical psychological disorders ranging from depression to anxiety, and from personality to mood disorders. If a mental environment dominated by negative emotions is not already demoralising enough, your physical health suffers too. If death isn't the first stop on the road down this desolate mode of existence, it's a stop awaiting your arrival sooner rather than later. Suicidality, high blood pressure, obesity, heart disease, and biological ageing are but a few physical manifestations. In the workplace the outlook isn't any better; salary levels and employment outcomes are telling signs. Unlike several of the other personality dimensions, where the sky is the limit, peddling backward as fast as you can from the upper limits of this one leads you toward a state of emotional bliss.

Changing traits

As we have seen, selectively changing typical thinking patterns and habitual behaviours is enormously beneficial. But is this even possible? After all, your personality defines and describes *you*. It is who you are and was shaped throughout your life by genetics, socialisation forces, parenting styles, and every other conceivable environmental factor along the way. Not only is personality infinitely complex, but is attempting a task as momentous as this – reinventing personal attributes of yourself – like opening Pandora's box? In changing these core aspects of yourself, are you fundamentally transforming your sense of self, your own identity? Is altering personality traits killing parts of you?

Personality change may make you think you are altering your nature, and in a sense you are; however, realise that morality, values, reasoning capabilities, personal connections, interests, intelligences (of which there are multiple types), and wisdom are other components that deeply align with your natural essence. Personality traits just describe an autopilot operating scheme, detailing how you tend to express yourself and behave on a day-to-day basis. A million and one people may act extroverted like you, but the essence of *you* is what makes you unique. Yet, for us to even entertain this philosophical debate it hinges on personality being fluid and malleable.

On this, the research is mixed. Some studies demonstrate personality stability over a four-year period, whereas others demonstrate changes in traits. Perhaps most insightful are the findings from a 40-year longitudinal study demonstrating that when personality is left to its own devices, extroversion and conscientiousness remain stable over a lifetime, whereas the remaining traits of openness, agreeableness, and neuroticism, change. From this we learn that there is a stable component of personality if we happily sit back and watch our lives unfold. Not helpful for those who wouldn't mind bumping some traits higher up and extinguishing the problematic ones that plague us. Fortunately, our freewill provides us with the choice to resist this passive life program. Aspects of personality do predictably change [2] due to many documented reasons, and we can renounce the passive progression of our personality profile through the calculated application of these reasons if we want to. Broadly speaking, personality can change in response to life experiences and situational factors, through applied philosophy and psychotherapy, and via the adoption of certain habits.

Behaviour change interventions

Life experiences and situational factors

As part of growing up, technically known as maturation, everyone's personality and psychology evolves. On average you become more conscientious, more agreeable, and less neurotic. It seems that becoming more responsible and better socially equipped while experiencing less anxiety, stress, and fearfulness, is a part of life. Aside from your personality profile maturing with age, there are certain life events that selectively dial up or down traits. Personality is much too volatile throughout adolescent years to draw any meaningful conclusions; however, after high school, when the neuro dust settles, research has some things to say.

Multiple studies have found that four years after high school, often the last year of college, individuals are higher in agreeableness, conscientiousness, and openness, and display decreases in neuroticism. Complementary studies also found that high-school graduates who started working increased in conscientiousness faster than those who began studying. Keeping with the demographic of young adults and occupational settings, those who are successful in careers increase in conscientiousness and decrease in neuroticism. Being promoted to a manager or leader causes further improvements in openness. It is evident that the social roles people step into and the responsibilities thrust upon them can catalyse changes in behavioural tendencies, subsequently influencing personality traits.[2]

For proof on the power of roles on our psychology and behaviour, we need look no further than the famed Stanford Prison Experiment, which took place in the 1970s (well before ethics were given due attention). Philip Zimbardo, the psychology researcher behind it, set out to determine whether prison guard brutality in American prisons was due to personality dispositions or situational factors. He wondered: do prisoners and guards behave in a hostile manner due to the social environments of prisons and their rigid power structures, or do they just have innate tendencies toward hostility and aggression? As part of the experiment, he converted the basement of a Stanford University building into a mock prison with barred windows and cells, at the same time putting out an ad to enlist volunteers into the two-week prison study.

After screening applicants through personality assessments and diagnostic interviews, 24 mentally and physically healthy volunteers were chosen to take part. Prior to the initiation of the study, participants were assigned to play the role of a prison guard or a prisoner, and, as they say, "the rest is history". Over the next six days, Zimbardo and his assistants closely observed "prison life". The atrocities that unfolded in this small Stanford prison literally made headlines. The otherwise normal, mentally healthy participants who were assigned the role of prison guards belittled, dehumanised, and psychologically tortured the "inmates" over the ensuing days. Keep in mind, the "inmates" were fellow study participants who had done no wrong, and who could just have easily been assigned the role of a prison guard.

The observed behavioural atrocities carried out by the pseudo-prison guards included placing paper bags on prisoners' heads, forcing them to do push-ups with other inmates sitting on their backs, stripping them naked, denying them food, placing them in solitary confinement, ostracising inmates through blame games, consistently waking them up to be counted using whistles in the middle of the night, taunting them with insults, and making them clean toilet bowls with bare hands. Reportedly, multiple prisoners suffered mental breakdowns, with some removed from the study. As a result of these issues, the entire experiment was shut down eight days early.

Aside from career-related areas of life, other events can cause slight changes to our personality profile. Researchers found positive and negative life events have corresponding influences on personality. College students who were subject to negative experiences, such as a friend dying, sexual problems, or having a sick family member, tended to increase in neuroticism. Those experiencing good events, like travelling to another country, getting promoted at work, and starting a relationship, tended to increase in extroversion, conscientiousness, and agreeableness, while their neuroticism reduced. These changes were relatively small, nonetheless still present. It's good news that a catastrophic event in your life will not transform and ossify you into a crumbling emotional wreck.

You have the ability to consciously choose to participate in, or undertake, certain social positions.

Relationships are one other notable area that impact personality, with multiple studies demonstrating an increase in conscientiousness and a decrease in neuroticism when someone settles into a stable romantic relationship.[2] Having a good spouse really does make you a better person, or at the least makes you operate more efficiently.

It is clear that social roles – whether representing an individual's first job after school, being an understanding and committed partner in a stable romantic relationship, occupying leadership or management positions, or even participating in a fictional power-imbued role – can affect how people behave. Situation-dependent behaviours occur soon after someone enters a role, as we saw from the prison guard experiment, and from longitudinal studies we can infer that these new role-dependent behaviours, when compounded over time, lead to alterations in personality traits. In this way, the study that highlighted a faster improvement in conscientiousness in high-school graduates after undertaking their first job likely came about through the compounded effects of daily participation in a job role filled with responsibility.

Imagine the Stanford Prison Experiment ran over four years; it would not be a stretch to guess at directional changes in the prison guards' personalities. Surely, continually dehumanising, insulting, and psychologically torturing others is not going to boost compassion levels. An increase in callousness is much more probable.

Roles have the ability to aggregate and emphasise certain tendencies in you, and you have the ability to consciously choose to participate in, or undertake, certain social positions. With this knowledge you can leverage role-based psychology to your advantage. If you want to become more responsible, take on a social role with more responsibility. If you want to become more open, inject yourself into a role that forces you outside your comfort zone and challenges your existing preconceptions about the world. If you want to develop empathy and conflict-resolution skills, commit to dating someone. Further refining social behaviours can be done if you enlist in a role with a heavy social component, say customer service. For me personally, I know that by adopting Baxter and opting in to raise him as a loving parent, I have become more responsible, organised, and patient.

Applied philosophy – today we call it psychology

Taking charge of your world and wielding power over external events, such as your occupational role, relationship status, and exposure to positive and negative events, to some degree is in your control; however, if you happened to discuss this topic with an ancient Stoic, they would implore you to re-evaluate where the locus of control in your life really lies. They would remind you that, in reality, nothing is in your control except your own thoughts and judgements as you can't compel others to hire you, love you, or count on destiny to grace you with a fortuitous event begetting beneficial personality adaptations. The Stoic would say that throughout your life fate is the true force behind all that happens. You, my dear friend, are simply an observer of the universe at work, and your ability to reason is all you have.

The following information is informed heavily by the insightful work of Donald Robertson, a cognitive psychotherapist and philosophy researcher.[45]

A Stoic is someone who practises Stoicism: a philosophy born in ancient Greece with roots dating back to the 4th century BC. The teachings of Stoicism are a continuation of the work of Socrates, who heavily influenced the Ancient Greeks' way of life and, ironically, ours. Stoics viewed life through a dichotomous lens. To a Stoic there were certain things that fell under our direct control and the rest simply fell outside of it, referred to as "externals". The things outside our direct control are said to be governed by "universal nature" or "fate"; the terms being used interchangeably in Stoic literature. The opinions of others, material goods, and wealth represent examples of "externals".

Importantly, unlike externals, in your direct control is your mind – the seat of reason – and your judgements. Judgements refer to the way you interpret and assign value to objects, events, experiences, people, and knowledge. Stoics placed the highest value on this "ruling faculty" because to them it represented the only true locus of control. Realising this changed how Stoics viewed and interacted with the world. Instead of being immersed firsthand in experiences and at the mercy of external events, they were able to take a step back and reformulate their reality.

They understood that emotions, feelings, and our overall experience is based on existing knowledge paired with our value judgements about people, events, concepts, and objects. Epictetus, a famed Greek Stoic philosopher from the 1st century, concisely summarised this through his quote: "It is not the things themselves that disturb people but their judgements about those things."

Value is something we place on things once they impress themselves upon our mind. We do this consciously and unconsciously, and it is because of these judgements that we react to things the way we do. To illustrate, a dormant lethal virus residing on a surface – part of objective reality – is neither good nor bad until we become aware of it and think about it. Our minds are responsible for giving it the label. Upon encountering the virus, we would initially process it based on our existing knowledge and value judgements, leading us to have an automatic emotional reaction to it, which we believe to be wholeheartedly justified and grounded in truth.

We may hold the belief that life is sacred and anything representing immediate danger to life is bad, scary, or evil (a value judgement), which would mean that encountering a virus we know to be deadly (existing knowledge) automatically manifests fear and anxiety, an emotional response that hijacks our system. The combination of our knowledge and value judgements have led us to believe the virus is *bad, scary, or evil* simply because it has the capacity to kill, and in doing so sends off alarm bells in our mind, whereas a Stoic would re-evaluate the first premise. Death is an inevitability and is controlled by fate. Instead of being anxious and fearful of the virus, they would respond with indifference. It is a part of objective reality, an external outside of one's control, and they merely accept it for what it is and what it represents.

Reason

This indifference doesn't mean they moved through life recklessly; they espoused proceeding with caution, which is a rational evaluation of circumstance, but relinquished the reigns of fear, which is an emotional, mentally destructive, and irrational guide to living. Stoics understood that approaching life with reason is much more conducive to long-term physical and psychological health than being a slave to emotions, especially when the majority of the time emotions are illogical. When faced with the circumstance above, instead of frantically jumping up and down, plagued with fear and anxiety, tripping onto this virus, and effectively signing a death sentence, a Stoic would remain calm and sidestep it, exercising full control of their "ruling faculty" and acting deliberately and purposefully. This logic can be extended to blindly succumbing to other emotions without first rationalising them. For example, if you were excessively excited, dangerously driven to further seek stimulating sensations as you sped down the freeway at 180 kilometres an hour, reason, should it make an appearance, would say, "For this transient pleasure you are jeopardising our existence, is this in line with your true purpose in life?"

Epictetus, like Stoics before him, was aware that the emotions we feel about things are based on beliefs and value judgements; that is, our cognition about external events. Epictetus knew that "externals" by themselves represented something completely objective; it was only in the mind they were interpreted to be bad or good, which led to strong emotional reactions in response to them. Because our beliefs are embedded in and precede the emotions we feel, Stoics advocated that by changing our beliefs we could change our emotional responses. A pithy aphorism to remember the difference between what we perceive to be real and what is physically real is, "The map is not the terrain." The map represents a subjective interpretation of reality and resembles the lens of consciousness we look through as we move through life. Separating subjective beliefs from external reality allows us to choose how to rationally interpret an event that has just occurred, allowing us to short-circuit automatic emotional responses to external events and bringing our mental state back under the dutiful control of reason.

Eudemonia

Fittingly, their philosophy set out to describe and achieve the "art of living"; a holistic approach that considered physical health and psychological flourishing as necessary for this end. Stoicism discussed what the "good life" was and how a person could experience fulfilment and true happiness, which they termed "eudemonia". In today's terminology, "eudemonia" roughly equates to mental wellbeing, as was suggested in the first chapter, where we deconstructed personal principles. To them, misery resulted from a mind that tended to place too much value on pleasure and the avoidance of pain. A hedonist, consequently, represents a mind that has been enslaved to passion and desire, which can no longer rationally function to achieve its moral purpose or protect itself through intellectual self-preservation. Eudemonia, the ideal of the Stoic, was achieved when they could master emotions to a point where negative emotions lost their ability to disturb inner tranquillity and positive emotions could be sensibly controlled.

Socrates, a revered Stoic sage, achieved the height of enlightenment and eudemonia and was one of the few believed to have truly mastered this philosophy. So much so it's reported that when facing his execution, he remained equanimous and willingly accepted his unjust sentence by drinking a lethal dose of poison, despite opportunities to flee. Stoics advocated for happiness and positive emotions on the condition they didn't lead to irrational indulgence, and as long as short-term pleasure didn't jeopardise longer-term psychological wellbeing.

Stoic happiness is not consuming a greasy hamburger, large bowl of fried chips, and a can of Coke when you supremely value physical health and are trying to shed some kilos; it is not having risky sex with a promiscuous person behind the back of your unknowing partner when you value commitment and honesty; and it's not taking a dopamine-stimulating drug when these actions clash with your reasoned purposes in life. Instead of transient, meaningless pleasures derived from "externals" (health, wealth, and reputation to name a few), effort should be directed to attaining self-awareness and self-control, forming the cardinal virtue of wisdom.

Wisdom to Stoics, along with happiness, represented the fundamental goal of life. According to Epictetus, externals were only valuable to the extent to which they serve this end, for what is the value of health if you are unwise and unhappy? Longer-term fulfilment should eclipse short-term gratification when your life is in accordance with the "highest good". Delaying gratification – being the ability to exert discipline in the face of temptation for longer-term wellbeing – describes a Stoic tendency. For them, the ideal life was characterised by an unwavering stream of reasoned, purposeful, and self-aware actions. A life of true integrity. Through a personality lens, it appears they would have been awfully conscientious.

There are four guiding principles of Stoicism:

1. *The all is one.* No individual human being exists in isolation; everything in the universe is connected.
2. *The only good is moral good.* The only things that should matter to us are those we control, such as our decisions, intentions, and acts of will. Anything outside our control bears little importance.
3. *The brotherhood of man.* Human beings are valuable in themselves for they possess volition and are capable of wisdom and virtue. All men and women are our brothers and sisters.

4. *The here and now.* The Stoic's sphere of control revolves around the present moment; hence, attention should be focused here. The past and future do not exist except as a figment of our imagination.

Here and now

I want to introduce the last principle and draw your attention to it. The Stoic concept of "here and now" is concerned with attending to oneself and being present in the moment; observing thoughts and judgements rather than mindlessly interacting with stimuli; and detaching from the past and the future, consequently relegating the negative emotions associated with them. Anxiety is an emotion born from future worries: depression usually stems from events in the past. Therefore, being present in the moment, the "here and now", frees you from their influence. This concept is echoed by another ancient philosophy – Buddhism. Buddhists refer to it as "mindfulness", the only difference being that Buddhism instructs people to focus not only on their thought processes and judgements in the present moment, but also on physical sensations such as the rhythmic patterns of their breath.

The pedagogy of Stoicism, including the above fundamental principles, all served one purpose: to improve the life of a Stoic through the achievement of psychological wellbeing. This included teaching strategies and practices to people that allowed them to control unhealthy emotions and impulses while achieving enlightenment and peace of mind. It highlighted a moral framework that people could subscribe to where everyone was equally valued and respected, it wound people together into a larger community, and it outlined noble life purposes individuals could adopt and enact. Already this philosophical system foreshadows the ingredients of enhanced mental wellbeing through fostering meaningful relationships and focusing on generating a sense of purpose in its followers.

In Ancient Greek philosophy there were no distinctions between spiritual, therapeutic, and philosophical practices; they were all grouped under the wider umbrella of Stoicism. In retrospect, Stoicism effectively described the earliest form of psychological therapy, and, perplexingly, 2,500 years later, modern civilisation has gone full-circle and now utilises this philosophy as the basis of one of its most effective psychological treatments. However, it is now referred to as cognitive behavioural therapy (CBT), known as a 21st century scientifically informed treatment modality, and instead of being administered by Ancient Greek philosophers it is delivered by westernised psychologists. Stoicism, Buddhism, other modern psychotherapies, and especially CBT, share common ground.

CBT

Today, CBT is used as an effective psychological treatment to combat anxiety, depression, substance abuse, marital problems, and mental illnesses. In many studies it proves to be more effective than other forms of therapy or psychiatric medications.

It is based on the following core principles:

1. Cognitive activity affects behaviour.
2. Cognitive activity can be monitored and altered.
3. Desired behaviour change may be affected through cognitive change.

As a consequence of these three premises, psychotherapists inspire change in patients by helping them challenge existing dysfunctional beliefs, thereby short-circuiting the more automated emotional responses. By putting a wedge between reality and emotional responses – the "cognitive" part of CBT – the therapist opens up a new possibility in the mind, helping the patient consciously choose how they experience life instead of being dragged mindlessly through it as a victim. This is Stoicism disguised and often it is paired with mindfulness practices stemming from the Stoic and Buddhist concept of the "here and now". Discussed below are three modern scientific examples illustrating how applied philosophy, or modern psychological therapy, whichever way you want to look at it, affects cognition, behaviour, and brain structures.

Obsessive compulsive disorder

The first study combined CBT and mindfulness strategies to overcome obsessive compulsive disorder (OCD). OCD is a type of anxiety disorder whereby sufferers are bombarded with upsetting, intrusive, and unwanted thoughts, referred to as obsessions, which subsequently trigger urges to perform ritualistic behaviours, termed compulsions. Around the time of the (1987) study, advances in neuroscience had determined certain brain circuits to be overactive in OCD sufferers. Using PET scans, an OCD sufferer's brain circuits involved in error detection, worrying, fear, and feelings of dread were found to be hyperactive when compared to normal people.

Not surprisingly, feelings associated with this dysfunctional circuitry evidently plague people with OCD.

The dysfunctional emotional circuitry and associated negative feelings are the reason OCD sufferers feel compelled to carry out irrational behaviours, such as turning the door handle left three times before opening it, washing their hands after touching any surface, or pathologically avoiding cracks on the pavement wherever they appear. The overactive region in their brain hijacks their attention, taking their seat of reason hostage, and bombards them with unbearable, irrational feelings to the point where they wholly believe refusing to give in to the impulse will result in disaster.

For example, someone with OCD may be affected by numbers and think that whenever they cross paths with the number 3 in life they have to drop down and walk on all fours for 3 minutes otherwise their family will die. As they encounter the number 3, upon not acting on this impulse, a feeling of extreme dread and anxiety washes over them; a result of their brain's faulty wiring. These emotions turn on like alarm bells and are so powerful and convincing that the individual obliges and carries out the "required" behaviour to shut them off. Sadly, situations like these become dreaded realities for some people.

Leveraging these findings, researchers forfeited conventional treatment options and tried a different approach. First, one of the lead researchers scanned the brains of participants to show them how their faulty brain wiring could explain the feelings and false beliefs they were experiencing. The rationale behind this was to try to assist patients to understand that the visceral emotions they felt due to their OCD urges were nothing more than manifestations of faulty neural wiring. In essence, putting a wedge between the emotional experience of the subject and objective reality. One of the participants understood straight away and exclaimed, "It's not me, it's my OCD!"

The researcher encouraged the group of participants to reflect on this point whenever they experienced OCD urges, hoping they would be able to overcome the emotional lure of the disorder through a higher level of awareness. After 10 weeks of this mindfulness-based therapy, researchers scanned the participants' brains again to compare them with initial scans, wanting to know whether physical changes in the brain occurred as a result of this therapy. Surprisingly, researchers realised the dysfunctional neural circuitry had improved and was no longer as hyperactive as it had once been. Furthermore, patients confirmed that symptoms had begun alleviating.

They were better able to regulate their behaviour and experienced less anxiety and distress.[46,47]

Depression

The second study used mindfulness-based CBT to teach people with depression how to break the vicious cycle of hopelessness. According to John Teasdale, a leading cognitive scientist at Cambridge, depressed individuals may escape the self-reinforcing thought patterns of depression by simply regarding thoughts as "events in the mind" and not absolute truths. Notice how the wording "events in the mind" also separates patients' feelings from objective reality, similar to the teachings of Stoicism. Teasdale continued this line of thinking in his study and equipped people with cognitive strategies, including alternate beliefs and value judgements, which could be substituted into existing thought processes. By substituting alternate beliefs and value judgements, participants were better able to understand the fallibility and transience of depressive thoughts through a higher level of awareness. Meaning that eight weeks later, once therapy was complete, these subjects fared better than another group of depressed individuals who were put on pharmacological-based depression treatments. Furthermore, similar to the first study, they too demonstrated changes in their neural functioning. The metabolic activity of key brain regions in depressed patients changed for the better.[47]

Neural adaptations

The final study, providing yet further evidence in favour of our mind's power, looked at neural adaptations in response to playing a piano. In this experiment, researchers had people practise a five-finger piano sequence two hours a day for five days. There were three groups in total: a control group that did unstructured practice whenever they liked; one in a condition where they physically practised playing the piano in a structured sequence for two hours a day; and another group that was told just to imagine playing the same piano sequence as the structured practice group for two hours a day. The researchers were interested to see how the brain adapts to learning new motor patterns. Motor patterns refer to a sequence of nerves that activate in order to carry out a muscle-based movement; certain regions of the brain initiate them. To do this a patient's brain was mapped using transcranial magnetic stimulation (a non-invasive process that allows researchers to observe the functional region in a brain) before and after the experiment.

When people actually played the piano for two weeks the activity in their motor cortex changed, indicating that their brain allocated more neural real-estate to the areas of the brain involved in coordinating the fine finger movements seen in piano playing. In simpler terms, the brain region responsible for coordinating muscles involved in playing the piano grew after people practised playing it. In light of neuroscience research, this finding was expected. Your brain has plastic properties, meaning that it is forever changing and evolving depending on what you need it to get better at. The rather mystical discovery was that even when participants didn't physically play the piano, but merely thought about playing it, imagining their fingers carrying out the necessary sequence of movements and interacting with the keyboard, their brains also responded in the same way. *Thinking* alone was enough to cause the brain to reorganise itself and allocate more neural real-estate to better perform a given function. Even though it was imagined.[48]

The effect of conscientious thoughts repeatedly activating key brain regions can be seen through increases in grey matter volume.

OCD – an anxiety disorder – and clinical depression represent high-level manifestations of neurotic traits. Remember, neuroticism is characterised by a tendency to display higher than average levels of depression, anxiety, and fear in addition to inclinations toward impulsive and irrational behaviours. Having these disorders means someone will likely score highly in the trait of neuroticism. Additionally, the way they operate and behave in day-to-day life is tremendously affected by these pathologies, to the point where people could validly label them as a "neurotic". Through the application of Stoicism layered with Buddhist practices, otherwise known as mindfulness-based CBT in the modern age, individuals were able to effectively combat debilitating disorders by extinguishing negative emotions and behaviours and replacing them with functional, purposeful alternatives. In effect, they were able to change core aspects of themselves that closely resembled *personality traits*. Upon successful treatment, no longer would they be described as a "neurotic person" or "depressed". Their behavioural tendencies are no longer grounds for those *personality* labels.

From this last study we can further extrapolate the power of the mind and thoughts. Not only does it represent a cost-effective, convenient way to practise the piano, but it hints at something much bigger. This study confirms the existence of a potentially perplexing phenomena in the ability of our immaterial mind to alter physical brain structures. From this, we could even exclaim that "all is as thinking makes it so" (Marcus Aurelis, Roman Emperor AD 161 and Stoic). No wonder a conscientiousness brain looks different. The effect of conscientious thoughts repeatedly activating key brain regions can be seen through increases in grey matter volume, just like imagining piano playing reorganises neural tissue in the motor cortex! Moreover, since we're now on the topic of conscientiousness, it's interesting to reflect on the personality traits of a Stoic. Going off their philosophies, which included the idealisation of reason, self-control, and self-awareness, paired with their war on negative emotions and impulse management, we could make an educated guess that Stoics shared in high levels of conscientiousness and low levels of neuroticism. Choosing to engage in certain philosophical practices really did shape personality profiles, evident through historical Stoic writings.

Think through your responses

These three studies are extreme examples that illustrate the power of the mind and applied philosophy in changing some of the most rigid habitual patterns of behaviour, thinking, and feeling. If an OCD sufferer and clinically depressed individual can utilise Stoicism and Buddhism in the form of modern psychotherapy to change, there is no reason why you can't employ self-awareness, perspective, and rationality for your own ends. If you are usually a person who cowers in the face of change, sticks to traditional beliefs, and spends no time in the land of imagination (someone low in openness), you can make a conscious decision off the back of a higher level of awareness to reformat yourself. When someone asks you to do something that doesn't fit with your normal routine, questions a traditional belief you hold, or raises an abstract creative idea to you, instead of automatically discarding these requests due to an unacknowledged feeling you get, consciously step back and explore that feeling, peel away its layers and rationally decide.

Your friend has asked you to forego your usual Tuesday night Netflix binge and go out for dinner with them and, automatically, as an introvert, you resist. Why? Question why you do not want to break your routine. Is the series you're watching more important than friendship? Has a Tuesday night in become a habit as a result of a period in your life that you now unconsciously adhere to? Are you insecure about your appearance and prefer solitude, something your Netflix binge excuse conceals? When you automatically respond, acknowledge it and question where the feelings are coming from that precede the response. Then question if the beliefs you hold that are leading to those feelings are valid and beneficial to your higher purpose. Is there a different way of responding to this request to go out on a Tuesday night now you've examined your beliefs? What are the pros and cons of going out versus staying in? If friendship and quality time is your highest value, then going out with your friend on a Tuesday night is something you should opt for, not mindlessly discard.

Choose your personality profile – your operating scheme – and with some conscious effort it will end up becoming your baseline mode of existence. Imagine living an open, conscientious life devoid of negative emotionality; the building blocks of success and health. The power to self-select these traits lies accessibly in your mind. You just need to choose to choose them.

On habits

The power of habits is no secret. Multitudes of books have been written on the topic and quotes about habits find large audiences on social media platforms, and rightly so. After engaging in a certain behaviour for long enough, the effort, mental battles, and uncertainty associated with it begin to slip away. A sense of duty, confidence, and peace of mind soon replace them. With time and repetition, conscious actions – the early behaviours – turn into habits, and habits run on autopilot. Upon a New Year's Eve fitness resolution, the 1st, 2nd, and even 13th journey to the gym after work are much harder than the 147th.

The difficulty lies in consolidating the habit, in other words, predisposing yourself to behave in a certain way when presented with certain environmental and bodily cues. When it hits 5.30pm and you've arrived home from work, changed out of work clothes, and are mentally drained and tired, are you compelled to get into your car and go to the gym like you previously intended? Surprisingly, in this situation your conscious choice about your behaviour (going to the gym versus staying at home and relaxing) is unconsciously formed. Unconscious processes in your mind predispose you to behave in a certain way, and when certain environmental cues or internal sensations are detected, automatic behavioural patterns are triggered. When you don't get in your car to travel to the gym, it wasn't a conscious choice; your unconscious mind merely responded in its standard way and you found out about it after the fact.

Research backs this up, showing the conscious intentions we form about most things happen after we have already processed them unconsciously and begun responding. Seemingly, our intentions serve the purpose of rationalising and coherently narrating our behaviours, helping us to make sense of the world and how we interact with it. The important thing to realise is that most of the time our consciousness is playing catch up and not actually dictating our actions. Some philosophers label conscious intentions as artefacts of unconsciously produced actions, stating they are nothing more than irrelevant by-products. We think we raised our finger because we "wanted" to raise our finger, but, really, unconscious neural activity responsible for our finger movement happened before we were consciously aware of it. The action was put into motion outside of our awareness; we just came to realise it midway and then decided that is what we wanted to do.[49]

This explains why cultivating a habit is not as simple as willing it into existence. I'm sure everyone, including myself, wants to adopt healthy eating habits, rigorous exercise habits, and to eliminate negative habits that have detrimental health effects (pick your poison). However, evidently, our intentions do not always become reality. Reason being, there is an unconscious part of the equation we're all neglecting when we try to engineer habits, and it's an integral and rather mystical part at that. Fortunately for us though, when equipped with the right knowledge, habits become malleable, and even more reassuring is the fact that forming and deconstructing habits, even at the most rigid and pathological level, is achievable.

Addictions, for illustrative purposes, can be thought of as bad habits, according to Marc Lewis, a neuroscientist, and both everyday habits and raging addictions can be overcome. In sharing the same underlying brain changes, which essentially represent neural traces of learning, addictions and habits both "rewire" the brain to pursue attractive goals while diverting attention away from alternative goals. If the new, attractive, overarching goal is to achieve the rush from a drug, the excitement of gambling, or a runner's high, dutifully your unconscious mind will puppeteer you in that direction.

This is why former addicts in vulnerable phases of rehabilitation are instructed to remove from their life anything they once associated with their addiction, whether it be friends, drug paraphernalia, magazines, or even travel routes. Sometimes, driving past a casino is enough to hijack the ruling faculty of a reformed gambler. The former addict's unconscious detects these things, lights up old goal-directed circuits, and carries out behavioural programs as a means to an old goal's end. The mental turmoil of the reformed gambler walking into the casino is like an argument about spilt milk, for the damage was done long before. To reiterate, addictions and habits can't be broken consciously because when you're consciously aware of them, it's already too late.

Self-programming

As a result of habits and addictions, your brain has "learned" to respond automatically and unconsciously in a certain way to environmental cues or internal sensations. Therefore, to cultivate a habit you need to commandeer your unconscious, consciously. You need to change the automatic responses it activates when presented with things in the environment, or when it is subjected to characteristic internal body states. It seems like a paradoxical problem yearning for an out-of-this-world solution but, fear not, philosophers have an answer.

The theory behind this is called "self-programming" and was developed by a professor in the Philosophy of Mind, Marc Slors.[50] In his paper, Marc discusses differences between long-term implementation intentions and the pseudo-conscious intentions we form after carrying out preprogrammed behaviours. Pseudo-conscious intentions are those that are formed after a decision has already been made unconsciously. For example, as the reformed gambler walked back into the casino, they formed the conscious intention to do so after their unconscious had already "decided" and caused them to act. Therefore, it wasn't really a conscious intention but more of a pseudo-conscious intention that came after the fact. Implementation intentions, on the other hand, arise when agents consciously intend to carry out specific actions instead of mindlessly being pulled toward abstract and sometimes unconscious goals. To simplify, pseudo-conscious intentions can be viewed as reactive and short term, whereas implementation intentions are planned with a longer-term focus.

For instance, losing weight is an abstract goal that doesn't really outline any behavioural operating schemes. It's a goal that spans multiple environments in your life (workplace versus home), is subject to many different internal states (depressed versus excited), and it is influenced by various activities (dieting and training). Telling yourself that you want to lose weight doesn't change the unconscious process that happens in your body when you walk past a piece of cake, come home from work and choose the couch over the gym, or get asked to go out for your usual burger and milkshake lunch at work. Your unconscious and powerful mind doesn't know what behaviours are directly related to this abstract weight-loss goal until you consciously link them to it.

This is an implementation intention, it "specifies the behaviour one will perform in the service of achieving that goal and, crucially, the situational context in which one will perform the relevant actions".[50] Keeping with our example, in formulating a sub-habit conducive to weight loss, someone may outline the after-work routine necessary to get themselves ready to go to the gym. "After work, at roughly 5.30pm when I get home, I will drop my laptop off in the study, get changed into my gym clothes, have a banana for a snack, and follow through with a scoop of pre-workout just before I walk out the door." When you outline this process, defining the situational context and your behaviours, your chances of achieving the behaviour you set out to do improves.[51] In turn better setting you up to consistently carry out behaviours and to develop those unconsciously dictated habits that lead to fulfilment of your self-identified goals.

Unconscious power

As we'll discuss later in the book, the power of your unconscious is phenomenal. Unconsciously, us humans respond to a huge number of things in the environment, dramatically influencing how we behave and think. This ability stems from evolution and was conserved over time throughout our species as it serves an important purpose. If there is a subtle cue in your environment signalling danger, such as a person running past with a fear expression on their face or an ever-so-slight smell of smoke, your hypervigilant unconscious detects it and focuses your attention on it. If the unconscious could talk it would say something like, "Hey, give this your full attention, it could be dangerous to us."

In the same way the unconscious mind has been shaped by evolution, it has been shaped by your previous needs and wants. It is set to behave in a specific way, carrying out operating schemes that will help it achieve the goals you've consciously decided on. When it senses bodily cues and environmental stimuli that it has historically learnt to associate with previous goals, characteristic responses are automatically activated. For this reason, when in a depressed state you may be pulled down a predetermined journey of binge eating, self-isolating, and sleeping, as these behaviours once served a function. The unconscious is trying to implement the necessary behavioural steps that will help you achieve the goal of avoiding negative emotions.

Cultivating calculated habits is yet another way to transform your personality profile.

Behaviours triggered by depressive episodes are one example, but this information is transferable to absolutely any other aspect of life. By taking the time out to think about a new goal you'd like to become your highest priority, you are fundamentally altering your unconscious operating schemes. When you link your newfound goal to a set of specific behavioural responses, you're giving the machine the blueprints for the behaviours required to get you there.

The reason we've doubled down on habit formation is because certain habits, documented mostly in the field of psychology, have been shown to change personal characteristics. Characteristic aspects of yourself are weaved into your personality; therefore, cultivating calculated habits is yet another way to transform your personality profile. For instance, gratitude journaling increases happiness, a component of extroversion. Counting acts of kindness and keeping track of the kind things you've done for a week or two can increase your kindness, a component of agreeableness. This act additionally positively affects your happiness.

Exercise is a well-known antidepressant. Fittingly, regular exercise has been shown to combat anxiety and depression, components of neuroticism. Mindful meditation improves emotional regulation, a component of neuroticism, and self-control, a component of conscientiousness. Acting extroverted produces hedonic benefits, and these positive feelings in turn contribute to your extroversion scores. There is research behind all the above examples and an endless amount more on other habits, which you could effectively integrate into your life if you so wished. The point is, your consciousness gives you the ability to self-select personality traits through adopting habits and embodying philosophies that are conducive to your version of success.

The only requirements for operating in a successful way are that you:

- understand the baseline knowledge about how you function and operate on a day-to-day basis; in other words, your *personality*
- realise where certain tendencies are likely to take you in life; evidenced through *personality outcomes*
- identify the different ways you can alter your day-to-day operations; done via the *behaviour change interventions* outlined above
- determine your end goals and what success is to you; derived from your *principles*.

When you have determined your end goals and outlined what success is to you, you can trace your way back to the personality traits required to get there and utilise targeted behaviour change techniques to adopt and leverage specific tendencies. I've explained your personality, shown you where certain tendencies will take you, and outlined a variety of techniques you can use to evolve your personality profile, the only thing left to do is choose your destination and reverse engineer it.

Culture

Your personality really does reflect your day-to-day operations, and when you peer at this through the lens of traditional business it becomes apparent that it is eerily similar to the definition of a company's *culture*, which also dramatically reflects the operations of an organisation.

In social psychological terms, culture can be defined as a "set of cognitions and practices that characterise a specific social group and distinguish it from others".[52] Culture is something that is transmitted to members via traditions, rules, artefacts, and expectations, highlighting that it is a learnt behaviour. On transmission, culture influences the attitudes, beliefs, and, in some cases, deep cognitive functioning of members. In business settings, a social group bound by organisational ties forms the culture of an organisation. Decades ago, social scientist and management consultant Dr Elliott Jaques first described "corporate culture" as:

The customary or traditional ways of thinking and doing things, which are shared to a greater or lesser extent by all members of the organisation and which new members must learn and at least partially accept in order to be accepted into the firm.[53]

The customary or traditional ways of thinking and doing things could literally be the definition of personality, except we move from the individual to a group. Culture shares further similarities with personality in that it is developed and shaped by the wider social environment and close peer relationships through learnt behaviours. Not only this, both culture and personality, as we've seen, dramatically influence how an individual, or member of a group, experiences life. However, the key difference is that unlike the mind being an emergent property of an individual, culture is an emergent property of human beings interacting with one another. It is a property that assimilates the personalities of all members, exerts social forces on all members, and in turn is reciprocally influenced by all members.

Culture, like a living organism, is always in a state of flux, constantly evolving and adapting to the myriad interactions happening in its atmosphere. Organisations themselves are mini behaviour bubbles, defining the boundaries of acceptable and unacceptable standards and reinforcing these through social forces, operant conditioning, behavioural modelling, and value structures.

Cultural influences

Organisational culture, apart from prescribing behavioural norms and shared beliefs, is also influenced by the vision, mission, and values of a business. These were introduced in the first chapter and could easily be remembered as the future destination you dream of reaching, how you're going to operate to reach this destination, and the values assigned highest priority throughout your journey, respectively. To illustrate, say we have an organisation called Company X comprising five employees, all of whom behave highly conscientiously. When tasks land into the lap of Company X personnel, whether insurance paperwork, processing client onboarding, developing products for new customers, managing projects, drafting legal agreements, or outlining and organising marketing campaigns, it is likely that whichever task is completed will be delivered in a timely manner and to a high standard. This is the power and predictability of the organisation's behavioural sphere. It outlines the characteristic response of the organisation's members across different tasks, toward different stakeholders, to chance events and circumstances, and is relatively stable over time.

Organisations, however, in the same manner individuals do, differentiate themselves in their vision, mission, and values. Where Company X may value web technology, innovation, and personal branding, other organisations with a similar behavioural profile may value mental health, equality, and human flourishing. While Company X may have a vision to create a 21st century résumé replacement through an interactive personal branding document, another organisation may be driven by the desire to achieve a vision that sees the psychological health of humanity improved. The Company X mission outlines a process for continual technology innovation that allows an individual to advertise themselves to the best of their ability with the best available tools; the other describes an oath to develop and compile psychotherapeutic techniques and informational resources that can be frequently distributed to members.

Personal reflection

If you are starting your own business, you need to pay close attention to how you operate in life. It is extremely important, when formally moving into the world of business, to understand and identify your personality and principles, which are integral components of your personal brand. Businesses are a second-order structure, an outgrowth of the human condition, and if your first-order structure – your human body comprising biological and psychological processes – is not healthy, optimised, well-understood, and flourishing, the foundational architecture of your professional success lacks integrity. For example, when organisations are created, the founders are deemed to be major influences on the formation of its culture.[54] The values, assumptions, beliefs, and behavioural norms of the founder are transmitted to organisational members and become characteristics of the group. They are learnt, adopted, and transmitted to future employees. The unwritten guidelines of group behaviour are observable and mimicable through your actions and attitudes. To understand the business you build, you first have to understand yourself.

Culture prediction

In the same way that certain behavioural tendencies point you in the direction of foretold outcomes, the culture of a business also represents a crystal ball. For example, let us entertain a scenario where a business is overrun by narcissists, who in personality terms are known as the extroverted disagreeable people. The narcissists will breed a toxic culture because the characteristic behaviours and social norms they create and reinforce in the workplace are a pollutant. It would not be hard to imagine workplace dramas waiting to unfold as narcissists emotionally and irrationally overreact to perceived threats, orders, or challenges. Clashes of the titans will frequent the workplace as the team-driven atmosphere transforms into unhealthy competition when rival "kings" and "queens" cross paths.

Apart from colleagues having to walk on eggshells, the high-performing, humble, good-natured, and cooperative employees will be exploited, silenced, and eaten alive by the narcissists. Some of the best workers will lose interest, enjoyment, and psychological security, meaning organisational creativity and innovation will suffer. Not to mention the overall drop in the organisation's productivity that results from unnecessary interpersonal conflict encroaching on valuable office hours. Instead of a cooperative, well-meaning employee culture that fosters a community of brand advocates, the organisation and its workplace now top the list for complaints. Flustered employees vent about the bewildering workplace behaviour they deal with to friends and family, further damaging the once-reputable brand of the organisation. What was a team-oriented, values-driven, flourishing organisation, soon turns into a drama-fuelled reality TV show.

This example is used to demonstrate how behavioural tendencies in the form of personality traits can pervasively impact an organisation's culture. These narcissists were chosen by management, but the same story unfolds when the founder of a company transmits their own traits throughout the organisation. An unadventurous, middle-aged accountant who avoids change, sticks to traditional processes, and is infused with a micro dose of curiosity, someone low in openness, can still build and run a successful company. And given it's their company, they have the final say. When screening prospective employees, they bend toward those who are similar to them. The conservatives, the rigid operators, the safe bets. The founder is already reinforcing their self-culture.

The few new employees who aren't like them silently look for guidance and, soon after, the unwritten guidelines, the fence posts around the culture, are interpreted and adopted from observations of the founder's behaviour. At this company, when a young employee is presented with innovative accounting software that has the potential to radically change current accounting processes, instead of opting in to learn more from the sales rep, they say, "Sorry, we've already got established processes that work well, and I know my boss wouldn't be interested." The employee begins to succumb to and reinforce the culture, innately understanding and enacting the boss's attitudes to things of this nature. Unbeknownst to them, there will be a point in time when society evolves, technology changes, and new markets emerge, and decisions like these that are based off the amplification of the founder's behavioural tendencies – the culture – spell organisational suicide.

A drama-fuelled toxic workplace. A corporation scared of change waiting to be fossilised. A benevolent and universally respectful environment. A group of risk takers, innovators, and big thinkers. A motivated community of autonomous professionals. An ecosystem of high performers who reliably deliver on time. An organisation infected with deceit, manipulation, exploitation, and counterproductive workplace behaviour. Each group description comes from the amplification of individual human tendencies, which can be described as personality traits. Personality traits in organisations come together to form the behaviour bubble known as culture, which influences its operations. So much so that the organisation could be described by its prevailing personality traits, as evidenced above. It is because of this that traits are obviously indicated in personal outcomes, professional outcomes, and up the chain for business-level outcomes. In light of the information provided in this chapter, certain traits are demonstrably antecedents of success for each of these three levels as well.

Contrasting personality traits with organisational cultures clearly outlines the business-as-usual for both individuals and companies. When a community of employees comprises workers who are open to new ideas, born neophiliacs, and display an anti-traditional thinking style, should we be surprised when they launch a succession of innovative products? When you have a group of people who are altruistic, well-intentioned, empathetic, and cooperative, it's not with sorcery that we are able to assert that the organisation has good customer relationships, it's with psychological science.

The traits of individuals are magnified and transmitted through company cultures and explains much of the organisation's behaviour. The personality of every employee combines and interacts with others; is focused through the values, vision, and mission statements of the organisation; and is both influential and reciprocally influenced by the wider social environment of the organisation. If we can use personality traits to predict the outcomes of individuals – and cultures are largely magnifications of group personality traits – through a company culture you too can glimpse its future.

To sum up

In this chapter we discussed how your personality describes your characteristic patterns of behaviours, thoughts, and feelings across situations and time. We examined the theoretical basis of personality and explored how genetics, socialisation forces, parenting styles, rewards, and punishments can shape it. We looked at the formation of personality dimensions and the types of tendencies that fall under them. Using personality research, we teased certain traits into the future and correlated them with occupational and career success, academic achievement, health, wellbeing, and social impact. We examined behaviour change techniques that could be employed to give you the best possible chance at success, whatever that means for you.

Subsequently, we applied this information to your professional pursuits, mainly by exploring how personality traits can manifest as a business culture and can be used to describe the operations of your company when combined with values, visions, and missions. Be aware of your traits – the behaviours, feelings, and thoughts that are unique to you and persistent over time. Excellence is a daily process, and Rome was built day by day, brick by brick. Small, compounded actions over time have outcomes of exponential magnitude. Traits are your bricks.

What's next?

Strategic partnerships between organisations and networking at the personal level are both tremendously beneficial for a number of overlapping reasons. In the following chapter we'll explore why pharmaceutical companies seek out small, innovative biotech companies and why bookstores seek out partners in other industries. From there we'll further uncover how networking is the key to unlocking dream jobs, boosting longevity, and skyrocketing your personal brand sales. In many ways, your network is your worth.

> *If you want to go fast go alone, but if you want to go far, go together.* —African proverb

Chapter 4:
Networks and Partnerships

You're at the epicentre of a world of people

Next, we explore strategic partnerships between organisations and contrast them with connections formed in personal networks. In line with the theme of this personal branding framework, this chapter draws awareness to the similarities between networking at an organisational level and networking at the personal level. The benefits of networking at an organisational level are magnifications and slight iterations of the benefits arising from personal networks. If you are functioning as an entrepreneur or independent professional, personal networking benefits and organisation-level benefits usually directly align. An example of this is when you meet someone at a party – traditionally thought of as a more social or personal circumstance – and, after exchanging information, you enter a formal business arrangement that sees them becoming an investor, business partner, employee, or customer.

At a personal level, you may have bonded with this person because they showed personality traits you regard as favourable; shared similar interests to you; reflected components of your personal principles, such as shared ethics, values, philosophies; possessed similar technical skills and knowledge to you; or, simply made you feel good through their interpersonal communication style. This then elevated from the personal level to the business level, whereby a new formal exchange occurred. This same process can happen in reverse whereby business associates grasp the ladder and step down from the superficial atmosphere of business into more intimate, personal levels. Consequently, your personal brand is crucial to developing your networks and, in a reciprocal fashion, is positively affected by your network.

Strategic partnerships in business

A strategic partnership refers to the relationship between two commercial entities, usually formalised by single or multiple business contracts. Despite the challenges associated with these partnerships, the benefits are of much greater significance. In a 2014 PwC CEO survey, more than half of the respondents had entered into a strategic alliance or joint venture in the last year, and 69 percent planned to do so in the coming 12 months.[1]

Partnerships, also referred to as alliances, are fostered for multiple reasons:

- Through successful partnerships, organisations can draw on each other's strengths, allowing them to grow their businesses more rapidly and effectively.
- Through leveraging partner resources, innovations, and subject matter expertise, each business can streamline their processes to better meet customer demands and target new markets, in doing so gaining a competitive advantage. Knowledge sharing itself increases the rate of learning for both organisations while providing fertile ground for new innovations.
- Partnerships enable businesses to co-advertise each other and participate in further forms of professional collaboration, increasing exposure and positively influencing brand image through associations.
- Risk distribution represents another tangible benefit derived from partnerships. Partners share the risks associated with developing new products, funding new research, and finding and capturing new markets, all of which can be financially and resource intensive to the point where it is sometimes unachievable in isolation.
- Alliances between two organisations can be used as a defensive mechanism to squander efforts from competitors that try to enter their market through imitation or the development of alternative offerings.

The following examples are provided to highlight some of the above points and to explore how they unfold in the real world.

Nestlé utilised partnerships as a strategy when their inhouse innovation department was unable to sustain annual growth of five to six percent. Realising this was opening them up to disruption from other competitors, who were openly collaborating and using public sources of innovation, they implemented a special business unit solely focused on developing strategic partnerships. Shortly after, through this unit's efforts, Nestlé developed an effective method for identifying and sourcing viable partners. By the turn of 2009 they'd formed alliances with other businesses, universities, start-ups, and venture capitalists, which acted as a defence mechanism against their competitors while providing them with a competitive advantage with regard to product innovation and talent sourcing. It was through a partnership focus that these benefits were achieved.

Starbucks – a world-renowned coffee brand – experienced extreme growth in the 1990s and provides a perfect business case for exemplifying the benefits and reasoning behind strategic alliances. Early on in its journey, the company understood the value of relationships and was interested in expanding its market reach for coffee drinkers. To do this, Starbucks had to find a way to put its brand of coffee in front of more people without being restricted to its existing retail sites. A simple but powerful realisation provided the answer they were looking for: books. Coffee and books are a match made in heaven and, given the naturalness of the fit between the two, it wasn't long before they formed a strategic partnership with Barnes & Noble Inc., the largest US bookstore chain. The way Starbucks set up shop inside Barnes & Noble allowed customers to enter from the street or directly from the bookstore, creating a mutually beneficial arrangement through shared foot traffic. Barnes & Noble received more morning traffic through early-bird Starbucks customers who flowed into their store, turning what was once a quiet period of store activity into a lively customer-fuelled environment. Starbucks benefited from Barnes & Noble shoppers when they took coffee breaks from their regular shopping activity. Together, these companies drove each other's revenues up while simultaneously contributing to a community-driven atmosphere that offered more to the customer.

Strategic partnerships are also driven by entire industry ecosystems. In the biotechnology industry this is fast becoming the norm. Biotechnology deals with the exploitation and manipulation of living organisms to create commercial products. For success in this industry, multiple aspects of business need to come together for a biotechnological intervention to be developed and subsequently gain market share. Big pharmaceutical companies become gatekeepers for drug entry into markets powered by their global reach and deep pockets. However, due to their size they can suffer from institutional inertia and have difficulty predicting the future, meaning that at any point their turf could be ripe for technological disruption. Advances in medical, nano, genetic, and countless other life-science technologies prove to be real threats, potentially leading to the demise of a pharmaceutical company that promotes archaic products reminiscent of another era.

On the flipside, research laboratories – commandeered by world-leading scientists and interdisciplinary teams, fuelled by excitement, entrepreneurial energy, and access to the latest research – provide a breeding ground for creative solutions and disruptive biotech innovations. However, they lack the funding, resources, and global networks to effectively manufacture, distribute, and reach global markets. The problems of both become the solution for the other. The big pharma companies strategically partner with biotech start-ups and cutting-edge research labs, essentially hedging their bets as they try to capitalise on disruptive technologies instead of being consumed by them. The smaller and more agile research labs need the funding, resources, and global networks afforded to them by the gatekeepers if they are ever to bring their ideas from lab to life. It is the trade of product innovation and disruptive technologies developed in labs for the market-capturing abilities of big pharma that makes this relationship symbiotic and necessary.

Notice that the overarching, unifying force that brings organisations into alliance comes from an overlap of each partner's strategic plans and goals. Although businesses may differ in their vision and customer base, along the way there are common steppingstones that allow them both to flourish and progress toward their master plan in a collaborative manner. Teamwork, even at an organisational level, makes the dream work.

Personal networks

Developing personal networks is one way to directly improve your personal brand. Notably, a good personal network not only works wonders for your personal brand, but directly flows over into health benefits as well. What's more, as a result of the internet and other technological innovations, the personal connections that confer the greatest benefits might even come from people you've not yet met in person. For example, in 2020, the second year of my company's existence, I was tasked with trying to make sales and develop business partnerships in the middle of a pandemic. Geographical limitations were in place, meaning no one was allowed to leave their house let alone engage in a personal discussion over coffee. Yet, surprisingly, despite being forced online, I formed some of my most pivotal and unlikely relationships. Many of which were not even in Victoria, my home state. This anti-traditional method of network development, despite the traditional network focus of this section, is important to keep in mind given we're in a continually advancing technological world.

Similarities are essential ingredients for fast-tracked relationship development.

In a more traditional sense, whenever you leave the house there is an opportunity to network. You can meet someone waiting for a coffee, develop a new friendship with a university peer while studying, or ignite a new connection with someone at your workplace. When you attend a party or event, you are exposed to a cocktail of individuals, some of whom could end up becoming friends, lovers, or business partners. Other places that provide a solid ground for new networks are the environments your interests or hobbies pull you toward. A person who regularly exercises will meet people at the gym, in much the same way as individuals in a sports team are bound to one another through other social factors. Circumstances such as these provide exposure to likeminded people who share similarities with you, and similarities are essential ingredients for fast-tracked relationship development.

More settings to develop networks could include a new business venture, the family gatherings you attend – which expose you to individuals who, at the least, share baseline familial ties – and, lastly, friends of friends, who represent an opportunity for fostering new connections because being a friend of a friend usually signifies a degree of existing commonalities between you and that third person. If you're friends with John because he shares your values, loves to read fiction, is fun to be around, plays sport, and is a good person, chances are his other friends share at least some of these attributes, meaning you and his existing friends share an underlying compatibility.

As mentioned, the evolution of technology presents novel ways to network and is increasingly important in the 21st century. Many social media platforms, online games, and digital communities already exist and provide fertile ground for new connections to be made. In fact, their purpose is to connect people with others. Understanding the avenues of network development gives you a different level of awareness when encountering these situations, and ensures you're equipped to capitalise on any and every opportunity that presents itself. While sounding platitudinal, the benefits arising from these newly formed networks are powerful and the reason for the existence of the personal networking element.

Networking, viewed another way, could simply be described as the people you meet throughout life. Although the word networking has professional and business connotations, many of the benefits of networking don't stay in the business world and aren't contained in your professional atmosphere. Frequently, people you network with in the traditional business sense, and the benefits attached to them, diffuse across many areas and have the potential to intricately intertwine themselves into your personal matters and life. At some point, this newfound business connection may be exposed to your friends or family through a dinner or a party. Upon getting to know each other and interacting further, you may engage in philosophical debates, participate in recreational activities, cross-promote each other's businesses, and even engage in a romantic or sexual relationship, if spontaneous sparks arise.

All of the above demonstrate the potential for "professional networks" to traverse the false dichotomy of business and personal life and entangle with personal areas in the form of introductions to personal social groups; engagement in personally relevant philosophical topics; the combined action of both parties' personal interests; the advertisement of an existing personally relevant business; companionate love between two people; and through mutual personal pleasure. Further, you may even start a new venture together or join existing businesses, effectively merging your life's work with the other person's, representing one of the most intimate personal relationships, since everyone knows entering a business partnership with another is akin to marriage without the sex. Co-founderships are as personal as it gets.

The point is, the people you meet, even in the traditional networking sense under the umbrella of professionalism, could end up becoming your best friend or an important aspect of your personal life. It is for this reason that networking encompasses many benefits that may not fit with the traditional perception of it. Everyone you know fits into the diagram of your personal network. Some may spend most of their time hanging out in the professional domains of your life, but at any point people can jump from professional to personal domains and vice versa. You, and your personal brand, are the common factor underlying all domains. Remember, professional existence in the world of business is merely a slightly filtered projection of your personal qualities.

Networking is good for you

At one point, your soul mate was a stranger. The force that brought you from stranger to lover happened through networking. If they came as a warm introduction from a friend, they entered directly through someone already in your personal network. If you walked up to them at a bar, sneakily chatted up their friend to make them jealous, and coincidentally found yourself in a conversation with them that you happened to initiate, you directly sourced and added that person to your personal network yourself. Arguably, one of the best reasons to network is for your physical and mental health.

Developing meaningful relationships and having a healthy social network is the key to these improvements, and since humans come preprogrammed to be ultra-social, it makes sense that subverting our creator's wishes leads to cracks in the matrix and causes our mental health to suffer. The fact that our body consists of an interplay between our physical and metaphysical matter means that detriments to physical health, stemming from emotional trauma and social dysfunction, come as no surprise.

The Harvard Study of Adult Development – the world's longest study of adult life – found that "good relationships keep us happier and healthier". The director of the study, psychiatrist Dr Robert Waldinger, in a TED talk,[2] said the "study has shown that people who are more socially connected to family, to friends, and to the community, are happier, they're physically healthier, and they live longer than people who are less well connected", also suggesting that "loneliness is toxic".

In a study of 7,000 men and women in Alabama, researchers found that "people who were disconnected from others were roughly three times more likely to die during the nine-year study than people with strong social ties".[3] Another study cited compelling evidence that linked a low-quantity or quality of social ties with a range of conditions, including the development and worsening of cardiovascular disease, repeat heart attacks, autoimmune disorders, high blood pressure, cancer, and slowed wound healing.[4] Psychologically, social connections and good mental health have been shown to improve self-esteem, improve psychological wellbeing, and reduce symptoms of anxiety and depression.[5,6,7] Healthy, platonic, and romantic relationships demonstrably rival traditional medical interventions.

The happiness pill walks past you every day. For me, one example springs to mind of someone I met through one of my close friends; a bubbly undergraduate psychology student who subsequently became my partner for three years. During the time we spent together, I went through some of the hardest and most depressing times of my life. Single-handedly, this person helped me get through, and, in doing so, positively influenced my mental wellbeing, quality of life, and happiness, for which I will be forever grateful. However, in case you are wondering, you don't need a romantic partner proficient in psychology to get this effect. Of course, a bit of psychological knowledge never hurt anyone, but I could equally describe select family members – my mum comes top of mind – and any of my closest friends as happiness pills too. My reason for using this example is because a romantic partner usually epitomises a happiness pill for most people, and it helps to get my point across. Such is the power of networking. Being open to new experiences with new people is a catalyst for your happiness and health.

Personal brand preachers

Networking also confers direct business benefits; a lot of them at that. From a marketing standpoint, whenever you bring a new person into your network, assuming you have effectively sold yourself and told them a bit about what you do, you may have just onboarded a personal sales rep. If you can clearly articulate your values to that person, develop a meaningful relationship, and give them confidence in your abilities, these people will end up becoming your brand preachers. They believe in you and your capabilities and they want to see you succeed. Not to mention you make them look good if they can provide people with your details in their time of need.

When referring to your brand, remember we are talking about your personal brand stemming from your personal qualities, not the company's brand that you work for, nor the brand of the product you started selling when you were 16. The side hustle you've been involved in for the last 10 years isn't even your brand, it is merely a product in your product suite, a small component of your overall personal brand. You and your personal qualities are the constant; these transient business ventures and side hustles usually are not.

You, collectively captured by your personal brand, are the central force behind every job, service, or product that entangles itself with your life. Under your personal brand you will deliver an array of constantly transforming services and products, which may traverse industries, change knowledge domains, target different demographics, and even service new geographical regions. This is why it's important to realise that the people you meet can end up becoming your "personal brand" sales reps, forming part of your overall marketing strategy for many of your business ventures. We are not talking about the marketing campaign for your product, we're talking about the strategic marketing plan for your whole life.

These people will tell their friends and family about you, if you make a good enough impression on them, and through their pre-marketing will potentially source you customers for your next business venture. In three years you could train to be a lawyer, but at this point you are not. Your network can't sell your legal services because they do not yet exist. However, when the time comes, all your close friends and brand preachers will be the first to put the word out. Not only this but you've arrived warm to their network as they've brought you up to people before. They are on team "you", and legal services are just another juicy addition that you've added to your dollar-generating toolbelt.

To explore this form of personal word-of-mouth style marketing, let's use an example. Let's say Jane meets someone who has just started an online fitness business where he livestreams his workouts to clients from his house. His name is Jedd, he has an athletic build, and his business is LIFE fitness. He is passionate about fitness. He values health and wants to positively impact as many people's lives as possible. He's been studying for the last three years and has nearly finished his exercise science degree. A day later, Jane meets another person, Max. Max is a personal trainer, is overweight and appears at first glance inactive, has held degrees in exercise science for the last five years, and is currently enrolled in an exercise science-related PhD. He too has an online fitness business, SCIENTIFIT, and sends weekly workouts to his clients, much like Jedd. SCIENTIFIT is approaching its five-year anniversary, but Max isn't celebrating because he lost his passion for fitness long ago. Unlike Jedd, Max comes across as arrogant and rude. He seems rather apathetic when talking about his online business and merely references it as necessary to pay the bills. He is looking for an out, but for the foreseeable future he must reluctantly monetise his existing skillset, which happens to be personal training and fitness coaching.

A week later, Jane arrives at her aunt's birthday party. While engaging in small talk with her aunt, the aunt says that she has been searching for an online personal trainer for workouts in the comfort of her own home. Jane thinks back to her encounters from the previous week and refers LIFE fitness. "You'll love Jedd, he's a really nice guy and I know you'll be in good hands. He cares about people he works with and it looks like he practises what he preaches." Notice, the basis of Jane's referral decision was impacted by the personal attributes of Jedd, Jedd's *personal* brand.

Although the brand of a business will hold influence in referrals, the personal brand of the people working with, or on, the business are equally, if not more, important. It was Jedd's personal brand that caused Jane to refer his services, which was in the form of LIFE fitness, despite Max's business being backed by experience, superior educational knowledge, and running for a longer time. LIFE fitness was a brand under the umbrella of Jedd's personal brand, and this is why it was referred.

Aside from selling services that are linked to your personal brand, there are also services directly attached to you. If you look at yourself as the product that is delivering services, a company hiring you is essentially paying for your personal services. In this sense, your networks have the ability to sell your personal services by recommending you for a job opening. They are sourcing your next personal customer in the form of an employer. Via this process, your networks can bring business to you through connecting you with people who will pay for different outputs of your personal services. In some cases it may be the product you are selling, such as Jedd's online video workouts; however, in others they can sell your services directly to an employer through a job recommendation.

Employee referral programs

To add to this job recommendation train of thought, networking proves to be a statistically more effective way to land yourself a job. Let's tease it out. Most people's dream job is to work for a respectable, successful, and well-known company. Statistics floating around on job boards on the internet suggest the average number of applicants for each corporate role is 250, then four to six of these people get interviewed and only one of them is hired. An extreme example, Google, a dream company for most, reportedly gets 2–3 million applicants per year for 7,000 open roles. A one in 428 success rate. As you can see, unless you are applying for a job at your local yoghurt factory, the landscape is competitive.

In this situation, the power of networks is most easily epitomised through nepotism. Knowing someone with influence can enable you to skip everyone in the queue, all 428 of them. For nepotism to work these wonders, you need to know a top dog, and they're usually hard to get to and in high demand but, luckily, this is not the only way personal networks prove superior in employment settings. Did you know, companies like Infosys, Coca Cola, and Deloitte have historically hired 40 percent of their employees through employee referral programs?

There are benefits to this method, including saving on recruitment costs, getting due diligence partially completed as employee referrals are similar to reference checks, and improving the quality of life for workers who now have meaningful relationships at their workplace. As a consequence, many other companies are implementing large-scale referral programs and following suit. Not to mention Gallup, a global analytics and advice firm, through their research has found that when employees have best friends at work they are more likely to be engaged, less likely to be actively searching for other employment, feel more connected to co-workers, tend to have more positive experiences throughout the day, are more likely to take risks that lead to innovation, and report fewer negative experiences at work.[8] In short, organisations further benefit from cultural improvements through this networking-based method of employment.

My dad, an executive in a tier one international organisation, intuitively understands the importance of a supportive and meaningful culture and places family values at the centre of the organisation. For him, hiring a relative of an astute, reliable, and disciplined worker is a no-brainer. Knowing this, make sure to develop meaningful relationships with as many people as you can. There is a better chance of getting your dream job through your network than coming in cold from a ridiculously crowded job advertisement. People are the key to your job-hunting success, so it's time to start making friends!

Word-of-mouth methodology

Surprisingly, or perhaps not, this word-of-mouth referral methodology, applied to sales, drives huge amounts of business. In 2017, Engagement Labs, a predictive analytics company, examined the effect of word-of-mouth activity on consumer purchases in the US. They found that 19 percent of all purchases in the US could be attributed to offline or online word-of-mouth referrals, equating to $10 trillion of economic impact. On the B2B end of the equation, the impact of word of mouth is even greater, with 91 percent of B2B sales being influenced by it in some way.[9]

When a company is looking for a new technology to purchase or integrate, and you've got a product contender, you best be making friends with people around your target. This is the sales funnel; friends of decision-makers are what will cause them to buy. Jay Bear and Daniel Lemin's book, *Talk Triggers*, describes three main reasons why word-of-mouth marketing works so well:

1. It is hyper-relevant. Meaning that when you have someone advocating for your brand or product, they can customise recommendations and alter their pitch based on the receiver's needs. It is like a personalised sales campaign.
2. Positive word of mouth saves the receiver time. By having someone experienced with a product or brand advocate them to you, it saves you time because you don't need to research and compare the market for alternatives.
3. It comes independently, meaning the person referring something has no financial interest in the purchase. This gives credibility to a brand or product and helps generate more trust in the buyer, making the referral more persuasive.

As mentioned, word of mouth can take place offline or online. A person is no longer limited by their grounded physical connections. Whenever your brand preacher comes across a post from someone on social media looking for a recommendation, and it fits the context of your service or product, guess who is getting a referral? Someone in your network can advertise your product to their friend in Poland if it is a good fit. Everything is moving online, and globalisation means online word-of-mouth activity is even more relevant. Build your brand through people.

An important consideration here is reciprocity, a social norm prominent in the field of social psychology. It states that a positive action will be responded to by another positive action, and it's grounded in the premise that reciprocal behaviour benefits both parties. For you to build your own brand you must be the cheerleader for other people. This means advertising them, supporting them, networking for them, and believing in them. They will reciprocate and do the same for you unless their moral compass is backwards. If you need a reason for supporting people other than benevolently advertising others out of the goodness of your heart and making your mum proud, the principle of reciprocity is your reason. To get referrals, give referrals. Make your network your team.

Sharing is caring

Other direct business benefits derived from networking come in the form of sharing. You can share resources, risks, and costs with another. To better illustrate this point it helps to use examples of people. On the one hand, let's assume we have a professional, Jill, who has spent the last few years actively involved in recruitment companies. Due to their years in the trenches, they have developed a Rolodex of industry-specific networks, possess arcane insights, demonstrate an in-depth understanding of recruitment processes, evidence high-quality interpersonal skills, and, of course, have saved a notable amount of dollars in the bank from their hard work as a head-hunter.

On the other hand, let's assume we have another professional, Jack, who instead of spending their years arming companies with talent, has spent the better part of the last decade cooped up in their basement building web technologies through self-taught coding skills. A stereotypical introverted coder, focused on automation, Jack has developed iPhone applications and powerful computer software that shaves days of time off of what were previously manual processes. Via interactions with forums and online communities housing other like-minded professionals, Jack also has a flywheel of tech-lovers and experts to call upon should he get stuck or find himself in a position of needing more hands on keyboards. Discovery-driven processes have led Jack to develop his own unique and valuable insights into automation, web development, and user-experience. It's paid off, too, as he has a few residual incomes, which means he is living comfortably.

The two are glaring opposites. Jill, a personable, interpersonally sensitive, extroverted recruitment professional, possesses refined people skills built through interviewing thousands of applicants that Jack is sorely lacking in. Instead, Jack, a logic-driven, process-oriented, computer-whispering introvert, speaks the language of code and isn't too caught up in the niceties of society. Jill's network hangs out at social events and hits the town, while Jack's move from house to house playing Dungeons & Dragons. Developing a website and coding for automation is as alien to Jill as sitting in a room involved in an intimate conversation with someone across the table is to Jack. But this is where the magic happens.

When Jack and Jill are put in contact by a mutual friend, who sees the potential for a tech-heavy, automated, recruitment start-up to be birthed, it is through sharing resources, risks, and costs that these two unlikely heroes stand the best shot at success. Sharing resources means the recruitment and web development-specific documentation, frameworks, and processes both are privy to, now become jointly owned by the parties. It means, the cost of a tech-heavy recruitment start-up is halved, as both contribute the required capital. Together, they hammer down the risk as all the tools on both of their toolbelts are used in conjunction to build a better product – ensuring the best chance of sustainably monetising their business. Not to mention, networks – once isolated – have become a more diversified pool of professionals waiting to be called upon by either of the dynamic duo. Sharing resources, risks, and costs really is a step up for any journey.

Effective collaboration

I've alluded to "combined consciousness" in previous chapters. Collaborating with another in the form of mind sharing is a recipe for problem-solving and creativity. Every time you encounter another person there is the added potential for innovation. Larry Page and Sergey Brin were both studying computer science at Stanford University when, after completing a research project together, they came to the realisation that popular search results on the internet were the most useful to people. This realisation, born from their connected minds, is the reason you can jump online and access the information you need immediately. Google arose from their combined consciousnesses.

In 1971, two people, both named Steve, met through a mutual friend. The friend had introduced them because they were both interested in electronics. Steve Wozniak and Steve Jobs both saw the advent of personal computing. Steve Wozniak's genius in software and computing combined with Steve Job's passion for his vision in delivering personal computing to the world, together, complimentarily transformed into the brand Apple. Introduction through a friend of a friend made possible the sharing of the resources, insights, vision, and values necessary for the achievement of stratospheric success.

Mike Krieger and Kevin Systrom cofounded Instagram. Garrett Camp and Travis Kalanick, Uber. Nobel prizes are regularly awarded to multiple researchers for their combined efforts and joint discoveries. Successful companies and Nobel Prize-winning discoveries are often an outcome of multiple minds, and in a world fast approaching 10 billion people, the chances of developing and bringing to life a unique and original idea independently are slim. Combining your consciousness with new people leverages the creativity and expertise of both to create completely novel connections between concepts that are underdeveloped and unachievable in the mind of one.

Personal and professional development

Personal and professional development occurs as a direct result of networking. The people you meet, having all had different journeys, educations, and life experiences, possess their own unique wisdom. People are like walking books; self-authored masterpieces, brimming with knowledge and evolving with time. Their life lessons can be made available to you once you cross the chasm from stranger to teammate. By tapping into people's wisdom and knowledge, you may find that their personal philosophies, insights, and perspectives about life are relatable and transferrable to your own.

What may be obvious to someone in their life may cause you to undergo a fundamental perspective shift, forever changing your attitude to a belief or topic. Someone might say, "I don't want to start a business and spend money," to which their friend may reply, "The only risk you face is that of being trapped in a career you despise because you didn't have a crack at starting your own successful passion pursuit when you had the chance." Diverse perspectives, sourced from other people, are the cure to the dogmatic lens of the world that your own consciousness permits you to look through. Understanding how another person deals with failure may offer you strategies. Observing how others solve problems, exert discipline, manage emotions, interact with the world, and find purpose can provide customisable clues usable for your own journey.

The knowledge sharing arising from natural interactions in personal and professional domains could really be described as informal symbiotic consults. Not to mention, being exposed to a new norm has the ability to change your perspective instantaneously. The aspiring gym goer struggling to go to the gym once a week can no longer live in the delusion that there is no time for additional sessions after having met someone who gets up at 4.30 am every day to train. Exposure to a new norm makes possible that which was previously perceived as impossible.

Perspective shifts, apart from changing lives, are powerful enough to save lives. This is precisely the mechanism whereby psychologists prevent suicides. If system resets and software upgrades were a person, the psychologist with a new perspective script would be its archetype. Psychologists and gym addicts are extreme examples used to illustrate the potential for your network to lead to personal development; however, everyone you meet has the potential to teach you something.

Learning from others is rooted in our biology and developmental psychology, evidenced through mirror neurons in the brain and the ground-breaking Bobo Doll experiment involving children, which was carried out by psychologist Albert Bandura in the 1960s. On one hand, biologically, mirror neurons in our brain light up with activity when we observe someone doing a behaviour or action and simulate the brain activity required to carry out what we have just viewed. Hence the term "mirror neuron". It's like our brain is learning and practising the neural gymnastics required in case we ever need to emulate the behaviour or action ourselves.

On the other hand, psychologically, in the Bobo Doll experiments, when young children observed behaviours of older "models", they went on to mimic the witnessed behaviours shortly after. The point being, we're physically hardwired and mentally equipped to observe and learn from others. Learning from others is so important that evolution has refined and conserved this process over time. Personal and professional development brought about through learning from others can be catalysed by simply diversifying your network and exposing yourself to new people and new experiences. Your body and mind will do the rest.

Associations

Another key consideration for personal networks presents itself in the form of "associations". This refers to the psychological associations, or mental connections, we generate between things. Associations are a powerful psychobiological force that can work in mysterious ways.

The power of associations has been demonstrated in well-known psychological experiments that explored classical conditioning. Pavlov, a famous researcher who contributed immensely to the field of behavioural psychology, was able to generate salivation in dogs, which is a typical response to food, through the presentation of a non-food stimulus in the form of a bell. When dogs are presented with food they will naturally salivate. When presenting food to dogs and ringing a bell every time the food is presented, the dogs will still salivate. After a while of pairing the bell and food together, the dogs will salivate in direct response to the sound of the bell, even if no food is presented! This is classical conditioning and describes a situation where involuntary physiological responses can be conditioned through associations to a neutral stimulus. Simply put, body mechanisms outside our conscious control can be conditioned to react to certain things through associations to something that already brings about that reaction.

If you tease out this concept further you will logically arrive at the conclusion that if an involuntary physiological response can be generated merely by pairing two things together over a short period, it stands to reason that the brain will leap to conclusions based on exposure to paired stimuli. It will be influenced, and learn from, the relationships it perceives between objects, people, experiences, and any other forms of stimuli.

Negative associations

In line with this logic, the examination of social associations was tackled by Robert Cialdini, a leading social science researcher in the field of persuasion. In his book, *Influence*, he uncovers the hidden power of associations and discusses in depth the association principle. This refers to the tendency for people to link things in their mind that in some way appear to be connected to one another, and because of this an "innocent association with either good things or bad things, can influence how people feel about us". Just like a dog can be conditioned to respond in a certain way toward something through previous associations, so can humans.

For example, as Cialdini evidenced in his book, it is common for weather reporters to cop hate mail from news viewers when they report bad weather.[10] The viewers associate the weather reporter with storms and destructive weather, merely because they present the information. Even though they do not cause the hurricane that destroys someone's house, they deliver the information, which is enough to warrant a personal vendetta. Further, if someone is working for a company recently featured in the news for their unethical use of data and currently undergoing legal proceedings, they may be engulfed by the shadow of negativity cast out by the entity they dutifully and honestly serve.

Other forms of negative associations may occur if you had begun to like someone and recently found out their mates were the cause of the recent crime wave in the area or were up-and-coming criminals. Despite being fond of the person you were talking to, you may begin to disassociate and distance yourself because their mates – their "associations" – manifest as shady characters with questionable morals, tainting the person you were once fond of. After all, research shows that people are usually assumed to have the same personality traits as their friends. If someone is a less than respectable person with questionable values who enjoys engaging in antisocial behaviour, we can make an educated guess that their friends may too share in this anti-authoritative nature with a bent toward disrespectful and dishonest conduct.

Your value is readable through your network.

No wonder our mums were always vigilant about the new friends we made growing up! They instinctively knew and understood the power of association, perception, and social conformity. On an individual level, spending time with less-than-honest rule-breakers can eventually rub off on you and poison your good nature through social conformity and peer pressure. But even before that happens, random onlookers can see something from afar that you cannot, and it is the negative web of associations that surrounds you, hinting at the destination of your morals, ethics, and interests. As such, you are intuitively avoided by virtue of your associations. Benjamin Franklin made it known that "the rotten apple spoils his companion".

Jumping to conclusions based off associations, which in this example happens to stem from people, is automatic and evolutionarily indicated. Extrapolating key and potentially lifesaving information from a safe radius betters our chance of survival through risk mitigation. If Jerry the Sociopath's best mate invited you over for pizza in the woods you could avoid a potentially 50-shades-of-grey-gone-wrong bad time by intuitively realising that if Jerry the Sociopath enjoys doing harm to living things, maybe it's not a good idea to jump into a forest cabin with his second in charge. Surely, long beach walks and pink sunsets aren't what these two misguided souls have in common?

We act on these associations because we have a feeling, and half the time we aren't even consciously aware we are doing it. For example, at a personal level, the intuitive gut feelings you get about someone are nothing more than the unconscious, and sometimes conscious, associations you are forming based on the consistency and integrity of their speech, the congruence between their verbal and nonverbal body language, the words and stories they use, and the interpersonal signals they give off during your interaction. A conversation with someone who hides their hands from sight, avoids eye contact, has closed body language, and has inconsistencies present in their speech, could lead you to have a bad gut feeling about them; an association born from red flags nested in their interpersonal communication behaviours. Interpersonal communication is explored in more detail toward the end of the book.

Positive associations

Positive associations exist too, and their influence is ubiquitously displayed throughout society. Sports fans are prime examples of this. Think about when a team makes the grand final: people go crazy, they cover themselves head to toe in their team's colours, chanting and shouting while using the pronoun "we" because it attaches them to their winning team ("we are the champions", "we won this year's grand final", "we're better than you"). The outcome of a sporting event, if successful, is enough to cause people with no personal relationship to the team or players, and in some cases no pre-existing connection to the sport in general, to turn into walking preachers with a new self-identity. They voluntarily enlist as cheerleaders because through their self-identified association to the winning team, they leverage and "share" in their success.

Utilising this logic, positive associations are exploited in the realm of advertising all around us. Attractive models are paired with absolutely anything because they lend their positive attributes to the product. Attractive women are used to advertise sports cars, just like males with muscly bodies are used for underwear packaging. Whatever it is, pairing the product with an attractive person creates positive associations around what is being sold. Even just being an attractive person, as we will explore later, causes people to associate you with kindness, talent, and physical health. Alongside negative associations, positive associations are prevalent and just as powerful in shaping the opinions of your audience.

Credible associations

The people in your network form part of your associations. Working with a reputable company, a domain expert, or a brand superstar allows you to be noticed and associates you with the positive attributes of the person you are working with. If a professor of innovation has endorsed your new product, onlookers will look at that title and associate your product with the esteem of the professor's domain-specific knowledge. If a large, well-known company uses your service, onlookers automatically conclude your service is at a quality high enough to meet the needs of large, well-known companies. Without knowing any prior information about you, people form judgements purely by looking at who is associated with you in a clientele, professional, or personal capacity. This is why websites feel the need to show off their most reputable clients, and it's why book authors usually try to source prestigious individuals for front cover quotes. Knowing this, you need to try to associate yourself with reputable and credible individuals, and, when possible, make it known to your network through collaborations, appearances at networking events, social media posts, or joint advertisements.

When people see your network associations, they deem you to share the common traits, capabilities, and values of those people. It fast-tracks your audience's perspective of you from unimportant stranger to someone they want to connect with and get to know. An extreme example of leveraging and exploiting positive associations comes in the form of podcasters. Million-dollar companies have been made off the back of podcasts because podcasters have brought enough reputable people onto their show that the audience slowly but surely knighted the podcaster with the accolades of their guests. Bring in enough famous people and people will think you're famous. That's the power of associations. Your value is readable through your network.

Network inception

Of course, there is one last benefit to networking, and, in an inception-like fashion, it is the entering of a new network from within your existing network. This, by the way, can form an infinite loop with endless possibilities. In a similar way that ground zero is the epicentre of a pandemic, the person you connect with is the central point of connection between a unique, resourceful, and rewarding bunch of others. All of whom view you favourably, trust you more, and are willing to do business or collaborate with you now that you are a "friend of a friend". You have come into their life already reference-checked, so the requirement for extensive due diligence becomes unnecessary.

Once you have added someone into your network, it is important to provide value to them as soon as you can to initiate the execution of the unspoken social contract stipulating the need for reciprocation. If you can do something valuable for them, they will do it back for you, and as you become more seasoned in the world of business, it is glaringly obvious that an introduction to the right person is the most valuable outcome that you could hope for, period! By sharing your network with new members of your network, you are inviting them to reciprocate and do the same for you. Despite this not always being the case, and the call to action for this sounding like a dishonest manipulation, sharing your network with other people benefits everyone and should be continually practised and engrained in you next to good manners and universal respect.

Six degrees of separation

When network sharing is practised, a person's whole life journey and the resulting concoction of awesome, high-quality, connected people they have come across and colocalised with are ready to be scanned, examined, and vetted for your needs, should you be deserving. It is the fastest way to find talented designers, investors with money, CEOs with decision-making capabilities, and people who will collaborate with you in pursuit of a common goal or ideology. Furthermore, if you set the standards for your network and surround yourself with the right people, your network will go out and advertise you while simultaneously scanning their world for people you should have met yesterday. Some dream teams shoot basketballs, but mine would be a group of vigilant people who recognise and action opportunistic introductions on my behalf. If this dream team existed in the next year, I could meet anyone on the planet, including but not limited to the Dalai Lama, Bill Gates, Donald Trump, and Elon Musk. And it all stems from the "Six degrees of separation" theory.

This theory states that any person on Earth could meet anyone else in the world with roughly six or fewer mutual connections. With five intermediaries we could get to anyone else on the planet, or so it goes. The theory initially came about in the book *Chain-Links* by Hungarian writer Frigyes Karinthy, published in 1930. The idea was based on the fact that the number of people known grows exponentially as the relationships in the chain increase. For example, assume that each person in the world knows 100 people. Each of these 100 people know another 100 people. There is now 10,000 people that you can access through any member of your immediate circle. As you move out to your third link, there is now 1,000,000 people you could access. In the fourth link, 100,000,000, fifth, 10,000,000,000, and by the sixth link you can hypothetically access 1,000,000,000,000 people, which of course exceeds the population of the planet. This comfortably combats any common connections people may share.

To conceptualise this theory, think about your friend who may know a police officer. The police officer reports to the chief commissioner, and the chief commissioner regularly engages with senior government officials. Some of these officials report to the prime minister. In five links you are now at the head of the country.

Unfortunately, theory does not always translate to reality, and if it did the field of science would see us living in space and possibly teleporting. In this case, though, it does. Researchers at Microsoft proved this theory to be accurate! Eric Horvitz and fellow researcher Jure Leskovec studied the records of 30 billion electronic conversations among 180 million people, scattered across various countries, and found that the average link between any two people in the database was 6.6 connections.[11] They also found that 78 percent of people could be connected in seven steps or fewer, and that some people were separated by as many as 29 connections. You are potentially five people away from the Pope and, holy shit, isn't that cool to know!

To sum up

In summary, there is an array of direct benefits that can be derived from strategic partnerships and networking. Benefits found in strategic partnerships include:

- leveraging each other's expertise and resources
- increased rates of learning
- co-advertisement and other marketing benefits
- risk sharing
- innovation.

Many of these, if not most, are directly transferable benefits to the realm of personal networking. However, there are additional benefits above and beyond those seen in the corporate world stemming from personal networking, a result of the hybrid personal and professional lens that we've used to analyse individuals through. Looking at networking in a more holistic way:

- The development of meaningful relationships and a strong social network confers physical and mental health benefits.
- People become brand preachers marketing you and your services in a way that traditional marketing cannot.
- Job opportunities prefer coming to you warm from the mouth of your associates and not through the cold, inefficient job boards congesting the internet.
- Sharing risks, resources, and costs makes the impossible, possible.
- New people bring with them a new mindset representing fertile ground for the genesis of revolutionary, disruptive, and paradigm-shifting realisations born from the combination of consciousnesses.
- Professional and personal development is expedited through learning from peers in your network.
- The people around you contribute to shaping the perceptions others form about you through "associations". Without people, the sociopsychological principle of reciprocity cannot be executed and leveraged for mutual advantage.
- Finally, every person you know has a network of their own, which means everyone you should know becomes everyone you could know if you know the right people.

This plethora of benefits is why networking is arguably one of the most important elements for the realisation of your personal brand's potential. Behind "hello" is a world of possibilities.

What's next?

Product suites contribute to the unique DNA of a business's brand, in much the same way they do yours. By zooming out on the economy, identifying global trends, aligning these with your interests, and developing necessary key capabilities, you can radically evolve the products in your product suite. Through immersive and vicarious experience, learning, and collaborations, you can transform your key capabilities into a valuable set of products. The next chapter explores how.

Chapter 5:
Product Suites

Biological manufacturing is limitless

Breaking down the economy into its constituent parts can provide a blueprint of the value that has been assigned to the needs and wants of individuals across different domains. Here, the term value refers to units of currency, which in this case is represented by dollars. The dollar is special because instead of holding inherent value, its symbolism of value is what gives it value – it is not the material it is made from but the fact everyone believes it valuable that confers value to it. Another requirement the dollar solves is that it represents an agreed and objective value for all members of a society; therefore, creating an effective method to trade goods and services amongst one another while providing a reference value for each good or service traded.

Universal agreement on value is necessary for businesses to flourish while trading. How would a 17th century farmer, living in a remote town, know what 20 of his apples are worth without a standard currency to base it on? What value would he reference? Would he trade the apples for a bottle of moonshine? Maybe he could get a pair of boots or barter an exchange with a blacksmith? Of course, problems arise if the supply and demand for apples isn't reflected in the other goods or services being traded for them because this will create a bottleneck. The limitations of a currency-devoid environment meant that up until relatively recently in terms of modern civilisation, it would have been hard to create a profitable international empire that could run on a global scale. However, the advancement of civilisation has now led us to a time in which anything is possible. From the comfort of your own home, you can exchange goods and services with people on the other side of the world at an agreed value. All forms of business can flourish in this modern age because there are no longer geographical constraints, communication barriers, or isolated currencies that are unexchangeable outside of the societies that imagined them. How exciting!

In more technical terms, an economy encompasses all the activity related to the consumption, production, and trade of goods and services in a specific area. A free-market economy, specifically, is characterised by the voluntary exchange of goods and services based on the laws of supply and demand. The economy is an interrelated system of human labour, exchange, and consumption that can naturally form as a result of aggregated human action. It applies force on the individuals, corporations, and governing bodies that reside in it. However, forces from individuals, corporations, and governing bodies are reflected outwards, in turn causing changes to the economy itself.

Dynamic societies

Other factors contributing to economies around the world are cultural forces, laws, and their specific geographies. As a result, no two economies are identical, and even the economy of a given area can completely transform over time. This fluidity is important to understand, especially for capitalising on economic shifts. For example, the COVID pandemic completely halted certain industries (travel) while causing massive surges in others (entertainment and delivery services). By positioning your key capabilities in line with the transforming landscape, your business will be able to flourish.

A large contributor to the US economy is the media and entertainment industry. Breaking down this industry's market into consumers allows you to work out what the average spend of a US citizen is on media and entertainment. In other words, the average US citizen places a dollar value of "x" on fulfilling the need or desire that media and entertainment solves. A $20 movie may be justified to avoid boredom, temporarily hijack our attention, or to ensure that the person we've taken on a date has a fun time. In a similar manner, you can capture the value that individuals assign to their needs and wants across the board. This forms part of your market research, which ideally should be done prior to identifying the products you want to deliver.

Remember that the needs and desires of people, although individualistic in nature, are still shaped by the larger environment of society and the world. Would there be a need for a selfie stick and portable lighting apparatuses for photos if Instagram and other forms of social media were not as popular in our culture? Given the rise of technology and the continual mutation of society, a common and consistent need will continue to demand newer, more-effective solutions. The problem of transportation has been around since humans could walk; however, as societies evolved technologically and culturally, the product delivered to combat this need has evolved from horses, to 19th century automobiles, to high-tech cars, to self-driving cars, and soon likely drones. As societies continue to evolve, new needs and desires manifest, while old needs and desires will expect new solutions offered through advanced products. This dynamicity is another important factor to consider.

Goods and services

To understand products, we need to understand what is meant by goods and services. Goods are usually tangible items and can be transferred in an instant, such as pens, computers, food, machinery, and other physical objects. Intangible goods don't have a physical nature and may take the form of digital or virtual goods, such as downloadable music or mobile apps. Services on the other hand refer to the provision of activities by another person. They're described as a transaction in which no physical goods are transferred to the buyer from the seller, and the benefits of the service are usually determined by the buyer's willingness to participate in the exchange. If a service was only slightly helpful and wasn't entirely necessary, a buyer would be less likely to make an exchange with the service provider. A professional who provides a service could be a doctor, lawyer, or waiter, and, of course, the benefits of these are well known.

In addition to goods and services being traded in society, there are small permutations and slight abstractions to the rule. Some companies differentiate themselves by offering a "solution", a combination of goods and services tailored to address a specific problem that their customer may face. A screwdriver sold in isolation is a *good* and repairing something is a *service*; however, a screwdriver in an IKEA box sold with accompanying materials like screws, pieces of wood, an instruction manual, and a warranty is a solution that addresses the problem of having no way to display your belongings on your walls. The shelf and its guarantee – the good and the service – are the solution to reliably solving this problem.

Ideas

An abstract commodity takes the form of an idea. The transmission of ideas through society causes waves of change that could massively transform the overall economy. However, these are not directly monetisable goods or services until they are made real. For example, if the idea that the meat industry was unethical, unnecessary, and unhealthy spread through society, overall meat sales would take a massive hit, while purchases of plant-based alternatives are likely to skyrocket. On this, hopefully the rise of tissue engineering and biosynthetic meats foreshadow a new paradigm where commoditising the slaughtering of life becomes a thing of the past. These ideas, or mind viruses, can be packaged and weaponised by companies, causing massive economic shifts in a heartbeat. Note, creative *individuals* are producers of ideas, which represent millions to billions of dollars for companies.

A perfect case study is that of Uber, the ride-sharing company, which was started because two people had an idea about how transport should and could work in the 21st century. Their idea – personal transport – toppled the monopoly of the taxi industry, which was based on a transactional transport service that didn't always satisfy customers. This skyrocketed Uber to billion-dollar status in a few short years. As of now, they are valued at $80 billion.

On ideas, the CEO of Hewlett Packard Enterprise even went as far as saying, "We're now living in an idea economy where success is defined by the ability to turn ideas into value faster than your competitors."[1] This is proven through venture capitalists and angel investors, who will often invest $100,000s to millions of dollars in an effort to reify an idea they believe in and can profit from. The consequences – whether financial, ethical, or desirable – of ideas are the reason for the esteem they are held in and the value attributed to them.

Products

When a good, service, idea, or solution is packaged up, marketed, and sold to a customer it becomes a product. Products can be tangible or intangible and can be made up of one or a combination of the above aspects. In marketing terms, a product seeks to serve the desires of a group of people, collectively known as its target market. The perceived benefits and attributes of the product create value for the customer, and that value is realised through the exchange of dollars. The exchange of products is vital to the economy; without it, goods and services could not be sold, and people would not be able to fulfil their needs and desires.

If we reverse-engineer products though, we can logically arrive at the conclusion that every product delivered is a direct result of a key capability, or a mixture of key capabilities that someone, or a group of people, possess. A key capability is what is required to deliver a market-ready version of a good, service, idea, or solution. If one of your key capabilities is communicating, you can deliver this as a customer service product. If one of your key capabilities is sewing, your product, a good, may be knitted socks. Here is where the product element of our framework becomes interesting.

Your product suite contributes to the DNA of your personal brand.

When thinking about the consumption, production, and trade of products throughout the world, companies like Apple, Amazon, Alibaba, and Ebay are probably top of mind. Individuals regularly buy from these companies to satisfy an array of desires and needs. The iPhone could satisfy the desire of someone to fit into their peer group, who are rocking the latest version. It could satisfy the need for handheld computing power and communication, which is becoming increasingly required in our technologically driven world. In the natural progression of using an iPhone, a cracked screen usually sends people to Apple stores in search of the screen repair *service*. Subscribing to Apple music further represents a product exchange between the company and the customer in the form of an intangible good, solving the need for music on demand.

Like Apple, throughout society there are multitudes of businesses that provide certain products or suites of products to serve specific demographics. If you need accounting work done, you can call an accounting firm that you find on Google. If you are looking for a birthday cake, there are many bakeries in your immediate area that you can visit. The logo for your new business can be done by the local graphic design company that specialises in digital art. Since you have a new business, you probably need a website as well, and luckily your friend knows someone who works at a web development company. And, to top it off, it's Friday, time for your fortnightly haircut at the local barbershop. Something important to consider here is that the products offered by these businesses fundamentally entangle with their brand. It's rare for you to be familiar with a brand without knowing the products they are offering, and sometimes you can even tell what product a brand offers just by looking at their name and slogan.

Product offerings are integral pieces of a brand, although they may change over time. Your product suite therefore contributes to the DNA of your personal brand. This is illustrated in the following slogans:

- Dollar Shave Club: "Shave Time. Shave Money" – shaving products.
- BMW: "Designed for Driving Pleasure" – driving products.
- *The New York Times*: "All the News That's Fit to Print" – news and printing products.

Here's the thing though, that accounting firm you contacted for services was itself paying a person to perform the accounting service for you. The bakeries pay bakers for their service; the end result being a cake that was produced. Purchasing the cake meant you bought the labours of the baker by exchanging money with the company that paid the baker for their time. When you contacted the graphic design company, a graphic designer, an individual skilled in creating digital art, delivered your product under the alias of the company brand. The web development company you were referred to tasked a web developer, whose services they paid for under an employment contract, with your website brief. As for your haircut by a barber, you paid the shop owner, which in turn paid the barber.

All products offered by companies are derived from the key capabilities of one or many people (except where this is automation technology or highly specialised equipment), and these people could deliver the same products independent of the company if they really wanted. Obviously, as an individual, you have the capacity to produce and trade your own personal suite of products.

Key capabilities

Slowly but surely the world is converging on the notion that key capabilities are not only conducive to personal success, professional success, and wellbeing, but are required by all as we stand at the dawn of an enigmatically evolving world. A report published in 2018 by Bill Lucas, Professor of Learning, highlights the need for educational institutions and frameworks to focus their efforts toward developing capabilities to suit this landscape.[2] Australia calls them capabilities; however, they can be referred to as

21ˢᵗ-century skills, competencies, attributes, soft skills, or traits. They are defined as a cluster of knowledge and skills and, in more specific terms, are referred to as "an interweaving of knowledge, skills, attitudes, and values that form the competencies that drive actions".[3]

To summarise, capabilities comprise two key components: "know how" and "know what". Simply knowing how to do something doesn't mean you are able to perform that action. Knowing what to do doesn't mean you can perform that action to a high standard. To be capable of something you need to know what to do and how to do it, a combination of theoretical understanding and practical application. The two main domains of capabilities – highlighted in the report as significantly important for the future of work – were "personal and social capabilities" and "critical and creative thinking". The report alluded to the fact that technical knowledge, as a standalone product, performs sub-optimally in the impending new world that enforces independent career management and professional autonomy for each of its citizens.

Realising this, pressure is being applied to policymakers to enact more practical experiences, extracurricular activities, and opportunities to develop universal transferable capabilities into curricula. When managing your own professional development, it's worthwhile understanding the current state of affairs, and that following the experts' lead ensures you remain competitive and relevant. Paying attention to the development of your own key capabilities is something you ought to do. If you don't want to listen to me, here's what the Organisation for Economic Co-operation and Development says about the future:

> *To prepare for 2030, people should be able to think creatively, develop new products and services, new jobs, new processes and methods, new ways of thinking and living, new enterprises, new sectors, new business models and new social models.[3]*

Capabilities to products

You have your own dynamic product suite and are continually exchanging this with others in one form or another. For example, if you are working as an independent graphic designer, you are selling products you have created from your key capabilities to customers, which could be other people or large organisations. Your key capabilities – your proficiency in graphic design software, your understanding and application of marketing and design principles, your technical knowledge required for the delivery of different design formats, your ability to communicate effectively with other people, the creative process you have developed and refined over time to come up with new, attention-grabbing visuals for your customers – all result in the unique product suite you offer: logos and brand design consulting.

Let us step into the role of the graphic designer. When someone comes to you for a logo for their new business, they are not coming to you for a logo. They are coming to you for a good logo that performs its function properly. A good logo is informed and targeted and conveys the unspoken message of the business and brand it represents. For this to happen, the logo needs to leverage industry knowledge, expert insights, and professional design skills that you as the designer possess. If your unique capabilities weren't valuable, the person would make their own logo or throw money at anyone who could vaguely navigate design software.

The initial engagement of you by the person takes shape as a consult, which is a service. As the graphic designer, you need to understand what the customer requires in their logo, what it represents, and how it matches their preconceived ideas. You need to guide them on what will and will not work. You need to provide expert input regarding the design parameters and colour schemes. You need to engage in a process of ideation to collaboratively generate new logo ideas if the initial ones are no longer feasible. In this initial phase of your service, you are leveraging your key capabilities through effective communication, collaboration, creativity, and your understanding and application of marketing and design principles.

The next part of your service is physically designing the logo concepts for your customer, which leverages your capabilities relating to graphic design software and the application of your technical knowledge. After some back-and-forth emails with your client, you arrive at the end result: a professional-looking logo that accurately represents the client's new business and brand while simultaneously aligning with their expectations. You deliver the logo to the client, an intangible good, and receive your payment upon completion of the job. The combination of the goods and services you delivered resulted in a product that satisfied the needs of your client. Your key capabilities are the prerequisites – the special ingredients you use to generate your goods, services, ideas, and solutions – which are then packaged and sold as products to customers in your target market.

Evolving capabilities

There are many different types of independent professionals with an enormous and consistently evolving suite of products that they deliver to customers. This idea is being realised by people all over the world, representing one of the reasons why the gig economy is surging ahead. Over one-third of the US workforce are already gig workers, with projections from 2020 onwards forecasting a dramatic increase. As discussed in the *Introduction*, the gig economy refers to a new economic environment characterised by a shift from traditional nine-to-five employment modes to one where independent professionals perform work on a task-by-task basis for various employers concurrently. Employers can be individuals, agencies, or corporate customers.

> ## Each of us has a completely unique suite of products to sell, derived from our key capabilities.

People are becoming disenchanted with the tedious routines associated with nine-to-five employment and are trading in normality, mundanity, and micromanagement for flexibility, autonomy, and independence. This paradigm shift helps to clarify the innate business capacity that we each possess as capable people. The products you offer form part of your personal brand, no different to the way products offered by businesses contribute to their brand. Each of us has a completely unique suite of products to sell, derived from our key capabilities. We all did the moment we landed our first job. Traditional employment is nothing more than an exchange of services from an employee to an organisation. Employers pay you for the products you deliver to them and their clients.

In the last example, we were an independent graphic designer working for ourselves. If our client is now our employer, there is not much difference. When we work for an employer as a graphic designer: we carry out our key capabilities on behalf of the organisation to their clients or provide work directly to the organisation itself (it is just one big client we are continually serving our products to). You are a business, whether you are working for yourself or an employer. In both instances, you are charging a nominal value for the products you deliver to your end customer. Therefore, in the traditional work environment, your employer is your customer, but in the gig economy, anyone and everyone can be.

The dynamic nature of the product suite we offer to the world is achievable through novel applications of our existing key capabilities and the acquisition of new capabilities. For instance, if we were to take the existing key capabilities from the previous example – a proficiency in graphic design software, understanding and applying marketing and design principles, an ability to communicate effectively with other people, and a creative process that has been developed and refined over time – we could offer a completely unique product by focusing our efforts in a different direction.

Instead of delivering a graphic design logo service, the culmination of these key capabilities focused through a different lens would enable us to perform well in the digital content creation space for social media (if we wanted to carve out a niche there). Thus, another product we could offer from our existing capabilities takes the form of creative digital content for marketing purposes instead of the traditional logo and business branding we were previously practising. In delivering this product we would be serving a new customer emerging from a new demographic. If we were to acquire yet new key capabilities, such as copyrighting knowledge and skills, proper research practices, and expertise in marketing analytics software, for example, we would be able to add even more goods and services to our product suite, allowing us to offer an advanced marketing product to customers.

We can design creative digital content to a high standard, deploy it alongside accompanying copy utilising knowledge of marketing principles, and further add value by identifying the psychographics of our ideal customer while monitoring and analysing the performance of the marketing campaign. This is the type of product a marketer sells to a company as an employee. However, this could be sold to many customers concurrently by an independent professional under the guise of a marketing consultant in the gig economy. And probably for much more than the marketer makes as an employee. But the lesser salary of the employee is the cost of comfort and security. Who knows when your next pay cheque is coming if you are the one responsible for sourcing your next client?

Needs and desires

Before you can offer products, you need to know two things:
1. The needs and desires of the people you can serve, especially the evolving needs and desires of society.

2. What products your key capabilities can give rise to.

Without understanding the needs and desires of your customers, you do not have a product. Without a market you cannot exchange the goods and services in your product suite. If you had a key capability that enabled you to throw a ball in the air and catch it, it would be hard for you to exchange this service with anyone because not many people find this valuable, and the majority can do this themselves. Consequently, this capability does not lead to a viable product. However, if you did it in an entertaining way, progressed from throwing and catching one ball to three balls, and put on a clown suit, you would now be offering a service, a product that a parent hosting their child's fifth birthday would pay for.

There is a spectrum that your key capabilities and the desires and needs that other people will pay to fulfil, sits on. For you to generate and refine your valuable product suite, you will need to spend time researching the economic landscape and explore different products that you could offer through key capabilities that you have or could develop. By identifying your key capabilities and understanding the needs of your customers, you can determine the products you can provide. Determining the value of these products relates to supply and demand and how much your customer wants to fulfil the desire or need you offer an antidote for.

Starting from the ground, imagine we have finished Year 12 and are about to start job hunting. To know what jobs we are eligible for, we first need to know what products our key capabilities will allow us to deliver. An average 18 year old may be capable of taking instructions and using a computer, communicating with others, and movement. If we package up the capability of "taking instructions and using a computer", it could be sold as services to a company in the form of a data entry product. We could transcribe words from paper to a computer database and be paid for it (assuming we have basic literacy capabilities). The key capability of "communicating with others" would see us eligible for a call centre job. We could sell our communication abilities to call centres as a product. Lastly, being able to "move" qualifies us for physical labour jobs, such as lawnmowing or pick-packing in warehouses. We can deliver these capabilities as products to customers. These jobs are all well and good, but there comes a time when career aspirations pull us forward, and for them to be realised we need to start adding new capabilities – the building blocks of our product suite.

Refining capabilities

Upon turning 19 years old, the once-enthusiastic warehouse pick-packer comes to a realisation: no longer do they want to be bossed around and treated as dispensable. A year in the trenches and maturity have slowly begun to alter their perspective. Instead, they want to feel empowered, important, earn more money, and consequently move up the proverbial ranks of the organisation to achieve a warehouse manager role. However, blocking their path is a key capability misalliance. Some of the key capabilities required for this managerial position are not the same capabilities our aspirational pick-packer currently possesses or can demonstrate. Warehouse managers are responsible for (amongst other things):

- maintaining the operational capacity of the warehouse by following procedures and policies
- achieving financial objectives by preparing annual budgets
- managing staff
- controlling inventory levels of the warehouse by conducting physical counts and liaising with key team members
- safeguarding the warehouse by establishing and monitoring security protocols and procedures.

In other words, to be a warehouse manager, capabilities are required, such as:

- running a business
- basic financial literacy and annual budget savviness
- leadership, empathy, and effective communication
- diligence and collaboration
- initiative, problem-solving, and vigilance.

Meaning that if there is any chance for Peter the Packer to secure this role, he must acquire and demonstrate these key capabilities.

Currently, the way employers or other potential customers understand your key capabilities is by looking at your work history, education, and life experiences. From an employer's point of view, it is easy to qualify someone for a job if they have previously worked in a similar role because they have already demonstrated the required key capabilities. Another easy way for them to be sure of your key capabilities is to upgrade you from role to role in a hierarchical fashion, because as you progress through each role you add another set of demonstrated key capabilities to your personal brand. Moving from a pick-packer at a warehouse, to team leader, supervisor, assistant warehouse manager, and then to a senior warehouse manager mitigates risk for employers as the amount of key capabilities you need to add for each subsequent role is minimal, therefore achievable and manageable. As an assistant warehouse manager, the only key capabilities you may need to refine or add in your quest for the warehouse manager role is improved organisational, project management, and problem-solving skills, while evidencing a newfound leadership capability. All other capabilities have already been demonstrated along the steppingstones of your career journey.

In this instance, the 19 year old would need to develop or acquire new capabilities while refining existing ones. Demonstrating these capabilities further adds credibility to their personal brand because actions speak louder than words. Platitudinal but relevant.

There are several ways key capabilities come into being. Disregarding the plight of Peter the Packer, let's tease out how anyone, including you, can develop, refine, and master new capabilities.

Immersive experience

First, experience. Experience is a teacher, a truly interactive and potentially unforgiving one at that, which may be why it is so effective. It follows then that to develop key capabilities you need to place yourself into new and challenging situations where you can learn and develop through experience. Public speaking is one example that hits home for me. I was terrified of public speaking from a young age, which was likely the result of a traumatic experience I had when I was six, where an assembly hall full of students laughed at me and my nervous, squeaky voice. However, this changed when I turned 22. I was faced with a difficult situation: pitch for investment in front of 500 people at a fundraising event and risk re-triggering an old trauma followed by severe embarrassment or, risk my first start-up company failing due to lack of funds. After a pros and cons analysis, where I weighed up each of pitching in front of 500 people, I concluded that the potential for severe embarrassment was a necessary risk given the abysmal financial state of my start-up company. I attended the event, ended up pitching rather well, and learned a lot. Much more than I would have had I not engaged in a novel and challenging experience.

At a neurophysiological level – or at the level of basic brain functioning – we hold attraction to novelty in high regard (unless the novel experience activates your phobia). As humans, we are naturally inclined to seek out new and unfamiliar stimuli and environments. In the neuroscience world this is referred to as novelty seeking and is mediated by our neurochemistry. There are many other ways our neurochemistry exerts powerful influences over the seemingly mundane nature of our daily lives. For example, when we experience eating food, our brain chemistry changes, and this impacts our future actions. In a similar way, sex can also change our brain chemistry. When we eat (or have sex) we feel pleasure, satisfaction, and happiness. These emotions are guided by molecules that are acting on our body and brain, and some of these same molecules motivate and guide our future behaviours. It's why food and sex are like drugs that some of us are unhealthily addicted to.

In all cases, when we experience something there is a cascade of events that occur deep within our brain, some of which are unconscious, which contribute to alterations in our future behaviour. This translates into what we know as learning and demonstrates the neurophysiological link between experiencing something and subsequently learning from it. In the earlier examples, we *learnt* at a neurophysiological level from our pleasurable experiences. We have been conditioned to enthusiastically chase down mating partners and binge on burgers, and we can give a lot of thanks to dopamine for this pleasure.

Dopamine is a neurotransmitter that modulates motivation and learning in the brain and is also responsible for the mysterious attraction we have for novelty.[4,5,6] New experiences often enable us to learn valuable information, which is why this powerful and influential molecule has lent its efforts to embedding this "novelty-seeking" drive deep within our mental machinery. The molecules that run your body are telling you something. If dopamine could verbalise its life mission, it would be something along the lines of: "to cause my human to learn valuable and new information through driving them to expose themselves to novel and challenging experiences". In support of dopamine, I would encourage you to pursue new and challenging experiences for exactly that reason.

We don't just learn at a neurophysiological level. We also learn at a psychological level through experience. This is an obvious one when we consider how people can make us feel and how this changes our behaviour. When we spend time with new people, we make judgements about them based on what they say, how they make us feel, and how they fit into our lives. If someone is conversing with us and we notice inconsistencies in what they are saying, and we pick up on some worrying nonverbal behaviours, we make a judgement call in our minds. We might put a mental sticky note next to them that says "untrustworthy, full of shit, and time waster". We've met people like this before and we know how it ends. As such, the labelling of this person is a result of our learning from previous experiences. We've already been down a road with shady characters who lack integrity, and the journey was archived and categorised in our mind. This judgement is therefore an informed psychological one, guided by previous experiences.

> # Many of our interpersonal skills are developed and refined through experiences with other people.

The importance of this aspect of learning is that many of our interpersonal skills, such as empathy, communication, leadership, active listening, and relationship management, are developed and refined through experiences with other people. These are processed and learnt at a psychological level.

It makes sense then that the best way for us to learn, develop, and demonstrate interpersonal capabilities is to put ourselves in a position where we can do this in real time, with real feedback, and real consequences. Firsthand experience is the most immersive type of experience. It's why volunteering and doing extracurricular activities that put you in these positions are beneficial for your employability. Not everyone likes the sound of volunteering at a charity for three months, but every employer and your many social capabilities will thank you for it. Trading three months of your time for a good cause, while learning, developing, and refining key interpersonal skills, is a perfect way to increase the amount of demonstrated key capabilities you have to offer. The personal growth you undergo that results from the development and diversification of your key capabilities is facilitated and expedited by real-world opportunities. Not to mention, the formal experience you can attach to your journey contributes to the overall unique value encompassed by your personal brand.

There are of course certain experiences that you can't have in the real world, and because of this your experiential learning capacity is capped. For example, there are geographical constraints, an absence of opportunities, and circumstantial limitations that restrict the experiences you can expose yourself to. Your remoteness may mean there are fewer opportunities to pursue and learn from. The business topography of your area may not support the kinds of industries or positions you're interested in. It's also hard to get someone to give you a chance to develop and gain experience when there's nothing in it for them and you've got none of the pre-requisite skills.

When you get to the later stages of your career, gaining experience for your next senior role comprises the same problems but for different reasons. How can you gain experience at a level above your current role when every time you make a vertical step toward the top of the hierarchy, the number of roles for you to develop in diminishes? Even if you have managed to source yourself an experiential learning position, like an internship, volunteer work, shadow role, or paid work (despite being paid, every position you do confers experience), there are still unforeseeable events that can occur, which can perturb the normal learning trajectory that you would expect. Meaning that despite tenure in certain roles, the learning you undergo and the capabilities you develop can differ depending on global, cultural, corporate, personal, and political forces. For instance, a web developer working during the dot com bubble in Silicon Valley for a large billion-dollar tech company will not learn and develop the same capabilities as their counterpart who worked in a bootstrapped start-up with a team of four, during a pandemic, in a country that, in contrast, didn't hold technology in high esteem.

The unique nature of these experiences can be viewed favourably or negatively. Novelty exposes us to new and potentially valuable lessons that we can archive for later. It helps us build new sets of key capabilities that we can develop and convert into monetisable products. But the roll of the dice experience we are subject to may mean we miss out on key learnings and neglect developing valuable capabilities. It is for these reasons that your experiential learning ability is capped, to your detriment. We need exposure to as many challenging, thought-provoking, and unique educational experiences as we can if we are to develop and refine key capabilities. The remedy for this problem is to experience as many situations, roles, industries, fields of study, and professional worlds as you can, vicariously, that is.

Vicarious experiences are real in your mind

Mirror neurons make vicarious learning possible. Mirror neurons, discussed in *Chapter 4*, were accidentally discovered in the 1990s by an Italian neuroscientist. After conducting a series of stock-standard experiments on monkey brains using electroencephalographs (which measure the electrical activity of the brain), it was discovered that whenever a monkey watched another monkey do something, its brain lit up with activity in much the same way it would if it was actually carrying out the behaviour itself. After this discovery, a large research effort followed. Many scientists have since realised we have neural networks that activate when we perform an action or experience an emotion, and that these same neural networks activate when we observe someone else undergoing these. Whether we observe it or perform it ourselves, our brain still activates in the same way. A pioneer of mirror neuron research, Marco Iacoboni, explains that the reason movies feel so authentic to us is:

> *…because mirror neurons in our brain recreate for us the distress we see on the screen. We have empathy for the fictional characters – we know how they're feeling – because we literally experience the same feelings ourselves. And when we watch the movie stars kiss on screen? Some of the cells firing in our brain are the same ones that fire when we kiss our lovers. "Vicarious" is not a strong enough word to describe these mirror neurons.*

Further reviews have even pointed out that our mirror neurons activate in response to a coach's demonstration of a technique, internal visualisation of proper form, and by television, film, visual art, and pornography.[7] Studies have demonstrated that sentences that describe action movements, such as, "I grasp the knife with my hand" or, "I kick the ball", activate systems in our brains resembling the systems we activate when we execute the described action.[8] This proves that narration itself has a mysterious ability to activate networks of mirror neurons in our brains. Building on this, Suzanne Keen, Professor of English, postulated that narrative fiction may be the key to building empathy through the activation of mirror neurons that occurs when we are exposed to, and identify with, new characters and narratives.[9]

Mar, Oatley, and Peterson went one step further and tested whether heavy amounts of fiction reading improved social skills. The outcome positively correlated empathy with fiction reading after extraneous variables were accounted for and causality was determined. In other words, improved social capabilities, such as empathy, was a proven result of reading fiction.[10] It's not a far stretch considering that processing emotionally laden sentences can activate facial muscles that express corresponding emotions, hinting at the inextricable link between language comprehension, emotional processing pathways, and motor system activation. Understanding happy sentences activates muscles in our face that are associated with smiling, while sad and angry sentences activate muscles that are associated with frowning.[11]

Neuroscientists now confidently demonstrate that emotions can be represented in a subject's brain by experiencing the emotion firsthand, seeing someone experiencing the emotion, or through an emotion-fuelled story.[12] If someone tastes something disgusting, sees someone else taste something disgusting, or hears a disgusting story, in all three scenarios their brain will activate a common area. One of the researchers stated, "This is why books and movies work, because they stimulate the area of the brain which is involved in what it really feels like."

I was always amazed by my introverted brother's superfast processing speed, ability to remember information, and natural wit, especially since he spent 95 percent of his time couped up in his bedroom bombarding himself with movies, games, and other forms of entertainment. But now it seems that his infatuation with the virtual world provided his mind with an unrivalled amount of simulations, and contrary to popular belief these comprised unique learning experiences. How can I ever win an argument with him when he has experienced and learnt from a thousandfold more social scenarios, conflicts, and heated arguments than I have?

This is scratching the surface of the science that points to humans as powerful walking simulators that can learn from firsthand experience, observations, spoken stories, books, internal visualisations, and forms of entertainment that mimic reality. We are built to learn vicariously, it is in our DNA, and the systems responsible for making it happen come hardcoded in our brains. The science even goes one step further and says that we don't just learn it vicariously, we embody it. We feel, experience, and internally represent much of what we are exposed to, and we can do this without a firsthand immersive, face-to-face encounter.

When people tell us a story about something that happened to them in a place we've never visited, in a situation we'd never experience, while performing actions foreign to us, we experience much of their experience through our built-in mirror neuron functionality as it processes the information they convey. We activate the muscles associated with the emotions they tell us about. We empathise with them, feeling what they feel. And we turn on neural networks of mirror neurons, mentally representing the actions they are displaying to us. We may not actually execute the flying kicks and frantic gestures that our friend dutifully demonstrates as they explain their story, but internally those gestures and the karate kick are happening; they are simulated, along with the emotions that were relayed to us through their narration. We may never have travelled to Zimbabwe and landed ourselves in a situation where we had to somersault out of a moving truck like our friend, but from our brain's point of view, or our "mind's eye", being there and experiencing it vicariously aren't all that different.

If you take a moment to think about it, it's clear that fictional scenarios nested in make-believe worlds can impact our psychological, physiological, and behavioural state. All the happy films you've watched, actually made *you* happy. Your psychological state changed. In the not-so-happy film, when an axe murderer hid behind a door and the naïve girl walked across the room oblivious to her impending bloody death, your heartbeat and breathing sped up, and your flight-or-fight mode turned on. Physiologically, you were affected. When a scary, developmentally challenged poltergeist-zombie hybrid jumps out from the shadows of the screen, you jump, behaving in a startled manner, as if the pixels can actually take a chunk out of your face.

Sometimes, the rolling credits of a movie or the earth-shattering implications of documentaries you watch sends your mind into overdrive. Forms of entertainment can lead you to develop new understandings, new feelings, and altered perspectives that impact life as you know it. Many a time, high percentages of people – after being mortified by documentaries showing the inhumane footage normally hidden behind the closed doors of the meat industry – decide to alter their once-carnivorous life path in pursuit of animal rights. This comes as a result not of firsthand experience, but of vicarious experience. They never did touch a sullen cow or see firsthand a pig take its last breath before it was transformed into a packaged good, but from what they experienced through their TV, they might as well have. This reinforces that there's little difference between vicariously experiencing something mentally or being physically there. We process it in the same way. So, how does this relate to you developing your key capabilities?

Virtual reality

To remedy the limiting problems we face in the "real world", we need to venture out with our minds. We need to identify and locate sources of information required for us to develop some of the key capabilities that our firsthand experience may be reluctant to offer. There are books on absolutely every topic under the sun, written by a diversified pool of experts, each with their own life experiences, personalities, and perspectives. There are nonfictional and fictional forms of entertainment from different genres and different eras, each conveying a unique message and feeling. Everyone you meet, or could meet, is a walking nonfictional, autobiographical storyteller who is often willing to share personal adventures with those willing to listen (assuming the person you meet isn't a pathological liar, otherwise you'd get a story strongly nested in fiction).

We can use the above to our advantage by understanding the power of our virtual-reality-simulating mind. In this sense, we can expose ourselves to an incomprehensible number of situations, assimilate facts and perspectives from different mediums of information, and gain unique insights and understandings to influence our key capability trajectories in much the same way real-world experience does. We may never gain the real-world experience we need to develop our management capabilities, but we can read management books, watch documentaries about great managers, and go for coffee with a manager to pick their brain. Not only are the lessons directly transferable, but doing these things may also present new paths of inquiry, leading to the expansion of our knowledge bank of relevant information. The above mediums contribute, in subtly different ways, to the development of our key management capabilities in similar ways to that of real-world experience. However, unlike real-world experience, we are not constrained by circumstantial limitations, an absence of opportunities, or geographical barriers. Reality is in the mind and our mind can go anywhere.

Education and micro-credentials

Aside from "real" experience and virtual simulations, education is another obvious way to develop key capabilities. Education differs from merely "experiencing" something; the delineation evidenced mainly by differences in outcomes. Effective education aims to bring about an inherent or permanent change in your thinking and capacity to do things. Learning, or educational experiences, are traditionally nested in classrooms, guided and facilitated by educators. However, without fundamental behavioural and knowledge shifts, such learning experiences can become nothing more than an experience. In the same vein, there are situations where experiences alone mimic educational learning experiences and, in some cases, result in more profound realisations and insights than any theoretical educational framework could ever teach.

Physically experiencing something allows you to apply theoretical understandings, which is why immersive activities grounded in reality are still of paramount importance. Targeted real-world experiences in conjunction with focused, high-quality education provide the recipe for key capability development, refinement, and mastery. What better way to demonstrate your scientific capabilities than previous work experience at a bioscience laboratory with a Master of Science behind your name?

One of the most influential frameworks dominating the structure of formal education was developed by educational psychologist Benjamin Bloom. The framework, widely known as Bloom's Taxonomy, is a comprehensive system that describes and assesses educational outcomes. Bloom created a hierarchy for human thinking capabilities and broke them down into six categories:

1. **Knowledge.** This relates to recalling or remembering previously learned information to draw out factual answers. A question testing this may be along the lines of, is this following statement true or false?

2. **Comprehension.** This is demonstrated when someone is able to grasp or understand the meaning of educational materials. For example, being able to "describe" or "explain" relevant information.

3. **Application.** This is the application of previously learnt information (or knowledge) to unfamiliar situations. Can you "demonstrate" how to use this information when presented with a new situation?

4. **Analysis.** This is evidenced when someone can break down information into parts and examine them by understanding the organisational structure of information. "Comparing", "classifying", and "arranging" information demonstrates this capability.

5. **Evaluation.** This involves judging or deciding according to sets of criteria without real right or wrong answers. When you "summarise" or "conclude" you are evidencing this level.

6. **Create.** This is demonstrated by applying prior skills and knowledge to combine elements into a pattern that did not exist before. "Creativity" in a specific field is the epitome of human learning capabilities.

As a student moves through the hierarchy and reaches higher levels, the extent of their "learning" improves. This type of framework underlies most of the formal education delivered by schools, universities, and TAFEs throughout the world, and testing an individual's learning using this hierarchy enables institutions to accurately assess where students are at. The result being that upon completion of a year level, unit, certificate, or degree, the educational institution can demonstrate that students have reached a certain level of education and now demonstrate a certain set of "key capabilities". Meaning they can now vouch for students' employability - their ability to monetise their capabilities as products, in said fields of study.

Up to 40 percent of existing university degrees will be obsolete, and post-study job prospects will continue to decline.

When you think of developing and refining key capabilities through education, more often than not universities will be the first to come to mind. Universities with established courses are usually a safe bet; however, we live in a radically transforming world. Moving forward, the economy could best be summarised as a volatile state of flux fuelled by the collective and unrelenting progressive efforts of humanity. As global disruptions happen at one end of the planet and are made readily available to the other end of the planet, within days or weeks entire industries may be severely impacted overnight. When an intelligent robot with machine-learning capabilities and heightened physical dexterity is developed in the labs of Japan, it's not just factory workers there who will soon be bowing out of their jobs, it will be Australian factory workers as well. Recently, whispers have been circulating that artificial intelligence may wipe out the accounting industry as a whole, or at the least, radically transform it.

A four-year, well-established degree, even when delivered by an innovative university, now bears risks that were alien to it a decade ago. By the time a student completes the degree, the industry they are looking to enter may not exist anymore or may have advanced so rapidly that the majority of their teachings are now obsolete. Take, for example, a marketing degree. Marketing now comprises email campaigns, social media advertising, SEO optimisation, and the exploitation of cookies (otherwise known as browser trackers). If you completed a marketing degree before the advent of the digital world, you would still be dealing with printed adverts in magazines. The void between your marketing capabilities and those required today would result in your professional obsolescence. Consider a computer science degree that teaches programming in a specific coding language only to have industry develop and refine their own, like Google's Go. Industry and innovation can evidently outrun traditional education models.

A 2018 report from EY titled, *Can the universities of today lead learning for tomorrow?*[13] explores the problem in detail. University leaders stated that up to 40 percent of existing university degrees will be obsolete, and post-study job prospects will continue to decline. The report highlighted five main global forces of disruption to the traditional education paradigm as we know it. These are:

1. the changing world of work
2. the rise of continuous learning
3. the blurring of industry boundaries
4. increased international competition
5. evolving digital behaviour.

The report draws attention to the fact that the educational value offered by a traditional university will need to completely transform to meet the demands of the new world. The highly sought-after remedy to these vexing problems is being realised through micro-credentials. The credentials, sometimes interchangeably referred to as nano-credentials or digital badges, are gaining significant momentum. So much so that they have overcome the institutional inertia of large universities and have forced their way into the curriculum, with many universities pivoting to adopt and integrate them.

Micro-credentials are certificate-like qualifications individuals can choose to study if they are looking to improve a skill found in a particular industry. You could think of these as targeted capability developers. Most of them are short, low-cost, online alternatives to the long, expensive, and content-heavy university courses. Upon completion, users are given a digital badge or certificate that contributes to their employability by demonstrating proficiencies in certain capabilities.

For example, a company looking for a web developer to code in Python doesn't need someone with a Master in Computer Science. Instead, they need someone who's completed an eight-week Advanced Python Coding micro-credential. As a result, academic transcripts are being traded in for digital badges. Given their agile nature, micro-credentials are developed with industry and employment in mind and aim to meet specific needs, which are sometimes neglected through higher educational courses. The laser-focused content, aiming to teach one capability well, leapfrogs the tedious and redundant content necessitated by traditional educational institutions. Nano study modes should be seriously considered when you are looking to develop and deploy your targeted set of products.

Capability mergers and acquisitions

Humanity has come a long way since the Stone Age, where basic tools and weapons were forged by the sweat off the brow of our primitive ancestors. Creating these low-tech hunter-gatherer tools required only one of the tribe to exert directed effort in pursuit of their spearheaded goal. As civilisation approached mediaeval times, specialists in this craft earned themselves the title of stonemason. These individuals were highly capable in this niche area of work and were regarded as the expert craftspeople of their time. The best and most experienced stonemasons went on to earn the title of a master mason and were regularly contracted to work in neighbouring towns, giving rise to their nomadic lifestyle.

Nowadays, genetic engineers, lawyers, psychologists, doctors, physicists, computer scientists, designers, biotechnologists, and web developers drive and fly around the world pursuing work that their professional titles crown them capable of doing. The difference between the mediaeval stonemason and the modern masterful worker are the interdependencies of modern-day professions and the infinitely complex state of affairs they operate in. This is fuelled by an unrelenting influx of new information. Unlike the stonemason, who lived in a pre-connected, dramatically less informed world that relied largely on their own skills and knowledge, the professionals of the future are standing on the shoulders of giants and peering down into seemingly infinite pools of information.

An illuminating example is the still-mystifying human body, despite how informed of it we supposedly are. We all exist as one individual. Universally, our anatomy and physiology hasn't changed over the 300,000-year period that marked the first fossilised discovery of *Homo sapiens*. Yet even with a 300,000-year runway – amongst the backdrop of a digitally connected world populated by over 7 billion bright minds, boasting an ever-growing pool of scientific research, and at a time when global collaboration and ultra-specialisation is the norm – we still can't overcome allergies, stimulate hair growth naturally, regrow organs, eliminate cancer, cure diabetes, or overcome viruses. There are hundreds if not thousands more conditions that currently have no effective treatments, and this isn't even touching on the psychological realms where even our own consciousness and the nature of psychopathologies still perplex us.

For a modern-day professional, especially those concerned with the human condition, to know all there is to know about their field of study, like their tool-crafting counterparts, they can only hope to do so if they are physically enhanced through advancements in technology and bioengineering. If they were able to upgrade themselves to a point where they had much more neural processing power and could access, process, retain, and synthesise all the information relating to their specialty area that was available, maybe then they would reach the limits of knowledge in their field, mirroring the accomplishments of the 15th century master mason. If, however, these human upgrades evade us, key capability interdependencies are all we have.

For example, the designers of the future will need to know how to design in augmented reality frameworks, will need to know what aesthetically appeals to constantly evolving societies and demographics, and will forever be engulfed by huge technological advancements and disruptions in their industry. Their craft will be influenced by computer science, psychology, sociology, and data science. How can a designer effectively deliver their design capabilities without collaborating with experts in their fields? Surely, there is no way they can single-handedly process and act on all the information found in these specialty fields themselves?

A psychologist of the future will need to adapt to the constantly evolving fields of psychology, cognition, and neurophysiology. What will happen if ground-breaking discoveries create new links between fields of computer science, emotions, and neurochemistry? The traditionally trained psychologist will need to work with a computer scientist and neurochemist to effectively treat a 22nd century patient; a therapeutic approach that would be reliant on capabilities rarely possessed by one person alone. Collaboration through key capability sharing is needed here.

Let's dive deeper and slide an oncologist under the microscope. This distinguished cancer clinician spends three years in undergraduate training, four years in postgraduate medical school, three years in an internal medicine residency program and follows through with a three-year clinical fellowship. Yet, at the end of this academic journey, none of these professionals reach the ceiling of their field of study, evidenced by the fact that cancer still exists and continues to make a mockery of the smartest minds on the planet (hopefully not for much longer).

Furthermore, there are thousands of oncologists and cancer scientists working daily to find a cure. Yet despite combined global efforts and the current state of technology and knowledge, they have been unable to achieve this end. Even though the cure for this apparently unsolvable complex series of physiological events that results in immortalised cancer cells still evades us, it is only through this combined global effort that the cure can be realised. Without collaboration, a cure for these misguided and unnatural cellular armies is unequivocally impossible.

Therefore, the capability of understanding and curing cancer is unachievable by an individual. Instead, it is an emergent capability generated by the global scientific research community, made possible by the key capabilities contributed by each individual that constitutes it. The point here is that no one individual in today's modern landscape can reach the capability limits in their own profession or field of research in which they are deemed an expert without being reliant on the key capabilities of others.

Another concept to think about is the merging of two niche professional worlds, each powered by the key capabilities of their professional inhabitants. The legal arena usually exists independently of genetic research, but sometimes they do collide. It is unlikely that a genetic engineer will ever become a lawyer and be able to effectively maintain and deliver both professional services to a high standard. If the genetic engineer is concentrating on delivering high-quality genetics research while remaining well versed on the constantly evolving genomics, bioinformatics, and genetics literature, it is likely their ability to deliver high-quality legal services will be negatively impacted. This is true for many other interdisciplinary scenarios and is why the aphorism "the jack of all trades is the master of none" is cemented in our societal diction.

There is a natural limit to *Homo sapiens*, preventing us from operating as supercomputers, and, as such, interdependencies are everywhere. In this scenario, what is the genetic engineer to do when they synthesise a novel sequence of DNA that proves to be an effective therapy for reconstituting the elasticity of skin? The synthetic nature of this DNA warrants it patentable, and the next logical step for the genetic engineer is to defend their IP, without which they cannot build a viable therapeutics company. The genetic engineer is unlikely to simultaneously be acting as a lawyer, and even if that was the case, presumably wouldn't be operating in this capacity effectively. It is at this point that there exists another key capability interdependency. To properly carry out their personal, professional, and research-related goals, this biological engineer needs to somehow acquire intellectual property-related legal capabilities. The genetic engineer can acquire these by partnering with a lawyer, contracting a lawyer for a service, obtaining a lawyer through employment, or by leaning on a friend who happens to be a lawyer for a favour. In all cases, for the engineer to be capable of formulating and delivering their skin-rejuvenating synthetic DNA therapeutic, they are reliant on another individual with a different set of capabilities.

Modern society is built on interdependencies similar to the nature of these types of relationships. However, the economic environment and globalisation means newer, faster, and more valuable interdependencies are continually being realised. In the absence of leveraging the key capabilities of other people, we would be back banging out our own Stone Age tools, unaware of what we could achieve through effective collaboration. It is for this reason that the acquisition of capabilities through relationships with others is highlighted. After all, if you own a software engineering company and want to move into web design, the first thing you're going to do is hire a web designer and bring that key capability inhouse. It's that simple.

The economy is in constant flux, but at this point in time humanity as a whole is functioning at superhuman capacity. The consequences of this are that, as a capable individual looking to flourish professionally, you need to always be observant of the rapidly transforming ecosystem that engulfs you, as this demands continually evolving products. Traditionally, goods and services were the footholds of trade, but in this newer age, solutions and ideas are becoming more impactful.

To sum up

Understanding the different types of products you can offer allows you to look down on the world from a different vantage point, illuminating areas of opportunity that you can capitalise on. Your key capabilities are what give rise to every form of product you can offer. Today, there is a universal push in the educational sphere to develop similar key capabilities in the youth to prepare them for the future of work. Just like the youth, you should also accept your status as a learner and aim to continually develop, refine, and master key capabilities. There is no room for stagnancy, and, as such, you should aim to experience (whether immersively or vicariously) as many novel, challenging, and relevant situations as you can to develop your arsenal of key capabilities.

You need to inform yourself through education in a mode of study that works for you, and you need to identify your limitations, leverage your networks, and attain the key capabilities that you require through other people, especially if the product you seek to deliver is born by the emergent capabilities of many. Hopefully, it is now clear that your unique and valuable product suite contributes to the DNA of your personal brand and is fundamentally important for personal flourishing and the realisation of your 21st century potential.

What's next?

In the whole world, of all the technologies that exist, *Homo sapiens* is the most advanced. Through an amazingly sophisticated interplay of biological and psychological forces, us humans perceive, interpret, and assign meaning to every waking moment, culminating them in a stream of experiences, which, when woven together, forms our consciousness. Our body has evolved over millennia; the conscious mind and language, however, are more recent additions. In the same way that understanding the mechanics and evolution of businesses leads to valuable insights, so too is it valuable to understand how individuals experience life. This experience is of growing importance.

Chapter 6:
Hijacking the Human Experience

Despite living in a shared social reality, biology still has a mighty influence

Modern-day marketing long ago transitioned from superficial, materialistic advertisements and now aims to generate *feelings* and meaningful connections in unknowing prospects. Marauding marketers in their quest to steal your attention utilise psychology, neuroscience, and emotional manipulation to effectively impact the experiences you are subject to in daily life, which, when done properly, signals big dollars for the companies they serve.

21st century experience-based marketing is like 1950s marketing on steroids and is as different as modern-day virtual reality simulators are to the primitive black and white movie reels of old. However, this shift to immersive experience also represents the evolution of marketing. Your conscious experience is as immersive as it gets, and despite being your personal and private interface with the world, to a marketer it is another opportunity to pull dollars from your pockets.

A large component of this experience is your feelings, and this is one way you are blindsided. The feelings generated when you interact with a company, product, or company representative (a customer service representative or salesperson, for example) are engineered. In most cases, modern-day marketing efforts are used to manipulate you in the hope you'll transition into a paying customer, and once there they aim to keep you there. Just as a marketer carefully crafts a personal experience for you, you too, as a biological business, possess the ability to engineer personal experiences for others.

This chapter provides the information you need to properly harness the power of a *personal experience*. However, to pull off a weaponised marketing experience, you first have to understand how humans, the living, breathing biological organisms we are, fundamentally experience the wider world. I refer to *human experience* when talking objectively about how human beings experience the world. *Personal experience* refers to the subjective experience of an individual and in the context of this book relates to an experience engineered consciously by another to improve someone's experience with a brand, whether it be a personal brand or business's.

Deconstructing the human experience involves explorations into neuroscience, psychology, philosophy, and physiology, and the findings are powerful. The underlying mechanisms that shape your reality, make you feel the way you do, and influence your decision-making processes, when known, can be applied and leveraged by you for future encounters with other people.

Grasping the mechanisms responsible for the human experience provides you with an insight into how you can positively influence and creatively encourage the people you interact with. Until artificial intelligence, advanced robotics, or aliens take over life as we know it, this ability represents one of the most valuable. It's time to understand how your external physical shell and immaterial mind cohesively function to bring about your reality, experience by experience. Not only is it good to know, but, most importantly, like any advanced software it can be hacked, and the knowledge in the back half of this book will teach you how. Engineering a person's feelings, experiences, reality, and judgements is something that can be done, and the human experience provides the gateway through which these processes take place. Information exchange is where the magic happens.

What an experience

Your life is made up of experiences woven together into what is called a stream of consciousness. Common definitions of experience converge around the following key points:

- It can be something you have gone through and gained knowledge of.
- It can be the act of directly perceiving or interacting with events or reality.
- It may have both mental and bodily states.
- It closely relates to feelings and emotional sensations.

As you read these words, you are undeniably having an experience. As you interpret and filter this information, you are perceiving and interacting physically and mentally with the external world. The understanding you derive is a result of your sophisticated mental machinery, and each word has the ability to transform your mental state. When you arrive at the end of the book, you will hopefully have learnt something new and will view yourself as a living breathing biological business capable of producing extreme value to yourself and the world. If all goes splendidly, the realisations you have may be so impactful that you "feel" different, hopefully more confident, knowledgeable, and enlightened from our deep dive into the science and philosophy of your own personal brand. If this happens, we've ticked off the categorical criteria necessary for you to truly experience an *experience*. Grasping the complexity of, and acknowledging, processes that our bodies and brains utilise to shape our subjective interactions with the world, experience by experience, is ground zero for your personal brand's marketing campaign.

While we wriggle our way through the rabbit hole of human experience, notice that personal experiences can push people down certain career paths, influence decisions regarding life partners, alter the trust and rapport in professional relationships, drive purchasing behaviours of consumers, and underlie the majority of our behaviours and decisions. To demonstrate, the power of a personal experience is evident through this book. By virtue of reading this, you have allowed me to take centre stage of your attention and have given me a chance to craft a powerful personal experience for you. Should you implement some of the creative strategies from previous chapters, and better understand the importance of your personal philosophy, or come to value personal relationships more so than before, then this book functioned well as a vector for the messages I wished to communicate and achieved what it set out to do. Consequently, if this were to happen, I have successfully engineered a personal experience in your life, an influential moment guiding your future behaviours and thoughts. For me this is already successful.

However, if any of those behaviours and thoughts leads you to interact with more of my products and services in some other way, and you decide to transact money for something valuable I or any of my businesses provide, then this experience, in hindsight, was in fact an upsell. In retrospect this book could even be considered a marketing tool delivered to you through a *personal experience*. Crafting calculated personal experiences means you can build better relationships, collaborate with others more effectively, better sell services and products, and influence others in any number of other ways. But first, it's time to unpack the human experience.

Tick tock

The philosophical concept of *human experience* is influenced by many variables, including sensations, feelings, meaning, memories, and even theoretical constructs such as time. Each contribute to our unique and subjective perceptions of the world. To date, the debate about whether time exists in the objective universe or is merely conjured up and perceived to be real by the minds of humans, continues. Notable experts, including British physicist Julian Barbour, argue that time is a psychological construct, a reflection of change. He argues that we perceive change occurring over "time" because it helps us make sense of our world. In contrast, the "block universe theory" in physics argues that time is as real as space and a fundamental reality. In the block universe everything has space and time coordinates, meaning everything that has happened or could happen exists right now.

Time, like Schrodinger's cat, appears to exist in a dual state where it could be argued to be a fixed reality or just another one of our characteristic human hallucinations. It is because of this that I dedicate a section to time when I deconstruct the nature of human experience. As you'll realise, whole industries have been warped by the construct of time, and despite its nebulous nature, the economic impact is real. For example, the travel industry sells you on a "future" experience; cosmetic companies "reverse the clock"; express couriers deliver parcels in "under 24 hours"; and watch companies sell instruments that "keep track" of it.

We humans have conceptualised and heavily rely on time as it allows us to measure, interpret, and interact with events that have passed, and events destined for the future. As such, the concept of time has been beaten into us and encoded throughout our existence because of the immense value it provides. It now forms an immutable part of our subjective world and represents a cornerstone of our experiences. What we think about and experience we weave into a temporal framework, and it is given meaning and is better understood through our personal sense of time.

For example, students graduating from college may experience happiness, relief, and excitement. During their graduation, a feeling of joy washes over them as they walk across the stage to shake the chancellor's hand in front of a crowd of people. The crowds' eyes eagerly follow them, and the graduates form the main attraction of the day. The crowd applauds, loved ones beam with pride, and the university chancellor, a revered god-like entity, joins in, smiling, shaking hands, and posing for photos. The formal ceremonial process taking place externally, in real time, coincides with each graduate's internal mental state. As these physical events rage on, the graduate simultaneously has a conscious experience that imbues the current events with further meaning. In addition to the positive feelings provided through the celebration taking place in the physical world, the graduate also experiences their own subjective happiness. They rejoice and embrace in social validation, a newfound sense of achievement, and tentatively permit feelings of mastery to wash over them. Equally joyous is the fact that an identity shift is taking place – the upgrade to "graduate status", a step up the ladder for many social hierarchies – and this is eagerly welcomed. Generally, this event is interpreted as positive from all vantage points, whether it arises from an internal monologue or from an objective appraisal of the external events.

This may explain the feeling of happiness. The feeling of relief, however, is inextricably tied to the past and stems from the graduates' perception of events that have previously happened. It stems from the years of effort they put into their studies. The anxiety they felt many times throughout their course as their capabilities were interrogated by the increasingly complex requirements of their units. The stressful years they persisted as they relentlessly fought an onslaught of university assignments. The years of financial hardship and missed opportunities they endured and no longer have to. These past events factor into the current interpretation of what they experience now.

An equally powerful temporal influence pulls from the nebulous land of the future. When we experience things in the present, we assign meaning, emotions, and feelings to them based on their perceived anticipated value for our future. The graduate felt excited because of their future career prospects. They felt excited about the income they were now worthy of. A future absent of stressful university assignments and looming deadlines was also exciting. Demonstrably, the excitement of this event stemmed from what it enabled and meant for this person's future. The processing of everything we encounter in the real world, or in the metaphysical corners of our mind, are often influenced by the omnipresence of time. Unless, of course, we are in flow state, where time no longer seems to exist...

Two forms of memory

Our archived personal data, which reveals itself as memory, heavily influences our experiences. For the purpose of this section, let's think about the mind and body as separate entities, much like Descartes did when he put the theory of dualism on the map. Dualism proposes that you can segment your existence into two distinct realms: the mental and physical. Your body inhabits the physical realm and obeys the physical laws of the universe and, by virtue of this, physics can describe its motion, how it generates and maintains heat, and why it doesn't float off into space.

On the contrary, your mind seems to be a phenomenon of a lawless realm. It is immaterial, doesn't abide by the laws of physics, can't explicitly be measured or examined, yet mysteriously influences the brain and body. The independent intelligences of the body and mind each contribute to the wholeness of our personal archived data, which goes on to shape our experiences.

Personal data

Our mental information – the information we are aware of and can manipulate with our mind – is one form of our personal archived data. The other form is physical and is made available through our body, most of the time unconsciously. Through our personal archived data, traditionally conceptualised as "memory", we access and utilise historical psychological data. This can be in the form of knowledge we have acquired over time, value and belief systems we have developed, and our evaluations of how external reality matches with the storyline of our own internally narrated world. These mental capabilities provide a layer of meaning to our interactions with the world and influence our experiences. For example, when we walk past a chair, we automatically recognise that we can use it to sit on because we've encountered objects like it before and recognise its function. In fact, most of our world has been architected and memorised in our mind already. We could change suburbs, social groups, organisations, or even situate ourselves in entirely foreign countries, and would still comprehend the majority of our environment thanks to this mental data.

Identifying the function of a chair is easy enough and is simply served by the object recognition capabilities of our mind, but if we find ourselves involved in a complex social issue, we revert to our values and beliefs. Unique to us, these will change how we interpret situations and, subsequently, can impact our experience. Our belief systems and values are what bring on many of our emotions. For example, a person valuing trust and loyalty would process and respond to betrayal differently than someone who did not hold such values. It's fair to say they would be much angrier than a person who didn't value loyalty and trust to the same extent.

It's also easy to see how violations to our beliefs and values can manifest as another emotion, regret. Upon making a mistake or doing something out of character that we feel bad about, we say to ourselves, "this isn't who I am", "that's not something I'd usually do", and we feel like we've "let ourselves down". This feeling can stem from personal actions that violated the beliefs and values we've developed over time and brought forward from our past. This is one example of how this mental subcomponent of our personal archived data can alter our experiences.

Narratives and cognitive dissonance

Another example is the stories we tell ourselves. Our self-authored narrative influences every aspect of our lives because, as the protagonist, we experience and feel each and every plot twist, climax, and feel-good moment. We are constantly comparing ourselves to where we think we should be in our fictional world. As an example, a single person between the ages of 25 and 35 may feel stressed, pressured, and anxious as a result of one of the common narrative threads society shares. In society, starting a family and settling down is extolled, however, to settle down, move in together, and start a family, individuals have told themselves that they need to be with someone for at least a few years, live with them for a couple, marry them, and then have their first child by a certain age. This storyline has been played out vividly by many individuals who live in societies where this is the norm.

If reality contrasts with the fictional narrative of the self, it can be a jarring experience.[1] The plot twist here comes if this person turns 30 and is still without a partner or child. The ensuing emotional rollercoaster is tethered to the congruence of their narrative framework with reality. Sure enough, this narrative is going to further shape other experiences they have. Interpretations of a brief sexual encounter provide one example. "Who does this person think they are to sleep with me and not want anything serious? Don't they understand the significance of this issue? My biological clock is ticking. I'm up to page 76 in my self-authored story, families and lifelong partners come on page 80 and they just want to mess around with no strings attached? They're delusional and I need a soulmate. What was a fleeting experience for one, who had a different story in mind, was certainly not for the frustrated individual who was much more interested in traditional tales.

Story congruence and cognitive dissonance add layers of meaning, and these internal feelings influence our experiences.

The psychological term used to describe the situation whereby people's behaviours conflict with their thoughts and attitudes is cognitive dissonance and it is akin to mental turmoil. To illustrate this further, if a personal trainer, who values health, fitness, and professionalism, is drawn to a social lifestyle full of unhealthy habits that sees them smoking, drinking, partying, and eating junk food regularly, they would experience cognitive dissonance. On the one hand, their thoughts and attitudes are geared toward an idealistic health professional narrative, but on the other their behaviours reflect a different narrative, potentially matching one where the protagonist is a rebellious socialite with impulsive tendencies who can't say no to partying.

There are two conflicting storylines here, and the current behaviours of the personal trainer match the former narrative of a party goer, which is not the narrative valued the highest. In this, cognitive dissonance has an adaptive value as it leaves us feeling tense, uncomfortable, anxious, and motivated to change when our behaviours contradict our thoughts and attitudes. After a while, the pressure exerted on the personal trainer to bring congruence to their behaviours, thoughts, and attitudes will likely reach boiling point and cause a shift. Either they will subscribe to a new narrative, reducing the value placed on health and fitness and increasing the value placed on a socialite lifestyle, or they will change their behaviours to match the narrative of a health professional.

Story congruence and cognitive dissonance add layers of meaning, and these internal feelings influence our experiences. When our stars are in alignment, we will be more satisfied and enjoy an experience more. On the contrary, when we deviate from our planned storyline, our experiences will be layered with feelings of tension, discomfort, and stress. This mental information stored in the chasm between the physical world and our immaterial mind contributes immensely to the human experience.

Physical data

Physical data, unlike our immaterial mental data, is stored in the body, interpreted, and frequently utilised independently of the mind. There are many examples of this in the form of somatic nervous system reflex arcs, autonomic nervous functions, immune system vigilance, epigenetics, and perhaps most obviously, in our DNA itself. A specific example highlighting this form of archived data is evident through reflexes. If you put your hand on a hot stove, before your brain processes that you are burning yourself, your hand will involuntarily pull away. This well-known reflex happens at the level of the spinal cord, which means it doesn't even use, or need, your brain. It's an automatic response occurring because of pathways that have transformed into a stored memory in your body, unlike the mental information floating around in the spectral realms.

The autonomic nervous system regulates the processes that keep you alive, including breathing, digestion, and liver functioning. The system operates automatically, outside of your consciousness, based on pressure signals, tensile forces, chemical levels, and gas concentrations to name a few. Your body has stored all the information that governs its functioning in an algorithmic way. For example, if carbon dioxide levels increase in your body, chemoreceptors (a specialised cell that responds to changes in chemical levels) detect the increase and signal your brain to increase your breath rate to protect your body from elevated acidity levels (breathing carbon dioxide out reduces the concentration of hydrogen ions in your body, hydrogen ions lower the pH of your blood and create an acidic environment). This pathway information is physically stored and conserved in the body and regulated by specific parts of your brain. All, of course, beneath the surface of consciousness.

Your immune system is even more intriguing and seemingly intelligent, and some immune cells are even named by their innate capacity to "memorise" pathogens. Whenever your body encounters a specific pathogen (a microbial organism that can cause disease), it creates a special line of immune cells whose sole mission is to destroy that pathogen should it ever re-enter the body. The cells are known as "memory T cells" and effectively mitigate the disastrous consequences that usually occur if an unchecked pathogen were to take your body hostage. Their memory of the pathogen means your immune system is hypervigilant to threats because "it knows what it is looking for". While your immune system is aware, you're surely not.

Epigenetics literally means "above genetics", represents "control mechanisms" for our DNA, and leads to different expressions of our genes. Certain experiences throughout life can influence our epigenetics, such as foods we eat, body fat, physical activity levels, alcohol, environmental pollutants, and psychological stress.[2] Changes to epigenetics arising from these factors can be long lasting and influence what genes our body turns on or off. In a sense, you could think of your epigenome (the entire spectrum of your epigenetics) as documenting environmental information at a level above your DNA, but concomitantly using this information to regulate what happens in your body. Your epigenome, then, has the potential to memorise the environment. One study proved this by showing that the nutritional status of a foetus (or infant) can result in lifelong epigenetic changes that may alter their lipid and carbohydrate metabolism, in turn potentially leading to obesity.[3] Here, the infant's epigenetics "remembered" the nutritional environment it was subjected to in utero, and consequently altered future metabolic functioning.

Below the level of epigenetics, DNA is another obvious vector for stored physical information. DNA is, by definition, "genetic memory". It is the reason for your heritable traits, idiosyncrasies, pathological predispositions, and it houses the code for absolutely every cell in your body. Unlike the conscious processing of your mental information, physical information stored in the body, despite frequently pinging your brain, is mostly processed unconsciously. The thousands of complex processes and events that happen every second in your body outside of conscious awareness to keep you alive still bamboozles the world's brightest minds. So, it seems fitting that in the world of psychology, the unconscious mind is beginning to be viewed as a pervasive and powerful influence over our higher-order mental processes.[4]

Consequently, arguments for its superiority over the conscious mind are passionately voiced. Some examples in support of this premise are provided below. The point to note here is that your body has its own unique form of intelligence that runs off physical data. This superintelligence is hidden away in our unconscious yet underlies most of our conscious experience. Despite the fact that you may be completely oblivious to signals from the environment, the vigilance of your body means that most of it is processed and stored. Your DNA, immune system, epigenetics, and conditioned patterns of behaviour will affect how you experience your world because your body is an inextricable part of the world and your consciousness. If stored physical data did not influence you, you would never have experienced an emotion.[5]

Environmentally friendly

One last input that contributes to our human experience is environmental data. This refers to the information absorbed from the external world in real time, consciously or unconsciously. The world around us is filled with valuable data that our brain processes, and, if necessary, pushes into our consciousness. For this to happen, our body's sensory organs react to specific signals in our environment, converting them into electricity so that our brain can decipher and assign meaning to them. Although you may see the world through your eyes, smell the roses through your nose, and feel sensations of touch through your skin, your experience of these events is determined by your brain. It receives electrical signatures of these events and creates a prediction of what is actually going on. Remember, the brain – the widely accepted platform for your mind – resides in a black box called a skull and never experiences anything but abject darkness. It never actually felt the touch of your lover, the mechanoreceptors in your skin did. It was never exposed to the fragrance of a rose, the olfactory receptors in your nose were. And it never saw the sky, the rod and cone cells lining the back of the retina did. Notably, through millions of years of evolution, our brain has excelled at detecting a huge number of environmental cues, many of which reside below the threshold of consciousness yet pervasively influence us. This illustrates another profound way our bodily intelligence can shape our subjective experiences.

The outside world contributes valuable information to us that we are constantly detecting, converting, processing, interpreting, and making decisions off. It is obvious when environmental data influences us consciously; real-time interactions with other people are one example. When we see, communicate, and bond with others we are clearly aware of most of the social information given off by them, as we are of the responses we give back. However, initially, for us to even know someone is there, our brain needs to pop up an alert to get our attention, for illustrative purposes it may be something along the lines of "person to your left, threat level minimal, perceived compatibility to mate with determined via attractiveness rating: high". This leads to us being aware of them, for if our brain didn't determine them important, we would be oblivious to their existence and they would reside in our unconscious, just like the house, the sign, and the natural landmark you drive past every day on the way to work that doesn't enter your awareness.

> ## Data from our environment consciously influences our decision-making, feelings, emotions, and, thus, experiences.

We are wired to be aware of and attend to the people around us because this is part of evolution. People can either be a threat to our survival or they could potentially end up the coparent of our child, and therefore represent a reproductive partner. Our fellow *Homo sapiens* are important for many more reasons in modernity, such as collaboration, psychological wellbeing, and utility, but in the primal tribes of our ancestors, reproduction and survival were paramount. Despite coming a long way from the primitive roots of our ancestors, our brain is still strongly shaped by evolutionary forces, and being extremely attentive to others in our environment is one example. In fact, a recent neuroscientific study confirmed that participants' brains have different activation patterns and lead to higher-level thinking when they think they are perceiving a face, despite no faces actually being in their view.[6]

Once we become aware of others, the ongoing interaction with them is mostly conscious. We can see their body language, we can hear the sounds, words, and vocal intonations layering their speech, we can understand the message they are conveying to us through their words, and we can interpret what they are communicating to us within a wider global context. We then respond with our own criteria and are aware of our behaviours and contributions to the conversation. These types of interactions are an obvious example highlighting how data from our environment consciously influences our decision-making, feelings, emotions, and, thus, experiences.

Other objects, stimuli, organisms, social interactions, and information can influence our conscious experiences to the same degree that a conversation with a peer can. This explains why you felt happy when you received a present for your birthday, were awestruck by a painting in an art museum, felt humiliated when you made a mistake in front of peers, and changed your mind after reading an article. Your conscious experience is inextricably linked to your environment in the external world and all it comprises.

The not-so-obvious way we are influenced by environmental data happens at an unconscious level. In the same way that your unconscious physical body stores, memorises, and intelligently processes historical information to shape your current experiences, it also picks up on real-time data and processes it, only providing your conscious mind with information it deems important. We will explore this in the following sections, but to give you confidence in the superintelligence of your unconscious, here are two perspective-shifting experiments.

In one study, a group of neuroscientists used fearful facial expressions to test the unconscious and conscious processing capabilities of humans. Their rationale was: "As fear is linked to danger, detecting fear in the environment, even unconsciously, enhances vigilance and alertness, which is essential to produce fast and adapted behavioural reactions." Essentially, to access the unconscious and the conscious, these researchers flashed images of human faces with fearful expressions to participants. In the conscious group, the images were flashed in the participants' central field of vision and lasted for 140ms. The participants were aware of these images. In the other group, fearful expressions were flashed to the periphery of the subject's field of vision and only lasted for 80ms. This was outside of their conscious awareness, meaning these participants didn't know about the fearful expression they had been flashed.

To give you some background, it's already well established in literature that humans have an arcane ability to interpret and process facial expressions and emotions of other people, consciously and unconsciously. What this study highlighted was that when a fearful expression is presented to your unconscious through your peripheral vision, your brain – through a specific sequence of events that follow a complicated neural pathway – seems to gear your body and brain to prepare, become aware of, and respond to this potential threat in a faster way than you would consciously.[7] This study highlights the superintelligence of your unconscious with regard to processing external information from your environment. If there's something you should know about that's going on in the environment, your unconscious mind will make sure it brings it to your attention.

The second study showed how your actual behaviour changes in response to unconscious processing of environmental cues. The Division of Psychology at the University of Newcastle, NSW, implemented an honesty box for drink payments, which means that whenever one of the faculty members wanted a drink, the payment they made solely relied on the honesty principle. If they took a drink, they were expected to pay by dropping their money into the honesty box. Nothing forced them to pay, and no one would know if they didn't. Little did they know, they were the unsuspecting subjects of an experiment in behavioural psychology. Above the counter, where the honesty box was, researchers used a banner with two different images to notify subjects of the honesty payment system.

Each week the image on the banner was alternated so that half of the time it had a pair of eyes that appeared to be looking directly at the participants, and half the time it displayed images of flowers. When the image of the eyes was on the wall, people donated significantly more money into the honesty box than on the weeks with the flower images. The researchers concluded that the image of a pair of eyes activates our perceptual systems and automatically and unconsciously affects how we behave.[8] In the experiment, the image of eyes increased the donations of participants for the public good. Since then, many experiments have demonstrated that images of eyes in the environment lead people to donate more to charity, behave more honestly with payments, transfer money to others, recycle appropriately, litter less, and increase prosocial behaviours.[9] Eyes in the environment affect human behaviour, so much so that it has been termed the "watching eyes effect".

By now, it should be clear that our *human experience* is shaped by many different forces. The construct of time is one, affecting many aspects of our interactions with the world. Another includes what we have mentally stored – the traditional concept of our memory – which alters every experience we have through existing knowledge structures, internal narratives, and belief systems. Arguably, despite not being realised for its capacity to remember, the body does most of the heavy lifting by physically storing important information, managing metabolic pathways, neural processes, and microbial armies in order to help us survive, thrive, and avoid danger. It is uniquely intelligent, frequently exerting hidden, powerful influences over behaviour and shaping many of our experiences. In addition, our current environment is always providing us with new information that we process, consciously and unconsciously. However, there is one more layer to this. Up until now we have viewed the physical and mental processes – the unconscious and the conscious – as two distinct operators. This is wrong. The sophistication of humans comes as a result of the *integration* between these two intelligences and their corresponding scaffolds: the body and the mind.

A super-intelligent processor

When we take a step back and think about the intricate connections between the mind and the body it becomes obvious. We could even test it right now. For this thought experiment, I want you to think of a memory. Specifically, I want it to be one of the funniest memories you can remember. When I think of some funny moments with my friends, I remember a time when one of my friends, who happened not to be the most athletic, tried to ride a bicycle off an elevated drain that had a two-metre drop on the other side. Gravity won and he nearly broke his rib. Regardless, the funny memory you conjured up would have done a few things to your physical state:

- The electrical activity in your brain would have changed, which is a result of physical electrical processes.[10]
- The electrical conductance of your skin, which is influenced by emotional arousal, would have increased, and muscles in your face would have been activated.[11]
- Your systolic blood pressure increased.[12]
- Your saliva would now have increased levels of IgA immune antibodies.[13]
- If you actually laughed, your body temperature, heart rate variability, and cortisol levels also changed.[14]

The spectral thought that entered your mind manifested in your body, creating a system-wide response comprised of electrical changes, pressure changes, tensile changes, temperature changes, and biomolecular concentration fluctuations. There are even whole nervous systems in your body that respond purely to the things you think about. For example, when you are scared you activate your sympathetic nervous system and this increases blood flow to muscles (to ready you for physical activity), decreases digestion and salivation (redirects blood to muscles, and it's why you have a dry mouth), dilates your pupils (so you can see better), increases your heartrate (to get more blood around your body), and increases your breath rate (to increase oxygen delivery to muscles and get rid of excess carbon dioxide).

On the flipside, the mental states that plague humanity can, and frequently do, arise from physical states of the body. Anxiety, for example, can be a result of numerous bodily dysfunctions. Studies show that changes in the composition of your microbiome, which refers to the trillions of microorganisms and their genetic material that live in your intestinal tract, can lead to anxiety-like symptoms.[15] Other studies demonstrate that breathing difficulties and hyperventilation can trigger anxiety through decreased oxygen levels in the body.[16] Thyroid dysfunction commonly manifests as anxiety,[17] and drugs, like cocaine, are widely known to trigger anxiety. The body and mind are quantumly entangled, and changes in one cause corresponding changes in the other.

Even stranger links between the body and mind make themselves known in the form of "embodied memory". Embodiment is explained as the body's influence on information processing through its sensorimotor state, morphology, and mental representation. In simple terms, embodiment refers to how our psychology can be influenced by our body. Embodied memory therefore details how the body contributes to psychological memory. In a scientific review, the body's memory was shown to significantly influence current experiences.[18] In one experiment, researchers asked subjects to judge the personalities of other people while at the same time holding a pen between their lips. Doing this pulls the face into a pattern similar to smiling. Another group of participants were asked to rate the personality of others too, except instead of holding a pen in their mouth, were instructed to bite down hard on a towel. This action mirrored the facial pattern seen in frowning.

The researchers found that the personality ratings from the participants were more positive if the subjects were unknowingly simulating a smile, and more negative if they were simulating a frown. Additionally, they noted personality evaluations were influenced unconsciously. The experiment concluded that participants' perceptions of others could be influenced through different facial muscle patterns that the body *remembered* and associated with corresponding feelings.

Further experiments show that people better remember positions of objects if they used their hands to point out where the objects were instead of just visualising them. Individuals also remembered the objects faster based on its location in relation to their body, demonstrating that the physical body's position in space influences memory retrieval of items too. Lastly, people remember performing actions better when compared to reciting descriptions, indicating bodily involvement in a task can contribute to how well we remember it. It might explain why your 80-year-old grandma will forget your name but will never forget how to ride a bike.

Previously, we knew that the mind and body were independently intelligent, and capable of remembering different information; however, now we know they work together to influence our memory. Our body, the seat of our unconscious, can pick up things in our environment that we aren't aware of and will store this information, only to offer it up to our consciousness when necessary. As a result of our body's memory, every experience we have is affected.

One obvious example of this is our "gut feeling". If I asked you to recall a time when you had a bad gut feeling about someone, and then quizzed you on the reasons why you had that feeling, you'd probably respond with, "I don't know, it was just a feeling I had... I can't explain it." This phenomenon is widespread and many a time leads to accurate judgements of a person. Your body, which includes rod and cone cells in your eyes, the sound-detecting machinery of your ears, neuronal circuits in your brain, and mechanoreceptors in your skin, most certainly detected some stimuli from that person that was processed unfavourably.

Through previous experiences, your body has catalogued deceptive characteristics and behaviours, and when interacting with others the information detected through your senses is vigilantly cross-referenced with this database of deception. In the scenario above, the unconscious processing of body language, handshaking behaviours, vocal characteristics, and eye movements trigger warning bells, and the bad gut feeling was your body alerting your mind to its findings. Did you know that when someone is lying their vocal characteristics change?[19] You probably didn't, but your body probably does.

Emotions, the intelligence of the past

Emotions, comprising all our feelings, contribute significantly to the human condition and are inextricably tied to how we experience every moment of our life. In the literature there are ongoing debates about whether emotions are the cause of consciousness or are an aspect of consciousness that's always there.[20] Early on, emotions were viewed as a substrate of cognitive processes, which essentially suggests emotions came about because humans thought up situations that caused emotional responses in our body. As time passed, science contributed more information toward emotion research and the theories evolved. Since then, many researchers have tackled the philosophical debate surrounding the nature of emotions and their relationship with consciousness.

Some fields of research prefer to look at humans in a more robotic fashion. Specifically, they propose that organisms have two different systems governing their behaviour: one is the cognitive system, which includes our ability to think, know, problem solve, and remember; the other is the emotional system. In this theory, the emotional system is considered an emergency system, which is able to interrupt the ongoing activity of the system (in this case, us) and rapidly select a new "operative scheme" for the organism. It does this by analysing sensory data, selecting an appropriate response pattern, and then transferring this information into appropriate memory systems.[21]

An example is when a person sees a snake. Humans are already hypersensitive to snakes as a result of evolution teaching us that they can be dangerous. When a snake slithers past, before we are consciously aware of what we have seen, systems in our brain activate and propagate information throughout the body. Upon detecting a snake, our body prepares the sympathetic nervous system, our flight-or-fight response, and shortly after becoming aware of the snake we are overcome with fear. This fear "feeling" has now taken over our system.

The emotion triggered in our body then causes us to choose from a preselected list of commands and executes one of them. For example, in response to "fear", our body has set operating schemes (or behaviour patterns, if you will), which include freezing like a statue, running for your life, or entering a state of hypervigilance. Each pattern would have served a valuable purpose as it was conserved through evolution. This auto selection is beneficial because dangerous situations requiring instantaneous decisions do not leave time for reason to deliberate the best outcomes. Pre-programmed responses fare much better. Following detection of the snake, and through the fear pathway, the "run for your life command" may be selected. When you have reached a safe distance, your body will update its memory systems so that it becomes even more efficient at detecting dangerous snakes and responding in the future. This view assumes that the emotional processes of humans are automated, pre-programmed systems that trigger when there is a recognised stimulus in our environment.

Algorithms

This line of thinking is similar to what Oxford professor Yuval Harari writes about in his book, *Homo Deus*, except he teases this theory out even further. After thoroughly analysing aspects of humanity, Yuval puts forward convincing arguments that humans, and most organisms for that matter, are nothing more than algorithms. Algorithms are methodical sets of steps that can be used to make calculations, solve problems, and reach decisions. His proposal, which is reinforced through advances in life sciences research, suggests that organisms are complex data processors that use information from the environment to make informed decisions and solve problems.

When using a baboon as an example, he notes that although it is hard for us to picture a baboon pulling out a notebook, pencil, and calculator to compute the probabilities of certain behaviours in specific circumstances, it need not be. The baboon itself is the calculator, and what the baboon *feels* is the consequence of all the algorithms and calculations that have occurred inside its body. Before the baboon decides to behave in a certain way, it will feel sensations throughout its body that arise from inbuilt data processing machinery. To illustrate how emotions govern behaviour, the feeling of hunger propels the baboon to search for food throughout its environment.

This view of emotions, decision-making, and *Homo sapiens* overall, if logically teased out, assumes that we may not be the truly free agents we think we are. We may, in fact, be slaves to our environment, purely responding to bits of data that, once processed, rise up and cause us to act programmatically. Even though we feel like we are making choices and behaving of our own volition, our body may have already chosen an operating scheme, in which case consciousness merely gives us the illusion of choice.

Interpreting emotions

Despite this, mechanistic views of humanity do not accurately explain the nature of consciousness as well as it explains the nature of emotions. Pre-programmed emotional processes make sense. Disgust, fear, surprise, happiness, anger, and sadness are widely cited as the six universal emotions exhibited by humans around the world, and we have been seeing and feeling these emotions for 100,000s of years. As a result, being able to immediately interpret and automatically respond to them has distinct survival advantages in human bonding, danger detection, and family protection, to name a few.

Highlighted previously, fear activates a pre-programmed neural response, leading us to respond faster than we would have had we perceived it consciously. In life-or-death situations, a delay of a few milliseconds could have spelled a bloody end for our hunter-gatherer ancestors and abruptly halted their river of DNA. Humans who processed and automatically responded to emotions may have been selected by natural selection. In this case, conserved algorithmic-like responses, such as the following, are a no-brainer:

1. Detect
2. Interpret
3. Respond
4. Live

Predetermined algorithmic-like responses don't make sense for the more complex thoughts, decisions, and multiple intelligences comprising modern human consciousness though. For instance, how does Aristotelian philosophy fit in with this view? What algorithms cause us to pursue our own unique purpose in life? If there was an algorithm for a unique life purpose, what stimuli would initiate it? Further, Newton's pursuit of mathematical sciences could not have been an inbuilt pre-programmed operative scheme activated through an algorithm. How could it be? How could his system know how to respond to relatively new mathematical stimuli – a subset of chronologically sensitive environmental data – let alone process it through a sophisticated algorithm?

Our bodies have evolved over millions of years. From an anthropological perspective, mathematics would appear on page 99 of the 100-page book of human history. That's not enough time for evolution to rewire our body and mind to make it math compatible through an algorithm. However, given enough time, this could occur. The problem is, the rapid advancements of our societies, philosophies, technologies, and relationships with the universe far exceed the rate at which our body could fine-tune its complicated, physically based, system-wide algorithms.

System updates

The world of metacognition and consciousness may have started from emotions, but how we acquire knowledge and mentally manipulate information – our logic and critical thinking – is vastly different and can potentially operate independently from our hardwired instinctive emotions. Here lies a key differentiator. Whereas emotional responses and their resulting physical manifestations, such as facial muscle integration, nervous system activation, and specific neuropeptide composition, are guided by millennia of evolution, enhancements to our mental intelligence, foundational knowledge, and reasoning faculties are powered by rocket fuel.

Every day represents unchartered territory because we're continually being exposed to new realms of knowledge.

To illustrate this, we can draw analogies between ourselves and sophisticated modern-day technologies like a Tesla. My friend owns one and despite waking up every day, walking to his car spot, and stumbling upon the same physical Tesla, the "intelligence" of the Tesla does not stay static. Some days, upon entering, he is notified of updates by a smooth robotic voice that says, "Hello, Marco, there were two new upgrades to the system installed last night." The system of the Tesla is like the intelligent component of our mind. The exterior, like our physical body that runs off emotions, doesn't really update, and if it does it takes a long time, but our minds – our systems – can be upgraded overnight through the input of new knowledge. The 21st century is an intellectually enriching environment and upon waking every morning your system update is complete; the events of the day passed are processed and encoded while you sleep.

Every day therefore represents unchartered territory for us as a species because we're continually being exposed to new realms of knowledge. Our intelligence upgrades at a far faster rate than our physical structure. There was a period when humans didn't have language technologies; however, over time, through the ongoing improvement and evolution of our cognitive abilities, this technology in us surfaced. Dogs bark, dolphins use high-pitched frequencies, apes use body language, and we began to use meaningful words. When we started bringing other humans into the world with language abilities, it vastly changed the mental landscapes and foundational knowledge of human minds, without much change to our physical bodies. How could our bodies have pre-programmed operative schemes to respond to an abstract thought that may have never been uttered before?

Our mental improvements outrun evolution; therefore, we cannot develop system-wide algorithmic responses. It is because of this that there is no way that our body could have a pre-programmed response to the new knowledge, new concepts, and novel environmental data we regularly encounter. Unless it relates to aspects of our survival, in which case it would be hijacked by the algorithm-like emotional processes characteristic of humans – the processes that were shaped over time, by evolution. The ability of emotions to command and control our body is super relevant to modern-day marketing, by the way.

Informational molecules

Other theories view humans in a more holistic light. Candace Pert, a famed neuroscientist, authored the book *Molecules of Emotion*, in which she puts forward the concept that the body and brain communicate through a network of informational molecules giving rise to emotion. The informational molecules, called neuropeptides, are small chains of amino acids released from the brain, and are what Candace conceptualised as "molecules of emotion". Interestingly, despite being made in the brain, these molecules have binding sites around the body, enabling them to interact with many other systems such as the immune system and gut. Candace proposed that our mind and our emotions arise from the flow of information as these molecules pass from our brain to different systems in our body, and the reverse.[22] Her research highlighted why it is possible for us to feel emotions in different parts of our body. In one example, she demonstrated how these neuropeptides had binding sites in our intestine, which provided a physical mechanism and explanation for our "gut feeling".

A similar theory, the Differential Emotional Theory, suggests emotions are a neurobiological process, and that the "feelings" we experience are merely a psychological phase that happens after biological events. This theory argues that our body and mind are constantly affected by emotional signals, supporting the view that consciousness evolved from our emotions. The consciousness we experience today is said to be influenced by the constant emotional flux of our body, which may reside in the subconscious or emerge into our awareness as a fully-fledged emotional experience. There is merit to this argument, with newer research proving there are unconscious processing pathways in the brain that respond to emotionally heavy stimuli,[23] thus demonstrating how there can exist states of emotional flux outside our conscious awareness. The interactions between our emotions and higher-order cognitive processes, such as thinking and reasoning, together, are what shapes our subjective experience.[20]

Our emotions can be activated in different ways, including through:

- sensory stimuli like facial expressions, body postures, and vocal characteristics
- our own behaviours
- language, speech, and sentences
- "drive" states in our body, such as hunger, sex, thirst, and interest.

In fact, it is said that we are motivated by drive states only because they affect us emotionally. Lastly, higher-order cognitive processes in the form of memories, beliefs, desires, evaluations, and decision-making processes trigger our emotions.[24] Holding true to its infinite complexity, the body also demonstrates reciprocal links between emotions and the things that trigger them. Emotions can produce facial expressions and body postures in their host and are affected by activities such as sex, interest pursuits, and food consumption. Additionally, emotions can influence memory recall, alter our evaluations of other people, and dramatically (and scarily) affect our decision-making capabilities.

Notably, the many theories and mechanisms behind and influencing our emotions share one thing in common. All allude to emotions representing a fast-tracked, powerful, and predictable influence over human behaviour. Viewing them from a more informed perspective allows you to better self-manage them as they arise, pushing you in the right direction towards a life of peace and emotional stability. Further to this, a better understanding of this universal component of behaviour leads to more productive, empathetic, and insightful interactions with people and the world. Lastly, this knowledge galvanises you against the immersive 21st century world, whose sole purpose is to hijack your attention, using molecules of emotions as trojan horses.

Logic and rationality

Here is where it gets interesting. Case studies that followed patients with brain damage uncovered some perplexing findings, so much so that it changed the whole direction of psychological enquiry into emotions and decision-making. One case study in particular, spearheaded by Antonio Damasio, an American neuroscientist, was the catalyst for this shift in gears and it was all thanks to his patient, Elliot. Elliot was an astute and smart man with an IQ in the top three percent. He held an upper-class management job in a large organisation and was a model husband and father, until he developed a small tumour in the frontal lobe that had to be removed. The tumour sat in the orbitofrontal cortex; the part of the brain responsible for connecting visceral emotions in the body to our stream of consciousness. When the orbitofrontal cortex was removed, Elliot's life crumbled. Soon after the operation he lost his job, got divorced, and went bankrupt after being conned by a "shady character". Despite his IQ remaining in the top three percent, and his high-level functioning remaining largely intact, he couldn't make a decision to save his life. Mundane tasks like deciding between a blue or black pen and where to park his car turned into endless deliberations. Damasio observed that Elliot often struggled to make effective decisions, and many a time he was unable to choose at all.

Further, Damasio noted that the middle of the day was remarkably difficult for Elliot. At lunchtime he would drive around for an hour trying to find a restaurant to eat at. Throughout this endeavour, he would become overwhelmed by decisional criteria, such as the time of day, the weather, and how busy the restaurant would be. Further deliberation about the lighting, seating, and parking ensued. Finally, upon settling on a venue that met his decisional criteria, he would open a menu, only to endlessly peruse the items on the list. Choosing a dish was like choosing a restaurant, albeit with different criteria. It turns out Elliot couldn't make a decision about anything because he didn't know what he "felt" like.[25]

Without emotions, humans short circuit. It is because of this case study that we now know that emotions drive human behaviour and are the basis from which most of our decisions are made. This is especially true when decisions relate to personal and social matters. The case study contributed immensely to the understanding of human behaviour. For one, it is why what we should do and what we end up doing are usually at odds. Logic and rationality tell us what's right, but our emotions are the reason we don't always do the right things. Evidence shows that logic usually takes a backseat to our emotions.

Technology, society, philosophies, and the nature of human relationships evolve much faster than the human body does. In a lifetime it's possible to move from primitive automobiles and Morse code to personal autonomous drone transportation and FaceTime. It is possible to upgrade humans through biotechnology, turning what was once the inner-workings of organic human life into a hybrid of technological processes and divine human intervention. The philosophies of human rights and civil liberties may be challenged abruptly when advancements in scientific instrumentation and technocracies lead researchers to argue about the existence and utility of "free will".

Although our intelligence is capable of adapting and evolving rapidly, our body and mind connections are not. This is worrying because despite the fact they spent millions of years co-evolving together, some technologists on the fringe are trying to leave the body behind, arguing it is a remnant of natural selection. However, the human body is needed. It is ultimately valuable. Emotions are its language, and it shares an intricate dialect with our mind at all times. The millions of years of emotional circuitry hardwired into our body still pulls rank over our decisions and determines what we find important in our environment. Our feelings are what make us human, and we owe a great debt to them. After all, emotions, our instincts, function to keep us alive.

There is one caveat though: as a result of emotions being triggered by predictable stimuli and powerfully acting on our body through evolutionary mechanisms, it means they are exploitable. As long as we inhabit human bodies we will be exposed through this weakness. In fact, this is exactly how our experiences in life are constantly being manipulated and exploited by companies, marketers, behavioural psychologists, and others, daily. Consciousness, our subjective experience, is a constant interaction between emotional bodily states and other aspects of our mental intelligence, but the emotional circuitry is the back door for hackers and the motivational launch sequence for all our behaviours.

This is how people and professionals can contrive your actions, feelings, and purchasing behaviours. Our faculty of reason does its best to make sense of everything, but when heartstrings are tugged or a marketer uses some well-crafted emotive copy for manipulation, we are at the mercy of our programmatical emotional circuitry, the massively influential operating system underlying our *Homo sapiens* technology. Although new eras of humanity are on the horizon, for as long as our physical body coexists with our mind, emotions fulfil an integral role in daily life and ultimately drive human behaviour. Our dependency on them creates vulnerabilities. Not only this, but we need to properly understand the inner-workings of the people we interact with if we want to deliver them an effective *personal experience.*

What's next?

With a better understanding of how we function as humans, it's now time to apply this knowledge to life in the 21st century. Especially since we have entered what experts refer to as an experience economy. The consistent exploitation of our attention and manipulation of our behaviour now forms the norms of the global ecosystem we operate in. Given accessibility, cost, and product quality are converging, the *experience* factor is now the magic bullet for company success. The simple fact is, this drives profits. Utilising your biology and psychology against you is how they engineer these experiences. Each and every one of them. But using this knowledge you can fight back and defend yourself against an onslaught of manipulation while simultaneously using it to ensure your personal brand's campaign is nothing short of remarkable.

Chapter 7:
Rise of the Personal Experience

Modern-day marketing

Up until this point the *human experience* has been under the microscope. Now, resulting from our deep dive into the mechanisms shaping how humans experience the world, we've reached a point where we can begin to apply what we've learned. First, let's recap: together, the mind and body form a super-intelligent system that can detect all kinds of signals from our environment, processing them consciously and unconsciously. The information we acquire, as a result of these processes, comes from our mental and physical intelligence. Our mental intelligence is the more obvious of the two. However, our physical intelligence, what we could refer to as our unconscious, is also powerful in shaping how we respond to our environment. On top of this, we have developed fine-tuned, body-wide operating programs called emotions that significantly influence every moment of our waking life. And, many a time, they are activated by stimuli outside of our conscious awareness.

The significance of our system-wide intelligence is evident in the absence of proper emotional processing. When our emotions don't properly weigh into our judgements, we experience a pathological inability to make decisions. In addition, it's widely known that emotions affect our memory, conscious decision-making processes, and significantly impact how our body functions. Further, scientists and philosophers have noted that emotions may have preceded consciousness, meaning emotions wield a significant influence over our decisions and behaviours due to the nature of their evolution.

To see how aspects of your mental intelligence can be influenced through emotional activation, look no further than flow states. In a flow state your creative potential and ability to focus are steered by *feeling* interested in something. In addition, emotions can prime your mind, guiding thought processes down different trajectories; can cause you to interpret events differently; and can influence how you evaluate knowledge and information you're exposed to. Our mental abilities, such as reasoning, knowing, and remembering, in conjunction with the feelings we derive from our emotional circuitry, form our stream of consciousness, and both are constantly interacting with each other.[1]

This stream of consciousness is how we experience every single moment in the world. Emotions are functional in your decisions, motivations, behaviours, responses, and physiological states. The fact that emotions are a result of evolution means they respond predictably to certain stimuli. People who understand this possess a unique ability to hack you and shape your reality. Your experiences can be manipulated through changing how you feel and changing how you feel isn't all too mystifying when you know how to short-circuit people's emotions.

> Nudging people into behaving in a certain way simply requires a target emotion to be triggered.

It is because of this that you and I are predictably exploited, manipulated, and coaxed into behaving in a certain way, purchasing a certain product, trusting a certain person, or aligning with a certain company. Whole fields of enquiry are dedicated to teaching these manipulative tactics and have infiltrated society. Think about it. Emotions rule decisions and lead to predictable behaviours. Emotions can be universally activated in people through common stimuli. Nudging people into behaving in a certain way simply requires a target emotion to be triggered. The target emotion can be found by reverse-engineering an individual or target customers' thought processes. When identified, this emotional trigger will activate that specific behavioural response. That is the secret behind mainstream manipulation.

Welcome to the world of marketing, brand strategy, and the realm of engineered experience, where this knowledge is used to exploit everyone, including you and I, daily.

Marketing, branding, and engineered experiences

If you picked ten marketers at random and asked them the question, "What is marketing?" you would be met with a variety of responses. Traditional marketers would say it's all about how you use your marketing budget to fund a campaign that advertises your product and its features. Some contemporary marketers would say it's about researching your customers, developing buyer personas, using this data to guide your marketing strategy, tapping into communities, and appealing to needs and wants. One or two of the most successful marketers would tell you it's about understanding human psychology, empathising with your audience, appealing to their most powerful emotions, developing an authentic connection with them, crafting a story they can relate to, and inspiring passion in them. When this is achieved, not only will they buy your products, but they'll voluntarily enlist themselves as a brand preacher, spreading the good word about your company and its offerings to everyone they know and anyone they meet. The most successful marketing campaign utilising this method resulted in Christianity, and the Bible is the most valuable book product in the world; this view on marketing works.

When the latter philosophy on marketing is adhered to it has flow-over benefits. In addition to becoming company disciples, it's unlikely the customers who were caught up in the web of this form of marketing will be once-off purchasers. These guys have strapped in for the long term and the lifetime value on them is sky high for the business. Like successful marketers, if you can achieve authentic connections, tickle emotions, and inspire passion with an audience or prospective customer, you too will have a devoted crowd in your wake.

Big brands

If you asked Steve Jobs about marketing, he would tell you it's about values. He never sold Apple products based on technical aspects and was adamant that Apple marketing employees should never go around talking about bits, bytes, megahertz, or processing speeds. That would not convince people to buy Apple Macs or invest in the company. History would eventually prove him right. The legendary saga of Steve Jobs and his tenure at Apple saw him being ejected from the board in 1985 and ultimately leaving the company that he passionately founded.

In 1996 he returned as the interim CEO and was met with a sombre state of affairs. The company was failing, sales had plummeted and there wasn't enough money in the kitty for them to experiment with different marketing agencies, new products, or new sales strategies. They had under a year to steer the behemoth of a ship back to the shores of success. One shot was all that remained for revitalising their brand image and regaining a foothold in the personal computing market that was once their playground.

Here is where one of the world's most successful and prolific marketing campaigns made its debut. One of the advertising agencies that Apple leaned on, TBWA\Chiat\Day, put forward an idea that resonated with Steve Job's company philosophy and values. The idea revolved around changing people's perspectives of Apple and the concept of personal computing. The agency proposed that Apple should honour the legacy of the "crazy ones", which they simultaneously labelled as the "geniuses" who thought differently. As such, "Think Different" was the message Apple broadcasted to its television viewership. The ad celebrated, with black and white photographs, some of the world's visionaries like Thomas Edison, Gandhi, Pablo Picasso, and dozens more. Accompanying the photographs was the text:

Here's to the crazy ones. The misfits. The rebels. The troublemakers. The round pegs in the square holes. The ones who see things differently. They're not fond of rules and they have no respect for the status quo. You can quote them, disagree with them, glorify or vilify them. About the only thing you can't do is ignore them. Because they change things. They push the human race forward. And while some may see them as the crazy ones, we see genius. Because the people who are crazy enough to think they can change the world are the ones who do.

The Think Different campaign is credited with turning the tide for Apple who, shortly after the campaign launched, recorded quarterly profits for the first time in two years. The campaign won numerous awards, developed cult-like followings, and became widely recognised as one of the most successful ever. Much of the campaign's success was attributed to the "strong emotional appeal". Individuals were able to empathise with Apple in its underdog role, align themselves with the values they espoused, and became excited about the change Apple was seeking to make. As a result of these value appeals, and the emotional manipulation engineered into the ads, viewers became motivated to buy Apple products. Viewers and existing customers *felt* something from the campaign that resulted in them buying Apple products and stock.

Big brands evidence this all the time; their marketing tactics tap dance right in front of us. For example, Nike, the shoe manufacturer, markets great athletes and honours athletic feats. Historically, despite their foothold on footwear, the marketing had nothing to do with shoes or the technology underlying them. Looking back, one of the major reasons for Nike's success is attributable to the fact that they consistently channelled their efforts into aligning themselves with great athletes. By doing this they were able to tap into the emotional part of the consumer and sell them on lifestyles, success, and healthy living. When consumers purchase Nike they do so because it makes them *feel* good and look cool.[2] Nike's competition also uses the widely available and affordable cotton, polyester, rubber, and synthetic leather to construct their shoes. Similarly, access to smart product designers, managers, and engineers likely isn't Nike's magic bullet. There is one thing that's peculiar to Nike though. It seems they add a dose of "feel good" emotion that others simply can't.

How do you feel?

Emotion, as discussed above, is the driver of human behaviour, and when the emotional part of our brain – the orbitofrontal cortex – isn't functioning properly, our decisions and subsequent behaviours are compromised. If you pull emotions over to the realm of marketing and realise that consumer behaviour is just a subset of human behaviour, the focus on emotional appeals makes sense. You can logically arrive at the conclusion that purchasing decisions are largely driven by emotion. Seemingly profound, this is already common knowledge to corporates. In fact, universities have been breeding professional manipulators for decades by embedding these teachings in marketing units, consumer behaviour courses, and psychology electives.

What started as naturalistic studies of consumer behaviour soon turned into the current marketing dogma we see today. Behavioural economists, amongst other professionals, quickly came to realise humans weren't the rational creatures they had previously thought. Logic, they too came to realise, took a backseat to emotions in purchasing behaviour, and because of this in marketing and advertising efforts an emphasis is always placed on how consumers *feel* and how to appeal to them through *feelings*. If purchases were driven by rationality and derived from the pure utility of the product, much brand-driven buying would not exist.

What is the point of paying $400 for a cotton T-shirt from Gucci when you could buy a similar cotton T-shirt from Kmart for $10? They are a similar fit, the same material, and fulfil the same function. Granted, the Gucci T-shirt may have a small, barely noticeable design stickered on it somewhere, but in rational, utilitarian terms, this design represents a complete non-necessity and should not affect the pragmatical function of the clothing. They could even have been made by the same person, exported from an underdeveloped country's factory.

The reason people opt for a Gucci label is because when they buy Gucci they are buying based on other criteria. It is a status symbol, it shows they have money, it talks to their values, it contributes to their social identity and self-image, and, as a result, it makes them *feel* a certain way. Emotions lead these purchases because it services a personal need, which makes the buyer *happy, proud, fulfilled,* or even *excited*.[3] How exciting for the guy who thinks, *This girl never loved me but wait until she sees me rocking my new Gucci flip flops and Louis Vuitton bum-bag.* To him, this brand is a babymaker, a family starter, it does not simply represent a rational decision based on functional, wearable material that can protect him from the elements; what a ludicrous notion.

Even though rationality could be said to be the sole driver for shopping at large, affordable retail chains like Kmart, equally likely is the fact that the shoppers are there because of their emotional leanings. Maybe Kmart is close to their house, it's convenient, and they don't *feel* up to travelling. Kmart's prices are cheaper than boutique retailers, and saving money at Kmart allows them to spend more on things they really love, such as gifts for family members, which would make them far *happier* than paying for similar overpriced and overvalued products offered up by other companies. The products are accessible and affordable, and, as a result, the purchases at Kmart are driven by *fulfilment, contentment,* and *relief.* The stress caused by the absence of the product that the person now has is extinguished, which no doubt also *feels* good.

Experience economy

Current thought leaders have proposed that we are now living in an experience economy where a person's experience matters more than the products and services they seek. Companies are paying keen attention to this shift and, in the name of delivering a better experience, are engineering people's feelings by hijacking their emotions. With the accessibility and availability that dominates the 21st century, is it any wonder the "experience" factor is another category of criteria that's now integrated into purchasing decisions? At this point in time, as a customer, I can get what I need from many companies on demand, conveniently, affordably, and at a similar quality, so why would I take a serving of an unnecessary, terrible experience if I could avoid it? In fact, if you treat me nice, remember my name, and show me you care, I'll pay more. Similarly, I am willing to pay for an overpriced café big breakfast and coffee because the accompanying experience represents a surcharge that justifies the worth, and I'm not alone.

In 2019, US consumers spent roughly the same amount of money on eating food at home as at restaurants.[4] By the look of it, the dining experience is surpassing homecooked meals, and it's an upward trend. Cooking and eating at your own kitchen table doesn't make you feel the same way the ambient environment of a local restaurant does. Dialling up a dose of experience, rather than products and services, is an increasing phenomenon throughout the world. People are focusing more on paying for *feelings* that companies can provide them through experiences. The travel industry, with a US spend of $1.1 trillion in 2019, and the entertainment industry, with a US spend of $678 billion in 2018, are two telling examples. Both are on the rise.

Just as McDonalds markets the *happy* family to sell burgers, so too does every other marketing agency and company hijack emotions when they sell their products. They capture and influence consumers through emotionally charged content and the ongoing use of emotional manipulation, gripping them through engineered video content, TV ads, and emotionally arousing images that pull at heartstrings. But most of the time they capture you through calculated copy at the top of their Facebook advertisements, in the text field of Google ad words, and in the product descriptions of their Ebay items. Next time an advertisement or post catches your attention on Facebook, pause for a moment and analyse the words they have used. In many cases they are emotionally charged words and sentences. If you press pause on your mind, you can see content marketers' manipulation in real-time, and this is how they orchestrate your experience.

The following are examples of well-crafted copy:
- "Furious Karen chases spiteful pigeon" – This is appealing because it sounds like it will be *funny*.
- "Shocking secrets of a marketing professional" – It's likely this post will be full of *surprises*.

- "Couple transforms homeless dog into loving pet" – Do you feel like an emotional rollercoaster ride while you eat lunch?
- "VIP 24-hour sale" – Can you feel the *fear* of missing out and the looming sense of *regret* if you do?
- "Mandatory vaccinations for all Australians" – That is a time-bomb. "Mandatory" and "human rights" don't go in the same sentence together. No wonder people posted thousands of *angry* emojis.

The use of well-crafted copy enables marketers with their targeted advertisements to hijack consumer attention. Their success is guaranteed when consumers click on their ad, read their content, visit their website, check out their products and services, and familiarise themselves with their brand. It is at this point that an innocent human experience, after being infiltrated by marketing efforts, becomes an engineered "brand experience".

Areas of experience

After companies realised the power of human emotion and became excited about engineering experiences, new professions were born, company spending was redirected, and universities hurried to cobble together courses to service this new demand. Currently, there are four major areas of experience that marketers and leadership teams identify as important in a company's success. Three of the four areas are Product Experience (PX), Customer Experience (CX), and Brand Experience (BX). In order, they comprise: the experience an individual has with a specific product; how the individual experiences the company over time through multiple interactions; and how a stranger or customer experiences the brand and everything it encompasses. The fourth area is User Experience (UX) and is concerned with a person's perceptions, feelings, and responses that result from the use or anticipated use of products, services, and systems. As a result, the user experience can occur during all other levels of experience. The "x" has been taken up by professionals in these communities and denotes the word "experience".

Brand experience can be described as an experiential strategy that uses touchpoints across multiple channels to build connection, affiliation, and trust between a brand and its audience. Even by seeing the brand multiple times, people become familiar with it and therefore begin viewing it more positively. This explains why companies continually attempt to put their brand in front of you any opportunity they get. Another way to think about brand experience is as a company's attempt to design sensory experiences that bring people into lasting and meaningful relationships with them. Wherever a brand exists, be it online or offline, there is a potential for you to encounter it. How you encounter it and the feelings you take away is the job of its branders, marketers, and advertisers.

Through the sensory experiences these professionals have architected, they hope to stir up feelings in you and win your approval. Most importantly, they wish to qualify as worthy of your ongoing business. But first, to get buy-in from strangers, the brand needs to become liked by them or, ideally earn the label 'friend', and finding common ground with their audience – a mechanism more well known for its involvement in relationship development between two people – is one sure-fire way to kick this off.

Remember, for a brand to be successful in fostering these positive feelings, it requires the development of personal, authentic, and meaningful relationships, which occur from value congruence, emotional appeals, and philosophical alignment. In fact, generating emotional connections with an audience is key in developing a strong brand, especially since modern consumers no longer just buy products and services but instead buy the emotional experiences being sold.[5]

Even though you may never have tried a can of Red Bull, going off content they post about extreme sports and record-breaking human feats, it's safe to say that if you've got an adrenaline-fuelled lifestyle, maybe these guys are the ones for you. They seem to understand your attraction to the extreme and share your passion, and because of this a camaraderie develops, and no longer will you perceive their brand as just another unimportant, unworthy energy drink company fighting for your attention. Unlike the others, they made you *feel* something.

For someone to arrive at this point where they are emotionally impacted by content requires exposure to the company in some way, shape, or form. Brand-awareness strategies implemented behind the scenes is how this exposure and your subsequent experience with them is engineered. Marketing and advertising campaigns, public relations efforts, eye-catching designs, published content, taglines, online and offline reviews, and word of mouth contribute to driving brand awareness and are regularly leveraged by organisations.

Using Red Bull as an example, at the time of writing, their video content has generated 1.5 billion impressions and commands an 8.5 million subscriber-strong YouTube channel. Individuals who view this video content are subjected to certain experiences and will consequently form opinions and feelings about the brand. It was hard not to feel a sense of awe when Red Bull uploaded a video of the stratospheric jump from space they sponsored and supported. In doing this, they broke world records, defied human limits, and changed people's perspectives about what is possible, all through a three-minute clip that was conceived and meticulously planned. In fact, that sense of awe was not an accident, they knew it was coming. They've always understood who they are and what they live for, now so do you. The branding has done its job.

Credibility

Importantly, these feelings and experiences can all happen before someone is a customer and can play a pivotal role in converting them from a stranger to a loyal brand evangelist. As part of these brand experiences an individual will form meanings and associations with the brand (known as brand image) and can be influenced by the esteem that society and other people hold the brand in (known as brand value). The Fred Hollows Foundation likely sparks feelings of altruism and compassion and brings humanitarianism to the forefront of your mind. This is their brand image at work. Microsoft, if they were to come knocking on your organisation's door, would probably be met with respect, and any of their requests, suggestions, or pitches would likely be honoured. Microsoft's brand value is why. A lesser-known technology-based company could walk in after them and follow the exact dialogue Microsoft engaged in, but their treatment and influence would significantly differ. Unlike Microsoft, the value of the other brand is still in its infancy and does not qualify for special treatment.

Highlighted above are two components of brand experience, and there are more. If brand experiences are positive, in other words, if an individual likes and feels good about the brand and the products they're offering, they will go to second base with them. "Take my money," they decide, and to that the company replies, "Welcome to the customer experience."

It's a pleasure doing business with you

Customer experience is hugely important in business and, of late, has been met with a rising interest since the corporate world evolved and became more human-centric. It encompasses the touchpoints, interactions, and overall journey of a customer with a company. For example, if an existing customer expresses interest in a new product a company has to offer, they will be handballed to a sales rep to seal the deal. After chatting with the sales rep, the sceptical customer may decide to venture online and conduct more research before exchanging money, in doing so visiting the company website and further interacting there. If all goes well, they end up purchasing the product, which potentially requires another point of contact in the company. Once purchased, questions about the product commonly arise, and a few days later the individual reaches out to customer support. Two weeks later the product unexpectedly malfunctions, creating a need to engage a manager at the company for a refund. A year on, the product's descent into obsolescence stimulates further contact with the company as new product upgrades and accessories are discussed.

Throughout this customer journey, multiple people and departments are engaged across different mediums spanning phone calls, Facebook messages, website chatbots, face-to-face conversations, and emails. This all-encompassing journey forms the customer experience. In forward-thinking, diligent organisations that understand the value of experience, like the one above, this process is carefully mapped out and engineered in such a way that a long-lasting and meaningful company–customer relationship develops. As such, after the exposure phase, when a customer touches any part of the business, through any channel, engages any person, and regardless of what stage of the customer lifecycle they are in, the organisation will endeavour to respond in a congruent, empathetic, and personal way so as to deliver a positive customer experience.

Recently published literature highlights the focus of companies on identifying customer emotions throughout the customer journey, understanding these emotions, and examining how they play a role at different touchpoints. This focus comes with good reason: customers' emotional responses account for cognitive judgements of the company, service performance outcomes, and return intentions.[6] A good cognitive judgement means a customer has a positive appraisal of the company and will likely refer them to a friend. Good performance outcomes lead to customer satisfaction. And return intentions manifest as brand loyalty. Taking advantage of this is surely beneficial, and experts have proposed that to deliver the best customer experience, customer needs must take centre stage.

Of course, this all sounds benevolent and altruistic. *How nice of companies to take so much care around crafting an ideal experience for me. What a nice organisation!* you think to yourself. It is nice, but it doesn't change the fact that they are puppeteering your experience through emotional manipulation so that you spend more money on them while ensuring you don't become a liability in the future. After all, manipulation is defined as "a clever way of controlling and influencing people". Through word-of-mouth referrals, customer satisfaction, and enduring brand loyalty, companies print themselves money from you and your friends' bank accounts. Not to mention that a bad customer experience can go viral now thanks to social media.

One incident involving a customer's bad experience with United Airlines went viral and resulted in $1.4 billion of company stock being wiped.[7] You, the customer, are always right, and it is more dangerous for a company not to acknowledge it than for the millions of people on social media to. Entitlement is the new norm. This is why companies try to humanise themselves as much as possible. We live in an age where fictional corporate entities are trying to personify themselves through the delivery of emotional experiences so that they can befriend you and manipulate you into caring about them. This is the only way they can survive and flourish. You are the centre of the universe, and the only thing they seek as much as turning over a profit is your approval, because the latter enables the former.

Product experience is narrower in scope than brand and customer experience. Whereas the former areas of experience are generalisable to all companies, product experience is prominent in technology companies that have software platforms and technological devices as products. The overall goal of the product experience is to engineer a customer journey that takes place within the confines of the product itself. The experience begins from the time an individual logs in to the product and is met by a welcome tour, right to the end of the session where the individual purchases the product and logs out. This represents an important area for businesses. Currently, free trials and freemium business models rely on a good product experience to convert people into paying, long-term customers.

Examples of online products and software systems include Facebook, Instagram, Snapchat, Active Campaign (email delivery system), Trello (team management software), and Hootsuite (social media management platform). A tangible example of an engineered product experience is probably sitting in your hand. If you joined the Apple cult and bought an iPhone, the moment you began to excavate your phone from the box, your product experience started. The cleanness, simplicity, and overall design of the white packaging comprised a sensory experience that formed part of your overall product experience. This then carried over into the usage of the product; simplistic and laboratory-looking user interfaces are hallmarks of iPhones. Throughout your whole in-phone journey, your experience was engineered through rigorous testing and unrelenting qualitative analysis. Apple spent a lot of time, resources, and psychological capital on that white box with your experience in mind, don't be fooled.

Lastly, the **user experience** details the experiences a customer undergoes as they interact with a company's products, services, and systems. As a result, this occurs ubiquitously throughout the other levels of consumer experience, be it through product interactions, engaging customer support, or navigating websites. User experiences, when engineered by companies, seek to increase the number of positive moments for the user while minimising the number of negative moments (otherwise known as pain points). In the case of an iPhone, a streamlined setup process and super-simple navigation are the engineered user experiences for that product, which, by virtue of Apple's rigorous product-testing processes, by design, result in positive experiences. The way an e-commerce store has set up their website to allow for easy product inspections and intuitive cart checkouts, evidences user experience at a system level.

Empathy mapping

Ideal outcomes for companies manifest when people are happy, satisfied, and proud as a result of their experience with a product or system. Achieving this relies on experience designers being tuned in to the emotions and mindsets of their users, so much so that a common method utilised to help design the user experience is empathy mapping. This is a way to visually represent what users say, feel, think, and do as they interact with company systems, products, or services. By understanding the emotions and thoughts that run through people's minds when they interact with elements of a product, designers can architect all the different touchpoints so that people transform into customers, and these same customers become loyal.

For an organisation to achieve meaningful, long-term relationships with its customers, it relies on an accumulation of positive user interactions and experiences. First impressions, consistency, associations, likeability, and empathy are underlying mechanisms that affect human psychology and influence human behaviour.[8] User experience design seeks to integrate and capitalise on all of these in their quest to convert you into a generous and loyal spender.

Examining the personal experience

Companies forever use values and emotions as social magnets and unrelentingly try to humanise themselves as much as possible. Online, they compete for your attention through their emotionally engineered content, comprising the bulk of their advertisements. First impressions matter here, and everyone knows there's only one chance to make a good first impression, companies too are keenly aware. If they come out a winner in the competition for your attention, provided they make a good first impression, without saying it they will invite you to learn about them further.

A click to some more of their content and your inevitable arrival upon their website is eagerly welcomed, and truth be told, half expected. In fact, they have been waiting for this moment, it is part of your predetermined engineered experience they have so meticulously planned. If you oblige, you begin the tentative early stages of your brand experience, exploring deeper levels of the brand than is displayed through superficial marketing material that has made its way into your field of vision. At this point, they will try to deliver you value, convince you of their integrity, and illustrate the superior quality of their products and services. Trust, integrity, credibility, and reciprocity need to be fulfilled for people to open their wallet and dish out its contents to an expectant company, and they know this is what needs to happen for them to win you over. To manufacture these feelings in you, they show off trust icons, testimonials, happy customers, and, much like a clairvoyant, they always seem to know your deepest dreams and desires. In fact, it's the basis of their appeal.

> What comes across as a caring personal relationship from a compassionate company to you, represents profits to them.

Companies know you are not buying team management software because of its underlying ingenuity and superior database architecture. You are buying it because it frees up your time and alleviates stress headaches. It is why product descriptions with dot points like "saves you time", "increases productivity", and "all-in-one system" are enthusiastically advertised. In the end, these are your triggers and the real reason for your purchase. Of course, they knew your buzzwords, they studied you and the people like you, you were their lab rats. You are not buying designer jeans because you need leg warmers. You are buying them for social reasons, status signalling, compliments, acknowledgement, and to feel and look like the model who's wearing them. How cool and confident are they, but how cool and confident will you be?

You are not buying scientifically formulated skin products to combat acne and remove blemishes. You're buying them for the feeling that clear skin gives you and what this now means for your self-esteem and social life. How coincidental that the models used to promote these skin creams always seem to be exuding confidence and happiness. Organisations can't dynamically respond or extract your desires in real time – the drivers of your purchases – but they've made educated guesses based on research and well-crafted assumptions. The feelings you get from stumbling upon your dream product were engineered, despite you feeling like they were a serendipitous coincidence. The truth is that most of the time businesses know what you want just as much as you do, perhaps even more. Going off the documentary *The Social Dilemma*, this isn't hyperbole, but more like a scary understatement.

As a result of the extravagant displays of trust, credibility, and the meticulously planned and targeted emotional appeals, they want you to like them. They understand you and your deepest desires, other people trust them, happy customers are plastered on their website, and rave reviews and ratings should alleviate your purchasing anxieties. Additionally, they have provided you with value through online resources, blogs, special offers, educational content, and informational videos. How nice is that? Not to mention the time and effort invested to ensure a positive first impression.

Engineering your whole experience was not cheap. Web designers, UX specialists, and web developers charge a lot of money. It is worth it for these companies though. What comes across as a caring personal relationship from a compassionate company to you, represents profits to them. Your relationship is a transactional commodity. They know that getting you to like them symbolises a positive emotional shift, and with your emotions in approval of them they can begin to play a different game. Through trust-building strategies, rapport development, empathy maps, and likeability techniques, they have qualified themselves as worthy of your impending payment. As long as they keep up their performance and continue to convince you of their integrity, quality, and value, you will remain a loyal customer, spreading the word to your disciples, and, as a result of your contribution, the company can ensure its own survival. After all, what are friends for?

The *you* experience

In the same way that companies continually fight for attention, respect, and camaraderie, so too are you when you are operating in a professional capacity. The competition is fierce, and if you don't care about the impression you make as much as the next professional, you are done. Insightful experts, universities, forward-thinking professionals, and executive leadership teams have even taken it one step further. After attention hijacking, they don't leave people high and dry, but instead they do quite the opposite by honouring the tectonic shift that is seeing cold, transactional exchanges being replaced with relationship-driven business philosophies. All lives matter, they say, as they carry out their humanitarian efforts.

> As a biological business, *you* are a product, and how people experience you matters.

Their ideology is fast becoming your reality, and if you choose to ignore it you will fall behind because the "experience" factor is the secret ingredient that makes a difference. Historically, only a few industries, such as travel and entertainment, dealt in experiences, but nowadays all organisations and companies must use emotionally charged experiences as their yardstick measurement for success. The emotionally experiencing consumer is the centre of every world, and in exchange for their dollar they want your product with a dose of serotonin. As a biological business, *you* are a product, and how people experience you matters.

The biggest and best organisations are forever creating attention-gripping content, are always aware of the impressions they give off, are excited to join the cult of experience worshippers, and place their customers at the centre of their universe. As a living, breathing business, everyone is your customer. You could aptly live by the motto "you never know". You never know when a friend or acquaintance will offer to pay you for something and transition into a paying customer. You never know who will offer you a job and exclusively buy your services. You never know who will refer their connections on to you, effectively marketing out your personal product suite. You never know if the brief interaction you just had with a stranger will reach fruition. Even people you haven't met yet could become your customer, and chances are this nebulous demographic will end up forming the bulk of your clientele. For them, the things you do today become part of your first impression when fate eventually intertwines your paths. Entire industries of customers are waiting to meet you. For the majority of customers, your first impression matters as much as a multinational company's does and represents the start of your *personal brand experience.*

Awareness

Ground zero for your personal brand is awareness. If no one knows, no one knows. The start of your whole journey begins with marketing and advertising campaigns. Alternatively, you could think of them as "awareness" campaigns. Organisations pay attention hijackers to generate brand and product awareness, foster engagement through content and posts, drive sales revenue up, and hopefully form cult-like communities that sell products on behalf of the company. It's no secret that these marketing specialists and content creators are worth every cent they charge. Start-ups lacking a chief marketing officer usually nosedive and burnout quite early in the game, which is testament to the fundamental role that marketers play in business. Proper marketing strategies are a maker or breaker. When you operate as an independent professional it may be a bit of a stretch to hire someone to do this for you, after all you'd need to find a marketing professional who is affordable, understands your personal brand and product suite as well as you do, and can post as regularly as you'd like them to. Further, they would need to be familiar with and know how to navigate all the social channels you use, and today there are hundreds in use.

Hopefully, you now realise that you are functioning as an independent professional whether you are an employee, a freelancer, an entrepreneur, or a contractor. Your personal brand, by virtue of its attachment to the deepest layers of your identity, seeps into the brand you emanate when acting in a professional capacity. For example, a self-employed freelance designer may provide a stock-standard graphic design service; however, elements of their personal brand will pervasively influence their service. How they communicate with customers is influenced by personality characteristics. How they come up with design ideas is influenced by their inherent creativity. The quality of their work is determined by their personal quality standards. The business's values are an extension of their personal values. The services offered by the business are an extension of the founder's unique product suite.

When you are an employee, your personal brand radiates outward, touching everyone you come into contact with: customer, boss, colleague, or subordinate. If you are an entrepreneur starting a company, your personal brand will heavily influence the direction, values, and culture of the company. In many cases becoming so intricately entangled it's hard to differentiate brand from founder. For example, Tesla and Elon Musk are practically interchangeable terms. Realising that you are an adaptable, independent professional with a personal brand that is always attached to you means you effectively operate in much the same way as a business does. Logically, the way you market and advertise yourself should be properly attended to. You need to solve this problem.

Common unity

Luckily, there is a solution that doesn't require employing an expensive professional to build and manage your social media accounts, although it does require a perspective shift. First, it's important to recognise that you are the centre of a community of people who are all attached to each other via you. Your Facebook friends, Instagram followers, Snapchat connections, YouTube subscribers, Reddit followers, LinkedIn connections, Twitter followers, real-life friends, family, and other social groups are all part of your community! In fact, you are the *common unity* that unifies them to each other. What's more, they have willingly opted in to be part of it by following you online or by accepting some form of social relationship with you. This is your audience. Marketers advertise to strangers, hoping to get the buy-in and emotional investment from them that your community is already giving to you. You don't need to pay anything to put your content in front of anyone because you already have all eyes on you and represent the epicentre of a universe of people.

Your personal brand and your professionalism are inextricably linked. Your social media channels represent the same online mediums that companies use to advertise their products and services. The networking events you attend are the type of events companies will pay to associate their brand with. The community you have is the receptive audience that companies wish they had. What you post is content that companies would pay other people to generate. You are the marketer of your own personal brand. Whatever you post to any of your personal social media accounts, and how you interact with others in real life, is directly attached to your personal brand. This can be curated by you, deployed by you, and reaches a receptive audience in your community. *This is the perspective shift.* You do not need to pay someone to manage your social media accounts, familiarise them with all the platforms you use, and continually vet their work because you already do this for your own social media accounts and everyday interactions anyway.

You are a marketer, an advertiser, an attention hijacker! Through navigating platforms, creating content, sparking engagement, and forming your own community, you have demonstrated the key capabilities of each one of these professionals. The only thing you need to do differently while you leverage existing social media platforms and internet technologies is to think about what you post and how it will be received. Ask yourself:

- Will it grab their attention?
- Is it valuable to them?
- What does it say about your personal brand?
- How can you leverage your community to improve your business?
- What associations will people form about you?
- What products and services do you offer?
- What are you interested in?
- What is your speciality?
- What are the emotional triggers that will stir people into action?

All personal posts from your social media accounts form an ongoing marketing campaign for your continually evolving and fluidic personal brand that is YOU!

If you wanted to take your marketing game further by designing, editing, and creating attention-grabbing visuals or videos, you only need to go to Google and say the word. Marketing technology, graphic design systems, video editing programs, and content management software are widely available and affordable on the internet. Simply type in the string of keywords in the above phrases and it manifests at your fingertips. Personally, I have no design or video editing experience, but after paying a yearly subscription of $60 to Filmora, a company specialising in video editing programs, I was able to navigate easy-to-use software to create video content for our company's YouTube channel and other social media accounts. Now that your marketing campaign is underway (and has been for quite some time), you need to think about how people experience you and therefore your personal brand. Ask yourself, what is the personal brand experience they are getting?

Hidden ingredients

How people experience your presence online and offline forms an integral part of your personal brand directly affecting your:

- brand loyalty
- word-of-mouth marketing
- brand image
- perceived value
- overall success as a business professional.

In the 21st century world of work fuelled by independent professionals and personal brands, irrespective of whether you're delivering products through goods, services, ideas, or solutions, you are intricately linked with your offerings, and so the experience people have with you matters. The first impressions they have of you, the extent to which they believe in your capabilities, how they appraise you consciously and unconsciously, the way you communicate, the confidence, trust, liking, and respect they have for you, how happy and comfortable you make them feel, whether you are able to impress them: all matter more than anything!

These are the hidden ingredients of your personal brand that win people over and keep them coming back to you in a professional capacity. Moreover, the universal elements of personal interactions begetting professional success traverses job roles, businesses, industries, countries, and likely the majority of humanity. In fact, the only time being a respected, capable, likeable, trustworthy, and impressive individual doesn't contribute to your professional flourishing is if you're an actor in a fictional movie playing the bad guy everyone should hate.

The personal experience

In light of its significance, I've created a framework for the important areas of your interactions that contribute to the experiences people have with you. We'll call it your *personal experience* since we're integrating you-as-a-business into the world of marketing, brand strategy, and engineered experiences. The framework encompasses neuroscience research, psychological techniques, marketing principles, and interpersonal communication strategies that have been cohesively pulled together to allow you to positively influence the people you interact with, many of whom are potential customers and brand advocates, on a conscious and unconscious level. This framework is detailed in *Part II*.

We have learnt that our conscious and unconscious minds are influential in shaping our experiences by altering how we feel and behave in situations. Both mental states even possess the ability to influence formal decision-making processes. In personal interactions, social information is processed consciously and unconsciously by brain areas responsible for decision-making. For example, your brain detects, processes, interprets, and converts people's social data to guide your decisions and feelings about them. This is what informs your judgements about people's trustworthiness, how much you like or dislike them, your wider appraisals of them, and how confident you are in their abilities.

Social data provides insights into people and their motives, highlights their values, and illuminates their feelings about you. There are definitive reasons why we feel we can't trust people and equally prevalent are the reasons we feel fond of others. Our mind and body pick up on information that leads to these judgements. Understanding the emotionally fuelled and intelligently guided decision-making processes that bring about these judgements will allow you to elicit the desired outcomes in other people by providing them with the available data they need to reach conclusions about you. At your disposal there are nonverbal behaviours you can use to make someone trust you, marketing techniques you can use to build confidence, and ways you can get people to like you by leveraging psychological principles.

Being believable

To create a tectonic emotional shift in our audience where they like and feel good about us, we need to be believable. We need to provide them with targeted information they consciously process as well as signals they unconsciously detect and emotionally respond to. Both need to be consistent with each other because emotions aren't easily convinced. We can't tell someone how excited and passionate we are about working with them while our voice is monotone, our shoulders remain hunched, and our previous social signals beg to differ. In the same way, we can't advertise ourselves as being punctual, conscientious, and respectful if we arrive late at meetings dressed in ill-fitting attire with no regard for the other. Warning signs like this will activate our audience's intuitive systems and will result in unfavourable evaluations. How people feel guides their decisions and behaviours. Knowing the source of their feelings and being able to positively influence them really does put you in a powerful position.

To sum up

Developing congruency with the information you deliver, your behaviours, and your presentation is an incredibly important precondition for people to trust you, like you, work with you, pay you, feel comfortable with you, positively appraise you, refer you, have confidence in you, and develop meaningful, authentic relationships with you. Especially in a business capacity.

Multinational corporations invest millions crafting convincing experiences to influence you. You don't need millions, but you do need this knowledge! The following information is grounds for manipulation, but if you are an ethical person, and if the framework merely represents a better way for you to advertise and evidence the honourable and moral pre-existing values and capabilities you already have, then my conscience is clear.

What's next?

Following, we unpack the first component of experience engineering: first impressions. During a first impression, within the first 30 seconds, there is a large exchange of social data happening, the processing of which can be conscious or unconscious. From appearances and colour psychology to handshakes and attractiveness judgements, engineering proper first impressions is one way to set the early foundations of a successful relationship. The many variables factoring into this early impression are explored and analysed so that they may be optimised and utilised for your *personal experience*.

PART II

Chapter 8:
The Hidden Art of Experience Engineering – 1

First impressions

In the corporate world, a bad first impression can deter partnerships and repel customers, effectively costing companies hundreds, thousands, or millions of dollars. In customer journey mapping at the level of product design, UX designers are keenly aware of the significance of a first impression; experts propose it takes ten positive interactions to resolve a negative one. The fact is that many a time there is no second chance to recoup the losses of a wayward deal or to lure back the valuable product user who exited an app due to a lacking experience. Billion-dollar international organisations and world-class experience engineers spend a lot of time and energy crafting a good first impression for precisely this reason.

The same esteem should be placed on the first impression you give to others. Research shows it can affect how much someone likes and trusts you, influences how likely they are to do business with you, alters the probability of them hiring you, and leads to them making accurate judgements and expectancies about you.[1] Some experts have even suggested first impressions can impact life partner choices.[2] Talk about catching someone's eye. In this section, we'll deconstruct first impressions into component parts and explore how to capitalise on each of them so that your personal experience starts off from a solid foundation.

It doesn't take long

We meet people every day and are constantly crossing paths with strangers, making new friends, and building new connections. Interestingly, the initial observation of someone, even if only brief, can have long-lasting effects.

It's been proven that the judgements and expectancies you form about people within the first 30 seconds of meeting them are accurate.[3] Other studies have demonstrated that observing snippets of someone's nonverbal behaviour for two seconds is enough for you to accurately judge aspects of their personality and their job effectiveness.[4]

The study that proved this videoed a teacher while they taught their class. After removing the audio from the video, the researchers picked out two-second snippets from the recording at random, referring to them as "thin slices of nonverbal behaviour". In total, three of the two-second recordings were used in the experiment. Researchers approached strangers and showed them the "thin slices of nonverbal behaviour" and asked them to make judgements about the teacher's work effectiveness and to assign them personality traits.

Later in the study, the experimenters compared the stranger's evaluations of the teacher with evaluations from the teacher's students and colleagues. Unlike the strangers, the colleagues and students knew the teacher intimately and therefore offered informed opinions about them. Surprisingly, the evaluations and judgements actually matched. Strangers were able to make an informed judgement about the teacher's work effectiveness and personality traits from two-second recordings of nonverbal behaviours, which was corroborated by the teacher's peers. The experimenters attempted to explain this by talking about the natural essence of a person being radiated through their body language.

What they call natural essence obviously refers to the personal qualities of your brand. To reiterate, in the first 30 seconds of meeting, people form judgements and build expectations about one another that surprisingly turn out to be accurate. Even from two-second slices of your nonverbal body language, people can absorb influential social information and reach valid conclusions about your work effectiveness and personality traits.

This is important because generating positive perceptions about your work effectiveness is a hurdle requirement for earning the business of your customers. Without inspiring confidence in customers, they will not feel comfortable engaging you, and if they hold any reservations about your quality of work, they will take their money elsewhere. We live in a professional surplus; others with your skillset are usually not hard to find. The social data emanating from you at the beginning of an interaction significantly influences people's perceptions with regard to confidence building and rapport generation.

In the last section of the framework, *Chapter 11*, we'll explore in-depth how nonverbal behaviours contribute to these impressions.

Trust

Noted previously, first impressions are a deciding factor in trustworthiness judgements, hiring decisions, and life partner choices.[2] The demonstrated ability to influence and impact many areas of your life hints at the universal importance and far-reaching implications of first impressions and, as we will discover, the sole ability to generate trust with someone, which can manifest in brief initial encounters, can completely alter the trajectory of subsequent relationships.

For example, in business settings, trustworthiness is a highly valued trait and may be the difference between landing a job at a new company or being promoted to a more senior level of management. It could be the deciding factor that causes a person to enter a joint venture with you or may represent a fundamental purchasing criterion from a new client. Behaviours that occur in the early stages of relationships play pivotal roles in bringing about these desired judgements.

Emotions

Your emotions also guide first impression judgements. Remember how we deconstructed the body and discovered that emotions were a way for the body to process and exchange information with different systems? Well, studies prove that your gut instinct about someone, which you base off their appearance on first meeting, over-rules what you already know about the person.[5] Your unconscious detects information from the first impression, converts it into molecules (neuropeptides) and relays this to the rest of the body. The gut has receptors for these molecules of emotion, and your gut instinct is simply the gut feeling you get when these neuropeptides bind to it.[6]

The body, your unconscious mind, is picking up information and conveying it to your consciousness through your gut. Despite someone having many credentials behind their name, working with big clients, having networked friends, and boasting a good social media following, your opinion may be dramatically swayed of them when you first catch a glimpse of their appearance and observe their early behaviours. Your intuition about them is an influential board member when you entertain decisions that involve them. With good reason, because if we don't let our instincts voice their opinions when we meet people, we may be more inclined to take the word of a suspicious-looking, trench-coat-wearing white van driver. Applying this to yourself means that your appearance alone can impact the emotional judgements and long-lasting impressions people form about you, so you need to get this right.

Head versus heart

First impressions are made up of two types of initial impressions: **explicit** and **implicit evaluations,** also known as decisions of the "head" versus the "heart". The "head" is logical and evaluative, whereas the "heart" is about how we feel. You may feel romantically attracted to a person but logically know it is not a good match. For example, a person may "know" you as a kind and respected professional (an explicit evaluation) but your appearance and behaviours, which unconsciously trigger stereotypes in their mind, may make them "feel" differently about you (an implicit evaluation). When the two evaluations contradict each other, such as the above, the discrepancy will affect the relationship trajectory. If you think positively about someone, but feel negatively about them, of course the relationship has predetermined limits.

Explicit evaluations can be measured directly and changed. For example, if I said, "I like you", that would be an explicit evaluation, but I can easily change it and say, "I don't like you" in light of learning new information.[7] You would be able to identify someone's explicit evaluation and attitude toward you through obvious behaviours and verbal statements. On the other hand, implicit evaluations are harder to measure because they are determined through emotional associations to other things. They are resistant to change and long lasting because they relate to how we truly feel about someone or something and are based off our deep and often hidden attitudes.[8]

Sure, bumping into the acting high-school principal who expelled me many moons ago I could explicitly state, "It's great to see you again, what a fortunate event." But, deep down, my implicit evaluation of their existence is anything but. My instinctive emotional circuitry and super-intelligent unconscious knows the unfavourable characteristics historically expressed by this person, and their reappearance on the scene has triggered deeply held memories and beliefs. It doesn't help that this evaluative system is not so forgiving. Even though my consciously monitored explicit evaluation of them has been altered to fit in with social norms and civility, the powerful, all-knowing associative machinery in my body will always respond to something it associates with a monkey in the same way, consistently over time. The cataclysmic clash of my two evaluations of the person most certainly boundaries the relationship's upper limits. Implicit evaluations matter.

Understanding what contributes to first impressions allows you to capitalise on your first encounter.

Can you recall a time when someone made you angry and frustrated for no apparent reason? What about the time you met someone and instantly felt a dislike for them without knowing why? That's your unconscious associative machinery picking up on signals from them that trigger unfavourable thoughts, associations, or attitudes in you. These implicit evaluations are intuitive judgements you make about someone or something, making themselves known to you through feelings. After all, the definition of intuitive is "understanding without the need for conscious reasoning" – something our emotional system has been a superstar at for many thousands of years.

The evaluations we form about people and how we behave and interact with them are based on both conscious and unconscious information, which is why being aware of the unconscious domains of interaction is crucial. Implicit evaluations can be heavily affected by the unconscious domains of communication and can subsequently influence the way we behave toward someone or the way they behave toward us. Not to mention, unconscious social factors have further been shown to influence a person's executive control,[9] which is implicated in governing and guiding aspects of human behaviour,[10] and in planning actions and updating goals.[9]

During the first impression, you provide the other person with information about you through your greeting, the way you shake their hand, the clothes and colours you wear, and how you present. That person may be oblivious to the hidden realms of explicit and implicit evaluations, but their super-intelligent unconscious is not. Understanding what contributes to first impressions allows you to capitalise on your first encounter and set the foundations for a healthy, successful, and trust-filled relationship. There's only one chance for a good first impression, and whatever else you do, don't forget to use their name!

Names and brains

Given the limited time you have to make a positive first impression, you should attempt to develop a rapport as fast as you can. The first thing to do is use the person's name, arguably the most important word in the English language for them, as it demonstrates that you acknowledge and attribute value to them as an individual. A study monitoring the brain activity in people when hearing their own name discovered an interesting phenomenon.[11] When a person heard their name compared to other names, researchers noted an increase in brain activation in the medial frontal cortex and superior temporal cortex. Interestingly, the medial frontal cortex is associated with making inferences about others, determining future behaviour based on anticipated value, and self-reflection.[12]

Using someone's name generates higher brain activity in social-related areas of their brain, resulting in that person being more attentive and receptive to you. Proof of this is encountered through the "cocktail party effect"; a psychological phenomenon demonstrating how your brain identifies and focuses on one auditory stimulus at a time. Usually, you will notice this effect when you're in a room full of people and somehow, from somewhere, you hear your name, which momentarily becomes the only thing you can hear. Your name represents a powerful stimulus, automatically pinging your brain and causing you to divert your attention in its direction.

Other research demonstrates that the medial frontal cortex includes areas involved in reward processing, reward-based learning, and reward-based decision-making.[13,14] Furthermore, a person's name can represent a social reward in the sense that it is an indirect way of showing someone that you value them. Activating a social reward system in the brain has been associated with positive feelings,[15] and this is probably why it feels nice when someone uses your name.

When you first meet someone, this is exactly how you want to influence them. You want them to be more receptive to you and to associate you with positive feelings, and you want them to know that you respect and value them, which is what the use of their name suggests. As a result of hearing their name, they become positively primed for future interactions with you. Meaning they will see you through a positive lens, giving more attention to all the good things about you while simultaneously turning a blind eye to the bad.

Priming relates to a bias in the brain whereby future information is interpreted based on perceived previous information. For example, the moment a person sees the word *doctor* they will faster recognise the word *nurse* from a string of letters as opposed to unrelated words such as *cat* or *dog*. Their brain uses previous information to activate related mental concepts, which guides future perceptions and behaviours. Superimposing the effects of psychological priming to human interactions essentially means that a person's evaluations of you will be more positive moving forward if the first impression was positive. For an in-depth exploration, I refer you to books and research papers by Daniel Kahneman, a leading researcher in human behaviour, who examines the concept of priming in detail.

Along with the more subconscious effects of using someone's name, research has also shown the obvious benefits of doing this. One study proved that by remembering someone's name they become more compliant with your requests.[16] It is like you're blowing magic dust in someone's face purely because you took the time to remember and voice the one word that's important to them. If you need a favour or are requesting something from someone, this small act significantly improves your chances of success. No wonder slippery salespeople and manipulative misguided souls feel the need to obsessively use your name. To avoid being perceived like this, don't use people's name excessively or for the wrong reasons because obvious attempts at manipulation are cringeworthy. We are just being polite and setting the stage for a mutually beneficial long-term relationship. We're not trying to con them into selling their parents' house and the family pet.

Repeating somebody's name after a first encounter and during a conversation does many things. Some of these benefits occur at a deep psychological level, whereas others can be directly perceived in business settings through compliance. A person's name is one of the most powerful words known to man and an awesome, influential secret weapon that is available to us. Use it wisely.

Appearance

Research presented at the Society for Personality and Social Psychology annual conference (2014) demonstrated that someone's appearance when you meet them can potentially alter the subsequent relationship you develop with them, including how much you end up liking them.[1] The moment you meet someone, you form judgements based off their appearance.[17] Inferences can be made about personality traits, social positions, biological characteristics, attitudes, emotions, and intentions. Clothing, in itself, provides information that people can, and do, use. Studies have related clothing to social positions, suggesting that, in organisations, higher-ranking people dress more formally when compared to lower-ranking members.[18]

Extrapolating from this, it stands to reason that your perceived social class can be hinted at through the formality of your attire. When trying to orchestrate a specific impression of yourself in someone's mind, altering the formality of your clothing can lead to you being perceived as more important, or less so, depending on the direction you choose. This isn't a hard and fast rule and doesn't change your inherent value; however, it's important to acknowledge that this is one way people reach conclusions about you. You can alter their reality by altering your formality.

When people observe you, the judgements formed based on your appearance can be guided by stereotypes, previous associated judgements, or based off superficial traits like attractiveness. This is an automatic process that is reinforced by the way our brains are wired. To get through life and avoid information overload, our brains have become really good at categorising experiences, people, and objects into buckets that "look the same". It saves us a lot of time, conserves our mental effort, and usually, but not always, provides accurate navigation of our world.

To illustrate this, imagine waking up in a fictional world where nice people wear blue shirts and angry, abusive people wear red shirts. After some time, the repeated abuse and aggression dished out by the red-shirted people begins to have repercussive effects. Merely glancing at someone in a red shirt would cause us to experience physiological, neural, and behavioural changes. Our stress hormones would ramp up, the flight-or-fight nervous system would activate, and we would exhibit avoidant or hostile behaviour in light of the impending interaction. In essence, we have learnt to associate red shirts with danger, aggression, antisociality, and negative feelings.

Even if we woke up back into the real world, we would still, for a time, assume all people wearing red to be angry and abusive. Our classification of red-shirted people is an example of a stereotype. As such, our behaviour would be influenced whenever crossing paths with someone wearing a red shirt, with a strong tendency to display hostile, timid, or vigilant behaviours in preparation for an aggressive interaction. This, as we know, is false logic. The people in the normal world wearing red aren't any more likely to be abusive than someone wearing a black, blue, or orange shirt; however, based on our previous experience, and the resultant associations we've formed, it's a viable conclusion for us to reach.

Historically, this stereotype provided an accurate and functional tool for us to navigate our social environment, but stereotypes can be flawed. In the same way that we can learn to stereotype other people and form biases, our unconscious mind and evolutionary urges influence how we assess others. The flipside of this is that others are automatically categorising and assessing us through potentially unfounded and illogical biases we may not be aware of either.

One notable example is attractive people. Unconscious biases fuelled by evolutionary psychology change how we perceive, interact, and value people we deem attractive. We can't help it. As humans we are forever using shortcuts to judge the people around us. We need to because streamlined judgements may save our lives, especially if we accurately judge someone as suspicious looking from aspects of their appearance we fleetingly observe. Identifying a crazy person when you're locked in their basement or in the back of a van is too late.

Despite this, judging someone off appearance alone does not always provide us with enough information to reach accurate conclusions. One study found that people were not able to make accurate character judgements about a person going off appearances and went on to conclude that "appearances may actually make us worse at predicting the characteristics of others".[17] This is important to underscore. Even though we spontaneously form superficial judgements and opinions about the people around us, most of the time we arrive at the wrong conclusions.

Other studies have demonstrated that 76 percent of people believe their judgements about other people, which they base off aspects of their clothing and external appearances, to be accurate.[19] Highlighted here is a precarious situation. People are constantly judging others based on superficial information. People's judgements are influenced via conscious and unconscious biases. These are fuelled by evolution and personal experiences. Frequently, this recipe leads to false judgements. However, most of the time people believe them to be accurate.

If we look at this from a different angle, we can use this knowledge to benefit us. People are always judging us based on our external appearance. They use previous associations, stereotypes, and how attractive we are to guide their judgement. As stated above, people believe their judgements to be accurate despite frequently being wrong. Knowing this, we could deliberately change the formality of our clothing to change their associations of us to a higher social class and elicit more respect. We could choose specific colours to wear depending on what traits we wanted them to associate us with. We could manipulate our appearance and alter our perceived attractiveness to generate positive judgements, in turn influencing how confident and successful we are perceived to be.

By insightfully manipulating our appearance and leveraging desirable associations, we paint their reality. The mental representation another person forms of us is no longer theirs, but ours. We have woven together seemingly distinct characteristics and advantageously used elements of social psychology to light their way, leading them to a destination of our choosing, one automatic judgement at a time. We are an artist, and their perception of us becomes our sculpture. Our immaterial creation holds no value except for the value placed upon another's impressions, which at times is priceless. Given that appearance provides the foundation for early judgements about us, primes subsequent interactions, influences many important relationship outcomes, and for the most part is largely alterable, the calculated control of it represents one social superpower.

Clothing

Clothing is an informative element of our overall appearance. Studies have demonstrated that personality traits such as extroversion and conscientiousness can be inferred through someone's physical appearance in a first encounter.[20] The researchers, when attempting to understand how these accurate personality judgements were achieved, postulated that conscientiousness was inferred through the formalness and neatness of a person's clothes. The reasoning behind it is: conscientious people have high standards in many areas of their lives; therefore, the way they dress is also subject to conscientious behaviours, and, as such, the neatness and formalness of clothing hints at this underlying trait.

Another aspect of our appearance influencing how we are judged is the fit of our clothes. This was demonstrated in a study that compared people wearing a tailor-fitted suit to an untailored ready-to-wear suit. A person wearing a tailor-fitted suit generated positive impressions within the scales of confidence, success, flexibility, and salary.[21] It appears that this aspect alone is enough to make people believe you earn a higher income and are more successful. Tailoring your attire to fit the contours and specific dimensions of your body is one way to radiate impressions of success. If we understand the law of attraction, dressing for success by wearing properly fitted clothes should be ground zero for every employee, business owner, entrepreneur, and anyone wanting to create a positive and successful impression!

Garner all the initial positivity you can by putting thought and effort into your attire.

Your shoes are another informative feature of your clothing that can contribute to impression formation. Some researchers believed shoes to be that powerful in predicting characteristics about a person they set up an experiment to test whether participants could predict the personalities of people solely by viewing their shoes.[22] Apart from participants accurately predicting attachment anxiety from footwear, their experiment did not confirm that shoes can contribute enough information about people to make accurate personality judgements. However, the fact that experts invested time and effort into this shows that there is reason to believe that shoes can convey a significant amount of information to other people. A person walking around in worn-out, unattractive shoes may be perceived as lazy or uncaring. Certain formal, polished shoes may allude to traits associated with conscientiousness. Vibrant, out-there shoes may hint at extroversion, and if someone consistently and unnecessarily wore red over-the-top designer high heels, it may signal narcissism.

This research is valuable for men and women. The formality and neatness of your clothes can transform perceptions to that of a highly professional person. Conscientiousness is a sought-after trait, no matter what profession you are in. The impressions given off by tailored, well-fitting clothes are favourable, with significant business ramifications. The shoes you wear convey information to onlookers and may leak personal characteristics that others consciously and unconsciously process. It is in your best interest to garner all the initial positivity you possibly can in your first encounters by putting thought and effort into your attire, and, in doing so, dramatically altering people's perceptions of you.

Before uttering a word, your clothing, appearance, and body language begin to paint a picture in the mind of your recipient. Their mental representation of you is taking shape, informing the trajectory of subsequent encounters through priming effects. To increase a person's confidence in their judgement of you, it's necessary to provide congruent pieces of information from all areas of first impressions, and here even colours have a place.

Colour psychology

Colour psychology has generated more interest in recent years as colours have been thought capable of influencing the psychological responses of people. Wavelengths of light are interpreted by specialised sensory organs in our body and broken down into information we can use. The colours we see can convey information to our brain about objects or people, which factor into our judgements. One notable example can be seen through pink and blue. Everybody knows that, traditionally, pink was for girls and blue was for boys, showing how feminine and masculine traits can be intermingled with the role that colours take up in society. Stemming from this association, you may automatically view a male outfitted in pink attire as feminine or homosexual.

The valuable data colours provide may also factor into our unconscious biases, moods, and decisions. There has been a longstanding belief that general emotional associations with colours exist, such as red for anger, green for envy, and blue for sadness. The association of colours to emotions has become so widespread that when people are sad, others describe them as feeling "blue", and when they are angry, others describe them as seeing "red".

Just like there are societally imbued generalised emotional associations to colours, there are evolutionary-fuelled responses too. We need look no further than frogs in the jungle. It is well known throughout the animal kingdom that bright colours symbolise poisonous or toxic species. A bright-coloured frog is therefore avoided by predators – evolution has taught them these colour characteristics represent a bad idea. This further exemplifies the importance of colour and hints at the complex information it conveys.

In the human world, colours play a role in personality inferences. Researchers suggest that colours can mediate psychological responses via the conscious and unconscious pathways of the brain.[23] Red has been shown to elicit perceptions of dominance, aggressiveness, braveness, and competition when it comes to achievement.[24] On the other hand, blue, when used in websites and company logos, is associated with trustworthiness, and viewing blue light has notable associations with increased subjective alertness and better performance with attention-based tasks.[25] Other experiments looking at personality inferences have demonstrated that lighter colours elicit more moodiness and could evoke perceptions of extroversion, wider interests, agreeableness, or disorganised personality impressions.[26]

Outside the realm of professional peer-reviewed journals, "colour experts" suggest blue has associations with intelligence, communication, and trust. Black is said to have associations with authority, sophistication, and power. Navy blue is said to elicit feelings of trustworthiness and professionalism while adding a degree of authority due to its darker shade, and white is associated with organisation and purity. Importantly though, these colour associations should be taken with a grain of salt as they simply represent the anecdotal opinions of self-appointed experts, the validity of their claims differing only slightly from palm readers and astrologers.

Scientific literature exploring colour psychology is rare due to the subjective nature of colour processing by individuals and their unique interpretations. For example, one person may associate green with nature and another with envy. One culture may associate red with anger, and another with prosperity. Despite this, scientific evidence does demonstrate that blue elicits trustworthiness, and, luckily for us, it just so happens that trustworthiness is a highly valued interpersonal trait, something we'd certainly benefit from engineering.

The recruitment industry aligns their support with the above findings, with 2,099 hiring managers in a CareerBuilder survey identifying black and blue as ideal interview colours. Science, not the subjective opinions of colour experts, also suggests red can elicit competitiveness between individuals, which should be considered depending on the social situation you are dropping into. For example, you may not want to bring about these feelings in a prospective employer when they are interviewing you. They may want someone submissive and obedient, not challenging and dominant. Come to think of it, I can't imagine any professional collaborative situations where red would be preferentially chosen. No other colour screams "look at me" as much as this one.

Human processing of colour is subjective and ambiguous. However, by reflecting on your own impressions of colour, you may be able to advantageously use this element in your appearance. Personally, if I walk past professionals wearing suits in the city, I find those wearing navy blue to be much more approachable and less intimidating than those wearing black.

Another way to think about colour is to think about its wider implications, irrespective of the traits and feelings it is associated with in literature. For one, consistently wearing a certain colour and style may contribute to the DNA of your personal brand. Steve Jobs was famous for his black turtlenecks. Lady Gaga is famous for the vibrant and outrageous colours and outfits she wears. Pink, the singer-songwriter, even named herself after a colour.

The colours you consistently associate with over time can contribute to your personal brand. Companies pay huge amounts of money to brand consultants and designers to get their colours right. Their logo, website, and product colours are meticulously engineered. They even colour-code their staff uniforms. In the same way companies sweat the details about colours, you should pay close attention to the colours you associate with. At any point in time, you may choose to knight a colour as a representative of your personal brand. Facebook, PayPal, Skype, Visa, LinkedIn, and Xero all chose blue as theirs.

Attractiveness

As superficial and irrelevant as it may seem, attractiveness significantly matters in human interactions and is especially important in our self-formulated judgements about others. Proof of this can be seen in employment settings. In mock interview situations, attractive people are more likely to be hired than less attractive people.[27] In real interview situations, the perceived attractiveness of interviewees had a higher predictive value of selection than any other examined criteria.[28] In other words, if you had a group of people walking through the company doors in the wake of their job interview, the best way to predict who would get the job would be to note their attractiveness and go from there.

Not only is it a game changer in employment outcomes, but some research shows that physically attractive individuals are also viewed more positively and more accurately during first impressions.[29] Outside of employment settings, Robert Cialdini, a world-renowned social psychologist, in his book *Influence,* reflects on how we automatically assign favourable traits such as talent, kindness, honesty, and intelligence to good-looking individuals.[30] He further cites evidence highlighting how attractive people are helped more in social situations and have more influence in changing the opinions of their audience. Perplexingly, Cialdini additionally references studies demonstrating how attractiveness can influence court outcomes, with handsome men receiving much lighter sentences than less attractive men. Literature corroborates this finding, showing the jury is influenced by the physical attractiveness of female defendants too.[31]

Building upon this, the field of social psychology confirms that attractive children receive higher grades from their teachers when their physical appearance is known,[32] and are more popular and better adjusted than unattractive peers.[33] In a meta-analysis, researchers found attractive adults differ from unattractive people in how they are judged, how they behave, and how they are treated. Findings found that attractive adults were more successful in their jobs and liked more. They presented as healthier and tended to have slightly higher intelligence and mental health. They were also more self-confident and had higher levels of self-esteem.[33] So pervasive and pre-programmed is our affinity for physical attractiveness that even newborn infants, ranging from 14–151 hours old, show a preference for attractive faces, measured via the amount of time they spent staring at attractive people compared to others.[34]

While unfair and completely unjustified, attractive people are treated as extra special; a product of evolutionary psychology. The reason we view people as attractive is because they demonstrate physical characteristics that appeal to the deep psychological mechanisms in our brain. Good facial proportions symbolise good genetics. Females with wide hips represent fertility and health, meaning they could be better equipped for childbearing. Males with chiselled jaws are attractive because a sculpted jawline indicates high levels of testosterone, which is linked to aggression and dominance. For females, testosterone-fuelled males are more likely to provide security and protection than males with lower levels.

In ancient times, educated guesses based on superficial characteristics were the best our ancestors could hope for. They didn't have electron microscopes, gene-mapping techniques, hormone therapies, or modern hospitals. Neither were social support systems, police forces, and online communities around. All they had were the physical aspects of people to base their life-changing mating decisions on, and those demonstrating positive markers evolution dubbed *attractive*. Deep down, our psychology still operates in the same way because that's what it has learnt over thousands of years. This is why we're hardwired to be attracted to certain individuals. Your brain subliminally tells you, "To ensure the best chance for your offspring's success, make sure to mate with someone attractive." Surprisingly, or maybe not so, this pervasive primitive urge still massively influences human interactions today.

If we take it a step further and explore attractiveness at another level, people who look good usually do so because they take care of themselves and put in effort to maintain a presentable appearance. This effort in itself may be attractive because it hints at positive personality traits, motivation, self-worth, and other aspects of psychology that modern humans deem important.

When you are seen as attractive, it means you are viewed more accurately, positively, honestly, and kindly during first impressions. It is assumed you are more talented and intelligent than your average-looking counterparts. The benefits of your attractiveness could include getting the job you applied for, receiving the help you needed, being able to speak your mind and persuading others into complying with your wishes, and, even if you violated the law by stealing, murdering, or raping, your sentence could quite possibly be lighter. Judges and jurors are not immune from the evolutionary forces that be. Although we won't benefit from that last point because we've got a proper-functioning moral compass, it's still valuable for us to impress favourable traits onto others.

To hack this aspect of our appearance and interlink these valuable associations with our personal brand, we need to deconstruct what exactly contributes to attractiveness judgements. Attractiveness is associated with:

- facial symmetry
- the averageness of the face to the general population
- the masculinity or femininity of the face
- good grooming
- youthfulness
- how much someone is liked as a person.[35]

In addition, white and natural-coloured teeth have been positively associated with attractiveness.[36] Full beards can lead to perceptions of dominance, whereas light stubble is rated as the most attractive [37,38] Different emotional expressions can lead to changes in your perceived attractiveness, with studies finding happiness to be the most attractive emotion in a female, and pride to be most attractive in males.[39] Less body fat, more muscle mass, and prominent female curves are obvious additions as well as lower waist-to-hip ratios.[40] This is a universal snapshot; however, despite what the above research says, individual preferences will clearly contribute to what people determine "attractive". The above criteria do not cater to those with foot fetishes, an affinity for plus-sized models, and addictions to BDSM submissives, to name a few. In the same way everyone has a favourite colour, everyone prefers certain looks, but some attributes are more universally popular than others.

Even though you cannot change the symmetry, averageness, or the masculinity and femininity of your face (unless you opt for cosmetic surgery and other procedures), there are many other things you can do to appear more attractive. The truth is that anyone can become attractive with a bit of effort. Although society unfairly overvalues a person's physical characteristics, it doesn't change the fact that there are clear benefits to being perceived in this way. Taking care of your teeth by employing whitening strategies to bring them back to an ideal colour is an easy way to improve your attractiveness rating. Moisturising your face and engaging in daily skincare can contribute to maintaining youthful skin. Being happy and proud advertises attractive traits to others. Good grooming such as tidying up facial and other body hair is impactful, and only requires effort. Makeup can be used to enhance the femininity or masculinity of your face and is why contouring is so popular. Females often contour their cheekbones (a hallmark of femininity) and make their eyes appear bigger and more noticeable with makeup. This is attractive to males because developed cheekbones are a sign of sexual maturity.

Hitting the gym and being active contributes to an optimal muscle mass to body fat ratio. Working on targeted musculature including glutes, pecs, shoulders, arms, and quads develops curves both sexes usually find attractive. Putting effort into yourself is another way. Finally, becoming more likeable makes you more attractive to your audience. This will be explored later in *Chapter 10* on Likeability. The recommendations listed aren't commandments, nor a one-size-fits-all approach; rather, they provide actionable points and real-life examples about how you can manipulate your perceived attractiveness to leverage the beneficial associations embedded in our minds through evolution.

You are beautiful whether you are fat or skinny, young or old, muscly or flabby, average looking or radically different. However, there are universal perspectives of aesthetic beauty, what we call "attractiveness", that can be capitalised on by implementing the above strategies. First impressions are extremely influential and important in judgement formation. Attractiveness alone – one aspect of a first impression – attaches to you a significant number of positive traits. Even though you may not value your appearance, simply be aware that others use it as a fundamental criterion when judging an array of your personal attributes, from intelligence to kindness, and employability to honesty.

Handshakes

Your handshake provides insights into the type of person you are and can leave a significant impression on the receiver. In fact, it is important enough to be a deciding factor in hiring outcomes. In mock interview situations orchestrated by researchers, people with firm handshakes received better appraisals by human resource professionals and were more likely to be hired.[41] Firm handshakes are slightly longer in duration, stronger, vigorous, and include a complete grip with eye contact.[42] Who would have thought that subtle nuances in our greeting behaviours could have such an impact? It could make or break your career.

Another experiment explored whether personality traits could be detected through handshakes.[43] Although researchers did not find all personality traits to be deducible from handshakes, they were able to prove conscientiousness as one trait that was accurately identifiable. In general, conscientiousness is associated with how well an individual can master a complex behaviour or skill. Researchers postulated that the reason behind accurate judgements of this trait came as a result of an individual's handshake appearing to be a mastered behaviour. Individuals with better handshakes gave off impressions that they had the ability to master skills, such as handshakes, which led others to detect this and perceive them as conscientious.

However, another study identified other personality traits correlating to handshakes,[42] finding that handshake characteristics could be related to personality traits. After completing personality surveys, self-reports, and undergoing handshake analysis, individuals with firmer handshakes were found to be more extroverted and open to experiences, while being less neurotic and shy. Not only this, but when trained research assistants participating in the experiment shook hands with these people, they also rated their personalities similarly. Meaning, if you naturally have a firmer handshake, you are more likely to score higher in the personality traits mentioned above, and others are likely to make accurate initial judgements of you regarding your personality.

As we discovered in *Chapter 3*, being extroverted means you are sociable and warm, openness to experience hints at intellectual flexibility and creativity, and being rated lower in neuroticism means others assume you are not depressed, anxious, and hostile. The study above also found that women who are more intellectual, liberal, and open to new experiences have a firmer handshake and make a more favourable impression when compared to women who are less open and have a softer handshake. Conveying personal qualities and behavioural tendencies to another person in the early moments of an interaction, within a three-second window, is certainly a difficult task. Although, you need not worry because a firm handshake delivers all this information, and potentially more.

From my research I've categorised eight types of handshakes and their meaning:

1. **Strong** handshakes are overly forceful, indicating your attempt to be domineering and powerful. Suggesting you are overcompensating for something you lack.

2. **Weak** handshakes are a sign you lack confidence and capability. It indicates to the receiver that there is mental weakness present, which may lead them to perceive you as neurotic.[42]

3. **Rushed** handshakes create the impression you do not care about the person you are greeting. Essentially, it is the same as brushing someone off.

4. **Long-lasting** handshakes are socially unacceptable, projecting an unwanted degree of immediacy, which can make the receiver feel uncomfortable.[44]

5. **Incomplete** handshakes occur when you give a handshake but do not acknowledge the person via eye contact, do not orientate your body in their direction, and do not present with a welcoming smile.

6. **Palm-down** handshakes can be perceived as domineering or controlling. When you force someone to shake your hand with their palm facing up, it implies that they are weak or submissive relative to you.[45] Offering your hand with your thumb up is the proper and neutral way to handshake.

7. **Informal** handshakes occur with friends outside professional settings. They often consist of a unique sequence of hand-smashing, chest bumps, and bro hugs resembling a form of modern art. It can convey unspoken messages.

8. **Perfect** handshakes are firm with the thumb oriented vertically, eye contact, a smile, direct bodily orientation, and the repetition of the receiver's name. This assures the receiver you are confident, capable, likeable, and independent (refer to the sections *Use their name* and *Eye contact*).[11,42,45,46,47]

In conclusion, a typical handshake lasts no longer than a few seconds, yet it transfers so much information consciously and unconsciously to the person shaking your hand. As highlighted above, having a perfect handshake leads people to believe you are more open, conscientious, passionate, extroverted, self-confident, and capable. Therefore, putting some thought into your handshake allows you to influence another's subconscious perspectives of you, allowing you to demonstrate traits that are viewed favourably and are highly valued by people and businesses.

Chronemics

Timing is another important factor that has a significant impact on your interactions with others. To put it into perspective, timing is the difference between life and death for a bomb diffuser. The timing of the market determines the difference between a company becoming a billion-dollar tech unicorn or a failed start-up. Time itself, as we have seen, can even completely alter human experiences. Moreover, the way you use time throughout social interactions, whether it be how early or late you arrive to job interviews, the time you allocate to see your friends, or if you regularly make others wait for you, provides illuminating social data to others by hinting at your traits, attitudes, and values.

Chronemics relates to the use of time in human interactions, such as being early, late, or keeping others waiting. By virtue of this, the way someone uses time can be linked to their social status. For example, a boss can call a meeting in the middle of the day without warning and the attendees are required to show up. Yet if the staff wished to speak to the boss, an appointment would need to be made in advance. In this scenario, the way time is commandeered changes depending on organisational rank.

Extending this outward into more general domains can allude to social positions of individuals. A fresh salesperson may spend 10 hours preparing for 30 minutes that a CEO of a large multinational company grants them. A mentee could spend 10 minutes waiting at a café for their mentor who is running late, which may be deemed acceptable granted the dynamic of the relationship. However, imagine the mentee was the one running 10 minutes late and the mentor wasted 10 minutes of their valuable time waiting.

Regardless of your social position, being late to an appointment, meeting, or interview gives the impression of carelessness, a lack of involvement, and quite possibly a lack of ambition.[18] Acknowledging and respecting other people's time is a sure-fire way to earn their early respect and convey that you are punctual, respectful, and reliable.

To sum up

First impressions set the foundation of your relationship with someone and can cause others to feel excited, impressed, comfortable, trustful, and pleased with you. Activating emotions such as these proves valuable for a plethora of reasons, regardless of the nature of the relationship you are forming. First impressions that are unable to manifest positive vibes, like those above, represent a lost opportunity and, more often than not, second chances are not granted. Via conscious and unconscious pathways, first impressions play a fundamental and universal role in shaping how relationships progress, influencing hiring decisions, life partner choices, personality inferences, social judgements, and perceptions of your character traits.

Within the first 30 seconds of meeting you, people are forming judgements and beginning to believe them. In fact, they may only need as little as two seconds of your nonverbal behaviour to accurately predict some of your traits. Along with early glimpses of nonverbal behaviours, they use your appearance, clothing choices, attractiveness, greeting behaviours, colour selection, and use of time as indicators of potential traits that you may or may not possess. Once they start to perceive you in a certain way, and start believing themselves to be accurate, this will influence how they respond to your requests, suggestions, business propositions, and overall presence.

It is impossible to read someone's mind (for now) and dispel all the inaccurate myths and assumptions flying around, so to save yourself time and headaches, implement these strategies to make sure their reality lines up with the one you prepared for them earlier. You are a person worthy of their attention, make sure they know it.

What's next?

After capturing someone's attention and priming them for a positive interaction, it is time to build their trust and confidence in you and the other products in your suite. In marketing, social proof is the weapon of choice used to persuade people for this end. The following chapter explores the neuroscience of social proof and how you can leverage this to improve your perceived value, generate more confidence in your prospects, and make people comfortable enough to do business with you.

Chapter 9:
The Hidden Art of Experience Engineering – 2

Social proof

The engineered first impression sets the foundation for a successful and rewarding relationship. As a result of the behaviours and techniques you implement, people will be primed to interact with you in a positive way, having a favourable evaluation of you and viewing you as talented, kind, likeable, respectable, and conscientious. A good first impression paves the way for trust formation and helps people to develop confidence in you and your capabilities. As we know, these conditions are fundamental for flourishing personal relationships to develop, and it is at this point, after a positive first impression, that the opportunity for business transactions may arise. Especially now since they are beginning to feel comfortable and are beginning to like you. But for people to take a step further and spend their hard-earned money on your products, they need to be convinced that your product is valuable. Making something appear valuable, credible, and sought after can be achieved through persuasive techniques, understanding and leveraging psychological research, and by commandeering brain circuits that were shaped by evolutionary forces.

As an independent professional with a personal brand and unique product suite, much like your corporate multinational counterpart, your existence relies on being able to sell. If you can't sell a product, you're in for a hard time. Money makes the world go round, and your world will stop without it. By employing the following strategies, you can make products in your product suite appear more credible and valuable to others while subliminally nudging them toward the purchase button. Remember, your products can be tangible and intangible goods, services, ideas, solutions, or yourself! When you apply for a job you are selling yourself as the solution.

If you are not a sole trader or entrepreneur, your whole career relies on your ability to sell yourself to an employer.

One of the greatest psychological hacks to generate confidence and persuade people to invest in you and your products comes from leveraging a psychological phenomenon called social proof. On the home pages of websites, in physical stores, during interviews, and through marketing campaigns, social proof is the underlying secret ingredient that weaponises sales efforts. Without it, customer purchases would drop significantly, and sales would plummet. As you know, without trust and confidence, people will not form positive evaluations of individuals or products. The absence of positive evaluations means people don't *feel good*, and if they don't *feel good* about something, they are not going to invest time and effort into it, let alone money!

> ## Social proof is what convinces you to push the purchase button and is the final nudge sending you over the edge.

For someone to buy something, anything, their ancient, all-knowing emotional circuitry needs to approve the purchase. Remember, emotions have the final say in our decisions, guiding our judgements about other people and manifesting in our consumer behaviour. In other words, if you put on a sales hat and venture out into the world with the hopes of selling products in your suite but are unable to build trust with your audience and do a lousy job convincing them of your product's value and credibility, chances are your target customer will not buy your goods, engage your services, or hire you. A negative response is expected given the lack of trust and abysmal appeal of the products. But, if someone likes you, trusts you, and holds you in high esteem, they will buy whatever you sell them. The magic wand of social proof waved over yourself or your products achieves all three and, in doing so, adds further irresistible appeal. Trust, likeability, and value are but a few of the perceptions beneficially distorted through the lens of social proof.

Engineering trust and confidence through social proof is how companies, individuals, and websites sell to you. Social proof is what convinces you to push the purchase button and is the final nudge sending you over the edge. In fact, the trust and confidence engineered through social proof are preconditions that need to be met for wallets to open in the first place. Understanding this means you understand one of the biggest secret weapons marketers around the world use to feed their companies the money they require to stay alive.

Think about it. Marketing professionals are employed by companies to boost sales to ensure the survival of the organisational kingdom they serve and all its inhabitants. In other words, marketers are paid to manipulate customers, people like you and I, into spending our money on their company and its products. Through weaponised psychology, consumers are frequently coerced into purchases; sometimes, that might not be in their best interest. Social proof is what makes this act possible. Demonstrably powerful enough to start crazes and fads, with the ability to steer crowds of people into buying trivialities such as fidget spinners, this cunning technique is one to watch out for.

Remember that you yourself are a marketer, marketing through your social media posts, conversations, and the content you curate and share. After this, there is another job for you to do. Once people know about you and your business, the next piece of the puzzle is to influence people to trust and value you and the products you sell. These ingredients are the essence of persuasion and drive purchasing behaviour. Social proof has been utilised by traditional marketers for aeons, but the time has come for you to learn the ancient secrets of such masterful manipulators. With great power comes great responsibility, so use this social secret wisely.

Social proof definition

Social proof is a psychological phenomenon whereby people mimic the behaviours of others to reflect the correct outcome in a situation. It can be illustrated as conforming to the general consensus and showcases how people are heavily influenced by the behaviours, decisions, and opinions of others. Simply put, social proof is evident in situations where people, seemingly automatically and almost blindly, copy the behaviours of others, leading to the phrases "herd mentality" and "following the crowd". For example, after entering a venue and seeing people sitting down quietly, you will sit down quietly. When you walk past a restaurant with 100 people lined up outside, a snap judgement about the quality of the food, an assumption born from social proof – the observed behaviour of others – will likely pull you toward that restaurant in the future. If your neighbours and friends have started meditation with rave reviews, guess who is about to tai chi their life away? Monkey see, monkey do; human see, human do. People are forever looking for *social proof* to guide their decisions and behaviours. Consciously or unconsciously.

Masterful marketers know how influential social proof is, and since the dawn of its discovery it has been used as a persuasive tool to influence purchasing decisions and consumer behaviour. In the world of marketing, they have identified and categorised different types of social proof, each having their own subtle nuances. One of these is known as expert social proof.

Expert social proof

This refers to a situation in which a credible expert is brought in to endorse the product you are selling. If I made rockets and a world-renowned rocket scientist rocked up and said, "Damn, that's a good rocket!" everyone hearing this statement will base their judgement of my rocket company off their commentary. If I was a smart, manipulative marketer, I'd record them as they said it, upload it to YouTube, then pay to advertise it. After all, they are an expert and most people don't know shit about rockets. Companies employ experts all the time to capitalise on expert social proof. For instance, food product manufacturers may pay an influential food blogger to endorse some of their products. The food blogger is a credible expert with a receptive audience who lives for all things food; the increase in sales was expected.

Celebrity social proof

This form of social proof can work wonders. It is the reason Nike sponsors famous athletes and pays them ridiculous sums of money merely to associate themselves with the brand. When Snoop Dogg did an advertisement for Menulog you can bet that, as a result, Menulog users skyrocketed. Companies associating with celebrities can tap into the celebrity's existing audiences, create trust instantly (celebrity endorsement automatically attracts trust from fans), and associate the company brand with the personal brand of the celebrity.

Everyone knows Snoop Dogg loves weed, so it's safe to assume some of his most loyal followers and supporters also share his passion for homegrown herbs. Not only would you associate weed with Snoop Dogg, but no matter who you are or where you come from, if you average out people's opinions, Snoop Dogg is widely regarded as a cool guy. His voice, luscious hair, and word acrobatics are smoother than a dolphin slipping in and out of the sea. Menulog not only associated itself with the "coolness" of Snoop but found one of its biggest markets in his personal audience. Stoners that have the munchies are the type of people who can't be bothered getting up off the couch to cook let alone leave the house for a Popcorn Chicken. How coincidental they've turned out to be the ideal demographic for Menulog's on-demand food delivery service. Weed smokers and munchies go hand in hand like a Big Mac and fries, or like Snoop and an on-demand food app.

User social proof

This is another avenue for mass-marketing manipulation. How do you know if something will work for you? By seeing it work for people just like you. Digital marketers urge customers and product users to share their success stories with the company and invite them to post videos of them using the product on their social channels for exactly this reason. It is hard to trust an online website and to evaluate products being advertised properly through a digital screen. However, when it comes out of the virtual world and becomes real and human, your ability to evaluate it, and therefore your trust in it, skyrockets. People use other people as guinea pigs, and companies know this. Real people using company products are manipulated by company marketers to be used as guinea pigs for future customers.

Leveraging the "wisdom of the crowd" is another popular marketing tactic. In a similar manner to herd mentality, the wisdom of the crowd is used to influence people's purchasing behaviours and decisions by showcasing the behaviours of the masses and contrasting them with the behaviours of purchasers. If 1 billion people are on Facebook, what are you not doing on it? The behaviour of 1 billion people exerts a large influence on you, whether you're aware of it or not. Companies use statistics with statements such as, "300,000 other people use our software, what are you waiting for?" to stir you into action, subliminally making you feel silly if you resist.

Friend social proof

The final tactic is the wisdom of your friends. Let's step back into the networking chapter where we spoke about word-of-mouth marketing and the powerful influence of friends' recommendations. Friends are trusted sources who tailor marketing messages to personally suit you, while at the same time having no vested interest in the company or product they recommend. With friends there are no conflicts of interest. Instead, friends come with a certificate of trust. Companies leverage this when they prompt you to share posts or tag them on social media.

The neurophysiological processes of social proof

Neurophysiology is the combined study of neuroscience and physiology. Neuroscience is concerned with the structure and function of the nervous system, whereas physiology is concerned with the functioning of biological systems in living organisms. In basic terms, neurophysiology is the study of how the human nervous system, which includes the brain, works. The powerful influence that social proof commands, as you may have guessed, comes as a result of evolutionary processes. A large number of researchers, in multiple settings, have explored how neurophysiology is associated with social conformity – and it's been observed in multiple settings. Essentially, this means you can see the changes in someone's brain activity when they encounter social proof. If you can see the effects of social proof, understand them, and predict how people's behaviour will change because of this knowledge, you've now got a powerful and influential tool in your toolbelt.

Let's tease out the underlying mechanisms of social proof and analyse available research. To observe social proof in action, one study attached a social influence onto an object.[48] In this case, the social influence was the opinions of music experts and the object was a song. While connected to an electroencephalograph – a machine that looks at brain function – participants were given a token for a song they liked and one for a song they didn't like. When a person received a token for a song they liked, a certain part of their brain lit up with electrical activity. The brain activity resembled the activity seen when receiving a reward. This makes sense because if you like a song and you acquire it, you feel happy due to this reward, and your brain activity should corroborate this. Interestingly, the same area of the brain lights up electrically when we agree with other people. As expected, when participants received a token for a song they didn't like, their brain activity was reduced.

The ground-breaking revelations of the study occurred when music experts' opinions were shown to participants. When the music experts liked the song the participant was given a token for, the participants experienced an increase in brain activity in these regions. Indicating that immaterial opinions of music experts bound to song tokens magically improved participants' perceived value of it. Participants now found the song more rewarding.

In technical terms, when people receive an object attached to positive social perception, their brain response mirrors a dopamine-mediated reward signal seen in reinforced learning responses. Our brains are hardwired to learn from social proof, as illustrated in the above study. If a music expert finds a song valuable, you will find that song more valuable. If your academic mentor raves about a book, you will now place that book on a pedestal. When your friends like your partner, you are going to like them even more. Other people's perception of value changes your own. You can test this on infants and toddlers. The moment you pretend something is important to you, they automatically become fixated on it and want it. A moment ago, they couldn't have cared less about the random toy on the floor they just rolled past, but now you've picked it up and seem to be making a fuss about it, it is, in fact, the only thing they've ever truly wanted.

This study demonstrated how a reward-like system that reinforces behaviour is activated in the brain when receiving an object attached to a positive social perception. When other people value something, we as humans are hardwired to attribute more value to that object. Our brains reinforce this behaviour at a neural level and, consequently, we naturally gravitate to sharing the same opinions as others and aligning our behaviours with theirs. We use social feedback to guide how we act and think.

A social psychology experiment by Solomon Asch in 1951 really drove home this point.[49] Famously known as the "conformity experiment", Asch demonstrated that when in a group of people, 32 percent of the time individuals will conform to the opinions of others, even when they know them to be wrong.

The music experiment showed how, at a deep neurophysiological level, our brains respond to social proof and can change our perceived value of objects based on social data. The conformity experiment demonstrated how social influence affects our higher-level decisions and behaviours. There is a reason evolution has wired us this way. We learn vicariously, safely, and much faster by observing and copying others. For example, imagine if you were suddenly dropped into a tribe in the Amazon jungle. Despite knowing nothing about the jungle nor the tribe's religious beliefs and laws, and regardless of being completely clueless as to what is valuable and what isn't in the jungle, within a short time you would learn all this from social data.

Observing a group settling into a spot near the river and casting out a line would provide information on how to get food. If we observed a tribesman falling into a bush surrounded by a configuration of sticks and stones, who was later sacrificed, we would infer the bush is sacred and the tribesman paid a hefty price for tripping into it. Similarly, if tribe members walked through a crowd holding a totem high above their heads during a formal ceremony, the sight of this would influence our brains' response to that object via social proof. Our brains now value the object more than before after seeing the value others have placed on it. Perhaps luckily so. We now know of its importance and understand the honour and respect mandated by the totem, lest we end up like the brother that tripped into the sacred bush. Social proof guides our future behaviours through learning processes. Through our fleeting experience of life in this tribe we'd already be motivated to seek out our own totem hidden somewhere in the Amazon, while ensuring we tiptoe carefully around sacred bushes.

Response to cues

In the modern world the principles are the same; humans are wired to learn from others through social data and respond to social cues in a semi-robotic manner. In a consumerist and materialistic society, when a product is perceived to be popular, observers eagerly jump in and mindlessly follow, creating crowds of people scrambling for bandwagons. The ancient evolutionary architecture of their brains that once saved them from sacrificial practices performs a much less important function in a modernised civil world, but it still influences them, nonetheless.

Social proof, when in the form of agreement or disagreement, also impacts us. If people disagree or respond negatively to certain actions, behaviours, or opinions, it will refine how we behave over time. In some Islamic countries, a woman who dresses inappropriately will fast be condemned, and in a short period of time will forego revealing attire for more modest clothing. Social data, positive and negative, shapes us in these ways.

The music token and sacred totem illustrate the power of social proof. The equation boils down to:

The object + social proof = change in perceived value.

Although humans are much more than inanimate, unconscious objects, this concept can still be leveraged in altering perspectives. From the product suite chapter, you'll remember that when you sell yourself to a company as an employee you are essentially functioning as a product. To explore how social proof can be leveraged to make you, the human product, appear more valuable, let's look at an interview situation. By relaying specific quotes, emails, opinions, and examples from others detailing your good traits to the interviewer, you are attaching yourself to positive social influences and effectively increasing your perceived value in their mind. Social proof has been leveraged and it's impossible for them to downplay your value after you've told them: "My last boss rated me as the top performer in my previous workplace"; "I was voted the most empathic customer support agent by my customers"; and, "My leadership team has personally recommended that I be promoted in my existing company, effective immediately should I want it". Using social proof to alter the value of yourself and other products in your suite is one of the secrets of social science.

In the same way you can leverage the opinions and behaviours of others, you can further benefit from attaching yourself to positive events and outcomes. Good and bad connections to information or experiences can influence how people feel about you. Research shows that being associated with something negative can cause a person to dislike you; however, the opposite is also true. For example, perceptions of the CEO of a charity may change if it became known the charity was fraudulently funnelling money to other companies. Conversely, graduating with a degree from a reputable university causes someone to be viewed favourably and valued more when compared to others who studied at a less-reputable one.

Revisiting an interview situation, a positive referenced statement, as well as providing a form of social proof, additionally generates positive associations to you. "I improved my team's productivity by 60 percent"; "The sales from my department were the highest they have been since the company launched our product, which is why management didn't want me to leave"; and, "Each of the previous organisations I've worked for has populated the list of Australia's top 50 largest companies", are statements that generate positive associations to you while leveraging social proof. Resultingly, people see you as valuable, likeable, and credible because others have already vetted you and because the web of associations around you injects further positivity.

Social media

Exploring social proof in the domain of humans can be a perplexing endeavour. Social experiments testing it unfold right in front of us, in our hand, on social media platforms, every day. In these realms, individuals leveraging social proof to sell products is such an obvious state of affairs they've decided they may as well embed it into their "professional title". "Instagram influencers" are people with many followers, and the special thing about them is just that – they have many followers. Users on Instagram with a large audience are perceived as popular, valuable for advertising, and in some cases famous. Yet in the real world, more times than not, there is nothing uniquely special or valuable about them. The perceived social support is the value in itself. When you see a profile with 100,000 followers, your mind automatically alters value perceptions and begins the internal dialogue, "100,000 other people can't be wrong; this person must be really important." In general, people who land on these follower-dense profiles assume that a lot of people value them, so they too begin to hold them in high regard, assigning god-like status to them. A curious state of affairs.

This is capitalised on, purposely, or incidentally, by Instagram users all the time. By buying fake followers, people purposely use social proof to their advantage. Additionally, individuals who are attractive instantly benefit, potentially unknowingly, from social proof via the royal treatment from the masses. Previously, we learned how aesthetic beauty is a hidden hack attracting more attention and rose-tinted judgements, consequently causing people to interact differently with those deemed good looking.

Whole businesses have been built around "influencer marketing", which reworded spells "the exploitation of social proof".

Funnily enough, regarding attractiveness, the other day I noticed some salespeople from India had weaponised their LinkedIn profile by choosing a female name from a Western country and uploading a profile picture of a beautiful woman, which no doubt would help them sell more internet security packages than before. Jarringly, there really is no value conferred when a longing man follows a random attractive female on Instagram; however, these behaviours form the status quo. After all, who doesn't like admiring an attractive person? As a result of gazing at an attractive person's profile, evolutionary biological urges will influence someone – usually a male as their hormonal drivers are stronger, to click the follow button. Attractive female influencers have largely built their following off the back of guys' genitals; after all, this is where testosterone (the horny hormone) is produced. No wonder 84 percent of Instagram influencers are women.[50]

When this happens though, influencers step up onto the pedestals of society, exploiting social proof for their own personal gain and for the gain of their sponsors. Whole businesses have been built around "influencer marketing", which reworded spells "the exploitation of social proof". This psychological mechanism is so profound that without it many people's lives would spiral into meaninglessness. Influencers have built their entire existence on this social phenomenon.

Attractiveness

Another experiment tested social proof's effect on brain activity in a different setting. Faces were shown to participants and they were asked to rate how attractive they thought the faces were. First off, faces were shown with no other information, so that the person's initial judgement was not influenced by other social factors like the opinions of others. After their initial judgement, participants were shown the faces again, but this time with social feedback agreeing or disagreeing with their decision. If a person had rated a face as attractive, and they were then shown social feedback that demonstrated other people rated the face in a similar way, positive social feedback would be present. The experiment found that agreeing or disagreeing with the majority led to different neurophysiological responses in the brains of the subjects. If the social feedback agreed with the participants' judgements, the neural response of the participant was different than if the social feedback disagreed with them. These brain studies provide evidence about how people respond differently when others agree or disagree with them, while highlighting that agreeing with the majority results in physiological and behavioural processes similar to learning.[51]

Experiments like these confirm that people are hardwired to learn to agree with the majority. As such, over a lifetime, the tendency to agree with others will continue to strengthen for people. The key findings of the research suggest positive social feedback, when processed, results in more thorough and attentive encoding in the brain. It also suggests a motivation to agree with the majority. If we extrapolate these results, we could arrive at the conclusion that how attractive we perceive people to be is impacted by how attractive other people perceive them to be. Over time, we gravitate toward social consensus. Isn't it interesting that a social phenomenon that automatically influences us, like social proof, changes our perception of another instinctive appraisal that automatically influences us in attractiveness?

Social proof is the backbone of herd mentality. Everyone is following crowds and aligning with peers because brains have evolved this behaviour to help make better sense of the world and reduce the amount of information they must process. If we go back to the example of the restaurant, seeing 100 people lined up outside, without any previous information about the restaurant, menu, or food, automatically sends the message that the food is good and worth waiting for. Further, social proof forms the implicit rules of society, everyone acts in accordance with what is defined as "acceptable" behaviour, yet this acceptable behaviour is based off how the majority are already behaving. Therefore, social proof functions as the connective tissue of a society's behavioural norms.

Generally, people show respect toward others, do not engage in profanity when talking in public, and willingly help the disabled and elderly, all of which is propagated and reinforced through social proof. This evolutionary universal law shapes everyone's behaviour, with the exception of people with autism or brain damage whose social data processing function is impaired. Knowing people generate reward-like systems in the brain and exhibit the hallmark of learning responses when aligned with social proof points to a powerful psychological hack, especially in the world of sales.

The multiple source effect

Social proof can be made more convincing by leveraging the "multiple source effect". This term was coined by researchers who set out to explore how to generate the most persuasive effect on someone else through the use of other people as "sources of information".[52] Their findings shed light on how structuring the opinions of others can persuade a person to differing extents. The study outlined four different scenarios. In the first scenario, one person presented one argument based on a single point of view. In the second scenario, one person presented three similar arguments based on a single point of view. In the third scenario, three people produced similar versions of an argument in support of a point of view. In the fourth scenario, three people produced three different arguments in support of a point of view.[52]

Taking the topic of abortion, we can illustrate this further. Let's assume we are in a country where abortion is illegal.

In the first scenario, a person presents an argument for legalising abortion (the point of view) stating, "Abortion should be legal because people have the right to choose whether or not they want to bring another human into the world".

In the second scenario, a person presents similar arguments for legalising abortion stating, "Abortion should be legal because people have the right to choose whether or not they want to bring another human into the world", "a female should have the final say regarding childbirth since it is her body", and "morally the decision should be with the mum, not politicians".

In the third scenario, three people present three similar arguments for legalising abortion. Person one states, "It is unfair to the future mum". Person two states, "It causes unnecessary stress to the future mum". The last person states, "The individual might not be ready to support a child". All are related arguments favouring one point of view.

In the fourth scenario, three people present three different arguments for legalising abortion. Person one states, "Abortion should be legalised because as a human being you have the right to choose the circumstance of your reproduction". Person two states, "Abortion should be legalised because economic studies have linked crimewaves to abortion laws, therefore stopping people from having abortions will increase crime rates".[53] The third person states, "It is unfair to the child if they were to be born in a cold environment that lacked love, which is bound to happen if people want to, but can't, have an abortion".

The fourth scenario may have been more convincing to you as a reader, and this is exactly what the study showed. This condition with three different arguments in support of a point of view presented by three different sources of information, was more persuasive than the others in the experiment.

To generate the highest form of persuasion, you need three different sources of information (such as three different people) to say three unique things supporting one specific point of view. This demonstrates a branch of social proof that you can utilise to help convince someone of the superior value that your products confer over the competition.

For example, in an interview situation, using three people's opinions (sources of information), you could persuasively market yourself (the product) to the interviewer as a highly capable manager. To do this, you would organise three statements from people prepared to attest to your superior work-related capabilities that you would deploy strategically. One might be, "During my time at my last company I was referred to as my boss as an emergent leader and had little interpersonal conflict with colleagues". Later, you could deploy another statement, "Senior management suggested that I apply for future senior management roles given my track record of management at the company". Lastly, you could end with the statement, "During stressful times in the company, my colleagues called on me to help with their workload. I was perceived as highly capable in stressful situations with good time-management capabilities". Statements from three different sources attesting to your exceptional management abilities are extremely persuasive.

Apply the formula to you or products in your suite by thinking of your argument (what you want to persuade people of), create three user personas (three sources of information), and then generate three different versions of feedback to contribute to the overall point of view you wish to push with your audience. If you want people to take up the view that your educational video courses are effective, ask three people how they benefited from the course and why they found it effective. Pick three distinct, unrelated answers, attach them to three real or fictional sources of information, advertise this on your homepage and socials, and, ta-da, this is your marketing strategy.

Social proof and ego depletion

When examining the effect of social proof, the mental state of the target is an important variable. In certain mental states, social proof's effect can be magnified. One study set out to explore this by looking at the effect of social proof when people are in low self-control conditions.[54] The aim was to determine whether someone in a "low self-control" state – also known as "mentally drained" or "ego-depleted" states – was influenced differently by social proof when compared to those in "non-fatigued" mental states.

Ego depletion refers to the loss of a person's willingness or self-control over a secondary task after participating in a prior task that was either tedious, included choosing from multiple options, or involved inhibition of impulses.[55] Social psychology researchers believe that there is a finite pool of mental resources available for "self-control" or "willpower" and, when depleted, the person's decision-making capability is affected. This explains why, after a big day at work or extended participation in mentally demanding tasks, your brain feels like mush and you resort to impulsive decisions. After a 12-hour workday, cooking and eating healthily can be a daunting task requiring willpower and discipline that you may not have, resulting in the automatic, impulsive decision to order takeaway. In the absence of willpower, your depleted brain looks for shortcuts, vigilantly searching for the easy way out. Social proof is a shortcut.

What is the interaction between social proof and ego depletion? To answer this, researchers examined the tendencies of people to purchase healthy food in a low self-control state.[54] In the experiment, mentally drained people, while grocery shopping, walked past a banner advertising a low-fat cheese as, "the most sold cheese in the supermarket". The statement represented social proof by subliminally suggesting that everyone buys the cheese, and this is how people should behave. The banner attached the low-fat cheese to a positive social influence and, as we know, people are hardwired to agree with the majority. It turns out that people in low self-control states – those who were mentally drained because they had either done tedious tasks beforehand, had to exert self-control to inhibit impulses, or had to choose from many options – were more influenced by the banner.

In summary, people who are mentally drained are more influenced by social proof because they lack the motivation to weigh the pros and cons of every choice and therefore resort to a more automated and impulsive form of decision-making. Instead of thinking for themselves, they let other people do the hard work for them and simply agree with what they say. Outsourcing thinking happens.

This information is relevant for selling yourself in an interview situation. With every job vacancy posted, companies can have hundreds of applicants. The interviewer has quite a job interviewing all the applicants one by one, over consecutive days, as well as going through résumés and contacting referees. Deliberations about which applicant is better, why they are better, whether they fit the organisation's culture, the risks of hiring them, and whether or not they meet gender quotas, are lengthy. The list of criteria goes on and on, not to mention that during interviews the interviewers have to inhibit their impulses, continually carrying out tedious filtering tasks associated with employee onboarding.

The point is, it is likely that your interviewer is in an ego-depleted state and will resort to a more impulsive, automated form of decision-making, one that leverages social proof because it does the hard work for them. This form of decision-making is like taking the "safe bet". Through social proof, the interviewer can already see how good you are by considering other people's views of you. Others have already vetted you and shown the interviewer the consequence of choosing you. Meaning, the interviewer who is currently overwhelmed with choice and lacking the motivation to thoroughly micro-analyse every applicant will be more receptive to, and heavily influenced by, the instances of social proof you strategically bring up in your interview.

HR managers and employers want to find the best talent for their workplace, so showing them positive social feedback about your abilities and attributes adds confidence to their decision. Like any other employee, interviewers have to answer to a boss, with their standard of work continually scrutinised. For them, having confidence in the recruit ensures they are not risking their reputation or job; another reason why incorporating some form of social proof into an interview contributes to an increased chance of securing a job role.

Social proof is a powerful tool of influence that you can exploit. When the time comes for you to sell your products, people you advertise them to need to be confident, comfortable, and trust that the quality and value of your products are exactly what you say they are. Essentially, social proof does this by allowing your customers to use other people as guinea pigs for your products and services. Previous experiences of your products, made available through social proof, highlights the future of your prospective customers' feelings. The customer knows that after their purchase, they will end up at the destination that others before them have been. Showing them that previous customers are happy with their spend, have benefited in some way, and highly value the products you have sold them, generates trust and confidence in the mind of future customers. Only with the approval of these feelings, will their wallets open for you.

What's next?

Having confidence in you and being comfortable with you is one thing, but it's not the whole story. Personal and professional success hinges on another core ingredient: likeability. If you are able to get someone to like you it further builds trust, improves rapport, mobilises people to act in your best interest, betters leadership abilities, and significantly influences the quality of relationships you have with others. Next, we unpack the science of likeability, analysing what it is exactly that leads people to like others, and how we can use this knowledge to fast track relationship development while simultaneously improving relationship quality.

Chapter 10:
The Hidden Art of Experience Engineering – 3

Likeability

Likeability is a key concept that is tremendously important for relationship development, influencing others, and your overall reputation. The likeability of an individual relates to the degree to which they are perceived as friendly, nice, polite, and pleasant to be around. Simply put, likeability refers to the extent to which someone likes you. Regardless of whether relationships are personal, familial, or professional, without mutual liking they go nowhere fast. Likeability significantly impacts how people interact with each other, and, as you'll see, this concept is associated with positive character traits, business opportunities, hiring outcomes, career successes, favourable attitudes, and can elicit specific behaviours in others that would otherwise be impossible if you were to try to contrive these.[30,56] Being likeable is a superpower that you can control.

The research behind this is strong. Likeability has been linked to personal success, professional success, and effective leadership.[57] Leading social psychologists have noted that your "likeability" can affect people's tendencies to do business with you.[58] Studies have demonstrated that:

- likeability can positively influence a business partner's willingness to engage collaboratively.[59]
- likeability incentivises people to act in the best interest of the liked partner.[59]
- a high degree of liking toward a partner or a partnership increases a person's commitment.[60]

Rather obviously, researchers conclude, "People will do things for people they like".[57]

It appears that, in the world of business, doing anything without likeability would be a dry and lacklustre affair. The bottom line is that business is fundamentally a personal endeavour. If you're going to be part of a winning team that steers companies, you're going to need leaders, or you'll need to be the leader yourself. Effective leadership requires the special ingredient known as likeability.

For any successful professional collaboration the old adage, "If you want to go fast, go alone. If you want to go far, go together", built on the premise that to achieve anything meaningful and long lasting you're going to need a team willing to work with you, applies. More importantly, not only willing to work with you but passionately involved in the team dynamic, sharing in a common vision, demonstrating an admirable work ethic, and operating on mutual respect. Finding the right people to join your team, whether you're an enterprise of one, or an enterprise of many, in a customer, colleague, or employee capacity, requires you to be likeable.

The impact of likeability in business is further signified when you realise people often quit their job, foregoing serious financial incentives, purely because they hate or strongly dislike their boss. Another telling example happens when businesses are born. You would be dreaming if you thought a collaborative and fragile start-up could ever metamorphosise into its final form without this core social ingredient present in the founders. Starting a business or working with anyone in a professional manner creates high-pressure environments ripe with disruption, personal debt, financial and psychological stress, challenging situations, and interpersonal conflict. You need your team on your side, willing to act in your best interests, and wholeheartedly committed to the professional relationship. Without this, people will be burned, businesses die, and the world loses out on innovation. Two likeable people are a force to be reckoned with.

Positive expectations

Likeability forms a web with other powerful and beneficial interpersonal traits. Evidence of a correlation between liking and trust was put forward in a scientific article suggesting that the concept of trust comprises two key elements, one of these being "positive expectations of the other party".[61] Positive expectations are closely related to benevolent intentions people infer about others when they think others like them.[62] When assuming someone likes you, you also assume they have your best interests at heart; a core ingredient in trust formation. In this way, by acting warmly to another, demonstrated either through body language, likeability boosting techniques, or elements of speech, you are able to lay down a steppingstone for trust.

One group of researchers went a step further, directly linking "liking" to trust and concluding that, "liking has a significant impact on trust".[63] Additionally, likeability and trustworthiness are characteristics associated with a credible source.[64] In business, credible sources have been shown to have stronger impacts on customer beliefs and opinions,[65] and even messages are delivered more effectively and positively during a conversation when someone is well liked.[66] A research paper on brand likeability proposed expertise, fairness, familiarity, credibility, justice, and equity are interpersonal traits and psychological evaluations that factor into likeability judgements.[67] Meaning, being likeable likely leads people to assess you positively on these dimensions. Finally, studies exploring emotions found that likeable people were more contagious in terms of their ability to transfer feelings to other people via emotional expressions. Respectively, people who were disliked were unable to influence the emotional states of others in this way.[68]

The above interpersonal traits, born from likeability, provide unquestionably superior benefits in the world of business than pay cheques and financial incentives. All things said, the world of business is dependent on the interpersonal relationships that first gave rise to societies. Without social cohesion, business, let alone modern civilisation, would cease to exist. Fundamental personal relationships are nourished through the positive traits that each party contributes, many of which are viewable in the preceding paragraph and are a consequence or relative of likeability.

Trust

Trust is incredibly important in any relationship. If you're interviewing a candidate and you don't trust them, you would never hire them. Research in the professional domain has demonstrated that hiring decisions are influenced by the amount of liking an interviewer has for the interviewee.[56] Increased likeability, with its tethering to trust, equals a better prognosis because employing someone represents a significant decision with potentially positive or negative consequences for the business, especially if the employee turns out to be unethical or unreliable.

Likeability and trust mesmerise interviewers during an interview; however, every other relationship depends on them just as much. The interpersonal traits of trust and liking, in an employee, are crucial for enabling managers and business owners to comfortably delegate important responsibilities. Moreover, employees need to be trusted with business secrets, client relationships, sensitive information, and work tasks. Outside organisational settings, a lack of trust in your romantic partner makes you overly possessive, fuelling a toxic relationship fraught with anxiety and psychological problems. If you can't trust your friend to keep your secrets, a convincing case could be made against the friendship even existing. And, joining forces with a business partner in the absence of trust is a recipe for disaster. Likeability, and its relationship with trust, is of universal importance.

Credibility

Apart from trust, the ability to be knighted as a credible person is also extremely valuable. Many times, someone's word is the only thing another has to go by. If a credible person gives their word, there is no fretting because the confidence they inspire extinguishes stress, shatters anxieties, and creates peace of mind in others. How powerful is that? This power extends further, whereby people will live their life based on the words you speak. Only because the Pope is credible will millions flock to hear him read from a book that many others could just as effectively read from. In job recommendations, if you're credible, when you vouch for someone there is nothing more that needs to be done. That someone no longer needs to be reference checked, trialled on the job, have their police records interrogated, or have their integrity probed. Credibility itself is enough for someone to invest $100,000s of dollars into a person's salary and likeability is one of its core ingredients.

People will go out of their way to sell you, just because they like you!

The nature of communication can radically alter another's interpretations of a message. For instance, managing a project team under pressure will be more effective and positive when you are likeable. When people like you they are willing to do things for you, act in your best interest, and commit more. Maybe this is why likeability boasts an ability to improve the effectiveness and positivity of communication.

Being a likeable person means you're emotionally contagious, and when you're emotionally contagious you have an uncanny ability to influence the emotions of people around you. The significance of this may not yet be apparent but building upon the information we now know, if people need to feel certain things for them to behave in certain ways, purchase certain items, or perform certain tasks, and our feelings are contagious, then to make them feel something we just need to make ourselves feel it. They'll catch it. When people are in a good mood, they will be more likely to comply with your requests, be receptive to your suggestions, and will likely evaluate you positively. To get them in a good mood, you just need to be in a good mood. Smile, and the world will smile with you (but only if you're likeable).

Examining likeability through a social lens offers you invitations to events where you can meet the right people. Moreover, when you are well liked, people are confident introducing you to others and passing on your details. You have a personal brand, and you can think of these introductions as "word-of-mouth advertising". People will go out of their way to sell you, just because they like you! Of course, your likeability also impacts the immensity of the personal network you can form. A likeable person's network is certainly more robust and reputable than that of a pessimistic, antisocial agoraphobic.

Business scholars have even conceptualised "brand likeability", a term used to describe how much a person positively perceives and psychologically evaluates a brand. They highlight that credibility, similarity, familiarity, expertise, trustworthiness, fairness, and how equitable a customer perceives their relationship with a brand to be, all contribute to liking a brand and the extent to which this occurs. The creators of this model identified brand likeability as a precursor to brand love, brand satisfaction, brand reputation, brand preference, and favourable brand attitudes.[67] Wouldn't these outcomes be great for your personal brand? Equipped with proper knowledge, these aren't just nice-to-have outcomes. The following science of likeability will ensure that your personal brand is the most likeable one on the planet. Trust me.

Self-disclosure

The Social Penetration Theory proposes that interpersonal relationships develop from shallow levels of communications to more intimate levels.[69] The theory is backed by experimental data demonstrating that as relationships progressed through different stages, there was an increase in the intimacies of self-disclosure between people. At the end of a relationship, self-disclosure was absent. The theory suggested that the level or intimacy of self-disclosure was correlated to the relationship strength between people; the more self-disclosure, the closer the relationship and the more you liked each other. Self-disclosure was therefore proposed to be fundamental to relationship progression and enhancing likeability. Self-disclosure encompasses the sharing of personal values, experiences, ideas, feelings, thoughts, and motives.

The relationship between self-disclosure and likeability has been further examined through studies on individuals with social anxiety disorders. These individuals are evaluated more negatively in social situations than people who do not have these conditions, meaning this population provided researchers with a good platform to test how self-disclosure influences likeability judgements.[70] Researchers created artificial social interactions where one of the conversating partners was an imposter and the other was the subject of the experiment: a socially anxious individual. Throughout the study, researchers noted how the participants communicated and documented how likeable each conversational partner thought the other to be. At the conclusion of the study, as determined by the imposter engaging with the subjects of the experiment, self-disclosure was found to be the "strongest predictor for the increase in likeability". Leading the researchers to conclude that self-disclosure leads to increases in likeability, even in individuals who aren't that likeable to begin with.

In other studies, experimenters explored the benefits of reciprocated self-disclosure.[71] This happens when individuals in a conversation engage in a balanced degree of self-disclosure. A fancy way of saying that people open up to each other and disclose information about themselves at a similar intimacy level. When reciprocated self-disclosure is present there is a higher degree of social attraction between people than when there is an unbalanced degree of self-disclosure. Social attraction is the attraction between two people, which leads to the development of romantic or platonic relationships. This study drew further conclusions from the research, suggesting that being involved in self-disclosure as a listener or a discloser could increase rapport between individuals.

Another study that explored self-disclosure specifically tested whether the perceived likeability of someone was enhanced if they were disclosed to by a person or if they had self-disclosed to that person.[72] Interestingly, the findings showed positive correlations between self-disclosure in both conditions, meaning that when someone self-discloses to you, you perceive them as more likeable, and they also perceive you as more likeable after having self-disclosed to you. It is a two-way street; you can make someone like you more by opening up to them or by listening as they open up to you.

The following scenario illustrates how social psychology principles can influence the relationship between two people:

Billy sits and listens to Jane as she self-discloses to him about her crumbling relationship with her boyfriend.

In this instance, Billy is the recipient of Jane's self-disclosure, and Jane is the person who has engaged in self-disclosure. As a result, Jane has become more likeable to Billy because she opened up to him. However, Billy has also become more likeable to Jane because he listened to the information she disclosed.

Understanding that self-disclosure provides a social lubricant and alters how people perceive you, means you can use this to your advantage in your quest to develop positivity-fuelled relationships with others. Sharing relevant personal information about your thoughts, feelings, opinions, and experiences when conversations allow for it is one way to boost your likeability factor. Though it is important to keep in mind the type of relationship you have with the person you are disclosing information to. You can't tell a stranger all about your daddy issues on day one, nor can you hijack conversations and overshare your life journey. Self-disclosure, in context, and in the right doses, is important.

Questions

Did you know that asking a question does more than just get you an answer? Questions asked by individuals in social interactions can facilitate communication and enhance the essence of conversation. It's no surprise then that recently released research revealed that people who asked more questions were more liked by their peers. The study, carried out by Harvard University,[73] consisted of participants engaging in conversation through an online platform called ChatPlat. On the platform, the number of questions asked by participants were matched to perceptions of "liking" by their partners. It was found that when participants asked more questions, they were perceived as more responsive by their partners. The researchers suggested that the increased perception of responsiveness was the main driver of the increase in liking. Question asking may also affect likeability through an increase in self-disclosure, as discussed previously.

Despite the obviousness of this concept, it may still be valuable to explore it a little more. Questions are a fundamental pillar of social interactions and are a catalyst to the collective intelligence of humanity. By asking the right question to the right person, you can assimilate their entire life's knowledge into a succinct takeaway, meaning that your rate of learning skyrockets. "How do I optimise my personal brand's experience?" you may ask, and I would give you this book. Aside from promoting knowledge sharing, questions can convey empathy and respect to a person. Thoughtful, considerate questions help show your conversational partner you are hearing them, empathising with them, and care about them.

A conversation absent of questions is cold and superficial. The key to a good question stems from the question's ability to elicit an insightful or personal response from someone. By asking a personal question, the person you are questioning will have to self-disclose information, subsequently enhancing the likeability between parties. Remember Billy and Jane? To add to this, it allows them to take centre stage in the conversation. Some people love being the centre of attention, talking about themselves, and it's probably why listening is a learned skill. Fear not, in the nonverbal communication section in *Chapter 11* we'll pull apart the elements of good listening so that you can apply the techniques in important situations, thus ensuring people you're engaging with feel like they are the centre of your universe.

The following story highlights the concept of asking questions. A salesman was applying for a job as an electrical engineer. Arriving at the building, the salesman walked toward the office where the job interviews were being conducted. As he drew closer, the interviewer popped outside and greeted him. Within a matter of seconds, both disappeared behind the office door. Walking past the door, an employee could hear the ebbs and flows of an enthusiastic conversation and commented to another colleague as she passed, "Must be a good fit for the job." An hour later, in good spirits, the interviewer and the salesman exited the office. The interview appeared to have gone well. When the salesman left, the CEO made a beeline for the interviewer and asked about the candidate. Excitedly, the interviewer raved about the candidate and relayed parts of their conversation. Confused, the CEO looked at the interviewer and asked, "So does he have the skillset we require?" The interviewer stopped talking and blankly stared at the CEO. The CEO continued, "We need someone to start as soon as possible. This department is struggling to keep up with the heavy workload." Swallowing nervously, the interviewer replied, "I don't actually know if he has the skillset we need, and I'm not quite sure if he's ever worked in this industry before. I also can't remember his name. He was just such a nice person… a really inquisitive fellow. He just had so many questions for me, a really genuine bloke."

On salespeople and questions, if you read *Secrets of Closing the Sale* by Zig Ziglar – one of the greatest salesmen in America – he clearly keeps a tally of the number of questions he's asked the reader throughout the book. "By the end of this book," he advertises, "I will have asked you 400 questions." What a nice guy.

Projecting "liking"

It has long been proven that we like those who express a liking for us.[74] This is a powerful form of social reciprocation. Showing or telling people that you like them automatically generates reciprocal positive feelings toward you. For example, if you were having a conversation with someone and they told you, "I like you and only have your best interests at heart," you would begin viewing them more positively. Social science confirms this.

Further research investigated reciprocated attraction through expressions of "liking".[62] It was found that benevolent intentions could be inferred about someone from a simple expression that elicited a reciprocal liking response. In other words, if you can tell someone you like them, in a direct or indirect way, they will assume you have good intentions. An expression of liking carries with it feelings of genuineness and positive regard. Essentially, expressing liking for someone leads them to form positive expectations of you, and these positive expectations are one of the fundamental components in trust formation between people.

Normally, understanding someone's intentions requires multiple social encounters where trust and rapport are progressively established, yet in an instant you can give people the information necessary for them to form positive opinions about you. Incredibly, it's as easy as directly or indirectly telling someone how much you like them, provided of course, it is believable. A subtle way of doing this is through compliments as they are an indirect expression of liking, whereas explicitly telling someone you like them is a direct expression of liking.[44] In general, we don't run around breaking and hurting things that we like, so it's not a far stretch that the little expression, "I like you," and its analogues, can be used by people to assume our benevolent behavioural intentions and subsequently like us more for them.

When someone assumes you have benevolent intentions it alters their attitude toward you, which means your interaction with them becomes more rewarding. An individual's attitude comprises three components that you should be aware of:

1. Behavioural
2. Cognitive
3. Affective

Behavioural attitudes are context specific and are defined by our tendency to behave in a certain way toward a person or object. Cognitive attitudes relate to our beliefs and knowledge about something. Affective attitudes relate to emotional responses that we generate toward people or things. In a nutshell, by expressing liking for someone, not only do you elicit a liking response back, but you also impart on them benevolent intentions, which makes them more likely to behave, think, and feel more positively about you. Warming up their emotional circuitry is necessary for them to confidently reach an internal decision where they reiterate to themselves that they like you. Additionally, the positive lens they adopt of you primes them to view you more favourably throughout your interaction, filtering out any negative associations or traits that may surface. As the saying goes, they are looking at you through rose-tinted glasses. In an initial meeting, developing a positive impression, getting someone to like you, and showing that person you have trustworthy attributes provides a solid base for a fulfilling relationship that can project far into the future.

Remember, when someone acts in a positive way toward you, there are other psychological phenomena at work relating to the need for people to reach cognitive consistency, which is achieved through alignment of their thought patterns, behaviours, and spoken words. A person who is inconsistent – saying one thing while doing another – is frowned upon by society. We may call them a hypocrite, accuse them of being a pathological liar, and would certainly never view them as credible. Imagine having a health-conscious friend who identified as a vegan and went around telling everyone about the benefits of veganism while condemning the meat eaters of society. Now imagine if you went out for dinner with this friend and they ordered a medium-rare steak, which, upon arrival, they barbarically hacked at and devoured before your food was even served. If people's words, feelings, and behaviours don't match up, we begin to negatively evaluate them on a number of traits.

Leading social psychologists have developed models demonstrating how our attitudes, beliefs, and behaviours are pulled into alignment as a result of internal emotional and psychological tension arising from conflicting attitudes and behaviours.[75] Even in experiments where people agree to a hypothetical question, they are much more likely to agree to that request should it be asked of them in real life.[30] Consistency, like many branches of psychology, is coded for in our brain, and if someone is being nice to you and acting positively toward you, their mind and body have all voted for you and are now on your team. They can't suddenly stop being nice to you now they've started. Those kinds of inconsistent tendencies are taboo in society, and it is much easier for them to choose a path and settle in. These likeability-boosting social strategies get the relationship rolling down a certain path, which, over time, is reinforced by the receiver's own psychology.

Compliments

Everyone loves a compliment. Who doesn't bask in being indirectly told they are liked? Flattery has been used by salespeople since the dawn of time. Think of the last time you went into a jewellery shop and the sales assistant helped you pick and choose. When trying jewellery on they always tell you how beautiful it is on you, that it suits your skin colour, matches your eyes, and even go further by suggesting it's simply perfect for you. Think back to those times when you were in a clothing store and the retail assistant made you feel like a fashion superstar with their flattering comments and surprisingly nice personality. How about that pop-up stall you walked past in the city where the two lively employees made a beeline for you to tell you how nice your outfit was, how much they liked your hair, or that they thought your tattoo was really cool?

The effect of compliments on liking is well documented. Studies have demonstrated that compliments generally enhance the amount of liking for someone, which is why they were tied to the previous section.[76]

Another aspect to think about when using compliments is the relationship of people to the organisations they work for. Researchers exploring employee identity found that through cognitive expansion, individuals are able to integrate the organisation they work for into their self-identity.[77] People's places of work literally become part of their metaphysical identity. Therefore, by taking this into consideration, compliments can be made to someone directly, or by complimenting the organisation they work for. As far as an individual is concerned, the organisation is part of them, and it doesn't matter if you put them or the organisation on a pedestal, it is just as personal and just as rewarding. The effect of compliments will still work their magic.

All the salespeople you bump into aren't just really nice people. The reality is, usually, they are just buttering you up to make a commission off you. They have been using an arsenal of social psychology sales techniques to make you like them more, some of which include self-disclosure, similarity, and flattery. They do this to extract the most money they can from you, and it works. They want you to like them so that you are comfortable giving them your money. That's why they tell you they like you indirectly through compliments. They do this to elicit a reciprocal response. It's a cruel world. But if it works for salespeople, it works for us when we are selling ourselves as an employee to an organisation, if we are selling ourselves as a cofounder of a business, and if we are selling our company to employees. Additionally, anything else in our product suite can be sold via the implementation of these sales strategies. People buy the experience, not just products and services, so how you make them feel matters.

Similarity

Robert Cialdini, a leading social psychologist in the field of influence, stated, "We like people who are similar to us." His writing demonstrated that similarities in areas such as opinions, personality traits, values, interests, or lifestyles can positively impact interpersonal relationships. In conjunction with Cialdini's observations, other researchers found that people consistently perceived that a "likeable person was more similar to themselves than a dislikeable person" and termed this the liking-similarity effect.[78]

Finding common ground with someone should be emphasised due to its ability to develop interpersonal liking and subsequently rapport. In an analogous way to implementing self-disclosure techniques, you can consciously attend to points of similarity and strategically use this aspect of social psychology to your advantage. When you talk to someone, if there are any shared opinions, values, or personality traits, recognise these. Both of you don't like communist governments? That's social lubricant. Your favourite colour is the same as theirs? Can you feel the bonding happening already?

Tony Robbins is a big proponent of finding common ground with people, and when talking about rapport he emphasises finding points of similarity. It's probably why when he walks on stage at an event he regularly opens with something along the lines of, "Hi guys, how you all feeling, what's happening? Do we like what is going on in the current environment? Yes or no? I mean, I like what you like. So…" He directly tells people that he likes what they like, and, in doing so, utilises the similarity principle to psychologically prime them for his incoming sales. If they like him, they are more likely to purchase from him. As long as he likes what they like, the audience likes him, even though the basis of their judgement was clearly contrived, emphasising the power and influence of the similarity principle.

> ## If you can tailor your application by incorporating their buzzwords, you may as well hand yourself the job.

The concept of likeability and similarity is present throughout all domains in life. If you take a moment to think about your friends or the people you like spending time with, you will realise that you've probably got something in common with them. Whether it be an activity, a belief, or even an interest. In business settings, especially in the realm of recruitment, the similarity plus likeability concept is massively important. Organisations and recruitment managers hide it in plain sight! When talking to HR managers it is common to hear things like, "We look for people with a good work ethic and who align with our organisational values." If you reword this, they are clearly telling you that they want someone *similar* to them.

In job adverts, employers tell you about the company, the culture, and the interpersonal skills that are heavily valued. In doing this they are trying to attract likeminded individuals; they are using these adverts as magnets for the right people – people who have things in *common* with them. If you can tailor your application by incorporating their buzzwords, you may as well hand yourself the job. You've shown them you are *one of them*.

If a biotechnology company advertises for a passionate and reliable individual, make sure you enter the interview proclaiming your love for microorganisms, modern metabolomic instruments, genetic engineering, and petri dishes. And, of course, demonstrate times in your life where people relied on you to get things done. Similarity builds rapport, and similarity can land you a job. At the end of the day, who doesn't like themselves?

Affect contagion

Affect contagion refers to the tendency of people to reflect the emotions of others through an automatic and unconscious transfer of feelings. Simply put, it is the capacity of emotions to be contagious. Research exploring the correlation between a person's likeability and the extent to which affect contagion occurred, found that people who were more likeable were more "contagious" in terms of their ability to transfer feelings to other people via emotional expression.[68] However, people who were disliked, did not change the affective state of the subject.

This is another interesting facet of likeability given that you can actually "transfer" feelings to other people if you are a likeable person. Everybody enjoys interacting with people who can make them happy, laugh, or feel good about themselves. If you are likeable, eliciting a mirrored response in others is as simple as generating this feeling internally. If you're likeable and you can make yourself happy, you can make someone else happy!

Your inner state can fundamentally alter the experiences other people have with you because when you're likeable you are a walking mood virus. Therefore, mentally preparing yourself for personal interactions should encompass positive, gratifying, and happy emotions. This will appeal to the personal values of your potential business partners, customers, colleagues, friends, romantic partners, and employers. Everyone strives to feel happy, valued, and appreciated. A well-known saying: "People will not necessarily remember what you did or what you said, but they always remember how you made them feel," hints at the importance of feelings. If you're likeable, you can always guess at how you made them feel. It's what you felt.

To sum up

Whenever someone has an experience with you, being able to generate positive and comforting feelings in them through the implementation of the above likeability techniques ensures your personal brand is poised for success. Strategically self-disclosing, inquisitively asking questions, projecting liking onto another person, complimenting, and finding common ground are methods you can use to get people to like you.

When people like you, they:
- trust you
- positively appraise you

- are committed to you
- appreciate your credibility
- act in your best interests
- are willing to be led by you
- receive your messages clearly and effectively
- are more likely to do business with you
- willingly collaborate with you in joint ventures
- have improved rapport
- will do things for you.

Just because they like you. No wonder your personal and professional success hinges on likeability.

Trust, credibility, and rapport are the key ingredients for success and come to fruition when people like you. Developing these qualities with people is a significant step in relationship development, affecting how people perceive and interact with you. For someone to vouch for you, advertise you, or spend any of their hard-earned money on you, they need to trust and like you, have confidence in your abilities, and feel a sense of mutual respect. Without trust and rapport, your relationships will not progress. Although the concept of trust is normally associated with romantic partners and friendships, professional relationships, too, require this.

Managers need to be able to trust subordinates at work, just like business partners in a company, and sellers and buyers in a capitalist economy. Without trust, nothing moves forward, relationships remain superficial holdouts with each party hesitating to absorb the first vulnerability. The other essential ingredient for relationship success is rapport, also made possible when people trust you. It is instrumental in properly connecting with people and signals an authentic and meaningful relationship. In general, the need for someone to like you and feel good about you is obvious. Would you ever elect to do business with someone you didn't like?

Successfully implementing likeability strategies means the potential of your personal brand exponentially increases. The way in which people perceive and evaluate your personal brand leads them to brand satisfaction, favourable brand attitudes, and improves your brand's reputation. Furthermore, brand likeability is an early and essential steppingstone on the path of a customer, leading them to brand love. Brand likeability is foundational for the flourishing of your personal brand.

What's next?

There's another layer to human interactions that significantly influences how people feel about others. This layer has been conserved over time through evolution and wields a dramatic influence over our emotions, and thankfully so. I'm speaking about unspoken communication. More specifically, the nonverbal communication we engage in from postural positions to eye contact, and from hand gestures to facial expressions. The super intelligence of our unconscious detects many subtle social signals and delivers to our consciousness an overall evaluation of others, it bases its decision largely off this unconsciously processed, unspoken social data.

Chapter 11:
The Hidden Art of Experience Engineering – 4

Nonverbal communication

We respond to gestures with an extreme alertness, and one might say, in accordance with an elaborate secret code that is written nowhere, known by none and understood by all. —Edward Sapir

In the early 1900s, Edward Sapir, a pioneering anthropologist and linguist, was on to something. Body language, he suggested, operated based on a secret code that everyone knew yet no one understood. Sounds like he was talking about our unconscious intelligence.

Nonverbal communication is defined as communication that does not rely on words or language and is understood to be the sending and receiving of thoughts and feelings via nonverbal behaviour.[79] Nonverbal behaviour includes body language, facial expressions, and can be related to paralinguistic aspects of speech; the tone and pitch elements accompanying spoken words.

The significance of nonverbal communication was first highlighted by psychologist Albert Mehrabian in his description of the 7/38/55 rule, demonstrating that:

- 7% of the message pertaining to feelings and attitudes is in the words spoken – verbal.
- 38% of the message pertaining to feelings and attitudes is paralinguistic (tone) – nonverbal.
- 55% of the message pertaining to feelings and attitudes is in body language – nonverbal.

Mehrabian's research showed that, during conversations, feelings and attitudes are primarily conveyed through nonverbal behaviour.[44] A word by itself has many potential meanings and can be dependent on the context it is used in. However, it is the information around the word that conveys most of what you are trying to say. For example, imagine someone saying the word "go" to you in a neutral tone. Now think of that same person shouting the word "go" while gesturing frantically to run. There is much more information in the second example. This is applicable to all other instances of communication.

Social interactions involve both verbal and nonverbal communication, but the importance of the latter is sometimes understated. Recent research proves that emotions are communicated far more through nonverbal forms of communication than verbal communication.[80] Furthermore, evidence demonstrates that people are more impressed by implicit or "nonverbal" information compared with explicit or "verbal" information.[81] People use nonverbal communication to form judgements about other people and to determine the feelings being displayed. As a result, body language can act as a window into someone's thoughts and feelings. Subconsciously, we pick up signals from people's facial expressions, gestures, tone, eye contact, and postures.[82] When the words we speak contradict our body language, others mistrust what we say and rely entirely on what we do. In his research, Albert Mehrabian stated "… nonverbal elements are particularly important for communicating feelings and attitude, especially when they are incongruent: if words and body language disagree, one tends to believe the body language".[44]

Body language gives us important information and clues about a person's intentions, emotions, and motivations via the integration of social cues in our brain's neural and semantic systems.[83] Our brain processes information about other people's body language in a complex, unconscious, and integrative way, delivering relevant information to our consciousness about that person. You know those moments when you feel like you can't trust someone or you're getting bad vibes? It's because your unconscious has figured something out about them via social cues and relayed it to your body through neuropeptides, the molecules of emotion. The feeling of trepidation you experience is the result of your consciousness finding out that something is wrong.

When someone is having an interactive experience with you, they are processing much of your social data. Even though you are verbally communicating one thing, the data they process from your body language and nonverbal behaviours is more informative, causing feelings to surface in them, which adds another layer to your communication. People automatically pick up inconsistencies between verbal and nonverbal messages. For example, if someone engaging you in a conversation told you how proud and excited they were for you, but remained monotone with crossed arms, a neutral facial expression, and no eye contact, their lack of movement, closed body language, paralinguistic behaviours, and absent eye contact would suggest they are not actually excited for you nor are they fully involved in the interaction.[18,84] Their words say one thing, but their nonverbal behaviour says another. This incongruency would be obvious if you experienced this. After all, behavioural science is something innate to you. Your human machinery comes pre-programmed with this software.

Your body language and the facial expressions you exhibit can dramatically alter an individual's perception of you. This becomes important upon realising they are largely controlled subconsciously and therefore "speak the truth": it's hard to hide your true feelings because they leak out.[85] When conversing with someone, you can try to convey a message, but if they don't believe you, it shows they don't trust you. You can tell a client you have their best interests at heart and will endeavour to deliver them an awe-inspiring product well worth their money, but if they don't believe you, the deal is off. If they don't trust you, it's because the message you are communicating is not convincing. It's not convincing because your verbal and nonverbal behaviours aren't congruent. They might not know why their gut feels the way it does, but it does, and their unconscious, emotion-fuelled evaluation of you is enough to sever the relationship. Effective immediately! Body language can make or break deals.

When acting in a professional capacity your nonverbal behaviours are forever being interrogated by partners, customers, colleagues, bosses, and friends. They all have the machinery required to thoroughly analyse and effectively interpret signals you are emitting. Remember, the feelings you experience when you talk to someone are evidenced through your nonverbal behaviours.

Also, nonverbal behaviours lead to predictable responses in others. In the same way that attractiveness generates automatic assumptions, a person's interpretation of your nonverbal behaviours can land you in different territories in their mind. Nonverbal body language is dependent on the context of communication; however, being aware of the universal messages sent without words is fundamental when generating positive feelings in others. There are actions that build trust, body postures that allude to liking, chameleon tactics that build rapport, and other nonverbal techniques that ensure your interaction with someone delivers them a first-class experience. These are explored in the following pages.

Postural behaviours

When you are communicating with people, nonverbal messages – some of which are decipherable from your posture – convey information to the recipient about the message you are trying to send. Not only does your posture add layers of information to messages, but certain postures can signal liking, rapport, and interest while others signal disengagement, non-affection, and urgency. The person you are communicating with can be impacted emotionally by how you hold yourself. You want to ensure this impact is positive. Subconsciously processed postural signals contribute to how people cognitively evaluate you, how they feel about you, and consequently how they interact with you.

Forward leaning

Leaning forward when you interact reveals liking for the individual,[86] a favourable attitude to the message you are communicating,[18] and more interest and involvement in the conversation.[87] However, in some instances it can imply a lower social status.[87] Adopting an involved posture when communicating with someone shows them you care about what they are saying. It underscores your interest in the conversation and conveys a favourable attitude on your behalf. Right now, if you were to conjure up a fictional scenario in your mind, this would become obvious. Imagine two people sitting at a table in a fancy restaurant waiting for their order. If one of them was leaning forward while they spoke to the other, who was sitting up straight, smiling, and listening attentively, you would deduce the two were sharing a positive flow of communication. The person leaning forward obviously has a favourable attitude to the other as they are leaning into them, and the other reciprocates this by approving the behaviour. If they disapproved, their nonverbal behaviours, and consequently the dynamics of the conversation, would be much different.

In certain situations, this forward-leaning behaviour can be symbolic of a lower status. This holds true in circumstances like that of a teacher and student, or a boss and subordinate, illustrating instances in which an excessive forward-leaning posture may hint at social hierarchies. Excessive leaning and attentive involvement are characteristic of someone who is learning, taking orders from, or overtly demonstrating respect for another. Despite excessive forward leaning potentially representing an ego blow and temporary backpedal down social ladders, in interactions there is nothing wrong with using it strategically to put someone on a pedestal. In fact, to be a leader you have to be a cheerleader. Supporting others is the business of leaders. However, if you are delivering a motivational speech, are an authority in a situation, or are trying to convey confidence and independence, restricting this postural behaviour may be best. The context of your communication matters.

Leaning forward makes the recipient of your message feel like they are the centre of the universe because they are the centre of your attention. Giving someone this valuable commodity is truly appreciated by another and leaning forward is the signal transmitting this. This occurs naturally in conversation when you stumble across a topic that interests or excites you. The trick here is to use this strategically for the purpose of conveying subconscious signals to the receiver at important points of the conversation. Imagine being able to show someone you're genuinely interested in their background and what they have achieved throughout their life. This is how. Furthermore, by leaning into a person when communicating, you are physically decreasing the space between you and them, which is important because the way we utilise space hints at our feelings. This explains why you push away something that smells disgusting yet lean into a flower when you detect its fragrance. The manipulation of space hints at your liking for the individual, and when we lean into someone – an indirect expression of liking – the laws of likeability are at work.

Backward leaning

Logically following on from the above, leaning backwards can signal your disinterest or lack of involvement in the conversation.[44] By leaning back, you effectively increase the space between you and the person, which is the opposite of what you do when you like something or someone. This suggests an unfavourable attitude to the message being communicated and can hinder your chances of fostering positive rapport with the individual you are communicating with.[18]

People unconsciously detect and interpret these signals. A lack of involvement and disinterest leaves them with an unpleasant evaluation of you. It's important to be mindful of the position of your body in space because this small act can unravel the integrity of your relationship with someone. No scene illustrates this better than the body language of a high-school troublemaker getting grilled by the principal after doubling down on mischief. As the principal interrogates the kid, the kid looks away, leans back in their chair and slumps down. The troublemaker may not be consciously aware of their reaction, but the unconscious intelligence of their body pushes them further from the object of their dislike – the angry, red-faced principal who might just blow a fuse.

Mirroring

This is one of the biggest secrets that manipulators, such as hostage negotiators, conmen, and enthusiastic salespeople, use to build rapport, generate trust, and facilitate likeability. Mirroring body language is something that can occur automatically or can be consciously mediated in conversations. In literature it has been referred to as the "Chameleon effect".[88] Mirroring or postural congruence occurs when a person's posture becomes visually identical to the person they are conversing with.[89] At the bar, two friends may adopt a similar self-assuring stance as they wait for the bartender to deliver their drinks. In between sets, avid gym goers deep in conversation may each rest one of their legs on a piece of equipment. At the beach, a group of friends all lay back, relaxing on their elbows as waves ebb and flow. The particular formations do not matter much, but the underlying synchronicity speaks volumes. The subconscious mirroring taking place influences the interaction on many levels.

Mirroring is a tool that can be used to fast-track relationship development.

Unbeknownst to those involved, these unconscious acts of mirroring are a signal indicating that positive speech and communication are present.[88] Interestingly, when someone subconsciously detects they are being mirrored, it can lead them to feel positively toward the other. In fact, mirroring is that powerful it's been established as an influential act in developing rapport.[87] As we know, developing rapport is critical to any form of personal and professional success, and without it meaningful, authentic relationships are elusive. Mirroring, then, is a tool that can be used to fast-track relationship development, nourishing it with the necessary ingredients to flourish.

The more significant finding regarding mirroring is that when a person observes someone mirroring or "imitating" their behaviour, they record higher brain activity in key regions of their brain, specifically, in the medial frontal cortex region.[88] The brain networks and regions highlighted in the study were reward-related areas in the brain, similar to those involved with processing primary rewards like chocolate.[90] Now you know why some people make you feel good. Note, just because this behaviour is associated with a plethora of benefits, don't go too hard when you are trying to leverage it to generate a personal experience for someone. If you are obviously mimicking their every action, things are getting weird. Instead, if you can pull this off nonchalantly or recognise positive rapport when it arises, you'll be better positioned for your future interpersonal endeavours.

The good and the bad

In general, body language can be broadly categorised as positive or negative. There are certain behaviours that give off impressions of openness, confidence, and enthusiasm, while others emanate tension, anxiety, and urgency. Some postural behaviours lubricate social interactions while others constrain them. Aiming to increase positive experiences while reducing negative experiences is the goal of a user experience designer. Therefore, when engineering the experience of your conversational partner you should aim to do the same.

Positive body language

In general, open body language is processed positively by others. It encompasses expansive postures that involve widespread limbs, a stretched torso, and the occupation of more physical space.[91] There is space between the arms and the body, the legs may be parallel with some space between, or if sitting, open and relaxed. Hands up and palms showing indicates openness to questions.[92] Overall, open body language presents a more effective means of communication, enhances your ability to influence others' opinions, and is rated as more positive.[93] It also conveys power to others,[94] produces power-related feelings and cognitions in the self,[95] and changes hormone levels in the body, creating a desirable physiological state.[96]

There are other variations of positive body language, each providing a unique impression for your audience. Standing erect with your shoulders back and head held high can signify self-assurance, confidence, and energy, resulting in more attention from your audience.[97] Relaxed, comfortable postures that lack stiffness indicate openness while facilitating free-flowing communication. Direct bodily and facial orientation paired with postural openness projects liking on to the other and is correlated with increased solidarity between individuals.[86] Essentially, when you are facing someone with your body and face, whilst using open body language, you will generate a feeling of togetherness between you.

The context of the interaction will guide how you strategically employ any of these positive behaviours, yet most of the time body language results naturally from how you feel. If confident, you walk with your head up and shoulders back, ready to tackle the world and show off your area of mastery. When completely comfortable, you might lounge around on a friend's couch with your legs up, hands behind head, and belly half out. When heavily invested in a conversational partner, you'll find yourself full frontal, standing to attention, and attentively hanging off their every word. If you want to create a positive impression or alter your internal state, consciously enacting these postures is an effective option. When tensions are high, pressure is rising, and interpersonal conflict is looming, altering your posture into a more relaxed and open one diffuses the situation and facilitates effective communication. Consciously preparing yourself for presentations by holding your head high and pulling your shoulders back will alter the audience's perceptions of you to one that is credible and authoritative.

Apart from actioning these techniques to alter perceptions, understanding this wordless language will allow you to identify with people and their emotions, the basis of empathy. Curiously, engaging in these behaviours can change your physiological state because your mind and body are bidirectional! What happens to one affects the other. In this vein, acting confident makes you confident!

Negative body language

In the same way you can ooze positivity, people can form negative impressions about you based on certain bodily behaviours. Closed body language is globally evaluated negatively and is hallmarked by contractive postures that minimise the amount of space the body takes up. Contractive postures are also characterised by limbs held closely to the body or crossed over each other, and the body looks as if it's collapsing in on itself.[91] A person sitting with their arms crossed, slumped over a desk exemplifies what you'd expect to see in this closed category of body language. Not surprisingly, this type of body language can imply coldness, distance, or a lack of confidence.[92] A closed, tense posture further carries feelings of dominance, hostility, and will likely lead to others forming negative evaluations of you. Broadly speaking, negative category postures carry messages of non-involvement and constrain social interactions.[84]

How you carry yourself provides information consciously and unconsciously to your audience, which they interpret and form judgements about. Slouching and looking down can convey you lack self-confidence.[18] A drooping posture may be associated with sadness whereas a rigid, tense posture with anger.[87] Other research suggests that tense, closed postures convey non-composure, non-affection, and immediacy.[84]Another way to look at this is to think of closed and tense postures giving off a feeling of coldness and urgency. Both of which are unpleasant feelings to the receiver.

It's important to be aware of any negative signals you may be emanating and to adjust your posture accordingly in order to maximise a relationship's potential. For example, confidence is one trait highly sought after in everyone, but unchecked postural behaviours can betray you. The person you are conversing with processes and factors posture into their evaluation of you. If they don't *feel* confident in you, it is because you are not displaying confidence in yourself, potentially ruining your opportunity to further develop that relationship personally or professionally. As discussed above, the simple act of mirroring someone's posture facilitates a meaningful relationship. This is how influential postural behaviours are.

Body language is powerful and although many people are not consciously aware of the small behaviours, movements, postural changes, and other nonverbal signals that are displayed in an interaction, their brain will still assign you a positive or negative evaluation. In other words, they will either come to the realisation that they like you or they don't through feelings triggered by unconscious social data. Emotions were around before words were, we don't need words to make up our largely influential unconscious mind and neither do others.

The power of the posture

In the world of body language, eminent researchers in social psychology have uncovered some fascinating links between a body's position in space and its influence on people's physiological and psychological states. Amy Cuddy and Dana Carney, the pioneering social psychologists behind the discovery, demonstrated this by using "power postures".[96] Power postures relate to how much physical space the body takes up and the expansiveness of the body. High-power postures are ones that take up a lot of physical space and are characterised by open body language. Low-power postures take up less physical space and are characterised by closed, contractive body language. Carney and Cuddy's research demonstrated that holding a high-power pose for two minutes provides physiological, psychological, and behavioural benefits associated with feelings of power. Therefore, by consciously manipulating your posture, you can change the hormone levels in your body and, in doing so, positively alter your psychological state.

Psychologically, holding high-power poses increases feelings of dominance as well as those of explicit and implicit power.[98] Meaning, if you engage in a high-power pose, you're outwardly displaying power to the social world around you while internally experiencing power from deep within yourself. As a result, the interactions you have with people change for two reasons: one, you feel more powerful and dominant internally, which changes how you interact with and respond to people; two, you are displaying power outwardly, which changes how others perceive and therefore interact with you.

Feelings of higher power are indicated in enhancing executive functioning of the brain by increasing the efficacy of goal pursuit and complex planning.[99] Complex planning involves updating new goals while inhibiting irrelevant goals, allowing you to better focus attention on the matter at hand while ensuring you're effectively working toward set goals. Members of stigmatised groups exemplify the manifestations of low power; fraught with feelings of devaluation due to being the subjects of social disapproval, they display worse self-control[100] and decreased performance when their lower status is made salient than when it is not.[101] In fact, neurophysiological correlates of low power, such as low levels of serotonin, also correlates with worse performance during complex tasks.[102] Being able to quieten the mind and focus attention, to think better, allows you to perform to the best of your ability, which is important in high-stakes social encounters such as networking events, presentations, partnership discussions, job interviews, and sales meetings.

Physiologically, holding a high-power pose for two minutes increases circulating levels of the hormone testosterone and decreases circulating levels of the stress hormone cortisol.[98] Holding a low-power posture for two minutes creates the opposite effect. Testosterone levels are closely linked to adaptive responses to challenges, dominance,[96] and social status.[103] All of which are viewed as favourable traits in the social realm.

Knowing that testosterone increases, cortisol decreases, and executive functioning improves is one thing, determining if it actually benefits people in the real world is another. To test the transferability of the findings, Amy Cuddy engineered an experiment to determine how the psychological and physiological benefits of high-power poses manifest in job interviews.[98] You would expect people in the high-power group to perform better. Participants were told to do a high-power or low-power pose for two minutes before an interview. People who did low-power poses decreased their circulating testosterone levels by 10 percent and increased their cortisol levels by 15 percent. People who did high-power poses increased their circulating testosterone levels by 20 percent and decreased their cortisol levels by 25 percent. Participants then participated in an interview and were rated on their performance by independent judges. The study found that "high-power posers, in contrast to low-power posers, appeared to better maintain their composure, project more confidence and present more captivating and enthusiastic speeches, in turn leading to higher overall performance evaluations". In conclusion, an increase in hiring recommendations made by the judges came about due to the enhanced social functioning of individuals who engaged in high-power postures through indirect hormonal and psychological benefits.

Teasing this further, knowing you can strategically engage in certain postures to positively influence your psychological functioning means you have a hidden hack you can use to better your performance in certain social interactions. Engaging in a power pose for two minutes before an interview demonstrably improves performance, representing the effectiveness of this technique and alluding to its transferability into many other social encounters. Standing for two minutes with your psychological state in mind changes the experience someone has with you because your presence and conversational performance improves. Standing with your feet apart, hands on hips and expanding your torso is one example of a high-power pose. There are many other high-power poses you can use as long as you maximise the space your body takes up. It may sound silly, but hacking aspects of your physiology, psychology, and communicative behaviours through convenient, inexpensive, and simple behaviours is anything but.

Listening

People have two ears and one mouth, yet most of the time the mouth is used twice as much as the ears. Poor listening behaviours become detrimental to the progression of interpersonal relationships, if left unchecked. On the other hand, good listening skills transform your conversational partner's experience to first class. Competent listening skills have been shown to benefit people in numerous ways. Researchers show that better listening leads to greater relationship satisfaction, more productive interactions, and enhanced work and academic success.[104] Good listening behaviours have also been associated with friendliness, understanding, responsiveness, and attentiveness.[105]

Active listening is a component of competent listening and is deemed the most effective listening technique.[106] There are three elements to active listening:[107] the first is associated with nonverbal communication cues demonstrating attentiveness and involvement; the second includes paraphrasing the speakers' message through our own words to communicate understanding; the third is associated with asking questions that encourage the speaker to elaborate on beliefs, feelings, or experiences. The superpower of active listening is its ability to build empathy and trust with the speaker.[107] When perceived by the speaker, it activates a reward-based system in the brain, creates positive feelings, and contributes to greater rapport between both parties.[15] It has been shown to facilitate agreements in negotiations,[108] is related to higher levels of social attraction,[109] and in the speaker feelings of being better understood have been reported.[109] In fact, FBI hostage negotiator Chris Voss, in his book *Never Split the Difference*, credits high-quality listening as an integral part of his negotiations with terrorists and other criminals. Through refined listening skills he is able to save lives and avert national disasters.

Since there are tremendous benefits associated with listening, it's imperative to understand how to convey we are listening to the person talking to us. Different levels of listening are "achievable" depending on the behaviours we choose to engage in. However, active listening should always be the goal. Implementing nonverbal techniques and elements of social psychology allows us to show the person we are interacting with that they have our undivided attention whilst creating an ecosystem of trust, respect, and empathy. Counterintuitively, to cause someone to feel a complex emotion, we don't really have to say much. Sometimes it's more what we don't say.

Components of active listening

1. **Nonverbal cues**: studies demonstrate that good nonverbal listening behaviours include maintaining and establishing eye contact, focused body language, and head nodding.[105] People who establish and maintain eye contact are likely to be viewed as good listeners because they are perceived as understanding. Focused body language, occurring when the body orientates toward the conversational partner, demonstrates attentiveness. Head nodding at appropriate times indicates responsiveness. Other nonverbal cues that can demonstrate attentiveness include leaning forward.

2. **Paraphrasing**: as mentioned, paraphrasing is essentially taking what someone says, putting it into your own words, then delivering it back to them. Studies have shown that paraphrasing the conversational partner's message results in them liking the listener more.[107] Paraphrasing what the speaker says demonstrates that you are listening and involved, and the message conveyed is the message being received. An example of paraphrasing can begin with, "What you're saying is that…" Psychologists and counsellors frequently use paraphrasing.

3. **Questions**: asking clarifying questions is a hallmark of active listening.[110] This was illustrated and supported by research using the example of storytelling. A person was asked to narrate a story to their peers. Upon completion of the story the audience then asked the narrator either generic or specific questions about the story. When asked generic questions, narrators had worse recall of the content they spoke about and rated the experience as less pleasant when compared to when they were asked specific, clarifying questions.[111] If you apply this to social encounters, asking specific questions shows you are actively listening to someone, whilst additionally creating a more pleasant and memorable experience for them.

Eye contact

The eyes, often termed the "window to the soul", are one of the most important aspects of nonverbal communication. They can express liking, intimacy, exercise control, regulate interactions, and provide emotional information about you and the people you are viewing.[82] Wide eyes indicate surprise, furrowed brows and squinting may signal anger, whilst a longing stare can hint at lust.

People who make eye contact are rated as more likeable, pleasant, intelligent, credible, and dominant compared to those who avoid or make little eye contact.[112] Another important finding highlights that without the presence of eye contact people do not feel fully involved in communication.[46] Furthermore, inconsistencies in eye contact or sporadic eye behaviour during conversations can lead to difficulties in trust formation, inhibit liking, and result in uneasiness.[82]

Direct or mutual gaze is needed to facilitate healthy social interactions.[113] Conversational partners need to know they have your attention and in turn must reciprocate for effective, inclusive communication to flow. If gaze behaviour shifts from an individual to something else, it demonstrates to them they are no longer the object of interest nor have the full attention of the observer. Despite the term "gaze" being used it shouldn't be taken too literally. Staring unflinchingly at someone for excessive periods of time will no doubt cause them to feel uncomfortable. The sweet spot is found somewhere in the middle where enough eye contact is maintained to facilitate positive communication, but not too much or too little.

Trust and rapport are only achievable with proper eye etiquette.

Research suggests that ideal eye contact varies in conversation depending on the role of the individual, whether they be the speaker or listener. The speaker and listener usually make intermittent eye contact during a conversation; however, the speaker looks at the listener less. The listener spends 80 percent of the time gazing at the speaker, whereas skilled speakers spend 45–60 percent of the time looking at the listener. Thirty percent of the time is spent mutually gazing at each other.[82]

The eye behaviour of the speaker can be explained by considering their inner thought processes. The reason the speaker spends less time looking at the listener is because, as they are talking, they expect the other's attention to be centred on them. The speaker's eye behaviour is a result of regular check-ups on their conversational partner to see if they are still listening to what they are saying. This provides a feedback mechanism to the speaker. If people are still looking at them, it's a positive sign, and they can infer that they still hold the other party's attention and the conversational content has earnt approval. However, eyes that have shifted away from the speaker indicate a loss of interest on the listener's behalf and potentially signals disagreement with the message being communicated.

Making sure you actively engage with appropriate eye contact does many things for your relationship with someone and consequently the experience they have with you. Eye contact confirms they have your attention and involvement and leads to you being perceived as likeable, intelligent, pleasant, and credible. Tellingly, some of the most valuable interpersonal traits – trust and rapport – are only achievable with proper eye etiquette.

An extreme example detailing the relationship between eye contact, honesty, and integrity, showed itself to me when I was 22 years old. During my first start-up, when I had engaged a reputable software development company to build my product, one of the sales reps I dealt with exposed me to a side of humanity that I was still blissfully ignorant to in my young age. This sales rep was a run-of-the-mill conman, the type of person who rips everyone off in their life to make a quick buck, without a drop of remorse. He had quite a good system too, albeit obviously not sustainable, and managed to do it to a lot of people before he was eventually found out.

In short, he would quote customers like me who needed software developed, then go back to the software company he contracted for, take out half the project brief before giving it to them, and then pocketed half of the customer's money that was allocated to the part of the brief he had taken out. The many people like me who had paid for technology development with all the whistles and bells ended up confused when the dysfunctional and unfinished software was finally delivered. The development company delivered only what it was presented with and received money for, oblivious to the other parts of the project the conman had taken out. It all came to a head when the software company and the customers interfaced directly, knocking down the Chinese walls this individual had put up between everyone, and connected all the dots.

Knowing what I know now, I would have been able to pick up on the warning signs. You see, whenever the sales rep was talking to my cofounder and I, his eyes would dart around the room, sometimes resting on the ceiling. He would close his eyes for extended periods of time, sometimes speaking whole sentences without opening them once. And very rarely was there direct eye contact, it was like my face was surrounded by an electromagnetic forcefield that his eyes couldn't penetrate. His eye etiquette was scattered, hidden, disengaged, and most of the time totally absent. In hindsight it makes sense: there's nothing open and honest about a conman, so why would his eye behaviour have suggested otherwise?

Facial mimicry

You are a chameleon, except instead of mimicking your environment, you mimic other people's faces. Facial mimicry refers to the process that occurs in human interactions where individuals undergo changes in their own facial expressions to mirror the expressions of the person they are conversing with.[114] Whether you're consciously aware of it or not, through muscle activation your face is spontaneously responding to, and mimicking, the people around you.

A study found that when participants were shown random images of people exhibiting emotional expressions, participants themselves elicited a similar facial response.[115] An electromyograph (EMG) was connected to participants' facial muscles, technically known as the orbicularis oculi, corrugator supercili, and levator muscles. An EMG is a machine that records the electrical activity of muscles it's attached to. In this case it was connected to facial muscles that are heavily involved in the formation of emotional expressions. When the muscles are electrically activated, the EMG detects this, and the pattern of activation is indicative of certain expressions being formed. For example, the corrugator supercili is the muscle responsible for frowning; increased electrical activity in this muscle would therefore be associated with this emotional expression.

The researchers found that when participants viewed an emotional expression, their facial muscles recorded electrical activity in the same way they would if they were actually exhibiting that emotional expression. So, if someone viewed a person who was surprised, their face would respond to and copy this expression. Mimicked expressions can occur on a micro timescale, known as micro-expressions, or can subsist over longer periods of time. Micro-expressions are not consciously interpreted by the receiver; however, those that last longer enter people's awareness.

Further research on mimicry also demonstrated that facial expressions can be mimicked even if the person is not consciously aware of the expression they have seen. A study showed participants images of happy and angry expressions for 30ms and recorded the facial muscle activity through EMGs.[116] At this speed, humans are not consciously aware of what they are seeing. Even though the participants were unaware of the image they had seen, their facial muscles still reacted to mimic the displayed emotion, despite it being flashed to their unconscious. In society and civilisation, the primary function of this type of mimicry is purported to foster affiliation and liking between people.[117] It doesn't stop there though, when you link facial mimicry to emotional contagion, things get kind of interesting.

Emotional contagion

This simply refers to the contagious nature of emotions. The process of emotional contagion is outlined diagrammatically as:

Perception → Mimicry → Facial Feedback → Emotion

Emotional contagion is a continuation of facial mimicry and refers to the ability of emotions to be transferable to other people.[47] When pondering emotional contagion, some experts even go as far as saying that people are "walking mood inductors".[118] The link between facial expressions and emotion was demonstrated in an experiment where participants were asked to make certain facial expressions and hold them for 10 seconds.[119] Afterwards, the emotional states of the participants were analysed, and it was found that facial expressions had the ability to produce corresponding emotional responses. For example, holding a happy expression correlated to subjective feelings of happiness in the individuals. However, of late, there has been some pushback on the effectiveness of techniques such as these for bringing about emotions.

In combination with the psychological responses derived from facial expressions, there also appears to be a physiological relationship between facial muscles and emotions. Holding facial expressions not only results in subjective reports of experienced emotions but can also change the activity of the emotional centres in your brain. In one study, botulinum toxin, otherwise known as botox, was used to denervate certain facial muscles involved in angry expressions. Essentially, the researchers blocked the activity of the muscles linked to angry expressions. They found that this changed the neural activity of brain areas involved with the representation of emotional states.[120] Hinting at the existence of a bidirectional relationship between emotions and facial musculature.

Another group of researchers looked into the link between facial muscles and emotion. When looking into the facial muscles responsible for an "enjoyment smile", they discovered that deliberate activation of these muscles resulted in changes in brain activity related to enjoyment.[121] If someone was able to replicate an enjoyment smile on command, there was associated physiological responses concerned with emotional processing. This proves that facial expressions that represent emotions have the ability to alter brain functioning and influence a person's emotional state. To sum up, there is physical evidence that the activation or inhibition of facial expressions can cause changes in your brain activity.

Interestingly, the concept of emotional contagion extends to group environments, whereby individuals can influence the moods, judgements, and behaviours of peers.[118] It's been suggested that the function of emotional contagion is to regulate social interactions by creating social warmth and social coolness, allowing people to bond more closely or create more distance with one another.[117] One point to draw attention to is that emotions are more "infectious" when you are liked. Implementing some techniques from the likeability section may improve your ability to transfer emotional states and leverage emotional contagion to your advantage.

Facial cues represent a shortcut to your conversational partner's emotional circuitry.

Understanding the hidden power of facial expressions and realising their corresponding significance in being able to influence the emotional states of others, provides you with the ability to generate better impressions and deliver exceptional personal experiences to your audience. Whoever they may be. Facial cues are important, not only due to their fundamental and expressive role in communication, but also because they represent a shortcut to your conversational partner's emotional circuitry. Especially if you are well liked.

In this way, a mechanism for empathy exists as I feel what you feel and vice versa. Mirroring facial expressions is implicated as an unmatched technique in fostering rapport and social attraction. Despite appearing to be some form of black magic, the information above clearly demonstrates that pulling certain faces can influence someone's brain activity relating to emotional processing. Like a virus, your facial expressions are responded to and mirrored by others, sometimes even outside of awareness, and quickly disperse throughout your social circle, partially or fully injecting doses of emotion into unsuspecting victims. Yawns are notably contagious, anger and tension fast leak into others, and giggles spread like wildfire.

Monitoring your mental environment and consciously fostering positive emotional states internally that radiate out into the world infecting others is one way to spread positive energy and start your own happiness epidemic.

The power of happiness

Smiling is a universal nonverbal behaviour recognised by everyone. What may not be so obvious is the fact that there are two different types of smiles. One relates to enjoyment and genuine pleasure whereas the other is fake and forced.

The genuine smile, relating to enjoyment, is referred to as the Duchenne smile and is characterised by the activation of the zygomatic major muscle and orbicularis oculi muscle.[122] The orbicularis oculi muscle is responsible for the wrinkling of the eyes, otherwise known as crow's feet, and only activates during a genuine smile.[123] A study comparing real smiles to fake smiles found that real smiles were perceived as more positive, genuine, and elicited more arousal in the receiver.[124] EMG analysis of facial muscles further demonstrated a higher degree of facial mimicry in people who viewed the genuine real smile compared to those who viewed fake smiles.

Given facial muscle activation and emotional responses are correlated, this suggests that genuine smiles are more emotionally contagious than fake smiles. It also demonstrates that people are able to discern between real and fake smiles even though they are consciously unaware of the criteria that separates the two. By now, the super intelligence of the unconscious shouldn't shock you. It does the majority of the heavy lifting and instead of teaching you the enormity of social cues to look out for, just gives you global evaluations after processing the cornucopia of social data you're exposed to. You've been able to spot fake people all along. True happiness, apart from being more contagious, benefits your physical and psychological health and represents considerable additional value for any 21st century product.

The importance of hands and gestures

Sign language interpreters speak whole languages with their hands, and, much like their audience, people watching you can pick up a lot of information from the behaviour of your hands. Hands are important in the realm of nonverbal communication and along with other forms of body language play a role in conveying messages and reflecting inner emotional states. If someone has clenched fists, we would instinctively recognise they were angry, the same way we would pick up on the nervous energy of a fidgeter.

Important traits your hands can display about you are openness and honesty, which are both necessary to develop trust with someone. Having your palms open when you are speaking conveys to the listener that you have nothing to hide.[125] This is intuitively interpreted. In contrast, hands hidden from sight are evaluated negatively and can give off impressions of untrustworthiness.[82,126] Think about someone lurking around with their hands in their pockets or hidden from sight and the types of impressions you would attribute to that person. Sly, suspicious, shady, or hiding something perhaps?

Apart from the face, the hands are the next most expressive and communicative part of the body. Given that 55 percent of feelings and attitudes are conveyed through body language, it's apparent that hands can make a message a lot easier to grasp.[44] Studies show this to be the case in multiple settings. Gesturing communicates more understanding of dynamic systems than words alone and can be used to help represent and resemble actions.[127] Dynamic systems are systems in a state of change with moving parts. Certain gestures can represent movement involved in the system, which increases someone's ability to comprehend the system. An example of this may be a teacher trying to explain the process of diffusion to a student. The teacher may use actions to resemble the flow of molecules from one part of the system to another. Apart from bettering another's ability to comprehend information, using gestures to explain something demonstrates a high level of knowledge of the subject matter. Gesturing has also been linked to more fluent passages of speech as it is thought to facilitate lexical word recall.[128] Using your hands as you speak may help you retrieve words from your memory.

Further research has even demonstrated that iconic gestures – hand movements that convey a meaning relevant to the semantics of spoken content, such as moving your hand up and down when talking about bouncing a ball – can contribute 8.2 percent more information than words alone when storytelling;[129] and that speech and gestures are processed together to increase language comprehension overall.[130]

As such, gesturing allows you to effectively communicate information, hints at your confidence in the subject matter, and demonstrates your openness, honesty, and willingness to accept questions. Trust development relies on these types of impressions being formed, and the behaviours of your hands play a fundamental role in this process.

To sum up

Communicating with others involves much more than just speaking. Your body language gives off important cues providing information about your emotions, intentions, and personal characteristics. How you lean during interactions tells people whether you are involved or disinterested. The presence of mirroring in your interactions signifies positive communication and is instrumental in developing rapport with others. Positive body language signals you are confident, open, energetic, and comfortable. Directly orientating your body toward your conversational partner projects liking and generates a feeling of togetherness. Positive power poses, additional to the beneficial impressions of open body language they generate, simultaneously improve your psychological and physiological functioning.

Negative body language constrains social interactions, gives off negative impressions, and detrimentally impacts your physiological and psychological functioning. It can portray a lack of confidence, non-involvement, and disinterest. It tells people that they aren't important, don't deserve your attention, and that you are not very likeable or capable. Without saying a word a never-ending stream of complicated messages is continuously conveyed to your audience. Unlike the English language, this form of communication speaks to our more primitive psychological needs, whose superiority is hopefully evident by now.

Actively listening to someone can make a world of difference. Demonstrating this through nonverbal behaviours such as head nodding, leaning forward, and focused body language, paired with inquisitive questions and paraphrasing, makes your conversational partner feel like they are the centre of the universe. It builds trust, empathy, develops rapport, leads to better understanding, and creates positive feelings for the recipient. The right amount of eye contact layered on top of this leaves nothing to chance. Once they have realised they have your eye contact, they know they are the centre of your attention. Being conscious of your own emotional state means you have a better chance at generating positive feelings in another. Your emotional state can be transferred to them through facial mimicry, especially if they like you. Prepare for interactions with others by manifesting positive emotions in yourself; they feel what you feel.

The experience someone has with you is significantly impacted through the many domains of nonverbal communication explored above. Knowing this, utilise nonverbal strategies in conjunction with first impression tactics, social proof applications, and likeability techniques, to ensure the personal experience people have with you is out of this world. Brand experience, customer experience, product experience, and user experience command millions of dollars in investment, require an army of professionals, and leverage research from around the globe. You don't have that, but you do have this information. Do your personal brand justice and give people an experience to remember. After all, in the 21st century, a good experience is a product in itself, and you're the only business with your unique offering.

Conclusion

What a journey it has been and thank you for staying the course. When you and I first met, many hundreds of pages ago, we were just beginning to touch on your hybridised biological and business nature. This duality, which is obvious by now, is by no means a bad thing. The fact of the matter is, we operate daily as a commercial entity; a result of civilisational progression. And by virtue of being human, are bound by the eternal laws of nature. Making better sense of this allows us to reconcile these two seemingly diametric identities into a more unified and potent whole. As evidenced, the world is changing. The fourth industrial revolution, gig economy, glorification of entrepreneurship, and millennial mindsets are accelerating the adoption of a new economic paradigm and dropping the future of work at tomorrow's doorstep. In a radically evolved 21st century, the individual, *you*, are placed at the centre of the universe by societies, employers, governments, and companies. The power is now in your hands and is only limited by the limitations you place on your own potential.

In a global village, amidst corporate talent wars, remote work, and gig norms, your personal brand is your value and puts you in charge. When companies try to copy us and humanise themselves, it's clear we are the epitome of a successful entity. No longer are people expected to give their life to a factory that breathes and thinks for them; an engrained image of the early industrial revolutions. Individuals – you and I – are now the metaphorical "factory", except our capital is the mind and, fittingly, we're in charge. We are whatever business we want to be; we codify the rules, have a vision, live a mission, subscribe to a framework of beliefs, are led by value structures, motivated by unique interests, capitalise on creativity, inform innovation, operate in a characteristic way, birth a culture, form strategic partnerships, develop personal networks, refine our capabilities to deliver an evolving suite of products, and naturally engineer experiences for other people every time we interact with them – something companies are fast trying to mimic and exploit. After all, as the saying goes, your life is *your business*.

Throughout this book, I have tried to focus your attention towards "elements" that I think contribute to the framework of a successful personal brand so that you can capitalise on them and leverage them for your own. I think a flourishing life in modernity definitely encompasses your human and business potential. This resource will position you well for the new world and, in doing so, I hope – along the lines of something my dad once said to me – you "achieve your potential" and become all that you can be. Here's to your success!

References

Introduction

1. Harvard Business Review, episode 762 'The Fundamental Human Relationship with Work' with James Suzman. https://hbr.org/podcast/2020/10/the-fundamental-human-relationship-with-work
2. Business.gov.au. Sole trader [internet]. Australia. Updated 05/05/2021. Available from: https://www.business.gov.au/planning/business-structures-and-types/business-structures/sole-trader
3. Australian Taxation Office. Sole trader [internet]. Australia. Updated 10/11/2016. Available from: https://www.ato.gov.au/business/starting-your-own-business/before-you-get-started/choosing-your-business-structure/sole-trader/
4. Parliament of Victoria. Births, Deaths, and Marriages Registration Act 1996. Updated 01/05/2020. Available from: https://www.legislation.vic.gov.au/in-force/acts/births-deaths-and-marriages-registration-act-1996/039
5. Births, Deaths, and Marriages Victoria. Why you must give us correct and timely data. Reviewed 21/07/2020. Available from: https://www.bdm.vic.gov.au/about-us/why-you-must-give-us-correct-and-timely-data
6. Victorian Law Reform Commission. Birth Certificates. Updated 06/04/2021. Available from: https://www.lawreform.vic.gov.au/content/4-birth-certificates
7. Schwab, Klaus. "The Fourth Industrial Revolution". Encyclopedia Britannica, 25 May. 2018, https://www.britannica.com/topic/The-Fourth-Industrial-Revolution-2119734.
8. Schwab, K. The Fourth Industrial Revolution. UK. Portfolio Penguin, 2017.
9. Bialik, K and Fry, R. Millennial life: How young adulthood today compares with prior generations. Pew Research Center; 30/01/2019. Available from: https://www.pewresearch.org/social-trends/2019/02/14/millennial-life-how-young-adulthood-today-compares-with-prior-generations-2/
10. Manpower Group. Millennial Careers: 2020 Vision, 2016. Available from: https://www.manpowergroup.com/wps/wcm/connect/660ebf65-144c-489e-975c-9f838294c237/MillennialsPaper1_2020Vision_lo.pdf?MOD=AJPERES

11. Reader, G. Around 550,000 people become entrepreneurs every month. Entrepreneur.com. 04/08/2021. Available from: https://www.entrepreneur.com/article/280212

12. Bosma N, Hill S, Ionescu-Somers A, Kelly D, Levie J & Tarnawa A. Global Entrepreneurship Monitor. 2019-2020 Global Report. Global Entrepreneurship Research Association, London Business School, London; 2020

13. Australian Bureau of Statistics. Characteristics of Employment, Australia, 2020. Available from: https://www.abs.gov.au/statistics/labour/earnings-and-work-hours/characteristics-employment-australia/latest-release

14. Bureau of Labor Statistics, U.S. Department of Labor, The Economics Daily, Independent contractors made up 6.9 percent of employment in May 2017. Available from: https://www.bls.gov/opub/ted/2018/independent-contractors-made-up-6-point-9-percent-of-employment-in-may-2017.htm (visited May 14, 2021)

15. Mills J & Jan C. The gig economy: structure, measurements, and opportunities. The Association of Professional Staffing Companies Australia, 2015. Available from: https://www.apscoau.org/sites/default/files/uploaded content/field f content file/the gig economy structures measurse oportunities discussion paper apsco 01 11-2017.pdf

16. Education and Training Policy team. The emergence of the gig economy. Australia, AI Group Workforce Development, 2016. Available from: https://cdn.aigroup.com.au/Reports/2016/Gig Economy August 2016.pdf

17. World Economic Forum. The future of jobs report 2020. Switzerland, World Economic Forum, 2020. Available from: https://www.weforum.org/reports/the-future-of-jobs-report-2020

18. Vaughan & Hogg, Human Social Behaviour (Custom Edition eBook). [[VitalSource Bookshelf version]]. Retrieved from vbk://9781488619113

19. University of Minnesota. Sociology, Understanding and changing the social world. 6.1 Social Groups, 2010. Available from: https://open.lib.umn.edu/sociology/chapter/6-1-social-groups/

20. Jobvite. Jobvite Recruiter Nation Report 2016. America, Jobvite, 2016. Available from: https://www.jobvite.com/wp-content/uploads/2016/09/RecruiterNation2016.pdf

21. Callahan, S. Picture Perfect: Make a great first impression with your Linkedin profile photo. 2018. Available from: https://www.linkedin.com/business/sales/blog/b2b-sales/picture-perfect--make-a-great-first-impression-with-your-linkedi

22. Airtasker. How do I add a profile photo to my account? 2020. Available from:https://support.airtasker.com/hc/en-au/articles/115015715188-How-do-I-add-a-profile-photo-to-my-account-

23. Human Capital Matters. Unconscious Bias. Australia; Australian Public Service Commission Australia, 2020. Available from: https://legacy.apsc.gov.au/unconscious-bias

24. Walter G. Stephan, & Cookie White Stephan. (2001). Improving Intergroup Relations. SAGE Publications, Inc.

Part I

Chapter 1: Principles

1. Humphreys, J. "Aristotle (384 B.C.E – 322 B.C.E)". Internet Encyclopedia of Philosophy. Available from: https://iep.utm.edu/aristotl/#:~:text=In%20 his%20natural%20philosophy%2C%20Aristotle,and%20behavior%20of%20 individual%20animals.
2. Shields, Christopher. "Aristotle", The Stanford Encyclopedia of Philosophy (Fall 2020 Edition), Edward N. Zalta (ed.). Available from: https://plato. stanford.edu/archives/fall2020/entries/aristotle/
3. Ryff, C. D. (1989). Happiness is everything, or is it? Explorations on the meaning of psychological wellbeing. Journal of Personality and Social Psychology, 57(6), 1069–1081. https://doi.org/10.1037/0022-3514.57.6.1069
4. Trudel-Fitzgerald, C., Millstein, R. A., von Hippel, C., Howe, C. J., Tomasso, L. P., Wagner, G. R., & VanderWeele, T. J. (2019). Psychological well-being as part of the public health debate? Insight into dimensions, interventions, and policy. BMC public health, 19(1), 1712. https://doi.org/10.1186/ s12889-019-8029-x
5. Vitlic A, Lord JM, Philips AC. Stress, ageing and their influence on functional, cellular and molecular aspects of the immune system. Age. 2014;36:1169–1185
6. Marsland, A.L. & Pressman, Sarah & Cohen, Sheldon. (2007). Positive affect and immune function. Psychoneuroimmunology. 2. 761-779.
7. Schroeder, M. "Value Theory", The Stanford Encyclopedia of Philosophy (Spring 2021 Edition), Edward N. Zalta (ed.), Available from: https://plato. stanford.edu/archives/spr2021/entries/value-theory
8. Kalleberg, A. (1977). Work Values and Job Rewards: A Theory of Job Satisfaction. American Sociological Review, 42, 124
9. London, M., Crandall, R.K., & Seals, G.W. (1976). The contribution of job and leisure satisfaction to quality of life. Journal of Applied Psychology, 62, 328-334.
10. Finegan, J. and Theriault, C. (1997), The Relationship Between Personal Values and the Perception of the Corporation's Code of Ethics. Journal of Applied Social Psychology, 27: 708-724. doi:10.1111/j.1559-1816.1997. tb00655.x
11. Fieser, J. "Ethics", Internet Encyclopedia of Philosophy. Available from: https://www.iep.utm.edu/ethics/

12. Agosta, L. "Empathy and Sympathy in Ethics", Internet Encyclopedia of Philosophy. Available from: https://www.iep.utm.edu/emp-symp/
13. McLaverty, T. "The Influence of Culture on Senior Leaders as They Seek to Resolve Ethical Dilemmas at Work" (2016). Publicly Accessible Penn Dissertations. 1569. https://repository.upenn.edu/edissertations/1569

Chapter 2: Interests, Creativity and Innovation

1. Van Iddekinge, C. H., Putka, D. J., & Campbell, J. P. (2011). Reconsidering vocational interests for personnel selection: The validity of an interest-based selection test in relation to job knowledge, job performance, and continuance intentions. *Journal of Applied Psychology, 96*(1), 13–33. https://doi.org/10.1037/a0021193
2. Hulleman, C. S., Durik, A. M., Schweigert, S. A., & Harackiewicz, J. M. (2008). Task values, achievement goals, and interest: An integrative analysis. *Journal of Educational Psychology, 100*(2), 398–416. https://doi.org/10.1037/0022-0663.100.2.398
3. Ryan, R. L., & Deci, E. L. (2000). Self-determination theory and the facilitation of intrinsic motivation, social development, and wellbeing. American Psychologist, 55, 68–78.
4. Duckworth, A. Grit. UK: Vermilion; 2017.
5. Csikszentmihalyi M. (1975/2000). Beyond Boredom and Anxiety. San Francisco: Jossey-Bass
6. Kuvaas, B., Buch, R., Weibel, A., Dysvik, A., & Nerstad, C. G. L. (2017). Do intrinsic and extrinsic motivation relate differently to employee outcomes? Journal of Economic Psychology, 61, 244–258. https://doi.org/10.1016/j.joep.2017.05.004
7. Zubair, A., & Kamal, A. (2015). Work related flow, psychological capital, and creativity among employees of software houses. Psychological Studies, 60, 321–331. https://doi.org/10.1007/s12646-015-0330-x.
8. Holland, J. L. (1997). *Making vocational choices: A theory of vocational personalities and work environments* (3rd ed.). Psychological Assessment Resources.
9. Pittenger, D. J. (2005). Cautionary Comments Regarding the Myers-Briggs Type Indicator. Consulting Psychology Journal: Practice & Research, 57(3), 210–221.
10. Anglim, J., Morse, G., De Vries, R. E., MacCann, C., Marty, A., & Mõttus, R. (2017). Comparing Job Applicants to Non–Applicants Using An Item–Level Bifactor Model on the Hexaco Personality Inventory. European Journal of Personality, 31(6), 669–684. https://doi.org/10.1002/per.2120
11. Anglim, J., Bozic, S., Little, J., & Lievens, F. (2018). Response distortion on personality tests in applicants: comparing high-stakes to low-stakes medical

settings. Advances in health sciences education : theory and practice, 23(2), 311–321. https://doi.org/10.1007/s10459-017-9796-8

12. Kashdan, T. B., & Silvia, P. (2009). Curiosity and interest: The benefits of thriving on novelty and challenge. In C. R. Snyder & S. J. Lopez (Eds.), Oxford Handbook of Positive Psychology (2nd ed., pp. 367-374). Oxford: Oxford University Press.

13. Todd B. Kashdan, Paul Rose & Frank D. Fincham (2004) Curiosity and Exploration: Facilitating Positive Subjective Experiences and Personal Growth Opportunities, Journal of Personality Assessment, 82:3, 291-305, doi: 10.1207/s15327752jpa8203_05

14. von Stumm, S., Hell, B., & Chamorro-Premuzic, T. (2011). The Hungry Mind: Intellectual Curiosity Is the Third Pillar of Academic Performance. *Perspectives on Psychological Science*, 6(6), 574–588. https://doi.org/10.1177/1745691611421204

15. Litman, J. A., Hutchins, T. L., & Russon, R. K. (2005). Epistemic curiosity, feeling-ofknowing, and exploratory behaviour. Cognition & Emotion, 19(4), 559–582. https://doi.org/10.1080/02699930441000427.

16. Hagtvedt, L. P., Dossinger, K., Harrison, S. H., & Huang, L. (2019). Curiosity made the cat more creative: Specific curiosity as a driver of creativity. Organizational Behavior and Human Decision Processes, 150, 1–13. https://doi.org/10.1016/j.obhdp.2018.10.007

17. Grace K., & Maher M. L. (2015). Specific curiosity as a cause and consequence of transformational creativity. Proceedings of the 6th international conference on computational creativity, Park City, UT.

18. Hardy, J. H., Ness, A. M., & Mecca, J. (2017). Outside the box: Epistemic curiosity as a predictor of creative problem solving and creative performance. Personality and Individual Differences, 104, 230-237. doi: 10.1016/j.paid.2016.08.004

19. Kashdan, Todd & Goodman, Fallon & Disabato, David & Mcknight, Patrick & Kelso, Kerry & Naughton, Carl. (2019). Curiosity has comprehensive benefits in the workplace: Developing and validating a multidimensional workplace curiosity scale in United States and German employees. Personality and Individual Differences. 155. 109717. 10.1016/j.paid.2019.109717.

20. Hagtvedt, L. P., Dossinger, K., Harrison, S. H., & Huang, L. (2019). Curiosity made the cat more creative: Specific curiosity as a driver of creativity. Organizational Behavior and Human Decision Processes, 150, 1–13. https://doi.org/10.1016/j.obhdp.2018.10.007

21. Celik, P., Storme, M., Davila, A., & Mzukisi, N. (2016). Work related curiosity positively predicts worker innovation. *Journal of Management Development, 35*,1184–1194.

22. Csikszentmihalyi, M., Rathunde, K., & Whalen, S. (1997). Talented teenagers: The roots of success and failure. Cambridge University Press.

23. Hardy, J. H., Ness, A. M., & Mecca, J. (2017). Outside the box: Epistemic curiosity as a predictor of creative problem solving and creative performance. Personality and Individual Differences, 104, 230-237. doi: 10.1016/j.paid.2016.08.004

24. Hughes DJ, Lee A, Tian AW, Newman A, Legood A. Leadership, creativity, and innovation: A critical review and practical recommendations. The Leadership Quarterly. 2018;29(5):549-569. doi:10.1016/j.leaqua.2018.03.001.

25. Ministerial Council on Education Employment Training and Youth Affairs. Melbourne Declaration on Educational Goals for Young Australians, 2008. Melbourne. ISBN 978-0-7594-0524-0.

26. Roberts, R. O., Cha, R. H., Mielke, M. M., Geda, Y. E., Boeve, B. F., Machulda, M. M., Knopman, D. S., & Petersen, R. C. (2015). Risk and protective factors for cognitive impairment in persons aged 85 years and older. Neurology, 84(18), 1854–1861. https://doi.org/10.1212/WNL.0000000000001537

27. Davis, M. (2009). Understanding the relationship between mood and creativity: A meta-analysis. Organizational Behavior And Human Decision Processes, 108(1), 25-38. doi: 10.1016/j.obhdp.2008.04.001

28. Pannells, T., & Claxton, A. (2008). Happiness, Creative Ideation, and Locus of Control. Creativity Research Journal, 20(1), 67-71. doi: 10.1080/10400410701842029

29. Schwab, K. The Fourth Industrial Revolution. UK. Portfolio Penguin, 2017.

30. Wark, M. Capital is dead is this something worse? UK. Verso, 2021.

31. Deep Knowledge Group. https://www.dkv.global/

32. Simonton, D. (2000). Creativity: Cognitive, personal, developmental, and social aspects. American Psychologist, 55(1), 151-158. doi: 10.1037/0003-066x.55.1.151

33. Jung-Beeman M, Bowden EM, Haberman J, Frymiare JL, Arambel-Liu S, Greenblatt R, et al. (2004) Neural Activity When People Solve Verbal Problems with Insight. PLoS Biol 2(4): e97. https://doi.org/10.1371/journal.pbio.0020097

34. Ritter, S., & Dijksterhuis, A. (2014). Creativity- the unconscious foundations of the incubation period. Frontiers In Human Neuroscience, 8. doi: 10.3389/fnhum.2014.00215

35. Ritter, S. M., van Baaren, R. B., and Dijksterhuis, A. (2012b). Creativity: the role of unconscious processes in idea generation and idea selection. Thinking Skills and Creativity. 7, 21–27. doi: 10.1016/j.tsc.2011.12.002

36. Davidson, J., & Sternberg, R. (2003). The psychology of problem solving. Cambridge, UK: Cambridge University Press. pp 150-160.

37. Sternberg, R. (1999). Handbook of Creativity. Cambridge: Cambridge University Press. pp. 191.

38. Simonton, D. K. (1991 b). Emergence and realization of genius: The lives and works of 120 classical composers. Journal of Personality and Social Psychology 61, 829-840
39. Pert, C. Molecules of Emotion. USA. Simon & Schuster, 1997.

Chapter 3: Personality and Culture

1. Bandura, A., Ross, D., & Ross, S. A. (1961). Transmission of aggressions through imitation of aggressive models. Journal of Abnormal and Social Psychology, 63(3), 575–582.
2. Carver, C. S., Scheier, M. F., Cloninger, S., M., J., Campbell, W. K., Friedman, H. S. (20191028). Personality Psychology Custom Book Edition. [[VitalSource Bookshelf version]]. Retrieved from vbk://9780655702078
3. Davis C, Patte K, Levitan R, et al. From motivation to behaviour: a model of reward sensitivity, overeating, and food preferences in the risk profile for obesity. Appetite. 2007 Jan;48(1):12-19. doi: 10.1016/j.appet.2006.05.016.
4. Allport, G.W., & Odbert, H. (1936). Trait-Names: A Psycho-lexical Study. No. 211. Psychological Review Monographs: Princeton.
5. Judge, T. A., Rodell, J. B., Klinger, R. L., Simon, L. S., & Crawford, E. R. (2013). Hierarchical representations of the five-factor model of personality in predicting job performance: integrating three organizing frameworks with two theoretical perspectives. The Journal of applied psychology, 98(6), 875–925. https://doi.org/10.1037/
6. Paunonen, S. V., & Ashton, M. C. (2001). Big Five factors and facets and the prediction of behavior. Journal of Personality and Social Psychology, 81(3), 524–539. https://doi.org/10.1037/0022-3514.81.3.524
7. Connelly, B., Ones, D., & Chernyshenko, O. (2014). Introducing the Special Section on Openness to Experience: Review of Openness Taxonomies, Measurement, and Nomological Net. Journal of Personality Assessment, 96(1), 1–16. https://doi.org/10.1080/00223891.2013.830620
8. Faruk Şahin, Hande Karadağ, & Büşra Tuncer. (2019). Big five personality traits, entrepreneurial self-efficacy and entrepreneurial intention: A configurational approach. International Journal of Entrepreneurial Behavior & Research, 25(6), 1188–1211. https://doi.org/10.1108/IJEBR-07-2018-0466
9. McCrae, R. R. (1994). Openness to experience: Expanding the boundaries of Factor V. European Journal of Personality, 8, 251–272. http://dx.doi.org/10.1002/per.2410080404
10. Ivcevic, Z., & Brackett, M. A. (2015). Predicting creativity: Interactive effects of openness to experience and emotion regulation ability. Psychology of Aesthetics, Creativity, and the Arts, 9(4), 480–487. https://doi.org/10.1037/a0039826

11. Feist GJ. A Meta-Analysis of Personality in Scientific and Artistic Creativity. Personality and Social Psychology Review. 1998;2(4):290-309. doi:10.1207/s15327957pspr0204_5

12. Helson, R., Roberts, B., & Agronick, G. (1995). Enduringness and change in creative personality and the prediction of occupational creativity. Journal of Personality and Social Psychology, 69(6), 1173–1183. https://doi.org/10.1037/0022-3514.69.6.1173

13. Barrick, M. R., Mount, M. K., & Judge, T. A. (2001). Personality and performance at the beginning of the new millennium: What do we know and where do we go next? International Journal of Selection and Assessment, 9, 9–30. doi:10.1111/1468-2389.00160

14. MacLean, K. A., Aichele, S. R., Bridwell, D. A., Mangun, G. R., Wojciulik, E., & Saron, C. D. (2009). Interactions between endogenous and exogenous attention during vigilance. Attention, perception & psychophysics, 71(5), 1042–1058. https://doi.org/10.3758/APP.71.5.1042

15. Japee, S., Holiday, K., Satyshur, M. D., Mukai, I., & Ungerleider, L. G. (2015). A role of right middle frontal gyrus in reorienting of attention: a case study. Frontiers in systems neuroscience, 9, 23. https://doi.org/10.3389/fnsys.2015.00023

16. Ramanoël, S., Hoyau, E., Kauffmann, L., Renard, F., Pichat, C., Boudiaf, N., Krainik, A., Jaillard, A., & Baciu, M. (2018). Gray Matter Volume and Cognitive Performance During Normal Aging. A Voxel-Based Morphometry Study. Frontiers in aging neuroscience, 10, 235. https://doi.org/10.3389/fnagi.2018.00235

17. Noftle, E. E., & Robins, R. W. (2007). Personality predictors of academic outcomes: Big Five correlates of GPA and SAT scores. Personality Processes and Individual Differences, 93, 116-130.

18. Wang, S., Zhao, Y., Li, J. et al. Brain structure links trait conscientiousness to academic performance. Sci Rep 9, 12168 (2019). https://doi.org/10.1038/s41598-019-48704-1

19. Lüdtke, O., Roberts, B. W., Trautwein, U., & Nagy, G. (2011). A random walk down university avenue: life paths, life events, and personality trait change at the transition to university life. Journal of personality and social psychology, 101(3), 620–637. https://doi.org/10.1037/a0023743

20. Lee, S., & Klein, H. J. (2002). Relationships between conscientiousness, self-efficacy, self-deception, and learning over time. Journal of Applied Psychology, 87(6), 1175–1182. https://doi.org/10.1037/0021-9010.87.6.1175

21. Kern, M. L., Friedman, H. S., Martin, L. R., Reynolds, C. A., & Luong, G. (2009). Conscientiousness, career success, and longevity: a lifespan analysis. Annals of behavioral medicine : a publication of the Society of Behavioral Medicine, 37(2), 154–163. https://doi.org/10.1007/s12160-009-9095-6

22. Judge, T., & Bono, J. (2000). Five-factor model of personality and transformational leadership. The Journal of applied psychology, 85 5, 751-65.

23. Stoeber, J., Otto, K., & Dalbert, C. (2009). Perfectionism and the Big Five: Conscientiousness predicts longitudinal increases in self-oriented perfectionism. Personality and Individual Differences, 47(4), 363–368. https://doi.org/10.1016/j.paid.2009.04.004

24. DeNeve, K. M., & Cooper, H. (1998). The happy personality: A meta-analysis of 137 personality traits and subjective well-being. Psychological Bulletin, 124(2), 197–229. https://doi.org/10.1037/0033-2909.124.2.197

25. Hill, P. L., Turiano, N. A., Hurd, M. D., Mroczek, D. K., & Roberts, B. W. (2011). Conscientiousness and longevity: an examination of possible mediators. Health psychology : official journal of the Division of Health Psychology, American Psychological Association, 30(5), 536–541. https://doi.org/10.1037/a0023859

26. Rich, B. (2010). Job engagement: Antecedents and effects on job performance. The Academy of Management Journal. 53. 617-635.

27. Costa PT Jr, McCrae RR (1980). Influence of extraversion and neuroticism on subjective well-being: happy and unhappy people. J Pers Soc Psychol. (4):668-78. doi: 10.1037//0022-3514.38.4.668. PMID: 7381680.

28. Carment, D. W., & Miles, C. G. (1965). Persuasiveness and persuasibility as related to intelligence and extraversion. British Journal of Social & Clinical Psychology, 4(1), 1–7. https://doi.org/10.1111/j.2044-8260.1965.tb00433.x

29. Gallagher, D. J. (1990). Extraversion, neuroticism and appraisal of stressful academic events. Personality and Individual Differences, 11(10), 1053–1057. https://doi.org/10.1016/0191-8869(90)90133-C

30. McCabe, K. O., & Fleeson, W. (2012). What is extraversion for? Integrating trait and motivational perspectives and identifying the purpose of extraversion. Psychological science, 23(12), 1498–1505. https://doi.org/10.1177/0956797612444904

31. Jensen-Campbell, L. A., & Graziano, W. G. (2001). Agreeableness as a moderator of interpersonal conflict. Journal of Personality, 69(2), 323–361.

32. Graziano, W. G., Habashi, M. M., Sheese, B. E., & Tobin, R. M. (2007). Agreeableness, empathy, and helping: A person × situation perspective. Journal of Personality and Social Psychology, 93(4), 583–599. https://doi.org/10.1037/0022-3514.93.4.583

33. Heaven PC, Ciarrochi J, Leeson P, Barkus E. Agreeableness, conscientiousness, and psychoticism: distinctive influences of three personality dimensions in adolescence. Br J Psychol. 2013 Nov;104(4):481-94. doi: 10.1111/bjop.12002. Epub 2012 Oct 26. PMID: 24094279.

34. Laursen, B., Pulkkinen, L., & Adams, R. (2002). The antecedents and correlates of agreeableness in adulthood. Developmental psychology, 38(4), 591–603. https://doi.org/10.1037//0012-1649.38.4.591

35. Barrick MR, Mount MK, Judge TA. Personality and performance at the beginning of the new millennium: What do we know and where do we go next? International Journal of Selection and Assessment. 2001;9:9–30

36. Kern, M. L., Duckworth, A. L., Urzúa, S., Loeber, R., Stouthamer-Loeber, M., & Lynam, D. R. (2013). Do as You're Told! Facets of Agreeableness and Early Adult Outcomes for Inner-City Boys. Journal of research in personality, 47(6), 10.1016/j.jrp.2013.08.008. https://doi.org/10.1016/j.jrp.2013.08.008

37. Spurk, D., & Abele, A. E. (2011). Who earns more and why? A multiple mediation model from personality to salary. Journal of Business and Psychology, 26(1), 87–103. https://doi.org/10.1007/s10869-010-9184-3

38. Yoon, K. L., Maltby, J., & Joormann, J. (2013). A pathway from neuroticism to depression: examining the role of emotion regulation. Anxiety, Stress & Coping, 26(5), 558–572.

39. Nolen-Hoeksema, S., & Morrow, J. (1993). Effects of rumination and distraction on naturally occurring depressed mood. Cognition and Emotion, 7(6), 561–570. https://doi.org/10.1080/02699939308409206

40. Shipley, B. A., Weiss, A., Der, G., Taylor, M. D., & Deary, I. J. (2007). Neuroticism, extraversion, and mortality in the UK Health and Lifestyle Survey: a 21-year prospective cohort study. Psychosomatic medicine, 69(9), 923–931. https://doi.org/10.1097/PSY.0b013e31815abf83

41. Beautrais AL, Joyce PR, Mulder RT (1999). Personality traits and cognitive styles as risk factors for serious suicide attempts among young people. Suicide and Life-Threatening Behavior 29, 37–47.

42. Mroczek, D. K., & Spiro, A. (2007). Personality Change Influences Mortality in Older Men. Psychological Science (0956-7976), 18(5), 371–376. https://doi.org/10.1111/j.1467-9280.2007.01907.x

43. Brydon L, Lin J, Butcher L, Hamer M, Erusalimsky JD, Blackburn EH, Steptoe A. Hostility and cellular aging in men from the Whitehall II cohort. Biol Psychiatry. 2012 May 1;71(9):767-73. doi: 10.1016/j.biopsych.2011.08.020. Epub 2011 Oct 5. PMID: 21974787; PMCID: PMC3657139.

44. Mathur MB, Epel E, Kind S, Desai M, Parks CG, Sandler DP, Khazeni N. Perceived stress and telomere length: A systematic review, meta-analysis, and methodologic considerations for advancing the field. Brain Behav Immun. 2016 May;54:158-169. doi: 10.1016/j.bbi.2016.02.002. Epub 2016 Feb 4. PMID: 26853993; PMCID: PMC5590630.

45. Robertson, D. The Philosophy of Cognitive Behavioural Therapy. New York, Routledge. 2nd edition, 2020.

46. Schwartz JM, Stoessel PW, Baxter LR Jr, Martin KM, Phelps ME. Systematic changes in cerebral glucose metabolic rate after successful behavior modification treatment of obsessive-compulsive disorder. Arch Gen Psychiatry. 1996 Feb;53(2):109-13. doi: 10.1001/archpsyc.1996.01830020023004. PMID: 8629886.

47. Begley, S. The Plastic Mind. NY. Ballantine Books. 2007. P173-174

48. Pascual-Leone, A., Dang, N., Cohen, L. G., Brasil-Neto, J. P., Cammarota, A., & Hallett, M. (1995). Modulation of muscle responses evoked by

transcranial magnetic stimulation during the acquisition of new fine motor skills. Journal of Neurophysiology, 74(3), 1037–1045.

49. Libet, B., Gleason, C. A., Wright, E. W., & Pearl, D. K. (1983). Time of conscious intention to act in relation to onset of cerebral activity (readiness-potential). The unconscious initiation of a freely voluntary act. Brain, 106(3), 623–642.

50. Slors, M (2015). Conscious intending as self-programming, Philosophical Psychology, 28:1, 94-113, doi: 10.1080/09515089.2013.803922

51. Papies, E. K., Aarts, H., & De Vries, N. K. (2009). Planning is for doing. Implementation intentions go beyond the mere creation of goal-directed associations. Journal of Experimental Social Psychology, 45, 1148–1151.

52. Vaughan & Hogg, Human Social Behaviour (Custom Edition eBook). [[VitalSource Bookshelf version]]. Retrieved from vbk://9781488619113

53. Jaques, E. The changing culture of a factory. London, Routledge. 2001

54. Edwards, R., Kumar, P., & Ranjan, R (2002). Understanding Organisation Culture and Innovation: A Case Study Approach. ResearchGate.

Chapter 4: Networks and Partnerships

1. Figgis, P (2014). Fit for the Future: Key findings in the Healthcare industry. PwC. Available from: https://www.healthworkscollective.com/wp-content/uploads/2014/04/pwc-17th-annual-global-ceo-survey-healthcare-key-findings.pdf

2. Waldinger, R. What makes a good life? Lessons from the longest study on happiness. 2015 Available from: https://www.ted.com/talks/robert_waldinger_what_makes_a_good_life_lessons_from_the_longest_study_on_happiness?referrer=playlist-ted_starter_pack

3. Berkman, L. F., & Syme, S. L. (1979). Social networks, host resistance, and mortality: a nine-year follow-up study of Alameda County residents. American journal of epidemiology, 109(2), 186–204. https://doi.org/10.1093/oxfordjournals.aje.a112674

4. Umberson, D., & Montez, J. K. (2010). Social relationships and health: a flashpoint for health policy. Journal of health and social behavior, 51 Suppl(Suppl), S54–S66. https://doi.org/10.1177/0022146510383501

5. Harris, M. A., & Orth, U. (2019, September 26). The Link Between Self-Esteem and Social Relationships: A Meta-Analysis of Longitudinal Studies. Journal of Personality and Social Psychology. Advance online publication. http://dx.doi.org/10.1037/pspp0000265

6. Kawachi, I., Berkman, L.F. Social ties and mental health. J Urban Health 78, 458–467 (2001). https://doi.org/10.1093/jurban/78.3.458

7. Santini, Z., Jose, P., York Cornwell, E., Koyanagi, A., Nielsen, L., & Hinrichsen, C. et al. (2020). Social disconnectedness, perceived isolation, and symptoms of depression and anxiety among older Americans (NSHAP): a

longitudinal mediation analysis. The Lancet Public Health, 5(1), e62-e70. doi: 10.1016/s2468-2667(19)30230-0

8. Mann, A. Why We Need Best Friends at Work. Gallup. Available from: https://www.gallup.com/workplace/236213/why-need-best-friends-work. aspx

9. Bear, J. Why Word of mouth is more important for B2B than for B2C. DemandBase Available from: https://www.demandbase.com/b2b-marketing-blog/word-of-mouth-talk-triggers/

10. Cialdini, R. B.. Influence: The psychology of persuasion. Harper Collins, USA. 2007.

11. Longer report: J. Leskovec and E. Horvitz. Worldwide Buzz: Planetary-Scale Views on an Instant-Messaging Network, *Microsoft Research Technical Report MSR-TR-2006-186*, Microsoft Research, June 2007.

Chapter 5: Product Suites

1. VanKuiken, H (2019) Delivering At Speed: The Art Of The Sprint. https://www.entrepreneur.com/article/336980#:~:text=As%20Meg%20Whitman%2C%20former%20Chief,relevant%20and%20strategic%20way%20is

2. Lucas, B. & Smith, C. (2018). The Capable Country: Cultivating capabilities in Australian education, Mitchell Institute policy report No. 03/2018. Mitchell Institute, Melbourne. Available from: www.mitchellinstitute.org.au

3. OECD. (2018a). The Future of Education and Skills: Education 2030. Retrieved from Paris: http://www.oecd.org/education/2030/E2030%20Position%20Paper%20(05.04.2018).pdf

4. Volkow, N. D., Wang, G. J., & Baler, R. D. (2011). Reward, dopamine and the control of food intake: implications for obesity. Trends in cognitive sciences, 15(1), 37–46. https://doi.org/10.1016/j.tics.2010.11.001

5. Glimcher P. W. (2011). Understanding dopamine and reinforcement learning: the dopamine reward prediction error hypothesis. Proceedings of the National Academy of Sciences of the United States of America, 108 Suppl 3(Suppl 3), 15647–15654. https://doi.org/10.1073/pnas.1014269108

6. Lieberman, D. & Long, M. The Molecule of More: How a Single Chemical in Your Brain Drives Love, Sex, and Creativity—and Will Determine the Fate of the Human Race. BenBella Books Inc, USA. 2019.

7. Gallese, "'Being Like Me': Self-Other Identity, Mirror Neurons, and Empathy.", cited in Keen, S. (2006). A Theory of Narrative Empathy. Narrative, 14(3), 207-236. Retrieved July 9, 2020, from www.jstor.org/stable/20107388

8. Tettamanti, M., Buccino, G., Saccuman, M. C., Gallese, V., Danna, M., Scifo, P., Fazio, F., Rizzolatti, G., Cappa, S. F., & Perani, D. (2005). Listening to Action-related Sentences Activates Fronto-parietal Motor Circuits. Journal

of Cognitive Neuroscience, 17(2), 273–281. https://doi-org.ezproxy-b. deakin.edu.au/10.1162/0898929053124965

9. Keen, S. (2006). A Theory of Narrative Empathy. Narrative, 14(3), 207-236. Retrieved July 9, 2020, from www.jstor.org/stable/20107388

10. Mar, R& Oatley, K & Peterson, J. (2009). Exploring the link between reading fiction and empathy: Ruling out individual differences and examining outcomes. Communications. 34. 407-428. 10.1515/COMM.2009.025.

11. Glenberg, A. M., Webster, B. J., Mouilso, E., Havas, D., & Lindeman, L. M. (2009). Gender, Emotion, and the Embodiment of Language Comprehension. Emotion Review, 1(2), 151–161. https://doi.org/10.1177/1754073908100440

12. Jabbi M, Bastiaansen J, Keysers C (2008) A Common Anterior Insula Representation of Disgust Observation, Experience and Imagination Shows Divergent Functional Connectivity Pathways. PLoS ONE 3(8): e2939. https://doi.org/10.1371/journal.pone.0002939

13. EY (2018). Can the universities of today lead learning for tomorrow? The university of the future. Available from: https://assets.ey.com/content/dam/ey-sites/ey-com/en_au/topics/government-and-public-sector/ey-university-of-the-future-2030.pdf

Chapter 6: Hijacking the Human Experience

1. Vaughan & Hogg, Human Social Behaviour (Custom Edition eBook). [[VitalSource Bookshelf version]]. Retrieved from vbk://9781488619113

2. Alegría-Torres, J. A., Baccarelli, A., & Bollati, V. (2011). Epigenetics and lifestyle. Epigenomics, 3(3), 267–277. https://doi.org/10.2217/epi.11.22

3. Lillycrop, K., Burdge, G. Epigenetic changes in early life and future risk of obesity. Int J Obes 35, 72–83 (2011). https://doi.org/10.1038/ijo.2010.122

4. Bargh, J. A., & Morsella, E. (2008). The Unconscious Mind. Perspectives on psychological science : a journal of the Association for Psychological Science, 3(1), 73–79. https://doi.org/10.1111/j.1745-6916.2008.00064.x

5. Izard CE. Four systems for emotion activation: cognitive and noncognitive processes. Psychol. Rev. 1993;100:68–90.

6. Liu, J., Li, J., Feng, L., Li, L., Tian, J., & Lee, K. (2014). Seeing Jesus in toast: neural and behavioral correlates of face pareidolia. Cortex; a journal devoted to the study of the nervous system and behavior, 53, 60–77. https://doi.org/10.1016/j.cortex.2014.01.013

7. Bayle DJ, Henaff M-A, Krolak-Salmon P (2009) Unconsciously Perceived Fear in Peripheral Vision Alerts the Limbic System: A MEG Study. PLoS ONE 4(12): e8207. https://doi.org/10.1371/journal.pone.0008207

8. Bateson M, Nettle D & Roberts G (2006). Cues of being watched enhance cooperation in a real-world setting. Biol. Lett.2412–414 http://doi.org/10.1098/rsbl.2006.0509

9. Bateson M, Callow L, Holmes JR, Redmond Roche ML, Nettle D (2013) Do Images of 'Watching Eyes' Induce Behaviour That Is More Pro-Social or More Normative? A Field Experiment on Littering. PLoS ONE 8(12): e82055. https://doi.org/10.1371/journal.pone.0082055
10. Vrtička, P & Black, J & Reiss, A. (2013). The neural basis of humour processing. Nature reviews. Neuroscience. Published Online. 10.1038/nrn3566.
11. Nakasone, A., Ishizuka, M., & Predinger, H. (2005) Emotion recognition from electromyography and skin conductance. ResearchGate. Available from: citeseerx.ist.psu.edu/viewdoc/download?doi=10.1.1.104.4937&rep=rep1&type=pdf
12. McMahon, C., Mahmud, A., & Feely, J. (2005). Taking blood pressure -- no laughing matter!. Blood pressure monitoring, 10(2), 109–110. https://doi.org/10.1097/00126097-200504000-00010
13. Dillon, K. M., Minchoff, B., & Baker, K. H. (1986). Positive Emotional States and Enhancement of the Immune System. The International Journal of Psychiatry in Medicine, 15(1), 13–18. https://doi.org/10.2190/R7FD-URN9-PQ7F-A6J7
14. Chang, C., Tsai, G., & Hsieh, C. J. (2013). Psychological, immunological and physiological effects of a Laughing Qigong Program (LQP) on adolescents. Complementary therapies in medicine, 21(6), 660–668. https://doi.org/10.1016/j.ctim.2013.09.004
15. Foster, J. A., & McVey Neufeld, K.-A. (2013). Gut-brain axis: how the microbiome influences anxiety and depression. Trends in Neurosciences, 36(5), 305–312. https://doi.org/10.1016/j.tins.2013.01.005
16. Dratcu, L. (2000). Panic, hyperventilation and perpetuation of anxiety. Progress in Neuropsychopharmacology & Biological Psychiatry, 24(7), 1069–1089. https://doi.org/10.1016/S0278-5846(00)00130-5
17. Bathla, M., Singh, M., & Relan, P. (2016). Prevalence of anxiety and depressive symptoms among patients with hypothyroidism. Indian journal of endocrinology and metabolism, 20(4), 468–474. https://doi.org/10.4103/2230-8210.18347
18. Glenberg A. M. (1997). What memory is for. The Behavioral and brain sciences, 20(1), 1–55. https://doi.org/10.1017/s0140525x97000010
19. Anolli, L., Ciceri, R. The Voice of Deception: Vocal Strategies of Naive and Able Liars. Journal of Nonverbal Behavior 21, 259–284 (1997). https://doi.org/10.1023/A:1024916214403
20. Izard C. E. (2009). Emotion theory and research: highlights, unanswered questions, and emerging issues. Annual review of psychology, 60, 1–25. https://doi.org/10.1146/annurev.psych.60.110707.163539
21. Oatley, K., & Johnson-Laird, P. N. (1987). Towards a cognitive theory of emotions. Cognition and Emotion, 1(1), 29–50. https://doi.org/10.1080/02699938708408362

22. Pert, C. Molecules of Emotion. USA. Simon & Schuster, 1997.
23. Schore, A. N. (2011). The right brain implicit self lies at the core of psychoanalysis. Psychoanalytic Dialogues, 21(1), 75–100. https://doi.org/10.1080/10481885.2011.545329
24. Izard CE. Four systems for emotion activation: cognitive and noncognitive processes. Psychol. Rev. 1993;100:68–90.
25. Damasio, A. Descartes Error. London. Vintage, 2006.

Chapter 7: Rise of the Personal Experience

1. Fisher, H. Why we love. USA. Henry Holt & Company, 2004.
2. Brohi, H., Khubchandani, R., Prithiani, Joti., Abbas, Z., Bhutto, A., & Chawla, S., (2016). Strategic Marketing Plan of Nike. Available at SSRN: https://ssrn.com/abstract=2760631 or http://dx.doi.org/10.2139/ssrn.2760631
3. Laros, Fleur J.M. & Steenkamp, Jan-Benedict E.M., 2005. "Emotions in consumer behavior: a hierarchical approach," Journal of Business Research, Elsevier, vol. 58(10), pages 1437-1445, October.
4. U.S Economic Research Service. Food prices and spending. U.S Department of Agriculture. Available from: www.ers.usda.gov/data-products/ag-and-food-statistics-charting-the-essentials/food-prices-and-spending/
5. Morrison, S., & Crane, F. G. (2007). Building the service brand by creating and managing an emotional brand experience. Journal of Brand Management, 14(5), 410–421. https://doi.org/10.1057/palgrave.bm.2550080
6. Verhulst, Nanouk & Vermeir, Iris & Slabbinck, Hendrik & LariviÃ"re, Bart & Mauri, Maurizio & Russo, Vincenzo, 2020. "A neurophysiological exploration of the dynamic nature of emotions during the customer experience," Journal of Retailing and Consumer Services, Elsevier, vol. 57(C).
7. Shen, L. United Airline Stock Drops $1.4 Billion After Passenger-Removal Controversy. Fortune. Available from: fortune.com/2017/04/11/united-airlines-stock-drop/
8. Kafanelis, J (2016). The Hidden Art of Interview Hacking, based on the on the paper "A theoretical model for interview hacking". Available from ZYGAVERSE.com.

Part II

Chapters 8–11: The Hidden Art of Experience Engineering

1. Society for Personality and Social Psychology. (2014). Even Fact Will Not Change First Impressions. Available: http://www.spsp.org/news-center/press-releases/even-fact-will-not-change-first-impressions. Last accessed 13/09/2017.
2. Gilron R, Gutchess AH. Remembering first impressions: Effects of intentionality and diagnosticity on subsequent memory. Cognitive, affective & behavioral neuroscience. 2012;12(1):85-98.
3. Ambady, N & Rosenthal, R. (1992). Thin Slices of Expressive Behavior as Predictors of Interpersonal Consequences: A Meta-Analysis. Psychological Bulletin. 111. 256-274.
4. Ambady, N., & Rosenthal, R. (1993). Half a minute: Predicting teacher evaluations from thin slices of nonverbal behavior and physical attractiveness. Journal of Personality and Social Psychology, 64(3), 431-441
5. Rule NO, Ambady N. First impressions: Peeking at the neural underpinnings. In: Ambady N, Skowronski JJ, editors. First Impressions. New York: The Guilford Press; 2008.
6. Pert, C. Molecules of Emotion. USA. Simon & Schuster, 1997.
7. Mann TC, Ferguson MJ (2015). Can we undo our first impressions? The role of reinterpretation in reversing implicit evaluations. Journal of personality and social psychology;108(6):823-849.
8. Mann, T. C., Ferguson, M.J., 2017. Reversing implicit first impressions through reinterpretation after a two-day delay. Journal of Experimental Social Psychology, 68, 122-127
9. Prabhakaran, R., & Gray, J. (2012). The pervasive nature of unconscious social information processing in executive control. Frontiers In Human Neuroscience, 6. doi: 10.3389/fnhum.2012.00105
10. Domenech, P., & Koechlin, E. (2015). Executive control and decision-making in the prefrontal cortex. Current Opinion in Behavioral Sciences, 1, 101-106. doi: 10.1016/j.cobeha.2014.10.007
11. Dennis, P. & Carmody M.L. (2006). Brain activation when hearing one's own and others' names. Brain Research, 1116(1),153-158.
12. Amodio, D. M., & Frith, C. D. (2006). Meeting of minds: the medial frontal cortex and social cognition. Nature reviews. Neuroscience, 7(4), 268.
13. Ridderinkhof, R., Nieuwenhuis, S. & Braver, T. (2007). Medial Frontal cortex function: An introduction and overview. Cognitive, Affective and Behavioural Neuroscience,7(4),261-265.

14. Rushworth, M., Noonan, M., Boorman, E., Walton, E., & Behrens, T. (2011). Frontal Cortex and Reward-Guided Leaning and Decision Making. Neuron, 70(6),1054-1069.

15. Kawamichi, H., Yoshihara, K., Sasaki, A., Sugawara, S., Tanabe, H., Shinohara, R., Sugisawa, Y., Tokutake, K., Mochizuki, Y., Anme, T. & Sadato, N. (2014). Perceiving active listening activates the reward system and improves the impression of relevant experiences. Social Neuroscience, 10(1), 16-26.

16. Howard, D. J., Gengler, C., & Jain, A. (1995). What's in a name? A complimentary means of persuasion. Journal of Consumer Research, 22(2), 200-211.

17. Olivola, C. & Todorov, A. (2010). Fooled by first impressions? Re-examining the diagnostic value of appearance-based inferences. Journal of Experimental Social Psychology, 46(2): 315-324.

18. Lunenburg, F. (2010). Louder than Words: The Hidden Power of Nonverbal Communication in the Workplace. International Journal of Scholarly Academic Intellectual Diversity, 12, 1-4.

19. Johnson, K., Schofield, N. & Yurchisin, J. (2002). Appearance and Dress as a Source of Information: A Qualitative Approach to Data Collection. Clothing and Textiles Research Journal, 20, 125.

20. Albright, L., Kenny, D. & Malloy, T. (1988) Consensus in Personality Judgments at Zero Acquaintance. Journal of Personality and Social Psychology.

21. Howlett, N., Pine, K. & Fletcher, B. (2013). The influence of clothing on first impressions: Rapid and positive responses to minor changes in male attire. Journal of Fashion Marketing and Management. Retrieved from ResearchGate 05/09/2017.

22. Gillath, O., Bahns, A., Ge, F. & Crandall, C., (2012). Shoes as a Source of First Impressions. Journal of Research and Personality, 46(4):423-430.

23. Railo, H., Salminen-Vaparanta, N., Henriksson, L., Revonsuo, A., & Koivisto, M. (2012). Unconscious and Conscious Processing of Color Rely on Activity in Early Visual Cortex: A TMS Study. Journal Of Cognitive Neuroscience, 24(4), 819-829. doi: 10.1162/jocn_a_00172

24. Little AC, Hill RA. (2007) Attribution to Red Suggests Special Role in Dominance Signalling. J Evol Psychol; 5: 1789–2082.

25. Elliot, A. (2015). Color and psychological functioning: a review of theoretical and empirical work. Frontiers In Psychology, 6. doi: 10.3389/fpsyg.2015.00368

26. Wu, Z. & Lin, T. (2016). Investigating the personality associations evoked by single colors: An exploratory study. Colour research and application, 42(3):388-396

27. Cash T. F., Kilcullen R. N. 1985. The aye of the beholder: susceptibility to sexism and beautyism in the evaluation of managerial applicants. J. Appl. Soc. Psychol. 15, 591–605

28. Chiu R. K., Babcock R. D. 2002. The relative importance of facial attractiveness and gender in Hong Kong selection decisions. Int. J. Hum. Resour. Manage. 13

29. Lorenzo, Genevieve L., et al. "What Is Beautiful Is Good and More Accurately Understood: Physical Attractiveness and Accuracy in First Impressions of Personality." Psychological Science, vol. 21, no. 12, 2010, pp. 1777–1782.

30. Cialdini, R. B. Influence: The psychology of persuasion. Harper Collins, USA. 2007.

31. Sigall, H., & Ostrove, N. (1975). Beautiful but dangerous: Effects of offender attractiveness and nature of the crime on juridic judgment. Journal of Personality and Social Psychology, 31(3), 410–414. https://doi.org/10.1037/h0076472

32. Landy, D., & Sigall, H. (1974). Beauty is talent: Task evaluation as a function of the performer's physical attractiveness. Journal of Personality and Social Psychology, 29(3), 299–304. https://doi.org/10.1037/h0036018

33. Langlois, J. H., Kalakanis, L., Rubenstein, A. J., Larson, A., Hallam, M., & Smoot, M. (2000). Maxims or myths of beauty? A meta-analytic and theoretical review. Psychological Bulletin, 126(3), 390–423. https://doi.org/10.1037/0033-2909.126.3.390

34. Slater, A., Von der Schulenburg, C., Brown, E., Badenoch, M., Butterworth, G., Parsons, S., & Samuels, C. (1998). Newborn infants prefer attractive faces. Infant Behavior and Development, 21(2), 345-354. doi: 10.1016/s0163-6383(98)90011-x

35. Rhodes, G. (2006). The Evolutionary Psychology of Facial Beauty. Annual Review of Psychology, 57:199-226

36. Hendrie CA, Brewer G (2012) Evidence to Suggest That Teeth Act as Human Ornament Displays Signalling Mate Quality. PLoS ONE 7(7)

37. Barnaby J. D. & Paul L. V. (2012). Beards augment perceptions of men's age, social status, and aggressiveness, but not attractiveness, Behavioral Ecology, 23(3), 481–490

38. Railo, H., Salminen-Vaparanta, N., Henriksson, L., Revonsuo, A., & Koivisto, M. (2012). Unconscious and Conscious Processing of Color Rely on Activity in Early Visual Cortex: A TMS Study. Journal Of Cognitive Neuroscience, 24(4), 819-829. doi: 10.1162/jocn_a_00172

39. Tracy, J.L. & Beall, A. T. (2011) Happy guys finish last: the impact of emotion expressions on sexual attraction. Emotion, 11(6),1379-1387.

40. Singh D. Adaptive significance of female physical attractiveness: Role of waist-to-hip-ratio. J Pers Soc Psychol. 1993; 65: 293–307

41. Stewart, G. L., Dustin, S. L., Barrick, M. R., & Darnold, T. C. (2008). Exploring the handshake in employment interviews. Journal of Applied Psychology, 93(5), 1139-1146

42. Chaplin, WF; et al. Handshaking, Gender, Personality, and First Impressions. Journal of Personality & Social Psychology. 79, 1, 110-117, July 2000. ISSN: 00223514.
43. Bernieri, Frank J. and Petty, Kristen N. (2011) 'The influence of handshakes on first impression accuracy', Social Influence, 6: 2, 78–87.
44. Mehrabian A. *1971* Silent messages. 1st ed. Belmont (CA): Wadsworth
45. Edwards, V. V. (2017). Captivate. 1st ed. New York
46. Argyle M., Dean J. (1965). Eye-contact, distance and affiliation. Sociometry, 28289–304
47. Hatfield E., Cacioppo J. T., Rapson R. L. (1994). Emotional contagion. Madison, WI: C.W. Brown
48. Campbell-Meiklejohn, D. K., Bach, D. R., Roepstorff, A., Dolan, R. J., & Frith, C. D. (2010). How the opinion of others affects our valuation of objects. Current Biology, 20, 1165–1170.
49. McLeod, S. A. (2018, Dec 28). Solomon Asch - Conformity Experiment. Retrieved from https://www.simplypsychology.org/asch-conformity.html
50. Statistica Research Department (2019). Share of Influencers posting sponsored content on Instagram 2019, by gender. Available from:https://www.statista.com/statistics/893749/share-influencers-creating-sponsored-posts-by-gender/
51. Schnuerach, R. & Gibbons, H. (2015) Social proof in the human brain: Electrophysiological signatures of agreement and disagreement with the majority. Psychophysiology, 1328-1342.
52. Harkins, S. G., & Petty, R. E. (1981). Effects of source magnification of cognitive effort on attitudes: An information-processing view. Journal of Personality and Social Psychology, 40(3), 401–413. https://doi.org/10.1037/0022-3514.40.3.401
53. Levit, S & Dubner, S. Freaknomics. England. Penguin Group, 2005
54. Salmon, S. J., Vet D. E., Adriaanse M. A., Fennis B. M., Veltkamp, M & De Ridder, D. T. (2015) Social proof in the supermarket: Promoting healthy choices under low self-control conditions. Food Quality and Preference, 45, 113-120.
54. Inzlicht M., Schmeichel B.J. (2012) What is ego-depletion? Toward a mechanistic revision of the resource model of self-control. Perspectives on Psychological Science, 7 (2012), pp. 450–463
55. Gallois, C., Victor J. Callan & Palmer, J. (1992). The Influence of Applicant Communication Style and Interviewer Characteristics on Hiring Decisions. Journal of Applied Social Psychology. 22(13) (1), 1041–1060.
56. Edward L. Nowlin, Doug Walker & Nwamaka Anaza (2019) The Impact of Manager Likeability on Sales Performance, Journal of Marketing Theory and Practice, 27:2, 159-173, DOI: 10.1080/10696679.2019.1577684
57. Cialdini, R. B. Influence: The psychology of persuasion. Harper Collins, USA. 2007

58. Pulles, N., & Hartman, P. (2017). Likeability and its effect on outcomes of interpersonal interaction. Industrial Marketing Management, 66, 56-63. doi: 10.1016/j.indmarman.2017.06.008

59. Tellefsen, T., & Thomas, G. P. (2005). The antecedents and consequences of organizational and personal commitment in business service relationships. Industrial Marketing Management, 34(1), 23–37. doi:10.1016/j.indmarman.2004.07.001

60. Oleszkiewicz, A., & Lachowicz-Tabaczek K. (2016) Perceived competence and warmth influence respect, liking and trust in work relations. Polish Psychological Bulletin, 47(4) 431–435

61. Montoya, R. M., & Insko, C. A. (2008). Toward a more complete understanding of the reciprocity of liking effect. European Journal of Social Psychology, 38, 477–498

62. Nicholson, Y. C. (2001). The Role of Interpersonal Liking in Building Trust in Long term Channel Relationships. Journal of Academy of Marketing Science, 29(1), 3–15.

63. Clark, J., Wegener, D., Habashi, M., & Evans, A. (2011). Source Expertise and Persuasion: The Effects of Perceived Opposition or Support on Message Scrutiny. Personality & social psychology bulletin. 38. 90-100. 10.1177/0146167211420733. (as cited in Nguyen, B. T., Melewar, C., & Chen, J., 2013)

64. Ho viand, C. I. and Weiss, W. (1951), 'The Influence of Source Credibility on Communication Effectiveness', Public Opinion Quarterly, Vol. 15, No. 4, pp. 635–50.

65. McGuire, W. J. (1985). Attitudes and attitude change. In Lindzey, G., Aronson, E. (Eds.), The handbook of social psychology (3rd ed., Vol. 2, pp. 233–346). New York, NY: Random House

66. Nguyen, B. T., Melewar, C., & Chen, J. (2013). The brand likeability effect: Can firms make themselves more likeable? Journal of General Management, 38(3), 25–50.

67. Monika Wróbel M., & Królewiak K. (2015) Is your mood more contagious if you are likeable? The role of liking in the social induction of affect. Polish Psychological Bulletin, 46(3) 413–420

68. Altman, I., & Taylor, D. A. (1973). Social penetration: The development of interpersonal relationships. Oxford, England: Holt, Rinehart & Winston

69. Voncken M.J., & Dijk K. L. (2012). Socially Anxious Individuals Get a Second Chance After Being Disliked at First Sight: The Role of Self-Disclosure in the Development of Likeability in Sequential Social Contact. Cognitive Therapy and Research, 37, 7–17.

70. Sprecher, S, & Treger, S (2015). The benefits of turn taking reciprocal self-disclosure in get-acquainted interactions. Personal Relationships, 22, 460–475.

71. Collins, L. N., & Miller, C. L. (1994). Self-Disclosure and Liking: A Meta-Analytic Review. Psychological Bulletin, 116(3), 457–475.

72. Huang, K., Yeomans, M., Brooks, W. A., Minson, J. & Gino, F. (2017). It Doesn't Hurt to Ask: Question-Asking Increases Liking. Journal of Personality and Social Psychology, 113(3), 430–52.
73. Lehr, T. A. & Geher, G. (2010) Differential Effects of Reciprocity and Attitude Similarity Across Long- Versus Short-Term Mating Contexts. The Journal of Social Psychology, 146(4), 423-439.
74. Festinger, L. (1957). A Theory of cognitive dissonance. Stanford, CA: Stanford University Press.
75. Grant, K. N., Fabrigar, R. L. & Lim, H. (2010) Exploring the Efficacy of Compliments as a Tactic for Securing Compliance. Basic and Applied Social Psychology, 32, 226–233.
76. Rousseau D. M. (1998) Why workers still identify with organisations. Journal of Organisational Behaviour, 19, 217–233.
77. Collison, B. & Howell, L. J. (2014). The Liking-Similarity Effect: Perceptions of Similarity as a Function of Liking. The Journal of Social Psychology, 154, 384–400.
78. Bonaccio, S. & OReilly, J. & O'Sullivan, S. & Chiocchio, F. (2016). Nonverbal Behavior and Communication in the Workplace: A Review and an Agenda for Research. Journal of Management. 42. 10.1177/0149206315621146.
79. Walker MB, Trimboli A (1989) Communicating effect: The role of verbal and nonverbal content. J Lang Soc Psychol 8 (3–4).
80. Proverbio AM, Calbi M, Manfredi M, Zani A (2014) Comprehending Body Language and Mimics: An ERP and Neuroimaging Study on Italian Actors and Viewers. PLoS ONE 9(3): e91294
81. Borg, J (2013). Body Language. 3rd ed. Great Britain: Pearson Education. 13–149.
82. Tipper CM, Signorini G, Grafton ST (2015). Body language in the brain: constructing meaning from expressive movement. Frontiers in Human Neuroscience. 9: 450
83. Burgoon, J. K. (1991). Relational message interpretations of touch, conversational distance, and posture. Journal of Nonverbal Behavior, 15(4), 233–59.
84. Jones, R. Jr. (2013). Types of Non-Verbal Communication. In: Communication in the Real World: An Introduction to Communication Studies. Minnesota: University of Minnesota Libraries Publishing 4.2.
85. Bickmore, T. W. (2004). UNSPOKEN RULES of SPOKEN INTERACTION. Communications of the ACM, 47(4)
86. Knapp, M. L., Hall, J. A., & Horgan, T. G. (2014). Nonverbal communication in human interaction. Boston, MA: Wadsworth.
87. Chartrand, T. L., & Bargh, J. A. (*1999*). The chameleon effect: The perception-behavior link and social interaction. Journal of Personality and Social Psychology, 76(6), 893–910.

88. Burgoon, J. K & Guerrero, L. K & Floyd, K. (2010). Nonverbal communication. Allyn & Bacon, Boston.
89. Small, D. M., Zatorre, R. J., Dagher, A., Evans, A. C. and Jones-Gotman, M. *2001*. Changes in brain activity related to eating chocolate: From pleasure to aversion. Brain, 124: 1720–1733.
90. Vacharkulksemsuk, T., Reit, E., Khambatta, P., Eastwick, P. W., Finkel, E. J., & Carney, D. R. (2016). Dominant, open nonverbal displays are attractive at zero-acquaintance. Proceedings of the National Academy of Sciences of the United States of America, 113(15), 4009–14.
91. Hale, A. J., Freed, J., Ricotta, D., Farris. G. & Smith, C. (2017). Twelve tips for effective body language for medical educators. Medical Journal, 39(9), 914–19.
92. McGinley, H., Lefevre,R., &McGinley,P. The influence of a communicator's body position on opinion change in others. Journal of Personality and Social Psychology,1975, 31, 486–90.
93. Carney, D. R, Hall J.A. & LeBeau, L. S. (2005). Beliefs About the Nonverbal Expression of Social Power. Journal of Non-Verbal Behaviour, 29(2), 105–123.
94. Zabetipour, M., Pishghadam, R., & Ghonsooly, B. (2015). The Impacts of Open/closed Body Positions and Postures on Learners' Moods. Mediterranean Journal of Social Sciences, 6(2 S1).
95. Carney, D. R., Cuddy, A. J. C., Yap, A. J. (2010). Power posing brief nonverbal displays affect neuroendocrine levels and risk tolerance. Psychological Science, 21, 1363–68.
96. Zho, H. & Zhang, T. (2008). Body Language in Business Negotiation. International Journal of Business and Management, 3(2), 90–96.
97. Cuddy, A.J.C., Wilmuth C.A. & Carney, D. R. (2012) "The Benefit of Power Posing Before a High-Stakes Social Evaluation." Harvard Business School Working Paper, No. 13-27.
98. Smith, P. K., Jostmann, N. B., Galinsky, A. D., & van Dijk, W. W. (2008). Lacking power impairs executive functions. Psychological Science, 19, 441–47.
99. Inzlicht, M., McKay, L., & Aronson, J. (2006). Stigma as ego depletion:
100. How being the target of prejudice affects self-control. Psychological Science, 17, 262–69.
101. Beilock, S.L., Rydell, R.J., & McConnell, A.R. (2007). Stereotype threat and working memory: Mechanisms, alleviation, and spillover. Journal of Experimental Psychology: General, 136, 256–76.
102. Park, S.B., Coull, J.T., McShane, R.H., Young, A.H., Sahakian, B.J., Robbins, T.W., & Cowen, P.J. (1994). Tryptophan depletion in normal volunteers produces selective impairments in learning and memory. Neuropharmacology, 33, 575–88.

103. Newman, M.L., Sellers, J. G. & Josephs, A. (2005) Testosterone, cognition, and social status, Hormones and Behavior 47 (2005) 205–211.

104. Bodie, G. D., & Fitch-Hauser, M. (2010). Quantitative research in listening: Explication and overview. In A. D. Wolvin (Ed.), Listening and human communication in the 21st century

105. Bodie, G. D., St. Cyr, K., Pence, M., Rold, M., & Honeycutt, J. (2012). Listening competence in initial interactions I: Distinguishing between what listening is and what listeners do. International Journal of Listening, 26, 1–28.

106. Jahromi, V. K., Tabatabaee, S. S., Abdar, Z. E., & Rajabi, M. (2016). Active listening: The key of successful communication in hospital managers. Electronic Physician, 8(3), 2123–28.

107. Weger, H., Castle, G. R. & Emmett, M. C. (2010). Active Listening in Peer Interviews: The Influence of Message Paraphrasing on Perceptions of Listening Skill. International Journal of Listening, 24 (1).

108. Fischer-Lokou, J., Lamy, L. & Dubarry, N. (2016). Effects of Active Listening, Reformulation, and Imitation on Mediator Success: Preliminary Results. Psychological Reports, 118(3), 994–1010.

109. Weger, H. J., Bell, G. C., & Robinson, M. C. (2014). The Relative Effectiveness of Active Listening in Initial Interactions. International Journal of Listening, 28(1), 13–31.

110. Jones, S. M. (2011). Supportive Listening. International Journal of Listening, 25(1/2).

111. Bavelas, J. B., Coates, L., & Johnson, T. (2000). Listeners as Co-Narrators. Journal of Personality & Social Psychology, 79(6).

112. Akechi H, Senju A, Uibo H, Kikuchi Y, Hasegawa T, Hietanen JK (2013) Attention to Eye Contact in the West and East: Autonomic Responses and Evaluative Ratings. PLoS ONE 8(3): e59312.

113. Itier R.J., Batty M. (2009). Neural bases of eye and gaze processing: the core of social cognition. Neuroscience and Biobehavioral Reviews, 33(6), 843–63.

114. Seibt, B., Mühlberger, A., Likowski, K. U., & Weyers, P. (2015). Facial mimicry in its social setting. Frontiers in Psychology, 6, 1122. http://doi.org/10.3389/fpsyg.2015.01122

115. Blairy, S., Herrera, P., & Hess, U. (1999). Mimicry and the Judgment of Emotional Facial Expressions. Journal of Nonverbal Behavior, 23(1), 5–41.

116. Dimberg, U., & Thunberg, M. (2000). Unconscious facial reactions to emotional facial expressions. Psychological Science (0956-7976), 11(1), 86.

117. Hess, U. & Fischer, A. (2013). Emotional Mimicry as Social Regulation. Personality and Social Psychology Review, 17(2), 142–157.

118. Barsade, S. G. (2002). The Ripple Effect: Emotional Contagion and Its Influence on Group Behavior. Administrative Science Quarterly, 47(4) pp. 644–75.

119. Flack W. (2006). Peripheral feedback effects of facial expressions, bodily postures, and vocal expressions on emotional feelings. Cognition & Emotion, 20, pp. 177–195.

120. Hennenlotter, A., Dresel, C., Castrop, F., Ceballos-Baumann, A., Wohlschläger, A. & Haslinger, B. (2009). The Link between Facial Feedback and Neural Activity within Central Circuitries of Emotion—New Insights from Botulinum Toxin–Induced Denervation of Frown Muscles, Cerebral Cortex, 19(3), 537–542.

121. Frank, M. & Ekman, P.. (1996). Physiologic Effects of the Smile. Directions in Psychiatry. 16 (1), 1–6.

122. Duchenne, G. B. A. (1990). The mechanism of human facial expression. R. A. Cuthbertson (Ed. and Trans.). Cambridge, UK: Cambridge University Press. (Original work published 1862.)

123. P. Ekman, R.J. Davidson, W.V. Friesen (1990). The Duchenne smile: emotional expression and brain physiology: II. Journal of Personality and Social Psychology, 58, pp. 342–353.

124. Krumhuber, E., Likowski, K., & Weyers, P. (2014). Facial Mimicry of Spontaneous and Deliberate Duchenne and Non-Duchenne Smiles. Journal of Nonverbal Behavior, 38(1), 1-11.

125. Barbara Pease and Allan Pease (2004). The Definitive Guide to Body Language: The Hidden Meaning Behind People's Gestures and Expressions. Australia: QLD: Pease International. 1-372.

126. Goman, C (2008). The Nonverbal Advantage. San Francisco, CA: Berret Koehler Publishers Inc. 1-206.

127. Kang, S. & Tversky, B. (2016). From hands to minds: Gestures promote understanding. Cognitive Research: Principles and Implications, 1(4).

128. Krauss, R. M. (1998). Why Do We Gesture When We Speak?. Current Directions in Psychological Science, 7(2), 54-60.

129. Beattie, G & Shovelton, H. (2001). An experimental investigation of the role of different types of iconic gesture in communication: A semantic feature approach. Gesture. 1. 129–149. 10.1075/gest.1.2.03bea.

130. Kelly, S. D., Özyürek, A., & Maris, E. (2010). Two sides of the same coin: Speech and gesture mutually interact to enhance comprehension. Psychological Science, 21, 260–67.

Acknowledgements

Thank you to Dr Betty Kafanelis, my talented aunty, for helping me to better organise my thoughts, for investing a huge amount of time and effort into the first edits of the book, and most of all, for believing in me and giving me the confidence to pursue this. Without this I don't know if I would have been inspired and energised to laser focus in on this project. Thank you to Claire McGregor for providing valuable structural advice, helping to organise sections, improving the readability, delivering world-class editing, and for allowing me to better convey the information in these pages. You have raised the quality of the book tremendously! Thank you to Gemma Saunders, for the support provided to me as I wrote the book, for providing me with a different perspective on some of my writing, and for weighing in on editing decisions that profoundly influenced the direction and readability of this book. And thank you to Kaitlyn McCabe, who helped me better understand some of the psychological concepts I was writing about and for supporting me in the earlier days of the manuscript.

www.ingramcontent.com/pod-product-compliance
Lightning Source LLC
Chambersburg PA
CBHW060024030426
42334CB00019B/2171